CAREERS
IN
MEDICINE

PLANNING YOUR MEDICAL CAREER:
TRADITIONAL AND ALTERNATIVE OPPORTUNITIES

T. Donald Rucker, PhD and Martin D. Keller, MD, PhD
Editors

CtE

PLANNING YOUR MEDICAL CAREER: TRADITIONAL AND ALTERNATIVE OPPORTUNITIES

BY T. DONALD RUCKER, PhD
MARTIN D. KELLER, MD, PhD
AND COLLABORATORS

About The Authors . . .

T. Donald Rucker is Professor and Head, Department of Pharmacy Administration at the College of Pharmacy, University of Illinois at Chicago. In addition, he is an Adjunct Professor of Preventive Medicine at The Ohio State University College of Medicine in Columbus, OH.

Dr. Rucker is a medical economist with degrees from the following Universities: BS, Miami; MA, Ohio State; PhD, Syracuse. He has held research positions with Michigan Blue Shield and the National Association of Blue Shield Plans. Before returning to academia in 1972, Dr. Rucker was Chief, Drug Studies Branch, ORS, Social Security Administration in Washington. Professor Rucker has served as a consultant to AARP, FDA, OTA, USP and the VA. His publications number more than 80 and include topics such as drug insurance, drug formularies, medical informatics and career planning.

Martin D. Keller is Professor of Internal Medicine and Chairman, Department of Preventive Medicine, The Ohio State University College of Medicine in Columbus, Ohio.

Dr. Keller holds degrees awarded by the following Universities: AB, Yeshiva; MS, New York; MD, Cornell; PhD, NYU; and MPH, Columbia. He has been employed as an epidemiologist in the U.S. Public Health Service and held important administrative positions in the Ohio Department of Health. In addition, he has been a lecturer in the Department of Preventive Medicine at the Harvard Medical School and Director of Clinical Services at Beth Israel Hospital in Boston. Dr. Keller has served as a consultant to state and federal government agencies, as well as foreign programs in Belgium, Bolivia, Colombia, Egypt, Jamaica, Nigeria, Portugal, Tunisia, and Yugoslavia. Dr. Keller has published works in numerous journals and been the senior or collaborating author of research monographs and papers presented at symposia dealing with technology, bio-medical engineering, environmental protection, and emergency medical services.

In addition, more than 40 medical experts contributed articles summarizing career opportunities within their specialized fields.

Published and distributed by the
Garrett Park Press
Garrett Park, Maryland 20896
301/946-2553

PREFACE

More than 40,000 Americans apply to medical school each year in the U.S. and abroad. Becoming a doctor, however, is far more complex than just getting into an academic training program and hanging out a shingle after graduation.

Further, as the projected physician surplus unfolds and an increasing proportion of jobs flow to the corporate/institutional sector of the delivery system, effective career planning will become a necessity for many medical graduates. Unfortunately, relatively few students seem to acquire reliable information about the numerous career opportunities associated with medicine or become familiar with methods for locating them.

To help remedy these deficiencies, this book describes specialty areas for physicians who aid individuals with health problems, i.e., work as clinicians, and enumerates positions held by many of the 50,000 physicians who are not directly involved in patient care. In addition, it offers numerous guidelines for improving the efficiency of the career planning process. Readers who pursue these recommendations may double or treble the probability of making a "right" decision about their future as opposed to those who proceed more haphazardly.

This volume has been prepared primarily for college juniors who are considering applying to medical school. The contents will also be valuable for medical students attempting to identify an appropriate specialty as well as physicians in practice who wish to explore non-clinical positions for their training and skills.

Chapter I introduces medicine as a professional discipline and furnishes an overview of the major source of employment, the health care delivery system. Chapter II outlines various techniques to help readers obtain maximum benefit from using this publication.

Chapter III describes fields in medicine where physicians may qualify for specialty board certification. It also covers certain sub-specialty and informal specialty areas where job prospects may be favorable. Chapter IV provides an original compilation of over 900 titles that indicate how medical school graduates currently serve society in a non-clinical capacity.

Chapter V scans the world of medicine from a broader perspective. Instead of the function/disease/training model adopted for the specialty areas, it discusses selected issues germane to the profession as a whole, including important aspects related to the delivery of medical care.

The final chapter analyzes how a general physician surplus may be turned to your advantage and reviews strategies to facilitate the transfer of professional credentials to the labor market under such conditions.

Because of their key role in supporting medical practice, details on more than 190 specialty societies are furnished in the Appendix. A number of these organizations represent a major resource that might assist students in clarifying careers available to those with medical backgrounds.

Since the number of differentiated career options for medical graduates exceeds 500, and most physicians work in an environment that is complex and dynamic, it is impossible for a single reference to include all the material relevant for evaluating a medical career. Consequently, numerous external readings have been cited throughout this volume. Moreover, an unique Medical Scorecard has been created to aid in translating your reactions and impressions into meaningful career planning hypotheses.

We are indebted to the expert collaborators who explained salient features of their respective fields. Without their cooperation, this task would have been more difficult and perhaps impossible. Further, several organizations, especially the American Medical Association, permitted us to reprint articles that seemed essential for helping readers understand the intricacies associated with medical practice and how it may evolve in the future.

Construction of this manuscript benefited greatly from the editorial and research assistance of Imogene Rettos as well as the word-processing skills of Gwen Smith, Jaqueline Parris and Danita Ellison. In addition, we appreciate the cooperation of physicians who referred us to experts who could survey various specialty areas.

April, 1986

T. Donald Rucker, Chicago, IL
Martin D. Keller, Columbus, OH

CONTENTS

Chapter I

DOCTORS IN OUR MODERN SOCIETY

Medicine is a venerable profession concerned with both the healing arts and the scientific basis supporting practitioner contributions. Most medical school graduates utilize their knowledge and skills as clinicians, i.e., they help patients cope with illness and disease. Currently, there are about 445,000 active clinicians in the United States. Since more physicians are entering than leaving the labor force each year, this figure seems likely to exceed 530,000 by the end of this century.

Medicine can also be viewed as a career option where the physician has little direct responsibility for patient care. More than 50,000 medical school graduates are employed in diverse roles ranging from clinical research investigators to administrative positions in government agencies and large pharmaceutical manufacturing firms.

Contemporary medicine can also be considered in terms of a major philosophical difference, the one of allopathic versus osteopathic medicine. Clinicians in both areas are concerned with the diagnosis, treatment and prevention of disease or injury. However, allopathists rely heavily on traditional treatment modalities (see Table I-6), while osteopathists utilize an additional technique, manipulation applied to the spine and joints. Because the latter[1] represent only about four percent of the total physician supply, this book stresses career options for those with the Doctor of Medicine degree.

Medicine may also be approached by the type of service rendered to patients. Some may wish to follow careers in primary care (such as family practice, general internal medicine and pediatrics) while others may find greater interest in specialized treatment (such as pulmonary medicine, neurosurgery or anesthesiology). Primary care physicians tend to see a variety of patient problems while specialists treat a much narrower range. Finally, the nature of surgical versus non-surgical intervention represents another basic dichotomy that may be employed when considering a medical career.

Estimates of the number of clinicians in each field are shown in Table I-1. While it is unnecessary to memorize the number of physicians reported in each area, the relative size of various professional options and proportion of Board-certified doctors provide valuable data for

---

[1] For information about training in the 15 osteopathic schools and practice opportunities in this field which is oriented toward primary care, contact the American Osteopathic Association, 212 East Ohio Street, Chicago, IL 60611.

TABLE I-1

ACTIVE FEDERAL AND NON-FEDERAL PHYSICIANS BY SPECIALTY AND CORRESPONDING
BOARD CERTIFICATION, DECEMBER 31, 1983, USA

PRIMARY SPECIALTY	TOTAL PHYSICIANS	CORRES-PONDING BOARD	CORRES-PONDING BOARD & OTHERS	NON-CORRES-PONDING BOARD	NOT BOARD CERTIFIED
Medical					
Allergy	1,551	89	297	713	452
Dermatology	6,315	4,169	243	208	1,695
Family Practice	35,952	19,832	269	340	15,511
General Practice	28,202	-----	-----	3,730	24,472
Internal Medicine	82,462	35,726	801	2,960	42,975
Cardiovascular	12,298	8,810	52	332	3,104
Gastroenterology	5,398	3,996	17	141	1,244
Pulmonary Diseases	4,696	3,295	31	189	1,181
Neurology	7,140	3,408	521	441	2,770
Pediatrics	32,831	17,524	289	253	14,765
Allergy	399	99	228	7	65
Cardiology	759	618	2	9	130
Psychiatry	30,763	14,117	287	537	15,822
Child	3,606	1,929	128	116	1,433
Surgical					
General Surgery	36,323	16,387	2,088	933	16,915
Cardiothoracic	2,169	42	1,464	328	335
Colon and Rectal	793	155	297	160	181
Neurological	3,873	2,290	43	28	1,512
Ob/Gyn	29,306	16,970	72	188	12,076
Ophthalmology	14,294	9,970	191	192	3,941
Orthopaedic	16,193	10,548	42	84	5,519
Otorhinolaryngology	7,051	4,819	44	42	2,146
Plastic	3,701	1,421	832	427	1,021
Urology	8,529	5,955	56	31	2,487

TABLE I-1 (continued)

ACTIVE FEDERAL AND NON-FEDERAL PHYSICIANS BY SPECIALTY AND CORRESPONDING
BOARD CERTIFICATION, DECEMBER 31, 1983, USA

PRIMARY SPECIALTY	TOTAL PHYSICIANS	BOARD CERTIFICATION STATUS			NOT BOARD CERTIFIED
		CERTIFIED BY			
		CORRES-PONDING BOARD	CORRES-PONDING BOARD & OTHERS	NON-CORRES-PONDING BOARD	

Other Areas

Anesthesiology	20,003	8,536	152	326	10,989
Emergency Medicine	10,375	880	176	2,365	6,954
Nuclear Medicine	1,295	383	538	172	202
Pathology	14,940	10,201	411	241	4,087
Forensic	291	215	4	5	67
Physical Med/Rehab	2902	1,379	64	105	1,354
Preventive Medicine					
General	871	266	32	161	412
Aerospace	695	161	17	140	377
Occupational	2,648	428	75	514	1,631
Public Health	2,112	467	54	534	1,057
Radiology	9,108	6,918	807	191	1,192
Diagnostic	11,345	6,828	570	189	3,758
Therapeutic	2,054	1,380	108	43	523

Miscellaneous

Other Physicians	6,497	-----	-----	2,524	3,973
Unspecified	7,057	-----	-----	492	6,565
Not Classified	12,643	-----	-----	5,297	7,346
Address Unknown	3,195	-----	-----	300	2,895
Total Active Physicians	482,635	-----	-----	25,988	225,134

Source: Physician Characteristics and Distribution in the U.S. Chicago: American Medical Association, 1984.

career planning. However, the data do not reveal that some specialists render primary services and that surgeons seldom spend all of their time at the operating table. Further, the content of practice varies significantly as illustrated by statistics that describe office visits reported in Table I-2.

Table I-2

Average Number of Patients Seen in Office Visits per Physician per Week, and Average Length of Visit, Four Medical Specialties, 1980-1981

Type of Practice	Average Number of Patients Seen per Physician per Week	Average Length of Visit (Minutes)
Internal Medicine	51.4	20.3
Obstetrics/Gynecology	68.5	13.9
General/Family Practice	86.8	13.5
Pediatrics	106.9	12.8

Note: Many physicians also see patients in institutional facilities.

Source: National Center for Health Statistics. Patterns of Ambulatory Care in Internal Medicine, USA, 1/1980-12/1981. NCHS Series 12, No. 80.

The Health and Medical Care Team

Recently, there has been an enormous growth in the number of paramedical or allied medical professions. Such professionals generally augment the care provided by physicians. In the United States, certain allied health professionals have been accredited to carry out some functions that, in the past, were exclusively those of the physician. Such tasks are usually performed under the direction of or by order of a physician. However, many allied medical professionals are seeking independence and licensure or certification to perform their duties without the need for a physician's order. A number of these professions have already gained independence and it seems inevitable that further change in the traditional prerogatives of the clinician will occur.

How, then, does this development affect the status and the role of the physician in our society? Does it shrink or limit the physician's control over patient care to the detriment of those who seek the physician's expertise, or, does it expand the role of the physician as the coordinator of a health care team? These questions can be troublesome and exciting to many physicians and medical students.

Among health professionals, the physician is the recipient of the most intensive education. Thus, it seems appropriate that he or she should be designated leader of the health care team. However, as an effective leader, the physician must acknowledge the contributions of other participants in the delivery system if this position is to be retained and patient health outcomes maximized.

This new role as team member and coordinator requires some reorientation of the function traditionally carried out by the "solo" practitioner. Here the clinician occasionally communicates with other physicians and all others are typically regarded as peripheral and clearly subordinate. Most successful physicians of the future will collaborate with non-physician members of the team, each of whom compliments the physician's contribution to patient care.

Unilateral decision making by the physician will be tempered by the participation of allied medical professionals who often carry out selected functions by themselves and with a proficiency that may equal or exceed that of the clinician. The physician's role becomes more that of the strategist who synthesizes the concepts, information and techniques of health care. In addition, this specialist monitors the specific care delivered to a patient to ensure results consistent with current health service standards and expectations. This broad responsibility holds no matter how unique the specialty of the clinician.

A Conceptual Framework of Health and Medical Care

The physician utilizes a complex combination of science and art. While diagnosis and treatment of illness are the mainstays of the physician's professional activities, there is growing emphasis on the preservation of health and prevention of disease. This change represents a logical extension of the growing understanding of the natural history of disease, a concept employed in the field of public health and in the introduction of new methods of health care delivery.

This broad framework provides the basis for the development of strategies to thwart the occurrence of disease by eliminating causal agents, preventing exposure of susceptible individuals or groups, protecting the susceptibles from the effects of the exposure, and altering the environment to favor health. Traditional public health programs are designed to clean up and protect the environment, provide proper nutrition and handling of food and water, protect persons by immunization, and enhance safety in the home, workplace, traffic and so on. With a growing emphasis on health promotion and disease prevention, the clinical responsibility of the physician may expand accordingly.

Despite the best efforts at prevention, we are not now, nor in the foreseeable future are we likely to be capable of avoiding the occurrence of many diseases. Since the preventive approach cannot eliminate the incidence of such illnesses, we move to early detection of the disease process before signs and symptoms are manifest. The aim is to detect disease in time to have the maximum likelihood of reversing, halting, or modifying deleterious conditions.

Early detection as the foundation for treatment has given rise to a large and complex array of screening examination and laboratory methods. While many tests are carried out by allied medical personnel, the strategy of determining the proper tests is the province of the physician. Further, interpretation of test results and the development of plans for early treatment, including mitigating risk and preventing disease, is a complex matter for which the physician is prepared by scientific and technical training.

Despite all our efforts, individuals become ill. Occasionally the onset of disease is abrupt and catastrophic, but in most instances the progression is sufficiently slow to allow the development of a medical plan to foster recovery or at least to limit disability and maintain reasonable comfort. This area represents the traditional realm of medical care - the diagnosis or assessment of disease and the development of a treatment or management plan.

The natural history of a disease thus extends from the period when primary prevention may be undertaken through the early stages of the pathogenic process, in which the disease is inapparent, through the onset of the signs and symptoms and the subsequent course to recovery, chronic conditions, and possibly death. The physician and supporting members of the health care team are thus poised all along this time line, applying strategies of prevention, early detection, treatment, limitation of disability, rehabilitation, and prolongation of life. As the health sciences become more sophisticated and the means of intervention become more powerful, these strategies may be applied earlier in the time sequence leading to more favorable outcomes. However, with the increased proportion of aged population, the efforts of medical care are being directed increasingly to the management of chronic conditions and end-stage disease.

The growth of knowledge and technology means that an individual physician cannot master all the requisite information and skills. Thus an effective clinician will need to avoid both inappropriate feelings of self-sufficiency and/or exclusivity as well as unjustified attitudes of inadequancy.

The physician must, therefore, know how to recruit the proper array of services to achieve optimal outcomes for patients. Otherwise, the patient facing the physician will enter the office with a silent prayer; "Doctor, I hope you can cure what I have," while the physician seeing the patient will think the obverse, "I hope you have what I can cure." With advances in communication and information retrieval via computer technology, the physician increasingly has access to current scientific information, proper facilities and personnel to augment the specific measures that may be undertaken in the patient's interest. In summary, the modern physician becomes the entryway but not the sole refuge of persons in need of health and medical care.

Medical Education

Medical education provides the scientific background and technical competence necessary for the practice of medicine. Training programs also attempt to inculcate values and attitudes which enable the physician to deal effectively with the medical problems of the patient. There is a continuing debate regarding the relative emphasis placed on technical information versus humanistic values and behavioral principles.

The education of the physician, of course, begins before medical school, continues through the medical curriculum and thereafter into the post-graduate or residency period. While most medical students in recent years have come to medical school with college majors in biology and chemistry, there is a growing interest in students from other academic disciplines, particularly the humanities.

Almost without exception, the 127 accredited medical schools in the United States have a four-year curriculum. Programs start with the sciences considered basic to the study of this field; anatomy, biochemistry (physiological chemistry), and physiology. These courses are followed by microbiology, pharmacology, and pathology. Generally, a course in human behavior or behavioral science is also presented.

Most medical schools have an offering in preventive medicine, stressing the principles of epidemiology, biostatistics, and public health. Recently, many curricula have introduced special courses in genetics and neurosciences. Because of the role of laboratory work, considerable time is spent studying anatomy, biochemistry, physiology, microbiology, pharmacology, and pathology. Students thus learn a vast new vocabulary and concepts that allow these "facts" to be organized into a useable body of knowledge. While it is certainly necessary to master this material in order to pass external examinations, including National Boards, few really expect that significant portions will be retained for very long. The objective here is not necessarily to inscribe all scientific knowledge on readily retrievable memory but to afford the medical student an operational set of terms, relationships, and concepts to support further learning and help absorb information from lectures and conferences.

The medical student must be prepared to approach patients with sufficient knowledge and skills to take a good medical history, carry out a competent physical examination, recognize laboratory tests and procedures that may be required, and formulate reasonable hypotheses regarding the nature of the patient's medical status and need for treatment. All medical schools offer an introduction to clinical medicine where students gain experience in interviewing and examining patients. In some institutions, this requirement is introduced in the first year (and intensified in the second) but in most it is deferred until the second. The objective is to prepare the medical student for the clinical "clerkships" in the third year of the medical curriculum.

Most schools have a full and prescribed curriculum, and little time is available for elective courses. Occasionally, students are given the opportunity to participate in research with members of the faculty. The summers between the first and second and the second and third years can be used for purposes of research and other special programs.

The clinical curriculum is reserved mostly for the third year. Major clerkships are required in internal medicine, surgery, obstetrics/gynecology, pediatrics, and psychiatry. There is a rapidly changing pattern of additional requirements for clerkships in sub-specialty areas, but most are still elective. An increasing portion of required time is spent on ambulatory medicine/primary medical care. The clinical departments that participate include obstetrics/gynecology, family medicine, internal medicine, pediatrics, and preventive medicine. The required time in medicine and surgery ranges from two to three or more months while student assignments in the others extends from one to two.

Most of the fourth year is devoted to selectives or electives. In many medical schools, students are given a choice of opportunities (selectives) including further study in the basic sciences to facilitate their integration with clinical sciences. Students may also follow assignments away from the medical school in order to gain a broader experience in other parts of the United States and to study subjects not readily available at their institution. Some students use this period to become acquainted with communities where they may wish to serve residencies. Departments of Preventive or Community Medicine frequently offer a great variety of elective programs in domestic or foreign health agencies. In the USA, these may involve programs for special populations such as those served by the Indian Health Service. Also, a variety of assignments can be arranged abroad where students become acquainted with cultures and health care systems other than their own.

Medical students often take courses in a number of specialty areas to see how they like them before making a commitment to a residency program. This strategy may have merit in some cases but it can also inhibit students from gaining a broad background. Students already committed to a particular residency are advised to seek different experiences while still in medical school. There is little value in eating a sandwich before going to a banquet.

In the current climate involving reappraisal of the medical curriculum, there are bound to be changes of emphasis and time commitment. Indeed, Table I-3 illustrates both this principle and career options that may be available to those wise enough to inquire further about such frontiers.

Table I-3

Relatively Rare Administrative Units Found Among American Colleges of Medicine

Basic Sciences

    Biocommunications
    Biophysics/Theoretical Biology
    Comparative Medicine
    Evolutionary Biology
    History of Health Sciences

    Interdisciplinary Toxicology
    Medical Genetics
    Neuroanatomy
    Pharmacology & Experimental
       Therapeutics

    Research in Health Education
    Structural Biology
    Tropical Medicine & Medical
       Microbiology
    Virology

Clinical Sciences

    Anesthesiology
       Intensive Care Medicine
    Clinical Engineering

    Family/Community/Preventive Medicine
       Clinical Social Work
       Health Services Research
       Medical Jurisdiction

    Medical Education

Clinical Sciences (continued)

    Medical Ethics
    Medical & Public Affairs
    Medicine
       Digestive Disease & Nutrition[1]
       Genetics & Human Genetics[2]
       Gerontology

    Neuropathology
    Otolaryngology
       Audiology & Speech

    Pediatrics
       Allergy & Cystic Fibrosis
       Behavioral Pediatrics
       Developmental Disabilities
       Maternal Fetal Medicine
       Perinatal Medicine

    Radiology
       Medical Physics
       Radiobiology Research
       Ultrasonic

    Reproductive Medicine

    Sickle Cell Disease Center
    Surgical Biology

    Transplantation
    Traumatology

---

[1] A recent National Research Council study reported that only a fifth of the 125 medical schools teach nutrition as a separate subject. Since patients seem increasingly concerned about anorexia, diets, food supplements during pregnancy, and vegetarianism, some medical students may find that clinical nutrition represents a viable career option.

[2] Contact the National Clearing House for Human Genetics, 1776 East Jefferson, Rockville, MD 20852.

Additional Practice Requirements

Although graduation from medical school represents a significant personal accomplishment, society regards it simply as one prerequisite for those who wish to practice in this field.

In order to treat patients, one must also obtain a license (via examination) from one of the 62 licensure boards. (Some jurisdictions still maintain separate boards for medicine and osteopathy). Successful candidates must have a degree from a medical school accredited by the Liaison Committee on Medical Education, obtain a passing grade on the medical licensure examination, and in most states, complete one year in an accredited residency program. The second step can be satisfied by meeting the requirements of the National Board of Medical Examinors, or, except for Louisiana and Texas, those established by the Federation of State Medical Boards. The conditions specified for U.S. citizens who graduate from foreign medical schools vary from state to state and details can be obtained from the respective jurisdictions.

More than 20 states also mandate that physicians complete approved courses in continuing professional education annually in order to maintain their license. Some clinicians find it possible to satisfy most of these stipulations by attending intensive two to three day sessions sponsored by national or specialty society organizations. The benefits of a personal continuing education plan, however, transcend the goal of just keeping up: "Acquiring new knowledge invigorates our professional efforts and recharges our energies; it is a helpful preventative against professional stagnation and the boredom of routine."[1]

Many specialty groups sponsor rigorous examinations covering both knowledge and skills to support certification by their Board (see the Appendix). While sitting for these examinations is voluntary, peer pressure and job market expectations combine to make this additional step almost universal for new graduates.

Health Care Delivery System

More than 90 percent of the medical school graduates are employed in organizations responsible for the provision of services to patients. This health care delivery system (HCDS) consists of three major components: (1) the resources (such as trained manpower, supporting workers, and facilities), including their quantity, quality and distribution, associated with the treatment of health problems; (2) the organizational structure through which care is rendered (such as various delivery mechanisms serving ambulatory and bed patients, and the referral

---

[1] Swogger, G & Grebenschikoff, JR, "Career Crisis," Group Practice Journal 33:39 (September/October 1984).

system); and (3), the financing mechanism utilized to reward providers (as influenced by insurance and out-of-pocket expenditures). Because of the increasing impact of externalities - government, consumerism and technology - some scholars contend these forces constitute additional components of our HCDS.

Effective career planning, therefore, depends not only on one's ability to select an appropriate specialty and master its scientific content but also to understand how these contextual factors may affect both professional performance and the opportunity to make a living. As noted by an American Medical Association report, "success in responding to the environment within which the profession must provide its services may be as important to health in America as any challenge we have ever faced."[1]

The remainder of this chapter introduces selected external considerations related to your assessment of a medical career. Because of the complexity of our task, and disagreement about system limitations, readers are encouraged to consult many of the citations at the end of Chapter I and throughout Chapter V.

Market-Oriented. Most health services (88 percent, based on dollar value) are delivered to individuals through the private sector of the economy where transaction terms traditionally are determined largely by buyers (patients) and sellers (providers such as doctors and hospitals). However, market prices may be influenced by the nature of insurance benefits and payment conditions established by third-parties. In any case, less than 12 percent of all personal health care is furnished directly through government agencies such as the Department of Defense, Public Health Service, and Veterans Administration. For example, the latter operates 172 hospitals, 226 outpatient clinics, 92 nursing homes and 16 other facilities. Moreover, the Defense Department operates 168 hospitals, 130 in the continental USA. An alert student, of course, will not view these figures as sterile statistics but as a potential source of employment for medical graduates.

With respect to physician income, 62.6 percent was supplied by third parties in 1982. A little more than 35 of these percentage points were accounted for by private insurance while 27.5 came from government-sponsored programs. This meant that physicians in private practice received, on the average, only 37.4 percent of their income directly from patients. Since group "purchasing of services in a competitive market requires that the health outcomes from those services be explicit and evaluable,"[2] not only reimbursement levels but various

[1] Report of the Council on Long Range Planning and Development. The Environment of Medicine. Chicago: AMA, 1984. p. iii.

[2] Tarlov, AR, "Shattuck Lecture: The . . . Supply of Physicians...," New England Journal Medicine 308:1238 (May 19, 1983).

other aspects of medical practice may be subject to regulation by third-party programs.

Pluralistic. A pluralistic system implies a diversity of organizational, political and economic components. Thus we find numerous delivery models such as solo practice[1], group practice (a growing form where nearly 16,000 units now account for more than 30 percent of all care provided to ambulatory patients), and specialized clinics that limit treatment to patients with particular medical problems (such as cancer or venereal disease). In addition, federal, state and/or local governments offer specialized care through mental health centers and prenatal programs for expectant mothers.

Because the HCDS developed from the perspective of programs rather than planning, various financing schemes exit. With respect to governmental units, federal and state agencies share the expense for Medicaid recipients - the poor on welfare - while individuals and Social Security share the cost of physician insurance coverage for those 65 years of age and over under Medicare. Although financial support is contributed by government sources, patient care under both is provided by the private sector. One of the best indices of the pluralistic nature of the HCDS is the proportion of personal health care expenditures - 39.6 percent - underwritten by tax dollars (Table I-4).

Complex. The pluralistic characteristic of the HCDS contributes significantly to its complexity. According to Roemer, its operation involves so many separate and largely autonomous components that it is sometime called a nonsystem.[2] This trait makes evaluation of clinical performance difficult, especially when some elements, such as the ability to deliver technically sophisticated care may be judged superior, while others are alleged to be in need of repair. Complexity is also increased by the proliferation of non-standardized nomenclature and the fragmentation of medical records.

Moreover, the delivery of patient care is supported indirectly by numerous groups such as pharmaceutical manufacturers, charitable foundations, professional societies (see the Appendix), licensure agencies, and professional schools. Others with an impact include the medical information industry (via reports on developments in science, medicine and health administration), self-help groups (e.g., Alcoholics Anonymous, Mended Hearts and United Ostomy Association), public interest groups, and voluntary health organizations (such as the American Cancer Association, American Lung Association and the Planned Parenthood Federation). Some voluntary health organizations go beyond the typical

---

[1] The Health Insurance Association of America predicts that solo practice will virtually cease to exist by the year 2000.

[2] Roemer, MI. An introduction to the U.S. Health Care System. New York: Springer Pub. Co., 1982. p. 1.

Table I-4

National Health Expenditures, United States, 1984

Type of Expenditure	Total Outlay (Billions)	Source of Funds (Percent)		
		Private	Public	Total
Health Services and Supplies	$371.6	59.3%	40.7%	100%
Personal Health Care	341.8	60.4	39.6	100
Hospital Care	157.9	46.5	53.5	100
Physician's services	75.4	72.3	27.7	100
Dentist's services	25.1	98.0	2.0	100
Other professional services	8.8	68.2	31.8	100
Drugs & medical sundries	25.8	91.1	8.9	100
Eyeglasses & appliances	7.4	84.0	16.0	100
Nursing home care	32.0	50.9	49.1	100
Other health services	9.4	21.1	78.9	100
Program administration and net cost of insurance	19.1	72.8	27.2	100
Government public health activities	10.7	----	100.0	100
Research & construction of medical facilities	15.8	42.7	57.3	100
Research	6.8	5.9	94.1	100
Construction	9.0	71.1	28.9	100
Total	$387.4	58.6%	41.4%	100%

Source: Health Affairs 4(3):101 (Fall 1985).

functions of providing health information and supporting research by operating clinics or providing care and equipment directly to patients. Such services, of course, add another layer of vertical and horizontal complexity to the HCDS and another potential source of employment as seen in Chapter IV.

Enormous Size. The economic significance of the health services field is evidenced by its 7.5 million workers. No other industry is larger. However, the 445,000 physicians currently active in patient care represent only about six percent of the total. The remaining positions are filled by individuals from more than 200 related occupations.

Clinicians play a vital role in caring for ambulatory patients. Nonfederal physicians in office practice handle over 600 million patient visits per year. Table I-5 furnishes a profile of the 20 most common principal complaints which induce individuals to seek treatment in this

Table I-5

Twenty Most Common Principal Reasons for Patient Visit to Physicians in the Office Practice of Medicine, USA, 1981

Most Common Principal Reason for Visit	Number of Visits (000)
General medical examination	30,222
Prenatal examination	23,501
Postoperative visit	18,071
Symptoms referable to the throat	15,098
Progress visit not otherwise specified	14,864
Well-baby examination	12,922
Cough	12,783
Blood pressure test	10,662
Back symptoms	10,318
Head cold, upper respiratory infection	9,185
Fever	9,160
Skin rash	8,882
Earache, or ear infection	8,745
Headache, pain in head	8,436
Chest pain and related symptoms	8,368
Abdominal pain, cramps, spasms	8,240
Eye examination	7,790
Hypertension	7,531
Knee symptoms	7,102
Vision dysfunctions	6,834
All other reasons	346,463

Source: National Center for Health Statistics. advancedata. Number 88, March 16, 1983.

setting. While the list excludes reasons that led to 60 percent of the visits, it cites problems seen most frequently by doctors whose practice is oriented toward primary care (i.e., family practice, internal medicine and pediatrics.) Table I-6 summarizes the modalities employed by clinicians in treating these individuals.

Table I-6

Therapeutic Services Provided by Doctors of Medicine and
Osteopathy Engaged in Office-Based Practice, 1976

Therapeutic Service	Visits	
	Number (000)	Percent
Drug prescribed	251,970	42.8%
Medical counseling	79,920	13.6
Injection	73,309	12.5
Office Surgery	41,497	7.1
Immunization/desensitization	31,287	5.3
Psychotherapy & therapeutic listening	24,249	4.1
Physiotherapy	17,590	3.0

Source: National Center for Health Statistics

Primary care in offices is augmented by doctors working in hospital outpatient and emergency departments where an additional 210 million visits are handled annually. Another 100 million patient encounters take place by telephone. However, the changing nature of medical practice is indicated by the fact that doctor visits to patient homes now account for less than 10 million contacts a year.

Turning to institutional care, some 6,900 hospitals admit nearly 40 million patients each year. Approximately 45 percent of these individuals will undergo an operation during their confinement. In 1980, the total number of surgical procedures performed only on hospitalized patients reached almost 25 million. The ten most common surgical cases are enumerated in Table I-7.

Table I-8 indicates physician employment in hospitals by type and ownership. While the figure of 53,130 has been adjusted to reflect full-time equivalents, an AMA survey for 1981 identified 78,600 doctors who actually had some financial arrangement with a hospital to provide

Table I-7

Most Common Surgical Procedures Performed on Patients Discharged from Short-Stay Hospitals Ranked by Frequency, 1983

Biopsy	1,495,000
Cesarean section	808,000
Excision of lesion of skin or tissue	680,000
Hysterectomy	672,000
Dilation & curettage, diagnostic	632,000
Extraction of lens	630,000
Bilateral destruction or occlusion of fallopian tubes	568,000
Insertion of prosthetic lens	516,000
Oophorectomy & salpingooophorectomy	512,000
Repair of inguinal hernia	510,000

Source: American College of Surgeons. Socioeconomic Factbook for Surgery. Chicago: ACS, 1986. p. 33.

services.[1] Pathologists and radiologists derive most of their practice income from this source, 96 and 87 percent respectively. On the other hand, general/family practitioners and internists with some hospital affiliation obtained the least, 40 percent. "Physicians most likely to have financial arrangements with hospitals are pathologists (78%), radiologists (58%), and those specializing in emergency medicine." Pluralism is illustrated again since these 78,600 physicians, averaged 38 percent of their practice income from non-hospitals sources, largely from patients seen in their private offices.

Study of the HCDS from the institutional perspective yields another method for uncovering possible employment opportunities. Table I-9 provides a statistical summary of specialized services furnished by American hospitals. Major responsibility for each function is usually exercised by a physician. One criterion for considering employment in such areas is the level of market penetration. Table I-9 identifies several low-penetration areas, such as genetic counseling, hospice, and psychiatric home care, which may represent a chance for qualified physicians to exercise leadership in creating new activities.

[1] American Medical Association. Socioeconomic Characteristics of Medical Practice 1983. Chicago: AMA, 1983. p. 11. Also see pp. 124-134 for unique insights about practice characteristics of selected specialties.

Table I-8

Number of Hospitals with Number of Physicians[1] & Dentists[2]
Employed According to Type of Facility, 1984

Type of Institution	Number of Hospitals	Number of Physicians & Dentists Employed (Full-time Equivalent)
Total: USA	6,872	53,130
Type of Care Provided		
General		
Hospitals	5,931	43,369
Hospital units	63	667
Psychiatric		
Hospitals	570	6,204
Inst. Mentally Retarded	28	199
Rehabilitation	76	323
Chronic Disease	41	406
Orthopedic	30	193
Eye, Ear, Nose & Throat	18	63
OB/GYN	15	19
Tuberculosis	7	43
Other	93	1,644
Ownership Class		
Federal	341	18,408
Non-Federal; Long-Term	717	6,607
State & Local Government; Short-Term	1,662	6,612
Community; Short-Term	4,152	21,503

[1] Excludes 337 professionals employed by 161 non-registered facilities, the majority of whom are employed by long-term psychiatric units operated by state governments.

[2] Dentists are believed to account for a very small proportion.

Source: American Hospital Association. Hospital Statistics - 1985. Chicago: AHA, 1985. Tables, 1, 5A, and 14.

Table I-9

Selected Hospitals Services likely to be a Major Interest
to Physicans, 1984

Type of Service (N = 6,302)	Percent of Hospitals with
Abortion	22.6%
Alcoholism/chemical dependency outpatient	18.0
Ambulatory surgical	81.0
Blood bank	67.0
Cardiac catheterization	16.3
Clinical psychology	36.8
Computerized tomography scanner	41.9
Diagnostic radioisotope	61.5
Emergency department	85.6
Family planning	12.3
Genetic counseling	7.6
Health promotion	46.7
Hemodialysis	24.0
Histopathology laboratory	61.6
Home care department	20.6
Hospice	9.8
Megavoltage radiation therapy	15.0
Occupational therapy services	45.4
Open-heart surgery facilities	10.8
Organ transplant	4.0
Organized outpatient department	50.6
Physical therapy	86.8
Premature nursery	25.6
Psychiatric consultation & education	31.3
Psychiatric emergency	34.6
Psychiatric foster and/or home care	3.5
Psychiatric outpatient services	20.5
Psychiatric partial hospitalization program	13.8
Radioactive implants	21.3
Rehabilitation outpatient services	35.7
Respiratory therapy	85.3
Therapeutic radioisotope facility	22.2
X-ray radiation therapy	16.2

Source: American Hospital Association. Hospital Statistics - 1985.
Chicago: AHA, 1985. Table 12A.

Less intensive medical services are furnished through some 17,000 nursing homes where approximately 1.9. million patients can be accommodated. Many of these residents, whose median age is 81 years, are visited by their physicians about once a month.

Economic Implications. One measure of economic importance is indicated by total outlays for health care services. According to Table I-4, these expenditures reached $387 billion in 1984 and government officials predict they may exceed $700 billion by 1990.

Three key economic issues related to the operation of the HCDS are (1) the relative percentage of national resources consumed by this sector, (2) persistent and excessive inflation, and (3) the efficiency of the overall system. With respect to the first factor, only 4.4 percent of all goods and services produced in the United States were allocated to the health area in 1950. By 1983, this proportion, after a steady rise, had jumped to 10.8.[1] The majority of this increase, though, did not emanate from an improvement in the quality of care or the amount of health services consumed. Instead, more than 70 percent stemmed directly from inflation where the rate of price increase in the health component has been at least twice that of the economy in general. While physicians ostensibly receive less than 22 percent of the personal health care dollar, services provided or ordered by doctors (e.g., who will be hospitalized, how long they stay there, and who will receive prescriptions) are responsible for around 70 percent of total system outlays.[2]

Most students will probably enter medicine because of the challenge of applying their technical knowledge and skills to the health problems of individual patients. However, relatively few will be able to escape the concomitant pressures, often generated by public and private insurance programs, to hold down the cost of care. This posture is supported by the general public which continues to believe that medical expenses are "outrageously and unjustifiably" high despite the fact that an overwhelming majority are satisfied with the quality of health care and its availability.[3]

Dynamic. While the HCDS is market-oriented, pluralistic, complex, enormous, and economically significant, it is also dynamic. One indication is shown in the growth of new medical knowledge which occurs at the rate of about five percent per year. Thus the ability of a clinician to provide optimal patient care depends not only on formal

---

[1] No other nation in the world devotes a larger share of its Gross National Product to expenditures for health care.

[2] Freeland, MS and Schendler, CE, "Health Care Spending - Can the Rate of Ascent be Slowed," HCFA Forum 5:9 (August 1981).

[3] Journal American Medical Association 248:2846 (December 3, 1982).

medical training but on systematic methods for keeping up with scientific progress upon entering medical practice.

Changes in the structure of practice were reported by Sydney J. Harris who noted that the number of "pain clinics" grew from one in 1970 to more than 300 in 1982. A similar phenomenon is manifest in the growth of walk-in, cash on delivery, free-standing health care centers. While there were around 400 in June of 1982,[1] it was expected that more than 3,500 would be in operation by the end of 1985. These urgent care centers are open seven days a week, 365 days a year, and from 12 to 16 hours each day. Fees generally run 40 to 60 percent less than rates charged at the local hospital emergency room.[2]

System Performance. In attempting to assess how well the HCDS functions, criticism depends significantly on the viewer's perception, goals and value judgements. In undertaking this brief review, it is essential to recall that physician responsibility varies along a broad continuum depending on the kind of problem being discussed. For example, no single doctor should be held responsible for the fact that some patients lack the ability to pay for their health care services or that a given community has excessive hospital beds. At the other extreme, though, clinicians do control the decision to undertake a surgical procedure or order a laboratory test.

Many experts contend that a satisfactory system should provide care that is comprehensive, accessible, coordinated, of high quality, economically justifiable, and capable of self-correction when deviations are recorded. Some of the shortcomings of our system relative to this model will be noted briefly.

Accessibility to comprehensive care may be impaired if citizens lack the economic resources with which to pay providers directly or purchase insurance coverage for this same purpose. However, even with insurance, patients may bear economic hardships that restrict their ability to obtain prescribed drugs or see a physician. For example, because of coverage gaps and patient cost-sharing features, Medicare beneficiaries still must pay for more than 60 percent of their health care expenses. Further, some 33 million Americans currently have no insurance coverage at all. Accessibility to health services may also be thwarted by a shortage or maldistribution of qualified providers (some inner city and rural areas have persistent shortages).

One problem involving the fragmentation of medical care arises when individuals, often on their own volition, see multiple practitioners during a short period of time. For example, a particular patient can

---

[1] Sorenson, L, "Hospitals and Doctors Compete for Patients with Rising Bitterness," Wall Street Journal, July 19, 1983, p. 14.

[2] "Business," New York Times, February 12, 1985, p. 1;20.

have diagnostic x-rays made independently by an internist, orthopaedist, podiatrist, hospital emergency room, chiropractor and dentist. In addition to the risk borne by the patient from uncoordinated exposure to gamma rays, one physician reported that "the most pervasive and dangerous diagnostic tool in the doctor's office is the x-ray machine."[1]

While supervision of medical care by a primary physician might introduce some element of control, this premise is difficult to satisfy because the last four providers in our example would probably be excluded. Further, data from a NCHS survey imply that more than 15 percent of the American adults under 65 have no regular source of care where a primary physician might perform this function. Our goal also becomes more elusive since some 15 percent of the population moves every year and the transfer of medical records under such circumstances becomes problematic.

Questions pertaining to the quality of medical care have been raised more frequently with respect to unnecessary procedures such as tonsillectomies and hysterectomies and the ordering of excessive or inappropriate prescriptions and laboratory tests. Studies have also cited hospitalized patients whose care could have been furnished on an ambulatory basis (thus saving money) and the confinement of bed patients for a period that exceeded medical necessity.

It is not generally perceived that care which fails to satisfy qualitative standards also produces serious economic problems as well. One direct manifestation of this principle is our national bill for malpractice insurance, a figure that totals more than one billion dollars a year. Prospective physicians may derive comfort from the finding that more than 50 percent of all claims filed are found to be without merit.[2] However, the problem is so pervasive that, according to the California Medical Association, it adds $5 a day to the cost of every hospital stay and $3-4 to the cost of every visit to the doctor.[3] The impact on particular physicians, though, ranges widely - 60 percent paid less than $5,000 a year in the early 1980s while 15 percent had expenses exceeding $10,000. Further, psychiatrists pay the lowest premium rates while neurosurgeons usually incur the highest.

When treatment decisions must be made rapidly at the patient's bedside, economics may become intertwined with moral/ethical issues. For example, the "intravenous technique that at a daily cost of $150 can provide complete nutrition for a patient temporarily unable to take food

---

[1] Mendelsohn, RS. Confessions of a Medical Heretic. Chicago: Contemporary Books, 1979. pp. 4-5

[2] Wall Street Journal, September 21, 1983. p. 33.

[3] Ibid., p. 45.

by mouth is also used to extend the lives of patients who have little or no prospect of ever leaving the hospital or resuming normal lives."[1] A doctor lamented recently, "The crying shame of modern medicine is the use of technology to prolong the act of dying, and we all know it."[2] Physicians who can help resolve this conundrum may enable society to cope with one of its most illusive problems.

Another limitation in the health services sector arises where contemporary professional educational stresses the technical sophistication of the medical specialist, an approach which "is increasingly less appropriate for the kinds of chronic illnesses to be dealt with today."[3] This emphasis in turn produces a mismatch between health needs and health care which "is a major cause underlying many of the more obvious difficulties of the system,"[4] including the economic burden which has attracted the most attention.

An additional cause of economic pressure on the HCDS stems from sources largely external to control by providers (thus improved patient health is more likely to result from inputs based upon prevention rather than treatment). The health status of individuals is influenced by (1) environmental pollution (e.g., the quality of our air and water), (2) personal behavior (e.g., life-styles that lead to obesity, alcoholism, drug abuse, smoking, veneral disease, worrying and motor vehicle accidents),[5] (3) genetic make-up (often the primary cause of conditions such as diabetes and heart diseases), and (4), income (which influences eating[6] habits and attitudes toward health maintenance).

These four factors are so significant that one investigator reported that "the medical system (doctors, drugs and hospitals) affects only about 10 percent of the usual indices for measuring health: Whether you

---

[1] Aaron, HJ & Schwartz, WB, "Hospital Cost Control: A Bitter Pill to Swallow," Harvard Business Review 63:161 (March-April 1985).

[2] Miller, AE, "They're Not Prolonging Life, They're Prolonging Dying," American Medical News 28:31 (June 14, 1985).

[3] Miller, AE & Miller, MG. Options for Health and Health Care. New York: John Wiley & Sons, 1981. p. 5.

[4] Ibid., p. 1

[5] Preventive efforts are likely to be hampered severely by the degree of confidence which the public has in warnings issued by government officials (only 23 percent) and organized medicine (only 43 percent). New York Times, June 12, 1977.

[6] The National Center for Health Statistics reported in 1980 that 26 percent of the population never ate breakfast.

live at all (infant mortality), how well you live (days lost due to sickness), how long you live (adult mortality)."[1] While the curative/palliative powers of medical care are applauded daily by millions of Americans, candidates for a career in this field may benefit from a realistic perspective about the legitimate domain of their professional contribution in the clinical mode.

Because of the complexity and size of the HCDS, as well as the micro-oriented training and practice experience of physicians generally, to say nothing of the fact that doctors are often very busy individuals, relatively few clinicians have had a major impact on improving its overall performance. Macro-oriented students, therefore, may wish to obtain additional credentials that stress system analysis rather than treatment techniques. This goal may be pursued by enrolling in certain programs that lead to the Master's degree in Public Health or Preventive Medicine. Given these qualifications, you would be able to seek positions in professional associations, medical schools and public and private insurance plans which often investigate how operation of the HCDS could be made more effective and less costly.

---

[1] Wildavsky, A, "Doing Better and Feeling Worse: The Political Pathology of Health Policy," In: Doing Better and Feeling Worse. (Knowles, JH, ed.). New York: WW Norton & Co., 1977. p. 105.

External Readings - Overview

Thomas, L. The Youngest Science. New York: Viking Press, 1982. 270 pp.

Robin, ED. Matters of Life and Death: Risks and Benefits of Medical Care. New York: WH Freeman & Co., 1984. 205 pp.

Cassell, EJ. The Healer's Art: A New Approach to the Doctor-Patient Relationship. Philadelphia: JB Lippincott, 1978. 240 pp.

Greene, RG. Medical Overkill: Diseases of Medical Progress. Philadelphia: GF Stickley Co., 1983. 310 pp.

Mendelsohn, RS. Confessions of a Medical Heretic. Chicago: Contemporary Books, Inc. 1979. 191 pp.

Israel, L. Decision-Making: The Modern Doctor's Dilemma. New York: Random House, 1982. 139 pp.

Bursztajn, H., et al. Medical Choices, Medical Careers. New York: Delacorte Press/Seymour Lawrence, 1981. Chapters 1,5, 9-15.

External Readings - Medical Education

Medical Education in the United States, 1984-85," Journal American Medical Association 254:1553-1656 (September 27, 1985). (Final issue published in September each year).

Bressler, DJ, "Notes from Overground: Fourth Year at Harvard Medical School," Journal American Medical Association 245:1637-38 (April 24, 1981).

"Report of the Changing Role of Residents in Hospitals," Bulletin New York Academy of Medicine 57:731-36 (October 1981).

"The Role of the Attending Physician," Archives Internal Medicine 142:698-99 (April 1982).

"Internship: Physicians Respond to Norman Cousins," Journal American Medical Association 245:2141-44 (November 13, 1981).

Bickel, JW, "The Role of MD/PhD Training," New England Journal Medicine 304:1265-68 (May 21, 1981).

Grimsley, WT, "Continuing Medical Education...." Southern Medical Journal 75:461-62 (April 1982).

"Who Shall Study Medicine?" Journal American Medical Association 245:1630-32 (April 24, 1981).

Association of American Medical Colleges. Medical School Admission Requirements (published annually). Washington: AAMC.

Virshup, B. Coping in Medical School. Chapel Hill: Health Sciences Consortium, 1981. 130 pp.

Klein, K. Getting Better: A Medical Student's Story. Boston: Little, Brown & Co., 1981. 284 pp.

Gusky, J. Ward Survival Manual. Dallas: Medical Student Pub., 1982. 180 pp.

LeBaron, C. Gentle Vengeance: An Account of the First Year at Harvard Medical School. New York: Richard Marek Pub., 1981. 272 pp.

Knight, JA. Doctor-To-Be: Coping With the Trials & Triumps of Medical School. New York: Appleton-Century-Crofts, 1981. 269 pp.

Fredericks, M & Mundy, P. Making It in Med School: Biography of a Medical Student. Chicago: Loyola Univ. Press (3441 North Ashland Ave.), 1980. 144 pages.

- 25 -

External Readings - Health Care Delivery System

"The American Health Care Delivery System," In: The American Medical Association Family Medical Guide. (Kunz, JRM, ed.). New York: Random House, 1982, pp. 728-53.

White, KL, "Life and Death and Medicine," Scientific American 229(3): 23-33 (September 1973).

Carey, LC, "Health Costs, Competition and the Physician," American Journal Surgery 143:2-5 (January 1982).

Borgenicht, L, "American Medicine: An Annotated Bibliography," New England Journal Medicine 304:1112-17 (April 30, 1981).

Tarlov, AR, "The Increasing Supply of Physicians, The Changing Structure of the Health-Services System, and the Future Practice of Medicine," New England Journal Medicine 308:1235-44 (May 19, 1983).

Roemer, MI. An Introduction to the U.S. Health Care System. New York: Springer Pub. Co., 1982. 134 pp.

Wohl, S. The Medical Industrial Complex. New York: Harmony Books, 1984. 218 pp.

McKeown, T. The Role of Medicine. London: Nuffield Provincial Hospital Trust, 1976. 180 pp.

Califano, JA. America's Health Care Revolution. New York: Random House, 1986.

Fuchs, VR. Who Shall Live? Health, Economics and Social Choice. New York: Basic Books, Inc., 1974. 168 pp.

Lee, PR, Estes, CL, & Ramsey, NB (eds.). The Nation's Health. San Francisco: Boyd & Fraser Pub. Co., 1984. 543 pp.

Jain, SC, & Paul, JE (eds.). Policy Issues in Personal Health Services. Rockville, MD: Aspen Systems Corp., 1983. 480 pp.

Medical Ethics and Cost Containment

. . . strategies developed to contain rising medical costs also connote a profound and rapid shift in the manner in which medical care is delivered . . . These proposals also have the potential to insidiously alter the factors considered in making life-and-death decisions for individual patients. . . .

A realistic approach would be the utilization of individuals, review committees, and others within the community who are familar with both the difficulty and the necessity of making life-or-death decisions but are specifically uninvolved and unaffected by the financial aspects of the particular decision . . .

- Johnson, DE, "Commentary," Journal American Medical Association 252:223-24 (July 13, 1984).

Chapter II

CAREER PLANNING: IMPROVING YOUR CHANCES

Selecting an appropriate career is probably one of the most difficult tasks that you will confront during your lifetime. If your personal satisfaction and contribution to society are to be maximized, little help seems likely to found in the revelation model which relies heavily on proclamation ("I want to be a doctor") and prayer ("I hope medicine is right for me").

Successful decision making is more likely to be associated with an extended process where you accumulate evidence about professional alternatives and adopt systematic methods for assessing their relative merit. As Doctor Harold Radwin notes, "there is a place for non-cognitive judgment." However, "this component is facilitated by a context of realistic expectations based upon as much information as is pertinent."

In searching for an ideal professional career, major choices include those of medicine[1] versus another area. If medicine is elected, will your medical training be used to engage in clinical practice or seek a non-clinical position? If the former, you will need to choose between a medical, surgical or related specialty field. Moreover, the question of a sub-specialty may arise as well.

Over 25 percent of the students admitted to medical school apparently select this field before enrolling as a freshman in college.[2] In addition, nearly three out of four medical students choose their specialty area while taking the clinical sciences curriculum,[3] usually in their third year of training. Since this decision can no longer be circumvented by opting for "general practice," all medical school graduates who expect to treat patients must elect an area for residency training. Moreover, many non-clinical posts seek doctors who have satisfied this requirement while some even specify "board certification." Many of the guidelines and techniques outlined below, however, seem essential regardless of when you decide upon a medical career or how you intend to utilize your medical education.

---

[1] An academic degree in medicine or a professional license implies a single career option. This book, though, recognizes a functional model involving more than 500 differentiated contributions. Thus the roles described below represent real rather than superficial career choices.

[2] American Medical News February 12, 1982, p. 25.

[3] "When Students Choose a Specific Medical Field," Journal American Medical Association 244:2813 (December 26, 1980).

Assumptions and Cautions

This book has been developed around several important assumptions. (1) Research indicates that job satisfaction generally is correlated closely with the interest that one has in his or her work. If perchance a medical degree is viewed as a means of enhancing your personal status or maximizing economic return, this volume has little to offer.

(2) We have provided a foundation for approaching the question, "What can I do if I decide to seek a degree in medicine?" No book, however, can guarantee whether a career in any field will satisfy your talents and ambitions. Careful examination of this reference though should double or treble the odds for making a sound choice.

Thus review of this book per se cannot serve as a substitute for the in-depth knowledge acquired through a four-year program of medical education, the three to five years of residency training, the guidance offered by a faculty adviser or preceptor, or the wisdom accumulated by an experienced clinician. However, the insights supplied by our expert collaborators, when buttressed by external reading, should furnish an overview of professional contributions and career options that may be difficult to replicate elsewhere.

(3) Sound career planning rests upon a broad understanding of professional opportunities and concerns. Consequently, the readings in Chapters III and V reflect a diversity of views prepared by clinicians in private practice, administrative officers of medical specialty boards, college faculty who engage in both teaching and research, an editor, investigators, professional association leaders and several non-physicians.

(4) Finally, this volume provides basic information about practice and non-practice options, outlines strategies to improve the reliability of career selection, and furnishes background material for asking meaningful questions about your presumed interests. These goals may not be realized, however, unless you invest adequate time studying this reference and following many of its recommendations. A more passive or haphazard approach to career planning introduces the risk that four to eight years of your immediate future will be wasted to say nothing about the dissipation of economic resources associated with this effort. Given a possible nationwide surplus of physicians coupled with high switching rates that characterize many residency training programs, as well as clinician movement between specialty areas (see Table I-1), more rather than less attention to career planning seems necessary.

Using This Guide Efficiently

Several guidelines may help to maximize the value of this book. First, do not attempt to digest its contents in one or two sittings. An extended period, therefore, should be employed to establish, test, and even discard hypotheses about your career plan.

Second, after completion of each numbered section, make a penciled entry of the assigned code in the appropriate column on the Medical Career Scorecard furnished on the inside of the rear cover. Next, test these impressions as outlined below in "External Readings."

Third, key information related to career planning is presented throughout this volume. Don't overlook some sections because of prior "knowledge" or a feeling that the unit seems irrevelant. For example, students interested in surgery can augment their impressions by a careful review of the external readings pertaining to anesthesiology and vice versa. Moreover, students attempting to choose between a medical or surgical specialty may gain invaluable perspective by examining how these approaches often complement each other - see Kra, SJ and Boltax, RS. Is Surgery Necessary? (page 284).

If you would like to learn more about the socio-economic-political environment which confronts doctors today (including aspects of medical practice as well), consider spending $45.00 for a two-year subscription to American Medical News. This valuable publication, issued 48 time a year, is available from the American Medical Association, 535 North Dearborn St., Chicago, IL, 60610. Read several back issues at your local library before making such an expenditure. The beginning of your sophomore year in college might constitute an ideal time for starting a subscription.

Organization of Specialty Information

The 33 medical fields described in the next chapter could have been organized according to various criteria such as availability of board certification, date of formal recognition for the specialty, number of practitioners, alphabetical, and so forth. Since our purpose is to highlight major career options, we have modified a traditional scheme, the tripartite classification utilized by the Association of American Medical Colleges. Thus the description of specialty areas were grouped initially under "Medical," "Surgical," and "Other."

While these categories are helpful in addressing our topic, medical practice does not necessarily conform to discrete models. For example, ninety percent of the patients seen by otolaryngologists, a "surgical" specialty, can be treated nonsurgically. At the same time, though, the average otolaryngologist operates two or three days each week.[1] Further, some obstetricians treat male patients, some surgeons derive more of their income from family practice than their primary specialty, and so forth. To summarize, your readings should be approached as

---

[1] Cantrell, RW, "Otolaryngology," Journal American Medical Association 245:1171 (March 20, 1981).

incremental snapshots of the complex world of medicine rather than a complete description[1] of every professional function.

In order to stress certain functional roles with promising employment possibilities, a fourth category, "Additional Professional Areas," was developed. Several fields in this more heterogenous section - especially units 27, 28 and 31 - represent areas where research may dominate the patient care component. Further, "Forensic Medicine," a legitimate sub-specialty of pathology (unit 23), has been placed here to highlight the unique population served. Finally, human sexuality (unit 33) has not been included under psychiatry because other specialists also treat problems of this type.

External Readings

To expedite assessment of professional options, numerous external readings are recommended throughout this book. Some stress the underlying cause of patient complaints while others review steps followed by a physician in arriving at a diagnosis. Additional selections focus on treatment options or the application of a single procedure. Certain references treat broader issues such as the concerns of an entire specialty or the organization of a quality assurance activity.

Each section includes articles and books, coded as (A) and (B) respectively, which were generated primarily by screening more than 200 medical journals. Since the universe of medical journals is more than ten times greater, and most books were excluded from the screening activity, your sample is biased with respect to both date of publication and scope of coverage. Thus recommended readings do not attempt to define the respective fields nor describe the latest scientific/clinical developments. On the contrary, they represent basic information which should faciltate more intensive investigation of the various topics.

In instances where a single report covers more than one subject, placement may be regarded as arbitrary. For example, a study that depicts how clinicians treat aged patients with arthritis could have been classified under either "Geriatrics" or "Rheumatology." Because cross listing was not employed, references pertaining to a particular topic may be found, on certain occasions, under another classification.

Since some libraries may not carry a given reference, or be able to secure it on an inter-library loan, each subject usually includes multiple citations. When consulting books, read the first 100-125 pages

---

[1] For a comprehensive analysis of the content of medical practice, see: Mendenhall, RC. Medical Practice in the United States. Princeton, NJ: Robert Wood Johnson Foundation, 1981. 96 pp.

from several volumes instead of the entire contents of one. [1] If a particular source captures your imagination, then continue to the end.

In order to facilitate comparative ranking of alternative career goals, many external references have been assigned an extended code. After the completion of such readings, transcribe these symbols to the appropriate column on your Medical Career Scorecard. Thus your level of interest in a primary area, such as Pathology (23), can, at a glance, be traced to the supplementary readings pertaining to the same field by noting the congruence or dispersion of similar articles (e.g., 23-A-1, etc.) and books (e.g., 23-B-1, etc.) on the Scorecard.

In attempting to interpret your profile, do not be dismayed if your preferred choice contains several selections rated as having "little or no interest."[2] Few if any occupations can be expected to yield complete satisfaction. The critical question for your purposes would seem to be whether medicine in general, or your current preference for a given specialty on balance, posesses sufficient appeal to warrant further attention.

Within each basic category, the numeric suffix suggests the relative ability of each selection to enlarge a student's perception. Those items with the lowest numbers (i.e., A-1, A-2 and B-1, B-2) represent the most important supplementary readings for establishing your interest in a given career area. On the other hand, recommendations classified at the upper end of the scale will probably yield less incremental value in helping to meet this objective. In addition, the latter may be more appropriate for students who have been admitted to medical school while citations at the preferred end of the scale may often be fundamental for career planning regardless of your status. Although relative rank may be critical in some instances, differences between adjacent listings (e.g., A-4 vs. A-5) are usually not significant, especially when moving toward items assigned a lower priority (e.g., A-11 vs. A-12).

In examining these external selections, it seems unnecessary to become preoccupied with the medical/scientific jargon which appears from time to time. Because the screening process endeavored to limit the number of sources characterized by technical complexity, difficulties of this nature should not be very great. Thus your purpose in reviewing the external references is not to master their content as in preparing for an examination. On the contrary, your goal here is simply to (1) determine any potential interest in the subject (can you envision

---

[1] Since few books that contain more than 450 pages seem likely to be read independently, this criterion was usually employed as a cutoff.

[2] Your scorecard may also be used to depict when a specialty area holds little or no interest. Thus, for some students, initial efforts in career planning may focus more on the elimination of certain fields than on attempts to identify an ultimate choice.

spending some 35 years dealing with such problems when they occur?), and (2), gain sufficient background for engaging in a dialogue with others who possess greater experience. If you are already enrolled in medical school, the meaning of unknown or obscure terms should be investigated.

Your overall objective is to review a minimum number of external readings sufficient to confirm the level of interest tentatively generated by the primary readings (i.e., contributions designated exclusively by a numeric code). In addition, uncoded bibliographic citations may serve the same purpose. Unfortunately, field research has not been undertaken to suggest the actual number of corroborating nominations that may be necessary to ascertain when a typical student may cross the threshold from "general interest" to "career goal."

Nevertheless, multiple positive entries on your Scorecard will help validate this critical decision. Thus you are encouraged to read additional articles/books until the incremental results no longer alter your feelings about a medical career generally or commitment to a particular specialty field. In summary, we believe that a judgment concerning your lifetime vocation is too significant to rest upon a single lecture, clinical rotation, description of a medical procedure, survey of a given discipline, or a sole reference such as this one.

Testing Your Impressions

The investigatory process should be initiated at least one year before applying to medical school or seeking a residency position. During this interval, the prudent student will strive to develop a tentative hypothesis concerning his/her career objectives and systematically review its validity by gathering new evidence to help confirm the current goal.

Some of the techniques that may aid in this two-stage process, such as heavy reliance on the external readings, were noted above. Also, set aside several evenings or mornings to visit a health sciences library. Most comprehensive facilities of this type carry 50 or more health newsletters that cover a variety of topics which range from "Aging" to "Women in Medicine." After the material in this book has been digested, your knowledge base will facilitate scanning the universe of newsletters. The next step is to identify several publications that correspond closely to your area(s) of high interest. Once these sources have been established, return several times and monitor six consecutive issues to determine if the reference tends to sustain or overturn your career hypothesis. Indeed, if one or two seem especially relevant, enter a subscription. Since the total expense of launching a medical career may exceed $100,000, investing $150-$200 to corroborate the wisdom of your choice could yield substantial dividends for many years to come. If you are enrolled in medical school, you may wish to spend $35 for a four-year membership in the American Medical Student Association.

Further, consider how your undergraduate major might be employed to strengthen performance as a specialist in medicine or even as a non-clinician. For example, a psychology major might contemplate the field of psychiatry, a pharmacy graduate might investigate clinical pharmacology, while a computer science major might examine epidemiology in the area of public health or pathology. While arguments can be advanced that diversity rather than synergism should shape the membership of a specialty, this latter strategy might represent an optimal solution for many students and society as well.

Another technique for appraising career interests involves careful selection of summer employment. Many pre-med and medical students seek a position with a private or public hospital to obtain funds and gain experience. Relatively few, though, serve as a research assistant for a large county or state medical society or the health department of a local or state governmental unit. Futher, the medical director of a health insurance carrier also might be contacted concerning the availability of a summer internship.

Finally, when the material and recommendations presented in this volume have been assimilated, seek the advice of a faculty member or community practitioner who can help evaluate your current preferences. Perhaps this expert can describe some job-related factors that may have been overlooked. If your evaluation of a career in medicine has been based upon many of the techniques advocated above, these discussions can be approached with both knowledge and confidence.

External Readings

Petersdorf, RG, "Some Perturbations in Medicine," Journal American Medical Association 249:2098-2101 (November 5, 1982).

"AMI Career Dialogue," Hospital Physician 18:25,29 (February 1982); 18:17,20 (March 1982).

Miller, GD, "How Career Decisions Are Made," Medical Student 9:9-15 (May 1983).

Roller, AC (ed.). The Pfizer Guide: Medical Career Opportunities. New Canaan, CT: Mark Powley Associates, 1983. 201 pp.

Rabinowitz, PM. Talking Medicine: America's Doctors Tell Their Story. New York: WW Norton, 1981. 319 pp.

Bluestone, N. So You Want to be a Doctor? New York: Lorthrop, Lee & Shepard Books, 1981. 241 pp.

Would you advise your child to go to medical school?

. . . Anyone going into medicine today would basically have to cope with different problems from those we coped with a generation ago - like the diminished expectations as far as power and status and money go. . . The basic attitude of helpfulness as well as the intellectual challenges are going to continue to be present throughout medicine - and, certainly, the changing technology is exciting. I can't imagine in good faith advising anybody not to be involved with it if they had an inclination to do so.

- Karleen Hammitt, MD, psychiatrist, Prescott, AZ.

Yes, but . . you must have a caring, compassionate concern for people . . . Medicine is a caring profession. Sometimes that mission gets lost in the mixture of all these new facets of marketing and entrepreneurship . . .

- Edward W. Reed, MD, general surgeon, Memphis, TN.

American Medical News 29:17 (January 3, 1986).

Chapter III

DOCTORS AS CLINICIANS

Section 1 - ALLERGY AND IMMUNOLOGY

Roy Patterson

Roy Patterson, MD, is Professor and Chairman, Department
of Medicine and Chief, Section of Allergy & Immunology at
Northwestern University Medical School, Chicago, IL.

The specialty of allergy developed gradually after the symptoms and
diseases related to environmental exposure were described. Originally,
allergic reactions were thought to be due to toxins in grass pollen, the
first pollen allergy identified. This malady was called "hay fever," a
misnomer still widely used.

Because the science of immunology was developing at about the same
time, it was thought that immunization against the presumptive toxin
would result in clinical control. Since initial attempts to treat grass
pollenosis with immunization appeared successful, this type of therapy
has continued to the present.

In later years it was recognized that the symptoms were not due to
toxins but some "altered reaction" or allergy of the host. This altered
reaction was then recognized to be on some type of immunologic basis due
to an allergic antibody. The field was inhibited because it lacked a
laboratory test to demonstrate such an antibody. The only clinical and
research tools were the allergic skin test, and subsequently, the
ability to transfer skin reactivity with serum from an allergic to
normal person. This was the major research tool for decades, known as
the Prausnitz-Kustner reaction.

Next, the effectiveness of allergy injection therapy was shown to be
associated with the induction of a new type of immune response
attributable to a different antibody, the "blocking antibody." The
evolution of the specialty was correlated with the recognition of
aeroallergens and with the correlations of symptoms of seasonal allergic
disease as well as the demonstration of allergic antibody. Thus, in
part, the specialty became strong in the U.S. due to the importance of
ragweed pollen as an allergen. Further, the high incidence and
chronicity of the disease led physicians to develop an interest in the
field, often because they or their family members had allergic diseases.
The subsequent history of allergy as a specialty is related to the
explosion of knowledge in the broad field of immunology.

The characterization of allergic antibody as being in the IgE immunoglobulin class, the development of assays for allergic antibody by in vitro techniques, the advent of new pharmacologic therapies, the recognition of new classes of bioactive mediators (leukotrienes and platelet activating factor, for example) have all advanced allergy as a scientific clinical sub-specialty.

The current practice of allergy is based on the traditional methodology using the newer scientific information available. The practicing allergist will spend much time in diagnosing the very common allergic problems in the population. These include allergic rhinitis, asthma, anaphylaxis, drug reactions, atopic dermatitis, contact dermatitis, urticaria and angioedema. Depending on the training and experience of the allergist, a significant part of the practice may be in other immunologic diseases such as diagnosis and treatment of immune deficiency diseases, occupational immunologic lung disease, the autoimmune disease and other less common problems such as the vasculitides.

The type of physician attracted to the specialty is generally comfortable dealing with chronic disease. Allergic disease can usually be diagnosed and treated very well. Cures are not often obtained except where an allergen such as a pet can be avoided. The clinical practice is a mixture of control of chronic recurrent symptoms by immunologic control and pharmacotherapy.

Allergists prepare for this specialty by training in either pediatrics or internal medicine. Subsequent to becoming board eligible in either of those fields, formal education in the subspecialty of allergy-immunology is done in a two, or occasionally, three year program. The training experience involves both children and adults as patients. A research experience should be included whether or not the individual plans an academic career or practice of the specialty.

Practice opportunities appear satisfactory. At times a physician may practice full-time allergy or part-time in combination with either pediatrics or internal medicine.

One advantage to the practice of allergy is the fact that it covers patients of all ages. Obviously, if the allergist is primarily an internist and is treating a sick child, this is done in conjunction with a pediatrician. Another of the advantages of the sub-specialty is the opportunity to do "medical detective work." The patient with unexplained acute allergic symptoms presents a complex problem to the experienced allergist. The allergist, by proper history and diagnostic tests, may identify an unsuspected pet hamster as the cause and obtain a cure by avoidance of the animal. Similar experiences are frequent.

The practice of allergy is complicated as it is possible for a physician to graduate from medical school, train in pediatrics or internal medicine without any significant experience in allergy. Such a physician in practice will usually realize the limitations of training and refer patients to the allergist for consultation and management.

In the same context, it is the allergist who knows what is and what is not allergy and how to manage the problems. Because urticaria and angioedema, for example, are common symptoms of allergic reactions to foods or drugs, physicians inexperienced in allergic disease will consider all cases of these clinical problems as due to an external allergen. It is the well trained allergist who can differentiate the non-allergic rhinitis, asthma, anaphylaxis, urticaria, and angioedema, review the patient's problems and provide proper pharmacologic control to patients who have at times been frustrated for years.

Newly developing fields, such as occupational allergic disease, the uncommon but challenging hypersensitivity pneumonitis, the continuing and ever growing problems of drug reactions all provide continuing intellectual challenges to the allergist.

For the physician who has the interest and talent for research, there are broad opportunities in appropriate medical schools and government and pharmaceutical companies. Often a combination of private practice and part-time academic work is possible.

Problems in the sub-specialty are typical of those associated with chronic disease. Because patients would like a "cure," the field is troubled by the use of unproven techniques. It becomes a frustrating case when the allergist has made the proper diagnosis and treatment plan but the patient goes to another practitioner for yet another therapy.

The changing economics of medicine will impact on the sub-specialty of allergy as it will on all types of practice in medicine. Because the best aspects of allergy practice include the prevention of illness, such as the prevention of hospital admissions due to asthma, the sub-specialty should remain competitive whatever the future holds.

In summary, the physician who enters the sub-specialty of allergy, after careful evaluation of the range and depth of the field, will be pleased with decades of allergy practice. It is recommended that any medical student or resident in pediatrics or internal medicine make every effort to have a rotation in an academic allergy program with both research and clinical exposure prior to entering the sub-specialty.

External Readings

1-A-1   Salvaggio, JE (ed.), "Primer on Allergic & Immunologic Diseases," Journal American Medical Association 248:2579-2772. (November 26, 1982).

External Readings (continued)

1-A-2   deShazo, RD & Salvaggio, JE, "Allergy and Immunology," Journal American Medical Association 254:2257-59 (October 25, 1985).

1-A-3   Fuacci, AS, "The Revolution in Clinical Immunology," Journal American Medical Association 246:2567-72 (December 4, 1981).

1-A-4   Postgraduate Medicine 72:134-85 (August 1982).

1-A-5   "Review of Procedures Used in the Practice of Allergy," Bulletin New York Academy Medicine 57:507-649 (September 1981).

1-B-1   Speer, F. Handbook of Clinical Allergy: A Practical Guide to Patient Management. Littleton, MA: John Wright - PSG, 1982. 258 pp.

1-B-2   Patterson, R (ed.). Allergic Diseases: Diagnosis & Management (3rd edition). Philadelphia: JB Lippincott, 1985.

1-B-3   Lawlor, GJ & Fischer, TJ. Manual of Allergy & Immunology: Diagnosis & Therapy. Boston: Little, Brown & Co., 1981. 504 pp.

1-B-4   Playfair, JHL. Immunology at a Glance. Oxford, England: Blackwell Scientific Pub., 1982. 70 pp.

1-B-5   Clark, WR. The Experimental Foundations of Immunology. New York: John Wiley, 1980. 372 pp.

Continuing Education

. . . Doctors who fail to keep up on an almost daily basis will very quickly wake up and find themselves Rip Van Winkles . . . .

- Black, D, "The Making of a Doctor," The New York Times Magazine, May 23, 1982, p. 62.

Section 2 - DERMATOLOGY

Edmund D. Lowney

Edmund D. Lowney, MD, PhD, is Emeritus Professor of
Dermatology at The Ohio State University College of
Medicine and former Director, Division of Dermatology.
His primary area of professional interest has been in
studies of allergic contact dermatitis in human subjects.

Dermatology involves the treatment of diseases of the skin, some of
the most common of which are psoriasis, acne, warts, and moles. Many
dermatologic disorders have systemic aspects, but these patients come
for treatment because skin lesions are of primary importance to them.
In the past, dermatology has been linked with venereology and clinicians
still treat a great number of patients with venereal warts, venereal
herpes simplex, and less frequently, syphilis.

Some dermatologic treatment is medical - therapy here involves drugs
given both by mouth (oral medication) and by application to the skin
(topical medication). Other treatments represent surgical care and
include removal of skin cancers, moles, warts, etc. The dermatologist
is also called upon to identify cutaneous signs of other diseases - for
instance, he or she might note jaundice and suspect that liver disease
was present and thus refer the patient to the proper specialist. Some
dermatologists also get involved in non-surgical cosmetic procedures
such as chemical "face peels" and injection of collagen into depressed
scars. There are several special surgical procedures in clinical
dermatology such as dermabrasion (trying to scrape away some of the
scars due to acne or wrinkles), hair transplants, special forms of
surgery used to remove skin cancers such as Moh's chemosurgery, and a
certain amount of plastic surgery.

Most of the patients who see dermatologists are self-referred,
possibly recommended by other patients. Perhaps twenty percent are
referred by other physicians for a variety of reasons although 50-75
percent of clinical dermatology may be done by physicians other than
dermatologists. Obviously, in areas where many dermatologists are
present, that percentage will fall accordingly. Closed panel practice
situations such as Health Maintenance Organizations (HMO) and military
medical facilities may have a host of dermatologists and patients go
directly to them. Other HMO's have few dermatologists and permit the
patient to see the specialist only if he is referred by a "primary
physician."

The laws of most states permit anyone who has a MD or DO degree, and
a license to practice medicine and surgery, to do anything from
prescribing a cough syrup to the removal of a malignant brain tumor.

Most dermatologists have completed four years of medical school, followed by one or two years of internship or residency in medicine and three years of dermatologic residency. After finishing these requirements, the trainee is eligible to sit for the American Board of Dermatology examination. However, the only legal status of the American Board of Dermatology is that certification may be a requirement for obtaining a staff position in VA hospitals and other government institutions. In practice, anyone with or without training, MD or DO, can practice dermatology in the U.S.A.

Most dermatologists find that the independence and pleasure of practicing in the field, coupled with the adequate income, are so attractive that relatively few have been induced to pursue non-clinical activities.

A common non-clinical activity for dermatologists involves teaching and research in a medical school, often with some time spent in clinical practice as well. A practice associated with a medical school is often more interesting than in a private office because a higher percentage of the patients represent referrals. While total income may be less, security is enhanced through the salary base provided by the school.

Compared with other medical specialities, dermatology offers many opportunities for research. Theoretically, all academic dermatologists are supposed to be engaged in research along with their teaching and clinical responsibilities. However, since there is a relative shortage of researchers in dermatology, many academic positions are filled by specialists with purely clinical interests. The lack of job security for a non-research dermatologist in an academic medical center, however, presents a problem which has not been solved.

Many pharmaceutical companies have active dermatologic development programs. On the surface, working for a large drug company, where one can do creative research developing new drugs with the backup of laboratory facilities of a large corporation, sounds quite attractive. However, dermatologists who take employment with these firms often leave after several years, quite disillusioned. The problem usually stems from the fact that the dermatologist is paid so much more than the other professionals who are associated with him, such as biochemists, that his tasks are confined to work that only a physician can undertake, namely, the design and setting up of clinical trials with physicians outside the company. Furthermore, the final decisions and management of the project always rests with the non-physician staff of the company. Thus with few exceptions, the dermatologist never gets to participate in this broader management function.

In addition to the drug industry, cosmetic and soap firms, such as Procter & Gamble, have enormous laboratories that offer many potential research opportunities for the dermatologist. Further, commercial contract firms may employ dermatologists as clinical investigators to test new pharmaceuticals/chemicals on patients or paid volunteers.

These investigations determine the toxicity, possible irritation, sensitizing potential, etc., of various compounds which drug and cosmetic companies market. This area has been exploited very happily by a few dermatologists; but the market can sustain only so many commercial organizations of this type.

Dermatologists see a wide variety of patients and usually see most of them very quickly. The practice of dermatology is fun because patients represent a broad cross-section of American society. Also, the stress associated with this specialty is relatively low. Few patients are likely to be seriously ill and the number of house calls at night is relatively small. Perhaps the most rewarding satisfaction, however, is the fact that the dermatologist can really help most of the patients seen.

Although a dermatologist usually sees more patients per hour than a family practitioner, the fees per patient visit tend to be similar. Consequently, the annual income level of the dermatologist often exceeds that of the family practitioner. On the other hand, it is very rare for a dermatologist to qualify as a "big earner."

Some dermatologists do a fair amount of cosmetic surgery and medical procedures which are not covered by most insurance programs. In these areas, the dermatologist is free to set his own fees without interference by regulations or price restrictions.

However, several limitations may be associated with this specialty. Treating nothing but acne and warts in an isolated office all day can be very boring if you have been trained to do complex procedures. Dermatology, just because it is relatively stress-free and lucrative, attracts a small number of people who are simply too lazy or irresponsible, or both, to make it in other areas of medicine. Further, dermatology involves looking at smelly, necrotic and pussy skin much of the time; in fact, a number of clinicians are helped by being relatively anosmic, i.e., they do not possess a keen sense of smell. Moreover, too many dermatologists may have been trained in recent years with the result that the specialty may be headed for financial and moral hard times. In spite of these drawbacks, most of which seem trivial, the number of applicants for dermatology residencies in the past few years has exceeded the number of places by a factor of three to four.

On the plus side, almost every person has one or more dermatologic complaints. Consequently, the number of potential patients is enormous. In the Soviet Union, where medical care is relatively free, there are about twice as many dermatologists per 100,000 population as in the United States. In short, the dermatologist can treat skin problems so much more efficiently than any other clinician that patients, given free choice, tend to prefer this specialist.

On the negative side, there is growing evidence that the market for dermatologists is rapidly becoming saturated. Young persons finishing their residency training often have difficulty finding a spot to practice. Ten years ago, new graduates could go anywhere and put out their shingle. Now one might have to journey to a small town in North Dakota or the coal mining region of Ohio to find an unopposed practice situation. However, in apparent defiance of the law of supply and demand, many dermatologists seem to be doing very well in places such as San Diego and San Francisco where the physician-patient ratio is extremely high. Further, pessimists point out that with the development of HMO's the free choice of the patient to seek dermatologic care may be decreased as these organizations require that a primary care physician be seen first. This problem may correct itself if dermatologists' incomes fall until HMO's can afford to hire them to work as primary care physicians.

As a general principle, it seems apparent that a prosperous doctor is a happy doctor. Because he is needed, he can practice on his own terms - do things he likes to do best, set his own hours, etc. For these reasons, financial security and overall happiness are closely correlated. But leaving aside financial considerations, what sources of intrinsic satisfaction can the doctor expect to find in the future? First, there will always be the pleasure of taking care of a delightful and varied group of patients. Secondly, the relative freedom from red tape as experienced in a predominately outpatient setting may survive. Other characteristics of the practice model, though, seem to lie beyond reasonable speculation.

Dermatology practice in an academic setting depends on the ability to obtain funds to support research. While several administrations have reduced federal support, Congress has often restored these cuts. Although academic dermatology has survived so far, the dynamics of the political scene may produce substantial retrenchment.

The dermatology matching program run by the National Resident Matching Program, One American Parkway, Evanston, Illinois, 60205, operates a service for interested applicants. Currently, interviews and applications are processed in the summer and matching results are announced in October of the internship year.

In general, dermatology residency directors are seeking bright young people with one or two years of training in internal medicine. Internships in surgery, pediatrics, general practice, or a mixed background, are often less preferable than one in internal medicine. However, any of the above seem superior to an internship in a nonclinical area such as pathology. However, almost no dermatology residencies will take candidates directly out of medical schools without at least one year of post-graduate training.

External Readings

2-A-1 "Skin, Hair, & Nail Disorders," In: The American Medical Association Family Medical Guide, (Kunz, JRM, ed.). New York: Random House, 1982. pp. 250-65.

2-A-2 Goodman, LJ & Swartwout, JE, "Socioeconomic Issues in Dermatology," Journal American Academic Dermatology 5(6):711-20 (December 1981).

2-A-3 Bigby, M & Arndt, KA, "Dermatology," Journal American Medical Association 254:2283-86 (October 25, 1985).

2-A-4 Tschen, E & Becker, LE, "Skin Infections," Continuing Education for the Family Physician 17:45-52 (July 1982).

2-A-5 "Symposium: Dermatology," The Practitioner 226:1221-1321 (July 1982).

2-A-6 "Dermatology," Postgraduate Medicine 72:164-246 (October 1982).

2-B-1 Pillsbury, DM & Heaton, CL. A Manual of Dermatology. Philadelphia: WB Saunders, 1980. 360 pp.

2-B-2 Roenigk, HH. Office Dermatology. Baltimore: Williams & Wilkins, 1981. 363 pp.

2-B-3 Stegman, SJ, et al. Basics of Dermatologic Surgery. Chicago: Year Book Medical Publishers, 1982. 134 pp.

2-B-4 Hall-Smith, P & Cairns, RJ. Dermatology: Current Concepts and Practice. Washington: Butterworth, Inc. 1981. 394 pp.

Section 3 - ENDOCRINOLOGY

Maurice Fox

Maurice Fox, MD, FACP, practices clinical endocrinology at the Palo Alto Medical Clinic in Palo Alto, CA and is a Clinical Professor of Internal Medicine, Stanford University School of Medicine. He is past Vice President of the American College of Physicians.

At one time a physician could master the current knowledge in medicine and deal with all patients' problems. Then technical procedures became possible, such as surgery, and it was recognized that one person could not be expert in treating all complaints and perform surgery as well. As surgery became more complex, it became clear that one individual could not master all the knowledge of surgery and sub-specialities developed for nervous systems, urological systems, gynecological systems, etc. Areas of responsibility thus narrowed so that one person might be expected to master current knowledge in the field.

This pattern was also true of medical specialties. One person could not master all the new knowledge of diseases of the heart, blood, nervous system and ductless glands. Thus were born the cardiologist (heart), hematologist (blood), neurologist (nervous system), and endocrinologist (ductless glands). The patient is not able to determine to which specialty his complaint belongs, so he goes to his physician, an internist, who is trained in the general area of medicine and can diagnose the nature of the problem. If diagnosis or treatment of the patient's problem proves to be obscure or difficult, the patient is then referred to a sub-specialist, such as an endocrinologist who is basically an internist with particular expertise pertaining to endocrine disorders.

The endocrine system consists of organs that have specific responsibilities for certain functions necessary for life such as growth, sexual development, reproduction, fuel availability and consumption, blood pressure maintenance, temperature control, and maintenance of an internal chemical environment necessary for life and functioning of the body. These organs (glands) secrete chemicals (hormones) into the blood stream in response to need. These hormones act only where their receptors are located, and it is the combination of a hormone (key) and its specific receptor (lock) acting together that causes the series of chemical reactions that characterize the hormone's action. For instance, insulin (hormone), secreted by the pancreas (gland) combines with the insulin receptor on a muscle cell and therefore acts to permit the entry of sugar into that cell. Sugar can then be used as a fuel and the muscle cell functions.

The purpose of endocrinology is to study which glands secrete which hormones, resulting in which necessary bodily functions. Diseases of endocrine glands are caused by too much hormone secreted by a tumor of a gland, or too little hormone caused by inability of an atrophic gland to secrete enough hormone. The job of the endocrinologist is to diagnose where nature has made a mistake. Usually there are three questions to be answered: (1) Are the patient's complaints due to an abnormality of endocrine gland function? (2) If so, which gland or glands are at fault? (3) Is the patient sick because the involved gland is producing too much or too little hormone and, if so, why?

The training of an endocrinologist begins in medical school followed by internship and residency training in internal medicine. This vast knowledge base is necessary for many reasons, not the least of which is to develop diagnostic acumen necessary to separate organic from emotionally based symptoms. Every endocrinologist must first be an excellent diagnostician. This requires a basic knowledge of human biology and psychology through comprehensive training in internal medicine. Subsequently, one spends several years as a "fellow" coping with and learning about specific endocrine diseases.

The practitioner of endocrinology must be fully trained as an internist because patients present nonspecific complaints such as fatigue, weight gain, and irregular periods. It is also essential that the clinician separate patients whose symptoms are emotionally based from those with life-threatening illness. For example, a patient with extreme fatigue and weight loss may be depressed or may have adrenal gland insufficiency. Failure to diagnose depression may result in an unsatisfactory response to therapy, but it is not life threatening. Failure to diagnose adrenal insufficiency may result in sudden death.

The endocrinologist thus assumes responsibility for making the proper diagnosis which may save the patient's life. Determining the correct diagnosis will lead the endocrinologist to order the proper tests which can substantiate the diagnosis and lead to life-saving therapy. If the physician does not consider the true diagnosis, due to lack of training or talent, he cannot make that diagnosis. Consequently, therapy is improper and the patient does not get well. This series of events makes the life of the endocrinologist rewarding as every patient is a diagnostic and therapeutic challenge. Life is never dull for the medical detective.

Some patients suffer from symptoms that lend themselves to explanations that are not supported by scientific facts. The endocrinologist will see many patients who suffer from dizzy spells thought to be due to low blood sugar - i.e. hypoglycemia. Extensive testing may not confirm the presence of a measurable low blood sugar. Other patients will complain vociferously of fluid retention but extensive testing may not reveal any basis for the fluid retention. In both cases, the patients are often very upset and demand relief whereas the endocrinologist cannot find any specific abnormality that he or she can correct. It is at these times that the true substance of the endocrinologist as a physician is tested. These patients are suffering, but no one can define why. The endocrinologist then must serve as a source of emotional support for the patient. The symptoms must be perceived as legitimate and every effort should be made to relieve the patient's discomfort, although not with therapies that may cause more harm than good.

Many patients present chronic diseases such as diabetes mellitus that require long-term, on-going contact between the patient and physician. These patients take the most out of the physician in terms of effort, time, and emotional contribution, yet also give the most to the physician in terms of the gratification that comes from the long term association and friendship that is the greatest reward the physician gleans.

New information is constantly developing in endocrinology. The thin bones and hip fractures that are the cause of much pain and illness in elderly women may be prevented by new diagnostic and therapeutic modalities unknown in previous years. A whole new specialty is developing in the diagnosis and treatment of causes of infertility and endocrinologists find immense satisfaction in enabling infertile couples to have children. Transplantation of pancreatic tissue may finally cure diabetes, possibly within our lifetime. Finally, insulin pumps may not only prove to be a more effective way of taking insulin but provide a reliable means of automatically adjusting the dosage as required.

The future will provide any number of new approaches to diagnose and treat ailments that human beings have had to suffer in the past. The diagnosis of these problems and their successful treatment will be the role of the endocrinologist of the future. It is a very exciting life.

External Readings

3-A-1   "Hormonal Disorders," In: The American Medical Association Family Medical Guide, (Kunz, JRM, ed.). New York: Random House, 1982. pp. 514-28.

3-A-2   Landau, RL, "Endocrinology." Journal American Medical Association 254:2277-78 (October 25, 1985).

3-A-3   Nusynowitz, ML & Taylor, TJ. "Endocrinology," Journal American Medical Association 247:2347-49 (June 4, 1982).

3-A-4   Federman, DD, "Endocrinology," Scientific American Medicine (1982).

3-A-5   Landau, RL, "All Obesity is Morbid," Contemporary OB/GYN 19:118-24 (May 1982).

3-A-6   Sims, EAH & Berchtold, P, "Obesity and Hypertension," Journal American Medical Association 247:49-52 (January 1, 1982).

3-A-7   "New Pathways to Diabetes Control," Patient Care 16: 131-79 (February 15, 1982).

3-A-8   Segaloff, A, "Managing Endocrine and Metabolic Problems in the Patient with Advanced Cancer," Journal of American Medical Association 247:177-79 (January 9, 1981).

3-A-9   Salans, LB, "Diabetes Mellitus," Journal American Medical Association 247:590-94 (February 5, 1982).

3-A-10 Gambert, SR, et al., "Interpretation of Laboratory Results in the Elderly," Postgraduate Medicine 72:251-56 (October 1982).

3-A-11 Postgraduate Medicine 71:116-68 (March 1982).

3-A-12 Hadden, Dr, "Endocrine and Metabolic Disorders," Clinics in Obstetrics and Gynecology 9:29-53 (April 1982).

3-A-13 The Practitioner 226:195-278 (February 1982).

3-B-1   Hershman, JM (ed.). Practical Endocrinology. New York: John Wiley & Sons, 1981. 284 pp.

3-B-2   Laycock, JF & Wise, PH. Essential Endocrinology. New York: Oxford University Press, 1983. 371 pp.

3-B-3   Schwartz, TB & Ryan, WG. Year Book of Endocrinology - 1982. Chicago: Year Book Medical Publishers, 1982.

3-B-4   Frasier, SD. Pediatric Endocrinology. New York: Grune & Stratton, 1980. 375 pp.

3-B-5   Hershman, JM. Endocrine Pathophysiology: A Patient-Oriented Approach. (2nd ed.). Philadelphia: Lea & Febiger, 1982. 316 pp.

3-B-6   Hershman, JM. Management of Endocrine Disorders. Philadelphia: Lea & Febiger, 1980. 259 pp.

Section 4 - FAMILY PRACTICE

Nicholas J. Pisacano

Nicholas J. Pisacano, MD, is Executive Director & Secretary, American Board of Family Practice. He was one of the founders of the Board and has been the only director since its beginning in 1969. Previously, he was Professor of Internal Medicine, University of Kentucky Medical Center, Lexington, KY.

Family practice is a relatively new specialty, approved in 1969 by the American Board of Medical Specialties. Not to be confused with general practice, family practice is quite different although its heritage can be traced to this source. Prior to 1969, general practice was what physicians did when they did not go into a specialty. Today, nearly all graduates of American medical schools enter some specialty now that family practice has become one of the three-year training options for postgraduate study.

With over 28,000 diplomates certified since 1970, family practice has grown into the second largest specialty in America. Currently, about 7200 residents are in training in nearly 400 accredited residency programs throughout the United States and about 2200 graduate each year.

The official definition of family practice, as adopted by the American Board of Family Practice along with its sister organization the American Academy of Family Physicians, is as follows:

Family practice is comprehensive medical care with particular emphasis on the family unit, in which the physician's continuing responsibility for health care is not limited by the patient's age or sex nor by a particular organ system or disease entity.

Family practice is the specialty in breadth which builds upon a core of knowledge derived from other disciplines - drawing most heavily on internal medicine, pediatrics, obstetrics and gynecology, surgery, and psychiatry - and which establishes a cohesive unit combining the behavioral sciences with the traditional biological and clinical sciences. The core of knowledge encompassed by the specialty of family practice prepares the family physician for a unique role in patient management, problem solving, counseling, and as a personal physician who coordinates total health care delivery.

To enter family practice, one should have certain attributes and

talents. Of course, all physicians need a base of scientific knowledge
to enter medical school and learn basic clinical skills in order to
graduate. Given the vast amount of medical knowledge today, the medical
student must make a specialty choice. The new specialty of family
practice retains the favorable and desirable attributes of the old "GP"
yet is a scientifically based, "people oriented" specialty. The
specialty of family practice focuses its training on characteristics
such as "first contact care; continuous care (continuity of care);
personal care (caritas); family care; and, above all, clinical
competence."

The American Board of Family Practice recently completed an
extensive examination of the content of family practice as depicted by
1,200 diplomates of the American Board of Family Practice who practice
the specialty. The results of the "Content Validity Study" defined the
eight major responsibilities of family practice as follows:

A) Helping patients and their families plan for maintenance of
good health:

   1. Providing basic health information
   2. Providing families with realistic expectations regarding
       health problems and health care results
   3. Providing information and guidance concerning the
       utilization of community resources

B) Collecting and organizing history, physical and family
information for the purpose of providing health care:

   1. Conducting a medical history, a family history, and a
       history of the patient's chief complaints
   2. Conducting a physical examination
   3. Generating an initial potential problem list which
       includes a differential diagnosis (sometimes called
       assessment)
   4. Identifying and acquiring relevant diagnostic tests (e.g.,
       laboratory tests, x-rays, etc.)
   5. Recording relevant information in a retrievable manner
   6. Organizing available information and integrating it for
       understanding and communicating

C) Identifying problems by assessing information with reference to
patients, their families and their environment, and established
standards for good health:

   1. Reviewing all available data pertinent to a patient and
       family
   2. Re-evaluating a problem list and differential diagnosis
       (assessment) with knowledge of accumulated data
   3. Identifying a patient's condition and/or needs by
       interpreting results based upon a concern for

patient and family history; local, regional and national norms; laws; culture; and environment

D) Selecting and offering plans to address problems:

1. Offering a specific management or treatment plan when appropriate
2. Implementing the appropriate treatment plan agreed to by a patient and physician with understanding of attendant risks
3. Following up on a patient's problem
4. Offering counseling in relation to the condition of a patient

E) Evaluating patients' health care progress and making necessary revisions to the management plans:

1. Carrying our re-assessment procedures
2. Determining the change and direction of a patient's health
3. Taking appropriate actions

F) Managing personnel, patient and personal resources:

1. Organizing people and space in the office efficiently
2. Evaluating the effectiveness of services
3. Using various health-related facilities in a community and region
4. Managing personal time

G) Continuing professional growth:

1. Participating in continuing medical education
2. Associating with peer groups, professional organizations, and institutions
3. Conducting quality care self-assessment
4. Conducting periodic career goal assessments
5. Modifying practice as appropriate
6. Participating in academic activities and research
7. Participating in self-renewal (professional growth) activities

H) Utilizing personal and professional skills to advance the quality of the physician's life in the home and the community:

1. Participating in civic or community activities
2. Participating in the political process on medical issues
3. Serving as a resource to schools and community groups on medical matters
4. Providing health-related leadership and instruction on as-needed basis
5. Recognizing and assisting impaired or at-risk physicians

Family practice shows a definite need and demand for research. Research can be of the purely scientific nature, clinical efficacy of drugs, other forms of treatment, management skills, etc. Most importantly, family physicians, with a large volume of patients with various disorders, diseases and problems, have the organizational network of the American Board of Family Practice and sister organizations (The American Academy of Family Physicians and the Society of Teachers of Family Medicine) to contribute significantly to epidemiologic research. We believe there is no greater potential for organized research in epidemiology than in the field of family practice.

The new concept of "wellness" is taught in all the residency programs as a prevailing philosophy - prevention of illness, maintenance of health through engendering the understanding of family dynamics, population, economic, social and psychological factors, nutrition, ethics, communication, and public health - to name just a few of the curriculum topics covered in the residency training program in addition to the other important disease processes.

It is important for physicians who expect to become Board certified to know that the American Board of Family Practice was the first of all specialty boards to require periodic recertification. Formal recertification every six years includes mandatory continuing education (currently 300 hours for a six year period); a computerized review of family physician's patient records to meet established criteria; and a written test covering recent medical knowledge as substantiated by the scientific literature. In short, a physician who selects family practice must understand that he or she must study continuously. The American Board of Family Practice also requires that all residents be evaluated by the training program faculty (including peers and other personnel) to ensure that proficiency is demonstrated in various psychomotor or procedural skills.

While all physicians should manifest certain personal traits such as honesty and integrity, this discipline requires that other attributes be demonstrated by the resident in training prior to being allowed to sit for the American Board of Family Practice certification examination. These attitudes and attributes, which are reviewed carefully by the program, include responsibility; initiative; reliability regarding patient care; rapport with patients and their families; relationships with other health professionals; self-initiated learning; acceptance of criticism; proper use of evaluative feedback; communication with patients; demonstration of concern; sensitivity and compassion; communication with the family and sensitivity to their needs; patient education skills; interviewing skills; and the effective use of consultants or faculty experts.

In short, the specialty employs various methods of assessment so that the public to whose well being we are dedicated will be assured. Thus young physicians seeking certification must have demonstrated cognitive knowledge, proficiency in procedural skills, and certain personal qualities or attributes which ensure that they have "head, heart, and hands."

The Board also reviews medical school and pre-medical school curricula. While science programs are absolutely essential in the training of any physician, it supports a strong liberal arts background as a requirement for admission to medical school. We also look forward to the day when these curricula will automatically include the study of the social behavior, ethical and philosophical disciplines.

For the student who may be interested in family practice, the following characteristics are regarded as important:

1. Cognitive Knowledge - analytical thinking; a mind that is trained to inquire, wonder, and be able to discriminate facts from non facts.

2. Desire to learn continually in a profession that is rapidly changing.

3. Hard work - family practice is not a "9 to 5" specialty five days a week. Family practice is not boring nor is it a leisurely specialty. It is truly a working specialty.

4. Availability is necessary with patient coverage provided 24-hours a day when the personal family physician is not on duty.

5. Rewards of great personal satisfaction - the joy of diversity of problems; the human "engagement" with people of all kinds, all beliefs, with a variety of problems.

6. An orientation to people - the family physician, to be satisfied and be satisfactory, has to understand, be tolerant, compassionate, and considerate at all times.

7. Materially rewarding, but frankly not as much as some other procedure-oriented specialties may be. It is unlikely that one can become rich merely by selecting family practice.

The family physician has the satisfaction of knowing when a job is done well. Every day as a caring, competent practitioner, he or she experiences the special feeling of being a part of the family that is cared for. Family practice should foster an equanimity in the physician as well as self-fulfillment as a human being.

External Readings

4-A-1 Taylor, RB, "Family Practice: The Specialty with Special Rewards," Physicians Management 22:205-19 (August 1982).

4-A-2 "Need Family-Oriented Care? Try a Family Practice Center," Patient Care 16:15-21 (October 1982).

4-A-3 "Want a 'People-Oriented' Doctor? Select a Family Physician," Patient Care 16:49-55 (October 30, 1982).

4-A-4 Rakel, RE, "Family Practice," Journal American Medical Association 254:2252-54 (October 25, 1985).

4-A-5 "How Competitive is Primary Care Today," Patient Care 16:23-94 (May 15, 1982).

4-A-6 Wechsler, H, et al., "The Physicians Role in Health Promotion: The Survey of Primary Care Practitioners," New England Journal of Medicine 308:97-100 (January 13, 1983).

4-A-7 Chatterton, HT, "Patterns of Health Care Utilization in an Academic Family Practice," Journal Family Practice 14:893-97 (May 1982).

4-A-8 "The Content of Family Practice: Current Status and Future Trends," Journal Family Practice 15:679-737 (October 1982).

4-A-9 Burkett, GL & Gelula, MH, "Characteristics of Students Preferring Family Practice/Primary Care Careers," Journal Family Practice 15:505-12 (September 1982).

4-B-1 McWhinney, IR. An Introduction to Family Medicine. New York: Oxford Univ. Press, 1981. 219 pp.

4-B-2 Diamond, N, et al. Ambulatory Care for the House Officer. Baltimore: Williams Wilkins, 1982. 258 pp.

4-B-3 Huygen, FJA. Family Medicine: The Medical Life History of Families. New York: Brunner/Mazel Inc,. 1982. 208 pp.

4-B-4 Geyman, JP. Archives of Family Practice: Selected Papers... New York: Appleton-Century-Crofts, 1981. 413 pp.

4-B-5 Dubovsky, SL & Weissberg, MP. Clinical Psychiatry in Primary Care. Baltimore: Williams & Wilkins, 1982. 292 pp.

4-B-6 Shires, DB & Hennen, BK. Family Medicine: A Guidebook for Practitioner of the Art. New York: McGraw-Hill, 1980. 512 pp.

Section 5 - INTERNAL MEDICINE

The General Internist

Warren W. Smith

Warren W. Smith, MD (deceased) was a general internist in
private practice in Columbus, OH. He had an interest in
writing and served as editor of the monthly bulletin of
the Franklin County Medical Society.

Formal specialization in the practice of medicine began in the last
century when surgery and obstetrics emerged as discrete disciplines.
Then around a hundred years ago William Osler convinced other medical
educators that certain young doctors should be encouraged to devote
themselves to a specialty now known as internal medicine. Their
training would consist of years in the wards and in the laboratory.
They would acquire a profound knowledge of clinical medicine and
biochemistry and be able to study as well as treat disease. Hence they
would be qualified as investigators as well as specialized practitioners.

At first the number of internists was small and most were associated
with medical schools and teaching hospitals. During the second third of
the 20th century, a number of factors combined to create an abrupt
increase in the number of all specialists. With the growth of medical
knowledge, some internists sub-specialized into hematology,
rheumatology, and other areas described below. The internist who has
not so sub-specialized is now referred to as a "general internist."

The general internist is a specialist broadly versed in the
diagnosis and medical treatment of adults. An important part of an
internist's practice involves seeing patients referred by other
physicians for evaluation of obscure symptoms. In this role the
internist serves as a "diagnostician." Many internists also function as
a primary physician where they are the first physician consulted by a
patient for a health related problem.

These days patients complain with considerable justification about
the depersonalization of medical care. New techniques have increased a
clinician's ability to evaluate and treat the patient - but they have
also spawned an army of doctors who seem more interested in the
technology than the individual. The patient needs and must have a
single warm, compassionate coordinator to guide him through the maze of
diagnostic tests and consultants. The general internist is the one
specialist who takes a comprehensive view of the whole person and who
can take a complete history, do a meticulous physical exam and know best
which consultants to call in. Much of the time he functions like a
conductor leading a symphony orchestra which is composed of fine
physicians. He causes the team to play harmoniously, and the individual
players of the orchestra cannot function well without this director.

Most new patients who come to see the general internist are referred by other patients, whereas most of the patients coming to the sub-specialist are referred by other doctors. Thus the general internist tends to attain a certain security in practice as patients continually refer others for care.

Patients of the general internist often manifest a strong loyalty and call him or her first with most medical needs. Patients who are not congenial may change to another doctor, and so in time, the internist's practice is composed of a high percentage of congenial individuals. Medical practice is therefore considerably more enjoyable for the general internist since your patients may include a high proportion of "friends."

What are the major components of an internist's practice? The most mundane activity might seem to be the routine physical. Actually, there is seldom such a thing as a routine physical; patients go to a doctor for a reason. If the doctor doesn't elicit this reason, he will miss an important lead. Every patient is unique and thus there is little chance for boredom. Many have habits that should be changed, for example, cigarete smoking. Persuading the patient to quit smoking tests and develops the doctor's skill as a salesman. Others have misinformation about cholesterol, fears of certain medicines or procedures that may be new or unpopular. The word doctor comes from the word teacher - the general internist is the patient's best teacher about general health matters.

During the past 40 years, an exciting era of chemotherapy has made possible the treatment of infection (the antibiotics), mood and emotional disorders (tranquilizers, lithium, the psychotropic drugs and antidepressants), and many tumors. The internist is in the midst of these new developments. Thanks to psychotropic drugs, many patients with mood disorders can be treated quite well by the internist, without need for referral to a psychiatrist. As another example, the writer is working with a series of patients with severe recurring headaches who have been relieved with amitriptyline given in appropriate dosage. Hypertension, the various rheumatic diseases, ischemic heart diseases, congestive heart failure, and a number of other syndromes may be treated effectively by the general internist. When cases appear that seem beyond his or her depth, the patient may be referred to an appropriate sub-specialist.

The task of keeping up with newly-developed drugs, however, is almost an impossible one. A patient may be taking several drugs for different diseases: The general internist monitors therapies given to the same patient by different specialists to ensure that these agents do not interfere with each other.

There is a canard often heard in academic circles to the effect that, in private practice, one deals solely with "hypochondriacs" and that clinical practice is dull and unworthy of the knowledge and skills of a highly-trained physician. Those who make such a statement have never practiced internal medicine.

As the primary internist develops a patient base, and knows them better and vice versa, he has a incredible therapeutic tool at his disposal - his rapport with the patient. A seriously frightened patient with chest pains can be given substantial reassurance over the telephone by the physician who knows him well. This ability to reassure, to persuade, to induce people to do unpleasant things, provides an enormous source of gratification to the practicing internist.

In sum, the general internist is a medical specialist with a broad view of human illness and its treatment. He is at the center of diagnostic evaluation and the non-surgical treatment of adults.

External Readings - Internal Medicine

5-A-1   "Consider Choosing an Internist for Your Personal Physician," Patient Care 16:25-32 (October 30, 1982).

5-A-2   "Your Practice is You - Reflections of a Diagnostician," Journal American Medical Association 247:1815-18 (April 1, 1982).

5-A-3   Griner, PF & Glaser, RJ, "Misuse of Laboratory Tests and Diagnostic Procedures," New England Journal Medicine 307:1337-39 (November 18, 1982).

5-A-4   "Therapeutic Choices Not Always Predictable," Journal American Medical Association 247:1231 (March 5, 1982).

5-A-6   "A Library for Internists," Annals Internal Medicine 96:388-401 (March 1982).

5-B-1   Fishman, MC, et al. Medicine. Philadelphia: JB Lippincott, 1981. 464 pp.

5-B-2   Weinstein, MC & Fineberg, HV. Clinical Decision Analysis. Philadelphia: WB Saunders, 1980. 351 pp.

5-B-3   Taylor, RL. Mind or Body: Distinguishing Psychological From Organic Disorders. New York: McGraw-Hill Book Co., 1982. 244 pp.

5-B-4   Major, D (ed.). Problems of the Medically Ill: New Agents and Approaches to Diagnosis and Therapy. New York: Grune & Stratton, 1981. 255 pp.

5-B-5   Proger, S & Barza, M.   Diagnostic Imperatives: The Timely Detector of Treatable Disease.   New York: Thieme-Stratton, 1981.   271 pp.

5-B-6   Comfort, A.   What is a Doctor?   Philadelphia: GF Stickley, 1980.   240 pp.

5-B-7   Bursztatn, H, et al.   Medical Choices, Medical Changes... New York: Delacortz Press/Seymour Lawrence, 1981.   456 pp.

The Sub-specialties

Earl N. Metz

Earl N. Metz, MD, is Charles A. Doan Professor of Medicine and Vice Chairman, Department of Medicine; Director of the Training Program for the Division of Internal Medicine; and Director, Division of General Medicine, The Ohio State University College of Medicine. He is also a member of the Board of Trustees for the Leukemia Society and a practicing hematologist-oncologist.

While it is important for patients to have a personal physician on whom they call for the majority of their medical care, it is impossible for any physician to have comprehensive knowledge and expertise in all areas of internal medicine.   Likewise, technical achievements in diagnostic testing and treatment have added to this complexity. Illnesses such as acute leukemia, obscure disturbances of cardiac rhythm, renal failure requiring dialysis therapy, etc., all necessitate involvement by sub-specialists with particular expertise.   The general internist or family practitioner may coordinate overall care and make decisions regarding the advisability of sub-speciality consultations. But if patients are to reap the benefits of modern medical diagnosis and treatment, participation by medical sub-specialists is often unavoidable.

This trend in the care of complex medical problems has been recognized by the American Board of Internal Medicine.   In addition to a certifying examination in general internal medicine, for about ten years ABIM has also offered examinations and supervised the certification of physicians in the sub-specialties of internal medicine.   To be eligible to take the certifying examination in general internal medicine, the physician must complete a three year residency in a hospital with an approved training program.

During this period, young doctors are actively involved in the day to day care of hospitalized patients.   They learn to perform a variety of diagnostic procedures and develop further their skills in obtaining an accurate medical history and performing a comprehensive physical examination. In many situations, they serve as the patient's primary physician. During these three years, the resident physician stays in the hospital one or two nights a week. While on night call, the resident physician may be responsible for the initial care of patients who are admitted to the hospital with acute medical problems and may serve as an emergency consultant to surgeons, obstetricians, etc. In addition to this intensive practical experience, a good training program includes formal teaching conferences each week and daily contact with senior staff physicians.

After completion of this post-MD training, the physician may elect to enter practice and pursue a career as a general internist. The majority of internal medicine residents, however, elect to continue their training for one or two years in a sub-specialty. By tradition, these additional years of training are referred to as fellowship training and usually take place in hospitals closely affiliated with medical schools. During these additional years of training, the sub-specialty fellow acquires the skill and expertise peculiar to that field and may engage actively in clinical or basic research related to this area of study.

At the conclusion of this period, a number of career options are open: In general, the more complete the training, the greater number of opportunities. For example, training as a sub-specialist does not preclude a career as a primary care physician. On the other hand, a physician trained in one of the sub-specialities may take full advantage of this intensive training and enter a practice which is restricted to patients with a relatively narrow spectrum of illness. Some may be invited to join the faculty of a college of medicine where their time will be divided between basic research in their area of expertise, direct care of patients, and teach medical students and post-doctoral trainees.

We turn now to a brief description of several of the sub-specialties of internal medicine. It is difficult to paint a true picture of how each sub-specialist spends an average day since function depends upon the setting in which the physician works. For example, the responsibilities of a practicing medical oncologist in a medium-sized city would be quite different from that of a full-time teacher and researcher at a large medical school and university hospital. Nevertheless, the problems faced by the sub-specialist in practice are not fundamentally different from those confronting his peers in the academic center.

Unit 5.1 - Cardiology. This field is considered by many to be the glamour specialty of internal medicine. There are several reasons why the life of the cardiologist can be both exciting and satisfying. First, heart disease is a common problem that affects all ages, from the youngster with a congenital heart defect to the elderly patient with chronic congestive heart failure. Coronary artery disease can, without prior warning, strike down young adults or middle aged patients in the prime of their productive years. Prompt intervention by a well trained cardiologist might make the difference between death and a return to full life.

Secondly, cardiology is on the forefront in the application of technical advances to clinical medicine. Many young physicians who have a background in engineering find this sub-specialty attractive when choosing a career. Diagnostic catheterization of the heart to study its structure and function has been applied for more than 40 years but practical application of this procedure continues to grow. For many years, this technique was used primarily to identify abnormal anatomy that resulted either from congenital heart disease or rheumatic fever. Now, however, it is commonly employed in coronary artery disease. Catheterization of the coronary arteries is used to identify patients who might benefit from coronary artery surgery and to directly infuse thrombolytic agents to dissolve blood clots in these vessels. It is also possible to inset inflatable balloons by the same technique and expand blood vessels narrowed by arteriosclerosis. Moreover, the same general techniques have been applied to studies of the electrical conduction system within the heart.

Cardiologists have also pioneered the use of so-called non-invasive techniques for the study of heart disease. These include the use of sonography, or echocardiography, to look at the heart and its function from the outside by use of reflected sound waves. Likewise, cardiologists may employ nuclear medicine techniques involving radioactive materials and external scanning procedures which can provide considerable information about cardiac structure and function.

Third, practical application of modern pharmacology may have its greatest impact in cardiology. The use of new drugs to stimulate a sluggish heart muscle or to quiet an electrically overactive area of the heart seems to be changing constantly. Study of the pharmacology of the heart muscle and its conduction system is without question an exciting area which promises to benefit many patients.

Finally, and perhaps most rewarding, there is still a place for the clinical cardiologist who must decide when to use the more sophisticated procedures, when to use the new pharmacologic drugs and, occasionally, when to do nothing more.

External Readings - Cardiology

5.1-A-1   "Disorders of the Heart and Circulation," In: The American Medical Association Family Medical Guide, (Kunz, JRM, ed.). New York: Random House. 1982, pp. 370-417.

5.1-A-2   Kauthamer, MJ, "Cardiology: The Heart of Medicine," Medical Student 9:8-14 (March/April 1983).

5.1-A-3   Alpert, JS, "Cardiovascular Diseases," Journal American
          Medical Association 254:2264-67 (October 25, 1985).

5.1-A-4   "Outlook 1982: Cardiology: Surer Diagnosis, Safer Therapy,"
          Patient Care 16:133-63 (January 15, 1982).

5.1-A-5   Tinker, JH, et al., "Management of Patient with Heart
          Disease," Journal American Medical Association 246:1348-50
          (September 18, 1982).

5.1-B-1   Goldin, AG. Your Guide to Care of the Heart. Philadelphia:
          GF Stickley, 1984. 150 pp.

5.1-B-2   Wong, CB. Learning to Live with Angina. Boston: Medicine in
          the Public Interest, 1981. 70 pp.

5.1-B-3   Cohn, PF & Wynne J. Diagnostic Methods in Clinical
          Cardiology. Boston: Little, Brown & Co., 1982. 377 pp.

5.1-B-4   Eich, RH. Introduction to Cardiology. New York: Harper &
          Row, 1980. 346 pp.

5.1-B-5   Yu, PN & Goodwin, JF (eds.). Progress in Cardiology 9.
          Philadelphia: Lea & Febiger, Inc., 1980. 193 pp.

Unit 5.2 - Gastroenterology. Like the cardiologist, the modern gastroenterologist is likely to be a procedure-oriented practitioner. Development of the thin flexible endoscope permits direct visualization of areas of the gastrointestional tract that were examined previously only by indirect techniques such as barium contrast x-rays. With these instruments, the gastroenterologist can look directly into the esophagus, stomach, and upper small bowel and identify disease much more precisely. He can also cannulate the bile ducts via their opening into the duodenum and, after injection of contrast material, obtain x-rays which outline the bile or pancreatic ducts with a high degree of resolution. Similar flexible scopes have been developed for examination of the large bowel. Biopsies of suspicious lesions can be obtained by direct visualization.

A gastroenterologist is the physician to whom other physicians refer patients with complicated liver disease. These illnesses can be evaluated by a variety of biochemical and immunological tests as well as a direct needle biopsy of the liver. Ulcerative colitis, and other inflammatory diseases of the bowel, peptic ulcer, cirrhosis of the liver, diseases of the esophagus and malabsorption syndromes are among the diseases treated by the gastroenterologist. Availability of these new diagnostic techniques have introduced more precision in the sub-specialty, thus enabling the skilled gastroenterologist to serve as a valuable consultant to surgeons and other internists.

External Readings - Gastroenterology

5.2-A-1   Ostrow, JD & Vanagunas, "Gastroenterology and Hepatology," *Journal American Medical Association* 254:2267-71 (October 25, 1985).

5.2-A-2   Burnstein, AV, "Peptic Ulcer Disease: Medical and Surgical Considerations," *Critical Care Quarterly* 5:1-7 (September 1982).

5.2-A-3   Lewis, JH, "When Your Patient Has Epigastric Pain," *Contemporary OB/GYN* 19:54-73 (May 1982).

5.2-A-4   Perkel, MS, "Acute Inflammatory Bowel Disease," *Critical Care Quarterly* 5:21-26 (September 1982).

5.2-A-5   Siegel, JH, "Newer Developments in Gastrointestinal Endoscopy," *Practical Gastroenterology* 6:29-31 (March-April 1982).

5.2-B-1   Davenport, HW. *Physiology of the Digestive Tract: An Introductory Text*. Chicago: Year Book Medical Publishers, 1982. 245 pp.

5.2-B-2   Grant, AK & Skyring, A. *Clinical Diagnosis and Gastrointestinal Disease*. St. Louis: Blackwell Mosby Book Dist., 1981. 401 pp.

5.2-B-3   Korentz, RL. *Practical Gastroenterology*. New York: John Wiley and Sons, 1982. 395 pp.

5.2-B-4   Bateson, M & Bouchier, I. *Clinical Investigation of Gastrointestinal Function*. St. Louis: CV Mosby, 1981. 232 pp.

Unit 5.3 - Geriatrics. Older people have always been with us. However, acceptance of the fact that elderly patients may have impaired ability to cope with life in general and illness in particular has been a slow process led by a few crusaders. Geriatrics is not a generally recognized sub-specialty. Thus, most physicians currently practicing geriatrics are general internists or other sub-specialists who have decided to devote their careers to care of the elderly.

The purist might argue that there is little unique about illness in an older person, that the manifestations of disease in the elderly usually represent, at most, an exaggeration of those seen in a younger patient. To a degree that is true. However, the increasing number of people age 65 and over combined with the increase in frequency and severity of illness in this group constitutes a significant health care problem. Furthermore, there are some problems which are unique to the elderly. These include the devastating problem of senile dementia, the altered metabolism of drugs, degenerative changes in heart function, etc. Provision of adequate health care for this large segment of our population will require the devotion of many physicians and hence represents a potential career opportunity.

External Readings - Geriatrics

5.3-A-1   "Special Problems of the Elderly," The American Medical Association Family Medical Guide, (Kunz, JRM, ed.). New York: Random House, 1982. pp. 716-26.

5.3-A-2   "Sorting Out Elderly Psyche From Soma," Emergency Medicine 14:160-64 (May 15, 1982).

5.3-A-3   Freedman, ML, "The Effects of Aging on Emergency Treatment," Emergency Medicine 14:194-210 (January 30, 1982).

5.3-A.4   Hospital and Community Psychiatry 33:101-110;127-33 (February 1982).

5.3-A-5   Aging. (Review six recent issues of this bi-monthly.)

5.3-A-6   Steel, K & Barry, PP, "Geriatrics," Journal American Medical Association 254:2286-88 (October 25, 1985).

5.3-B-1   Hodkinson, HM. Common Symptoms of Disease in the Elderly. St. Louis: CV Mosby, 1980. 147 pp.

5.3-B-2   Libow, LS & Sherman FT (eds.). The Core of Geriatric Medicine: A Guide for Students and Practitioners. St. Louis: CV Mosby, 1981. 354 pp.

5.3-B-3   Schrier, RW. Clinical Internal Medicine in the Aged. Philadelphia: WB Saunders, 1982. 324 pp.

5.3-B-4   Somers, A & Fabian, DR (eds.). The Geriatric Imperative: An Introduction to Geronotology and Clinical Geriatrics. New York: Appleton-Century-Croft, 1981. 356 pp.

Unit 5.4 - Hematology. A hematologist is an internist who has taken two or three years of training following his medical residency to become an expert in the diagnosis and management of patients with diseases of the blood and bone marrow.

Any one or all of the three formed elements of the blood may be increased or decreased to a level that threatens life. These problems may be due to more rapid than normal destruction of blood cells or to failure of the bone marrow to make new blood cells at an adequate rate. The hematologist uses a variety of tests of the blood and examinations of the bone marrow to sort out the various diagnostic possibilities and plan treatment.

Leukemia is one of the major diseases which interferes with bone marrow function. In this instance, the overgrowth of malignant cells impedes production of normal blood cells. The hematologist uses a variety of chemotherapeutic drugs which are designed to be more toxic to the malignant cells than to normal cells. This goal is often a fine line to walk and requires considerable expertise in titrating drug dosage as well as the cooperation of a well organized blood bank facility in providing replacement blood products during the time the patient's bone marrow is not functioning. For some kinds of leukemia, this type of treatment is very effective; for others, the results are poor. Bone marrow transplantation offers new hope for some patients with leukemia and an increasing number of hematologists are becoming involved in this promising form of treatment.

In addition to treating patients with blood and marrow malignancies, hematologists take care of patients with sickle cell disease, clotting disorders (hemophilia), and various kinds of anemia and immunologic disorders. Hematology is a specialty with outstanding opportunities for clinical and basic research and for the care of patients with complex and serious illnesses.

External Readings - Hematology

5.4-A-1   "Blood Disorders," The American Medical Association Family Medical Guide, (Kunz, JRM, ed.). New York: Random House, 1982. pp. 418-33.

5.4-A-2   Bevan, DH, "A Field Guide to the Bleeding Disorders for the General Practitioner," The Practitioner 226:25-32 (January 1982).

5.4-A-3   Kasper, CK, E, "Hematology and Oncology," Journal American Medical Association 254:2259-62 (October 25, 1985).

5.4-B-1   Kapff, CT & Jandl, JH. Blood: Atlas & Sourcebook of Hematology. Boston: Little, Brown & Co., 1981. 147 pp.

5.4-B-2   Hughs-Jones, NC. Lecture Notes on Hematology. St. Louis: Blackwell Mosby Book Distributors, 1979. 164 pp.

5.4-B-3   Waterburg, L. Hematology for the House Officer. Baltimore: Williams & Wilkins, 1981. 135 pp.

Unit 5.5 - Infectious Disease. Internists who specialize in infectious diseases typically work as full-time members of a hospital staff rather than as private practitioners. They provide a valuable service to patients and other physicians as consultants in diagnosis and management of complex and life-threatening infectious diseases.

Training in infectious diseases often includes extensive training in microbiology and epidemiology. Expertise in these areas widens the scope of career opportunities by including hospital infection control and epidemiologic research on a broader scale. Investigations of Legionnaires disease and acquired immunodeficiency syndrome (AIDS) are examples of the latter activity. Physicians involved in this kind of work may have an impact on health care which extends far beyond the usual one-on-one relationship between physician and patient.

The expanding development of new antibiotics and antiviral agents has provided important research opportunities in infectious diseases and, for the average physician, made consultation with an infectious disease expert a common occurrence.

External Readings - Infectious Disease

5.5-A-1   "General Infections & Infestations," In: The American Medical Association Family Medical Guide, Kunz, JRM, (ed.). New York: Random House, 1982. pp. 558-69.

5.5-A-2   Holmes, KK, "Infectious Diseases," Journal American Medical Association 254:2254-57 (October 25, 1985).

5.5-A-3   The Practitioner 226:1477-1548 (September 1982).

5.5-A-4   "Infectious Disease," In: Medicine (Fishman, MC, et al., eds.). Philadelphia: JB Lippincott, 1981, pp. 381-424.

5.5-B-1   Mims, CA. The Pathogenesis of Infectious Diseases. New York: Academic Press, Inc., 1982. 297 pp.

5.5-B-2   Marr, JJ. Infectious Diseases in General Medical Practice. Reading, MA: Addison-Wesley, 1981. 460 pp.

5.5-B-3   Primary Care. 8:545-751 (December 1981).

5.5-B-4   Sanford JP & Luby JP (eds.). Infectious Disease. New York: Grune & Stratton, 1981. 426 pp.

Unit 5.6 - Medical Oncology. Medical oncology is closely related to hematology in the care of patients with malignancy. For many years hematology encompassed both diseases of the blood and chemotherapy of other malignant tumors. The explosion of new methods of treatment for cancer has led to the recent emergence of a separate sub-specialty - medical oncology. There is still a considerable overlap in both research and patient care and the two sub-specialties are combined in some training programs. A post-doctoral trainee may elect to take three years of training in a combined program and take the American Board of Internal Medicine sub-specialty examinations in both hematology and medical oncology.

A medical oncologist spends most of his time treating cancer patients with chemotherapeutic drugs. This form of therapy is not nearly as precise nor as effective as antibiotic therapy of bacterial infections but the principle is the same. For some forms of malignancy, such as lymphoma or testicular cancer, chemotherapy may be curative. For other types of cancer, it is difficult to demonstrate any benefit.

Medical oncology is changing constantly as researchers look for new chemotherapeutic drugs, better combinations of available drugs, and new forms of therapy. It is a career best suited for those who are willing to become involved in clinical investigation and in the care of patients whose prognosis may be bleak.

External Readings - Medical Oncology

5.6-A-1   Bulkin, W & Stein, CA, "Medical Oncology...," Medical Student 8(1):8-9 (November/December) 1981.

5.6-A-2   McKelvey, EM, "Oncology," Journal American Medical Association 245:2209-11 (June 5, 1981); 247:2969-70 (June 4, 1982).

5.6-A-3   "Outlook 1982: What Tomorrow Holds For Cancer Care," Patient Care 16:17-89 (January 15, 1982).

5.6-A-4   "Detecting Breast Cancer Early," Patient Care 16:47-147 (March 15, 1982).

5.6-B-1   Creasey, WA. Cancer: An Introduction. New York: Oxford Univ. Press 1981. 271 pp.

5.6-B-2   Graham, J. In the Company of Others. New York: Harcourt Brace Jovanovich, 1982. 131 pp.

5.6-B-3   Cady, B. Cancer: A Manual for Practitioners. Boston: American Cancer Society, 1982. 444 pp.

5.6-B-4   Nixon, DW. Diagnosis and Management of Cancer. Menlo Park, CA: Addison-Wesley, 1982. 304 pp.

5.6-B-5 Skeel, RT (ed.). Manual for Cancer Chemotherapy. Boston: Little, Brown & Co., 1982. 304 pp.

5.6-B-6 Cassileth, PA, et al. Practical Approaches to Hematology - Oncology. New York: Medical Examination Pub. Co., 1982. 360 pp.

Unit 5.7 - Nephrology. A nephrologist is an internist who has special interest and training in diseases of the kidney. Renal function can be impaired by a variety of diseases which affect those organs primarily, e.g., glomerulonephritis. The kidneys may also be affected seriously by systemic illnesses such as shock, diabetes, toxemia, pregnancy, and severe hypertension. These situations make a nephrologist a valuable consultant in the overall care of such patients.

Normal renal physiology and the alterations that occur with disease are complex and are often difficult to study except by indirect and relatively imprecise methods. The nephrologist relies on changes in blood chemistry and proteins, the excretion of electrolytes and protein in the urine, the contents of the urine sediment, various radiographic procedures, and occasionally a needle biopsy of the kidney to arrive at a diagnosis and plan of treatment. Perhaps because of this, nephrology has often been an attractive specialty to physicians more interested in the intellectual or academic side of medicine than in a more direct interventional approach to patient care in which results are apparent immediately.

This concept of nephrology is now outdated. Two developments, which occurred almost concurrently, have changed the therapy of choice. First, the use of chronic intermittent dialysis for renal insufficiency has made it possible for many persons with virtually no renal function of their own to carry on with some semblance of a normal life. Second, the use of kidney transplantation has obviated the need for chronic dialysis for many patients and, when feasible, is a better alternative than dialysis. The nephrologist does not do the transplantation but works closely with the transplant surgeon before and after the surgery, often maintaining the patient on the dialysis program for an extended period until a suitable kidney becomes available for transplant. The procedures for ensuring successful transplantation are undergoing continual refinement, especially in the area of immunologic modification to prevent rejection of the grafted kidney.

Investigation of normal and abnormal renal physiology and mechanisms of renal injury continues to occupy many academic nephrologists, but renal dialysis and transplantation have thrust nephrology into the forefront of clinical medicine. Dialysis and transplant programs represent a major commitment of many larger hospitals and it is likely to remain so until new treatment programs are effective in preventing chronic renal failure.

External Readings - Nephrology

5.7-A-1   Glassock,   RJ,   "Nephrology,"   Journal   American   Medical
          Association 254:2273-76 (October 25, 1985).

5.7-A-2   "NIAID   Study   Identifies   Factors   That   Affect   Renal
          Transplantation Outcome," Journal American Medical Association
          246:1663-64 (October 9, 1981).

5.7-A-3   "The High Price of Federally Regulated Hemodialysis," Journal
          American Medical Association 246:1909-11 (October 23/30, 1981).

5.7-A-4   "Renal Disease," In: Medicine (Fishman, MC, et al., eds.)
          Philadelphia: JB Lippincott, 1981, pp. 145-77.

5.7-B-1   Sullivan, PA & Grantham, JJ. Physiology of the Kidney.
          Philadelphia: Lea & Febiger, 1982. 236 pp.

5.7-B-2   Schrier, RW. Manual of Nephrology: Diagnosis and Therapy.
          Boston: Little, Brown & Co., 1981. 292 pp.

5.7-B-3   Brenner, BM & Stein, JA. Chronic Renal Failure. New York:
          Churchill Livingstone, 1981. 337 pp.

Unit 5.8 - Pulmonary Disease. Internists specializing in pulmonary disease are the medical descendants of physicians who devoted their careers to the care of patients with tuberculosis. Tuberculosis is no longer the terrible public health problem it once was in the United States. The disease is still with us and the large hospitals committed solely to the care of patients with tuberculosis have been converted to other uses and the disease now emerges in individual cases, often in the elderly or immunocompromised.

There is still enough pulmonary disease to keep these specialists busy. Sadly, much of it is self-inflicted by cigarete smoking. Emphysema and lung cancer are serious health problems directly linked to smoking. The specialist in pulmonary medicine does his best to help such patients cope with their illness and many are active, through their professional organizations, in trying to modify patient habits which lie at the root of the problem.

Pulmonary medicine also includes the care of patients with more reversible or treatable diseases. These include pulmonary infections, asthma and other immunologically mediated lung diseases. As in gastroenterology, new technology has had an impact on the practice of pulmonary medicine. Flexible bronchoscopes have made it possible to look at the trachea and bronchial tree, obtain cultures, biopsies, and, in some cases, even washout (lavage) the lung with saline.

Another development that has changed the practice of pulmonary medicine is the emergence of intensive care units in many hospitals. A patient ill enough to require treatment in an intensive care unit frequently needs mechanical support of his breathing with a respirator. Because of the technical complexity of management and the expertise of pulmonary medicine specialists in the use of respirators, these physicians are often called on the supervise the operation of such units.

External Readings - Pulmonary Disease

5.8-A-1   Hart, LL & Freston, JW, "Pulmonary Disease," In: Remington's Pharmaceutical Sciences, (Osol, A. et al., eds.). Easton, PA: Mack Pub. Co., 1980. pp 621-22.

5.8-A-2   Petty, TL, "Pulmonary Medicine," Journal American Medical Association 254:2271-73 (October 25, 1985).

5.8-A-3   Delaney, MD, "Tracking Down the Cause of Pneumonia," Contemporary OB/GYN 19:126-34 (May 1982).

5.8-A-4   Colice, GF & Matthay, RA, "Distinguishing Bronchitis From Its Mimics," Contemporary OB/GYN 19:136-48 (May 1982).

5.8-B-1   Williams, MH. Essentials of Pulmonary Medicine. Philadelphia: WB Saunders, 1982. 190 pp.

5.8-B-2   Kiss, GT. Diagnosis and Management of Pulmonary Disease. Menlo Park, CA: Addison-Wesley, 1982. 242 pp.

5.8-B-3   Bordow, RA, et al., (ed.). Manual of Clinical Problems in Pulmonary Medicine. Boston: Little, Brown & Co., 1980. 535 pp.

Unit 5.9 - Rheumatology. Arthritis is a major health problem which makes life difficult for millions of patients. Care of patients with rheumatoid arthritis constitutes a big part of the practice of most rheumatologists. Although this disease is seldom a threat to life, it can cause severe disability from joint swelling and pain - and eventually joint destruction. The job of the rheumatologist is to help control pain and maintain joint function, primarily through the use of medications designed to reduce inflammation. Most rheumatologists also work closely with other physicians and therapists in the overall management of these patients.

The complete health care team might include physical therapists, orthopedic surgeons, occupational therapists, and physical medicine specialists. Sometimes, remarkable restoration of function can be achieved by corrective joint surgery when done at the appropriate time and with all members of the team participating in the pre- and post-operative care.

Rheumatologists are also experts in diagnosis and management of a group of illnesses classified under the general heading of "autoimmune disorders." Systemic lupus erythematosus is one of the best known of this group. These illnesses can affect the function of multiple organ systems of the body and involvement of the joints may be only a minor component of the overall illness. Many of the illnesses treated by rheumatologists are, in a general sense, the result of autoimmunity against normal body tissue - much the same as the tendency of the body to reject a transplanted kidney. Because of this, rheumatologists study immunology and normal body defense mechanisms.

Researchers in this area are trying to clarify the normal mechanisms of antibody and cell mediated immunity so that the reactions can be successfully suppressed when turned against self and stimulated to greater activity to augment the defense against malignancy. Clinical and basic investigation in this area is among the most sophisticated and intellectually challenging research currently being done in medicine and holds the most promise for genuine modification of disease processes.

External Readings - Rheumatology

5.9-A-1   Langone, J, "The Riddle of Arthritis," Discover 2(8):26-30 (August 1981).

5.9-A-2   Hart, LL & Freston, JW, "Rheumatology." In: Remington's Pharmaceutical Sciences, (Osol, A, et al., eds). Easton, PA, Mack Pub. Co., 1980. pp 623-24.

5.9-A-3   McCarty, DJ, "Rheumatology," Journal American Medical Association 254:2262-64 (October 25, 1985).

5.9-A-4   Bole, GG, "The American Rheumatism Association, 1990," Arthritis Rheumatism 25:1-9 (January 1982).

5.9-A-5   Klinenberg, JR, "1984-2034: The Next Half-Century for American Rheumatology," Arthritis Rheumatism 28:1-7 (January 1985).

5.9-B-1   Bluestone R. Practical Rheumatology: Diagnosis and Management. Reading, MA: Addison-Wesley Pub. Co., 1980. 240 pp.

5.9-B-2   Gordon, DA (ed.). Rheumatoid Arthritis. New York: Medical Examination Pub. Co., 1981. 200 pp.

5.9-B-3   Golding, DN. Tutorials in Clinical Rheumatology. London: Pitman Medical, 1981. 133 pp.

External Readings - Rheumatology (continued)

5.9-B-4   Beary, JR (et al.). Manual of Rheumatology and Outpatient Disorders: Diagnosis and Therapy. Boston: Little, Brown & Co., 1981. 366 pp.

5.9-B-5   Talbott, JH. Clinical Rheumatology. New York: Elsevier/North Holland, Inc., 1981. 221 pp.

5.9-B-6   Gordon, DA (ed.). Rheumatoid Arthritis. Garden City, New York: Medical Examination Pub. Co., 1981. 200 pp.

5.9-B-7   Roger, M & Williams, N. Rheumatology in General Practice. New York: Churchill Livingstone, 1982. 266 pp.

Problems in Practice

One perspective on medical practice is indicated by a survey where 1,000 physicians ranked business problems that caused the most difficulty. In rank order, these were: Insurance, billing and collecting, taxes, conforming with government regulations, controlling overhead cost, personnel administration and retirement planning.[1]

In order to help minimize such burdens, and for other reasons as well, many physicians have foresaken solo for group medical practice. This latter arrangement includes three or more physicians formally organized to provide medical care, consultation, diagnosis, or treatment through the joint use of equipment and personnel, with income from medical practices distributed in accordance with methods previously determined by members of the group.

It is estimated that more than 15,500 such groups employed more than 140,000 physicians in 1986.

---

[1] American Medical News, December 26, 1980/January 2, 1981. p. 14.

Section 6 - NEUROLOGY

John S. Garvin

John S. Garvin, MD, is Professor and Head, Department of Neurology, University of Illinois College of Medicine at Chicago. His research interests have been primarily in epilepsy and electroencephalography.

Neurology is the medical specialty which encompasses the diagnosis and treatment of diseases of the nervous system. This includes the brain, spinal cord and the peripheral nerves. It is closely related to neurosurgery which provides the surgical treatment to patients with tumors, subdural hematomas, etc., and to psychiatry which sees patients with mental and emotional symptoms. Neurologists are frequently asked how they are different from neurosurgeons. This query may be answered by comparing internal medicine and surgery to neurology and neurosurgery. The majority of patients with neurologic diseases are not amenable to surgical treatment. Patients with changes in their personality or impairment of memory frequently are seen by neurologists for evaluation and it is not unusual for patients with organic neurologic disease to also have emotional problems which require the care of a psychiatrist.

In the past 30 years, there has been a marked change in the practice of neurology. Before World War II, most neurologists were associated with medical schools or large teaching hospitals where they taught medical students, examined pathological specimens and correlated clinical signs and symptoms with disease processes of the brain and spinal cord. Consultations by these neurologists were obtained for diagnostic and prognostic opinions with the general feeling that treatment was to little avail. With the diagnostic capabilities of the electroencephalogram, computerized tomography, angiography, electromyography, the newer techniques of nuclear magnetic resonance and the advances made in neurochemistry, however, neurologists of today not only make diagnoses but also treat patients with both acute and chronic neurologic disease.

What type of practice may a neurologists have? Although there are still solo practitioners, the majority of neurologists are associated with a clinic or group practice. If one desires a solo practice, he or she is ordinarily on a hospital staff where patients seen are referred by other doctors for neurological consultation and examination and then returned to the referring physician. Some patients with complicated problems such as convulsive disorders or Parkinsonism may continue with treatment by the neurologist. The neurologist in solo practice will also treat acute neurologic emergencies such as status epilepticus and myasthenic crises. In addition, this specialist usually will interpret the electroencephalograms and perform electromyographic studies at the hospital as well as maintain an office for seeing ambulatory patients.

Two or more neurologists may form a practice. Their practice is similar to that of the solo practitioner but has the advantage of more time available for teaching, research and even vacation. A neurologist in a multi-specialty group has the advantage of a built-in referral base and the availability of other specialties for consultation. The physician usually interprets the electroencephalograms, the evoked responses, performs electromyography and works closely with the neuroradiologist.

The hospital based neurologist frequently receives all or part of his or her salary from the hospital and is required to see patients in consultation for other physicians, direct the electroencephalographic laboratory, perform electromyograms, determine if there is a cessation of cerebral function, i.e., "cerebral death," etc. The neurologists also may have an office to see ambulatory patients. Such hospital-based physicians are usually affiliated with teaching institutions where they are active in instructing students and residents and conducting clinical research.

The academic neurologist is associated with a college of medicine with primary duties that involve teaching and research, and to a lesser degree, clinical care. The research may be primarily clinical or laboratory.

Pediatric neurology is a well-established sub-specialty of neurology. It requires training in pediatrics and neurology for a practice that may be either solo or associated with a group or medical school.

Although neurologists may restrict practice only to consultation or office practice, this is rarely the case except among individuals who have semi-retired.

Since neurologic investigations have changed the practice of this specialty so much, it is necessary to discuss basic diagnostic tools and what neurologists do with them. Electroencephalography, one of the most important tests for patients with epilepsy and syncope, is usually performed by a technician and the record interpreted by the neurologist. Similarly, visual evoked responses and brainstem auditory evoked responses are performed by a technician and interpreted by the neurologist. These results are useful in diagnosis of various neurologic diseases, especially multiple sclerosis.

The neurologist performs electromyographic studies and nerve conduction velocities on patients with diseases of the spinal cord and peripheral nerves. Various non-invasive studies involving blood supply to the brain are performed by neurologists. With the advent of computerized digital angiography, though, these tests will probably not be of as much value as they have in the past. With the increase of neuroradiologists and computerized tomography, the neurologist no longer performs air studies and myelograms. Computerized tomography is usually performed by the radiologist in the hospital although there are neurologists who also perform these studies. In all cases, it is the neurologist who has available the entire history and physical findings and who must review these x-rays in conjuction with the neuroradiologist to determine the clinical significance in a particular patient.

Lumbar punctures are done by many physicians; however, it is not uncommon for the neurologist to be asked to perform this procedure, especially if it may be difficult.

A typical day for a neurologist in private practice - either solo, group, or a multi-specialty clinic - will consist of seeing patients in the hospital, either his or her own as well as those being followed along with the patient's primary physician. When these rounds are completed, the neurologist will probably turn to interpreting EEG's or doing electromyograms. He or she will review x-rays on patients, make final diagnoses and advise on treatment plans. The afternoon may be spent in the office where both ambulatory referral patients and returning patients will be seen. One-half day a week may be spent in the out-patient clinic at a university.

The academic neurologist at a university or teaching hospital will spend considerable time with students and residents as well as research. Indeed, neurologists tend to spend more time in research than those in some other specialties.

Professional qualifications are rigorous since many neurologists take additional fellowships for sub-specialty training. Pediatric neurology has already been discussed and an examination for this sub-specialty is sponsored by the American Board of Psychiatry and Neurology. Fellowships in electroencephalography, which include training in evoked responses, are available. Certification of competence is made by examination by the American Board of Electroencephalography and the American Board of Qualification in Electroencephalography. These independent certifying groups are not associated with the American Board of Psychiatry and Neurology. Fellowships in electromyography are available and certification may be obtained through the American Association of Electromyography and Electrodiagnosis. Other sub-specialties in neurology consists of neuro-otology and neuro-ophthalmology. Many of these individuals are primarily otologists and ophthalmologists with extra training in neurology or vice versa. Some neurologists have special interest in other sub-specialties as neuro-oncology, neuropharmacology and neurochemistry.

Neurology is a small branch of medicine that has expanded greatly since the 1940's. The Graduate Medical Education National Advisory Committee Report of 1980 estimated a need for 5,500 neurologists by 1990, and given existing residency programs, predicted that 8,650 would be in practice by 1990. The Ad Hoc Committee for Neurology Manpower Survey of the American Academy of Neurology, however, estimated that only one percent of ambulatory patients with neurologic disease are cared for by neurologists. They projected a need for 12,000 to 13,000 neurologists by 1985 and thus a shortage of 5,000 to 6,000. Moreover, another investigation estimated a need of 14,520 by 1990.[1]

The financial aspects of neurology vary by type of practice. The usual financial rewards are similar to those of internists but many be considerably higher if procedures such a electromyography are included. The financial outlay for office and equipment vary considerably. If the electroencephalograph and electromyography are owned by the hospital or a group, the neurologists has only office expenses which may be shared with other physicians.

What type of individual makes a successful neurologist? This question is difficult to answer, depending on what type of neurology interests the physician. Generally all neurologists should have an inquiring mind, frequently asking themselves "why." They usually have an interest in history and are able to take many items of information and put them together to form an overall picture. Frequently they enjoy mysteries, which again indicates the use of information to solve a puzzle. Many neurologists are compulsive individuals which is helpful since a routine neurologic examination is necessary on each patient as some unexpected finding may represent a key diagnostic clue.

The localization of function in the brain and spinal cord is such that the logical mind is able to explain signs and symptoms more easily and accurately than is possible in other branches of medicine. Individuals who enjoy bridge frequently are excellent neurologists as this game again uses logic and requires the necessity of integration and memory. It is important that neurologists (unless they work only in basic research) like people and relate well to individuals. This trait is necessary since parts of the neurologist's examination depend upon the cooperation of the patient. In addition, good patient rapport is necessary for adequate treatment of chronic neurologic diseases.

Neurology is not as lucrative a specialty as others but offers a comfortable living. Further, many patients have diseases for which we have no specific therapy at present, but how long this will continue is not known. The improvement of therapy for those with convulsive disorders, Wilson's disease, and Parkinsonism has been remarkable. The research in cerebrovascular disease and dementia are such that within this generation new treatment should be available.

Neurology is intellectually stimulating and many new discoveries involving the nervous system and its functions are occurring at the present. Ten years ago treatment of Parkinsonism with drugs to supply deficient dopamine to the brain was just beginning. Recently the

---

[1] Garrison, LP, et al. Physician Requirements - 1990: For Neurology. Seattle: Battelle Human Affairs Research Centers, 1982.

transplantation of brain cells into rats has demonstrated that the cells not only live but will produce dopamine. The understanding of the chemistry of the brain will produce increased activity in neuropharmacology and new therapeutic regimens. The working hours for a neurologist ordinarily can be controlled. Although emergencies arise, these are not frequent and since the neurologist does not need unusual physical ability, he may continue to practice after the standard retirement age. All in all - a good specialty to consider.

External Readings

6-A-1   Norback, B, "Neurology: The Challenge of a Mystery, "Medical Student 8(2):7-9 (January/February 1982).

6-A-2   "Disorders of the Brain & Nervous System," In: The American Medical Association Family Medical Guide, (Kunz, JRM, ed.). New York: Random House, 1982. pp. 266-93.

6-A-3   Conrad, CD, "Sorting Out Depression's Many Faces, " Contemporary OB/GYN 19:150-63 (May 1982).

6-A-4   Donald, JO, "Treating Two Troublesome Headaches," Contemporary OB/GYN 19:164-75 (May 1982).

6-A-5   Joynt, RJ, "Neurology," Journal American Medical Association 254:2279-80 (October 25, 1985).

6-A-6   Ziegler, DK, "Presidential Address (1981): Thinking in the Brain," Neurology 32:276-79 (March 1982).

6-A-7   Menken, M, "Consequences of an Oversupply of Medical Specialists: The Case of Neurology," New England Journal Medicine 308:1224-25 (May 19, 1983).

6-A-8   VanAllen, MW, "Neurology," Journal American Medical Association 274:2965-66 (June 4, 1982).

6-B-1   Wells, CE & Duncan, GW. Neurology for Psychiatrists. Philadelphia: FA Davis, 1980. 241 pp.

6-B-2   Scheinberg, P. Modern Practical Neurology. New York: Raven Press, 1981. 360 pp.

6-B-3   Weiner, HL & Levitt, LP. Neurology for the House Officer. Baltimore: Williams & Wilkins, 1978. 180 pp.

6-B-4   Lou, HC. Developmental Neurology. New York: Raven Press, 1982. 291 pp.

Section 7 - PEDIATRICS

Robert C. Brownlee

Robert C. Brownlee, MD, is a pediatrician and Chief Executive Officer, American Board of Pediatrics, the organization responsible for the evaluation and certification of pediatricians. He is also on the pediatric faculty of the University of North Carolina School of Medicine.

To most pediatricians, their specialty is the most rewarding discipline in medicine. Dealing with children and their parents, guiding them through the mazes of childhood and adolescence, and seeing them emerge as healthy adults is an emotionally rewarding experience. In all other specialties, the physician is often dealing with a deteriorating individual and it is his or her job to make their remaining years as pleasant and healthy as possible. In short, pediatrics is basically an optimistic specialty.

Pediatrics also differs from other fields in the nature of the contact between physician and patient. In pediatrics, with young children, most of the communication is with the parent(s). As the child grows, one deals more and more directly with the patient. In providing anticipatory guidance (counseling) to the patients, the pediatrician helps them in their handling of the child and themselves. Thus, in many instances, the pediatricians provides much counseling to the whole family. In this setting, well-child care takes is an important part of the physician activities. In helping the family avoid problems or make changes in their handling of the child, there is great potential for affecting the whole future of the child, of breaking the cycle of repetitive errors from generation to generation in a given family.

Most contacts in a general pediatric practice are in an ambulatory setting. The majority of patients seen in the hospital by the general pediatrician are newborn infants. The time expended on the care of the sick patient in the hospital is disproportionally large relative to the number of patients seen. From the financial standpoint, the pediatrician makes most of his income from patients seen in the office.

The average pediatrician works between 50 and 60 hours a week. Most work in a partnership or group setting, usually with more than two pediatricians together. The solo practice of pediatrics has declined steadily for the past 30 years. Most general pediatricians spend a normal work day as follows: up early with a telephone hour from 7:30 a.m. to 8:30 a.m; hospital rounds from 8:30 a.m. to 10:00 a.m.; office hours from 10:00 a.m. to 1:00 p.m.; lunch on the run or while he or she writes or dictates charts and makes telephone calls; office hours again from 2:00 p.m. to 5:00 p.m. After 5:00 comes more work with charts, mail, and office business affairs. If not "on call" he or she leaves the office and makes night rounds at the hospital, answers telephone calls, and sees patients in need of emergency care. The latter are treated usually in the office or the hospital emergency room and on rare occasions at the patient's home.

A recent study from a large prepayment plan reports that 3.6 percent of the pediatrician's patient contacts are for initial hospital care, 2.6 percent for in-hospital follow-up care, and 2.5 percent for newborn care. Thus more than 90 percent of the patient services represented non-institutional care. The practice profile among pediatric sub-specialties, and even within the sub-specialties varies tremendously.

What are the educational training requirements for becoming a certified pediatrician? After a full medical school schedule which results in obtaining the Doctor of Medicine degree, the new physician must complete a three-year residency program accredited by the Residency Review Committee for Pediatrics (RRC) in the U.S. or a similar program accredited by the Residency Review Committee for Pediatrics and Surgeons of Canada. Training in other residency programs is not acceptable toward meeting the requirements of the specialty board in pediatrics, the American Board of Pediatrics (ABP). Upon completion of the residency, the candidate must take a day-long written examination. If successful, the candidate qualifies for the oral examination, a 30 minute session with each of four examiners. Satisfactory performance here completes the evaluation process and the ABP then confers a certificate indicating the individual has met the highest professional qualifications associated with pediatric practice.

It is possible to be a pediatrician and practice, teach or do research in this field without being certified. However, almost all aspiring pediatricians enter the certification process, and of those that do, the large majority complete it and obtain certification.

Five sub-specialty areas - endocrinology, hematology-oncology, neonatal-perinatal medicine, cardiology and neurology - have established formal certification processes as well. By this means, it is possible for the pediatrician to fulfill certain training requirements (usually two years of fellowship after the general pediatric residency) and sit for examinations testing the individual's knowledge of the area. Successful performance brings certification by the ABP that the individual is qualified in one of the sub-specialties as well.

Pediatricians may also be certified in allergy and immunology, neurology, and psychiatry through other Boards besides ABP. In addition to these areas recognized by formal certification, there are a number of areas of sub-specialization available to pediatricians. Among these are infectious disease, adolescent medicine, pulmonology, rheumatology, developmental disabilities, critical care, public health epidemiology, etc. Others no doubt will emerge as medicine evolves and becomes more complex.

The work of the pediatric neonatologist consists largely of in-hospital care, dealing almost exclusively with problems of very small premature infants and the sicker, full term infants. Treatment requires knowledge of the physiology of the newborn, particularly the special pathophysiology of the respiratory system, the central nervous system, of fluid and electrolytes, and of nutrition. Tremendous progress has been made in the care of the small, sick newborn the past 15 years with a considerable decrease in the mortality rate and any long-term consequences. One must be abreast of the innovations in ventilatory technology, of ultrasound, hyperalimentation, x-ray, blood-gas determinations, to name a few.

The pediatric cardiologist is also primarily hospital-based and many function within pediatric departments of medical schools. Their work involves a blend of clinical and laboratory effort, seeing patients and then using a variety of technical tools, electrocardiography, ultrasonagraphy, catheterization of the major vessels and the heart, including operative procedures via the catheter, various diagnostic approaches using fluroscopy, x-rays and cinemagraphic techniques. The pediatric cardiologist is intimately involved with the pre- and post-surgical care of patients with congential heart disease.

Most patients seen by cardiologists are referred by other pediatricians for diagnosis and treatment. Many of these cases require long-term follow-up as pediatric cardiologists follow patients with congential heart disease from birth into adult life. This continuity of care is desirable for the patient and also allows the physician to learn more about the prognosis and problems of these individuals as they progress through various stages of life.

Pediatric nephrology is another in-hospital sub-specialty. Much of the diagnostic work involves procedures done best in the hospital such as ultrasonography, radiology, angiography, clearance studies, and renal biopsies. Many of their patients have chronic renal disease requiring long-term treatment such as repetitive dialysis. Some follow-up visits can be done in an ambulatory setting but very few nephrologists practice in a private setting doing nephrology exclusively.

The pediatric endocrinologist most often functions in a hospital setting, but is not tied to the facility as are other sub-specialists. Much of his or her own work is clinical in nature with the necessary diagnostic work done in hospital laboratories. In many cases, the endocrinologist is also involved in research and this activity is facilitated if the office is located in a hospital. Endocrinologists become involved in disorders of growth and various glandular diseases and conditions of children. These include disorders such as diabetes, hypo- and hyper-thyroidism, growth hormone deficiencies, and disorders of sexual development.

The pediatric hematologist-oncologist deals with disorders of the blood and the various malignancies which occur in children. Leukemia is perhaps the best known of the disorders in this area. Others such as sickle cell disease, various anemias and solid tumors are also part of their field. Patients with these disorders present a variety of problems, many of which require hospitalization. While the hematology-oncology sub-specialist frequently is hospital-based for convenience of the patients and physicians, it is possible for such a physician to sustain an office outside the institution.

The fact that many patients have congenital disorders, hemophilia for instance, which will require life-long therapy, or malignant disorders, leukemia for instance, makes this an emotionally draining area in which to work. On the other hand, the progress made in improving the quality of life of these patients and decreasing the death rate makes for an emotionally rewarding profession.

Adolescent medicine is an area long neglected but which has received increased attention in the past 25 years. Pediatricians and internists both have been active in this field although pediatricians perhaps have been more so. Adolescent medicine is a natural outgrowth of general pediatrics since it still deals with a growing and maturing individual physically and emotionally. There are many opportunities and needs in this area. With the increase in teenage pregnancies, children are having children and oftentimes are responsible for their care. The divorce rate in teenage marriages is higher than in any other group, the potential for child abuse is high, and the probability for all sorts of emotional problems in children is great. Pediatricians need to be involved with these people. The increased use of street drugs by younger age groups may require pediatricians to be knowledgeable in this area as well.

Pediatricians generally need to be interested in people, to be kind, compassionate, and considerate. Considerable manual dexterity is required as many procedures have to be performed on tiny infants and small children, particularly when the patient may not be cooperative.

Perhaps because of certain basic personality traits common to many pediatricians, and perhaps because of the skills needed to deal with children and parents, pediatricians frequently find themselves involved in administrative work. An inordinate number seem to become deans of medical schools as well as assistant and associate deans.

Pediatrics and internal medicine have much in common. Many of the same illnesses are seen and treatment modalities are similar. The opportunities for research, teaching, and intellectual stimulation are almost identical. The major difference lies in the fact that in pediatrics the focus is on growth, development, and maturation while in internal medicine it is a matter of trying to maintain the status quo and prevent or correct the effects of the deterioration brought on by aging.

In summary, pediatrics is a field that holds great interest and rewards for that special physician who has the real interest of children at heart. The pediatrician, unlike any other specialist, may find it useful to live and work as the advocate for his or her patients. This commitment, not for the pediatrician but for the improvement of children everywhere, means involvement in medical, social, institutional, legislative, and political situations. Too few people act as an advocate for children. It is part of the pediatrician's sacred trust to do so.

External Readings - Pediatrics

7-A-1   Kunz, JRM (ed.). The American Medical Association Family Medical Guide. New York: Random House, 1982. pp. 644-715.

7-A-2   Austin, G, "A New Age for Pediatrics: Change, Challenge, and Cost," Pediatrics 70:643-45 (October 1982).

7-A-3   Fulginiti, VA, "Pediatrics," Journal American Medical Association 254:2293-95 (October 25, 1985).

7-A-4   "Children Are Different - And So Are Pediatricians," Patient Care 16:85-93 (October 30, 1982).

7-A-5   "Providing Follow-Up in Childhood Cancer," Patient Care 16:167-242 (June 15, 1982).

7-B-1   Gundy, JH. Assessment of the Child in Primary Health Care. New York: McGraw-Hill Book Co., 1981. 193 pp.

7-B-2   Fulginiti, VA. Pediatric Clinical Problem Solving. Baltimore: Williams & Wilkins, CO., 1981. 1982 pp.

7-B-3   Weinger, HL. The Children's Ward. New York: GP Putnam, 1980. 264 pp.

7-B-4   Schmitt, BD. Pediatric Telephone Advices: Guidelines for the Health Care Provider... Boston: Little, Brown, & Co., 1980. 279 pp.

7-B-5   Prensky, AL & Palkes, HS. Care of the Neurologically Handicapped Child: A Book for Parents and Professionals. New York: Oxford Univ. Pres, 1982. 331 pp.

External Readings - the Sub-Specialties

7.1-A-1   "The Smallest Patient," Medical World News 22:28-36 (September 14, 1981).

7.1-A-2   Galanter, M, "Peer Group Influence on Adolescent Alcohol Use," Bulletin New York Academy Medicine 57:370-77 (June 1981).

7.1-A-3   Strasburger, VC, "Who Speaks for the Adolescent?" Journal American Medicine Association 249:1021 (February 25, 1983).

7.1-A-4   Schohberg, SK, "Pediatrics: Adolescent Medicine," Journal American Medicine Association 245:2214-15 (June 5, 1981).

7.1-A-5   "Approaching A Child's Cancer Treatment," Patient Care 16:115-207 (April 15, 1982).

7.1-A-6   Oh, W, "Neonatology," Journal American Medical Association 254:2291-93 (October 25, 1985).

7.1-A-7   Crain, LS, "Neonatal Screening: An Overview," Contemporary Education for the Family Physician 16:53-63 (February 1982).

7.1-B-1   Blum, RV (ed.). Adolescent Health Care: Clinical Issues. New York: Academic Press, 1982. 297 pp.

7.1-B-2   Marshall, RE, et al. Coping With Caring For Sick Newborns. Philadelphia: WB Saunders, 1982. 292 pp.

7.1-B-3   Schreiner, RL. Care of the Newborn. New York: Raven Press, 1981. 308 pp.

7.1-B-4   Koocher, GP & O'Malley, JE. The Damocies Syndrome: Psychosocial Consequences of Surviving Childhood Cancer. New York: McGraw-Hill Book Co., 1981. 219 pp.

7.1-B-5   Sugar, M. Responding to Adolescent Needs. New York: SP Medical and Scientific Books, 1980. 254 pp.

7.1-B-6   Kellerman, J (ed.). Psychological Aspects of Childhood Cancer. Springfield, IL: Charles C. Thomas, Pub., 1980. 321 pp.

Section 8 - PSYCHIATRY

Lester H. Rudy and Joseph A. Flaherty

Lester H. Rudy, MD is Professor and Head, Department of Psychiatry, University of Illinois College of Medicine at Chicago. He has served for 15 years as Executive Director and Secretary of the American Board of Psychiatry and Neurology.

Joseph A. Flaherty, MD, is Associate Professor and Director of medical student and residency training programs in psychiatry, University of Illinois College of Medicine at Chicago. His major research interests include social psychiatry and in particular, the influence of social support on depression.

Psychiatry is one of the most diversified medical careers. Practice profiles may range from the full-time psychoanalyst working in an office doing in-depth analysis of the patient's early life experiences and character development with a few patients to the consult-liaison psychiatrist in medical and surgical wards, as well as psychiatric units, using the knowledge of neuroendocrinology, computerized tomography, and psychodynamics in making diagnostic assessments. The typical psychiatrist, though, works in a variety of settings and employs a wide range of therapeutic modalities. Before describing what psychiatrists do, it may be useful to start by answering some common questions raised by prospective medical students.

Perhaps the most frequent query concerns the distinction between a psychologist and psychiatrist. The basic difference is that a psychologist has received a masters or doctorate in some field of psychology while a psychiatrist has received an MD degree and has had three or four years of additional training in psychiatry. Although there are a variety of career options in psychology (industrial, school, experimental to name a few) it is the clinical psychologist who is most often confused with the psychiatrist. Clinical psychologists usually obtain training in group, family or individual psychotherapy. By talking with a patient over time, they try to help the patient through a crisis or become better equipped to handle day-to day problems. Psychologists have had additional training in psychological testing - tests which measure intelligence, personality, fantasy life and a variety of other functions.

Psychiatrists, because of their medical background, differ in two important ways: first, they are more suited for the variety of problems associated with physical illness and the interplay between mind and body; second, they are particularly trained in general pharmacology and psychopharmacology and therefore able to prescribe and monitor drugs. These two differences usually result in a psychiatrist being more prepared in the total treatment of patients with major psychiatric disorders such as schizophrenia, manic depressive illness and organic brain syndrome. It also makes them a more likely candidate for referrals of patients with medical illnesses such as delirium following open-heart surgery, impotence, substance abuse, and the mental complications of prescribed drugs such as steroids.

Another common question concerns the difference between a psychiatrist and psychoanalyst. The latter is a psychiatrist who has had five or more years of additional training in psychodynamics and psychoanalytic therapy. Psychoanalytic therapy requires a well motivated and insightful patient who, usually, is not suffering from a psychotic syndrome. Therapy generally consists of four to five sessions per week over several years; the patient usually lies on a couch and allows his mind to focus on anything that comes into it. By this free-association process, the analyst and patient obtain a deep understanding of the patient which ultimately allows a basic change in the individual's orientation and way of relating to others.

While many non-analytic psychiatrists perform psychotherapy as one modality in their treatment armamentarium, the intensive work done four times or more each week on the couch is usually reserved for one with psychoanalytic training. A general psychiatrist may refer patients for psychoanalysis just as he/she may refer a child to a child psychiatrist.

Each general psychiatrist receives training in a variety of services. Before discussing variations in career patterns, it may be helpful to describe briefly the basic competencies of the general psychiatrist.

Diagnostic Assessment. Modern psychiatric diagnoses rely on very specific criteria and employ a range of laboratory tests to determine the clinical functioning of the patient. Diagnostic assessment requires one or two depth interviews where the patient's past and present symptom history is reviewed along with a careful mental status examination which test memory, orientation, judgment, calculations, and notes the presence or absence of hallucinations, delusions and suicidal or homicidal ideation. Modern laboratory methods such as the dexamethasone assessment test are useful adjuncts to the diagnostic process. Diagnosis is obviously essential before any treatment can be planned.

Individual psychotherapy. This method varies widely according to the patient's problems and goals. It involves methods to help the patient objectively review past and current relationships, to accurately identify affect or feelings, to reformulate life goals, and to assess strengths and weaknesses. Psychotherapy can also be viewed as an educational process through which the patient learns to reorganize his or her life in a manner which leads to greater satisfaction and to maximize abilities, using Freud's criteria, to work and love.

Group therapy. The goals of group therapy may be similar to the individual method but this modality uses the other group members and the group process to provide feedback and advice on one's interpersonal style.

Consultation. The most common consultation is patient-centered where the psychiatrist does a diagnostic assessment on a patient referred by a medical colleague for the purpose of recommending treatment specific to the referring physician's concern. For example, open-heart surgery patients frequently experience extreme anxiety, depression or confusion following the surgery and the cardiologists and surgeons often want specific recommendations for their management. Consultee or program-oriented consultation is done when the psychiatrist does not directly see or treat the patient but works with health-providers. Psychiatrists specializing in this area in a hospital are often referred to as consult-liaison psychiatrists. Additionally, psychiatrists also provide both types of consultation to schools, nursing homes, prisons, and a range of social agencies.

Psychopharmacologic management. This type of treatment is offered by psychiatrists and can be combined with other modalities such as psychotherapy. Recent breakthroughs in pharmacology research place these treatments on par with any other branch of medicine.

In-patient psychiatry. Although treating hospitalized patients requires competency in the basic modalities previously described, additional skills are required for those who spend the majority of time in hospitals or clinics or who serve as coordinators of inpatient units. Hospitalized patients are usually more severely disturbed and require psychiatrists capable of handling patients whose status may change dramatically over 24 hours. The inpatient psychiatrist should also have basic administrative skills, ability to understand the group/milieu dynamics and process, and capacity to diplomatically resolve potential conflicts among the staff and patients. Inherent in these skills is the ability to coordinate the work of a variety of mental health professionals - social workers, psychologists, nurses - in a harmonious way that leads to optimal patient benefits.

Emergency psychiatry. All psychiatrists handle psychiatric emergencies such as suicide attempts, overdoses, panic attacks, acute homicidal ideation, manic episodes, delerium and social emergencies (e.g. rape). This requires sharp diagnostic skills and the ability to make prompt decisions without benefit of extensive diagnostic tests.

Although some psychiatrists limit their practice to one or two of the seven basic competencies outlined above, a recent study by the American Psychiatric Association shows that most regularly utilize all these modalities, though they vary in the proportion of each. A typical psychiatrist may have a few patients in one or more hospitals which he or she sees in the morning and then goes to an office to meet with outpatients for individual psychotherapy and/or psychopharmacologic management. A psychiatrist typically spends a few hours each week consulting at a school, social agency, or medical ward. The same psychiatrist then may see patients in group or families one evening a week or on Saturday morning.

In addition, a high percentage of psychiatrists participate in and enjoy medical student and residency teaching. The current system of medical education employs a broad base of region sites and community hospitals each of which need a qualified psychiatrist for on-site teaching and supervision.

Finally, a few psychiatrists select research as an area of their particular interest. According to most observers, it is this diversity in practice, the flexibility of one's schedule, as well as the control the psychiatrist has over this flexibility, that makes psychiatry emotionally rewarding for its practitioners.

Given this degree of diversity, one can only make comments about the type of patients psychiatrists see in very general terms. The specifics will vary with the interests, abilities, and location of the individual psychiatrist. In general, however, spectrum of depressive illness will be the most common disorder seen for all psychiatrists as depression is the most common psychiatric disorder across age categories. Geriatric psychiatrists will also see more individuals with delerium and dementia and deviation; child psychiatrists see more behavioral disorders and autism. Psychiatrists concentrating on psychotherapy will see more young adults commonly with personality disorders classified as borderline or narcissistic personality disorders. All psychiatrists see patients with schizophrenia and anxiety disorders.

The financial picture of psychiatrists obviously varies by type of practice. Psychiatrists are commonly reported to be on the low end of the spectrum for practicing physicians. Although it is clear that a psychiatrist does not charge as much for an hour's service as a neurosurgeon or cardiac surgeon, this data is misleading in two ways. First, psychiatrists usually continue to practice into their senior years, whereas older surgeons either retire or move into lower-paying administrative positions; therefore, figures on psychiatrists include more part-time semi-retired people. Second, many individuals, particularly women, have found psychiatry ideal for a part-time practice while raising young children; this also tends to lower the average income of psychiatrists. A recent profile shows the typical office-based psychiatrist sees 48 patients in a 58 hour work week and charges $55 per visit, earning a net median income of $59,000 per year.

Psychiatrists who specialize in inpatient work and/or psychopharmacologic management usually make significantly more. The majority of psychiatrists (61 percent) are not part of a corporation, although individuals in solo practice usually have agreements with other psychiatrists to share coverage for vacation and weekends. The expenses of the practicing psychiatrist are relatively low as many require no equipment, office supplies or even clerical help. The cost of malpractice insurance is considerably less for psychiatrists. Billing can be done by hand, through a personal computer or a billing service, while phone calls can be managed by an answering service and page system. The major expense for most psychiatrists is providing a comfortable and noise free office, without interference or threat to confidentiality.

Perhaps one of the most pragmatic considerations is the fact that psychiatry is now considered a shortage specialty. It is anticipated that the needs for psychiatrists in the next decade will not be met by current practitioners. Although this shortage is a serious concern to academic psychiatry, it bodes well for the young psychiatrists who is planning a career. There are currently a wealth of openings available in the public sector (e.g. Veterans Administration, state hospitals, mental health clinics, military and public health service) as well as a diversity of career options in the private sector including group or solo practice and health maintenance organizations.

Students, of course, will want to consider what characteristics may predict success and satisfaction in the field of psychiatry. Regardless of special areas of interest within psychiatry, there are a few characteristics that all educators would agree are needed. Foremost, perhaps, is a high tolerance for ambiguity. Much of what is troubling a psychiatrist's patient is not immediately apparent, even with the most careful assessment and laboratory data. Only through ongoing observation in a hospital or ambulatory setting is a clearer picture of the patient's symptom picture, history, and dynamics eventually seen. Psychotherapy requires that the psychiatrist frequently refrain from questioning the patient while awaiting for data to unfold at the patient's rate and in the patient's style. Unconscious feelings and memories cannot be dissected and removed for examination. One must proceed cautiously with a fair degree of uncertainty.

Psychiatry requires that practitioners be patient and accept lengthy delays in gratification. Physicians like to make people feel better right away; unfortunately this is rarely possible except in cases such as a fractured bone or appendicitis. The psychiatrist must also maintain a genuinely non-judgmental attitude by not allowing personal ethics or morals to interfere with his or her psychotherapeutic work. Although psychotic patients will often enjoy an immediate benefit in symptom relief with psychopharmacologic intervention, work with patients with characterlogic and neurotic disorders often requires a great deal of time, even years, before improvement can be seen by both the patient and the physician. During treatment the patient may become pessimistic or even angry at the psychiatrist. Such responses require a great deal of patience, which includes the ability to remain non-defensive. Patients with major psychiatric disorders may not achieve a complete cure in the sense of being permanently symptom-free. However, with proper treatment, they can often be greatly improved and return to a fully-functioning and rewarding life. Relapses, however, occur frequently requiring episodic or continued treatment.

Another characteristic often present among psychiatrists is a strong curiosity about what makes people "tick." Students can identify this trait in themselves when they ponder why friends or family members act in the way they do. A related trait is an interest in a patient's past history, i.e., in hearing the patient's "story."

Fellowships are now available in child, community and social, forensic, administrative, and psychopharmacology. Individuals who pursue child and adolescent psychiatry obviously like children, enjoyed their pediatric rotation more than medicine and surgery, and/or were successful in mastering particular difficulties or major life experiences in childhood or adolescence. Work with children is, in some ways, more difficult than adults; the patient does not sit down and provide a history or list of problems. Rather, through play, story-telling, drawings, and family interviews, the psychiatrist must piece together an understanding of the child's problem

Students who become social or community psychiatrists often have had an interest in the social sciences and humanities such as sociology, social psychology and history. Subjects such as racial bias, ethnic differences, immigration, and social class were particularly stimulating to them. Social and community psychiatrists are often involved in the planning and evaluation of mental health care delivery for entire communities and in planning programs to prevent mental illness or reduce the deleterious effects of psychiatric disorders.

Although administrative psychiatrists are well advised to become good general psychiatrists, individuals who pursue this field usually have an interest in group dynamics, business, and administration. They often have served in leadership positions in high school and college and may have coordinated activities such as fund raising or blood drives. The duties of administrative psychiatrists range from directors of psychiatric units, psychiatric hospitals, and mental health centers to department heads or coordinators of psychiatric education programs.

While it may be an oversimplication to say that forensic psychiatrists are those people who had difficulty in deciding between law and medicine, it is probably true that forensic psychiatrists have a special interest in legal matters and enjoy the logic manueverings of the legal profession. These psychiatrists spend their time in the assessment of patients to aid the court in determining the need for involuntary hospitalization, the patient's competency to stand trial, make a will, manage his own finances and to participate with his attorney. Service may also involve cases where the insanity defense is used.

Fellowships in psychopharmacology usually attract students with a strong background in science and who found the basic science courses in medical school to be particularly interesting. In the past, most psychopharmacologists have performed clinical research on psychotropic drug efficacy and laboratory research on the neurochemistry physiology of drug actions. However, there is currently a growing number of clinical psychopharmacologists, based in private and university hospitals, who provide consultation and treatment of patients who have not responded to drugs prescribed by general psychiatrists.

Psychoanalysis, as a separate career, attracts students with a strong interest in the unconscious as shown through interest in their own dynamics and in literature that emphasizes dynamics, and character development (e.g., Dostoevsky, Hesse).

Research opportunities are available in all the above fields as well as in general psychiatry. Students pursuing research should have an interest in the analytic process of defining a problem, making hypotheses, designing an appropriate methodology, and the systematic collection of data. In addition, interest and ability in statistics and computers are becoming essential to the research psychiatrist.

Medical students often wonder if psychiatry may be too emotionally draining for them. Difficult patients, the continuing possibility of a patient suicide, the negative feelings that a patient sometimes "unloads" on the psychiatrist and the length of treatment before improvement is seen are concerns that many students express about entering the profession.

However, a recent survey of psychiatrists showed that the vast majority were satisfied with their field, would not consider switching to another specialty and would readily recommend psychiatry to one of their children. As compared with another medical specialty, more psychiatrists were favorable about their life style, the flexibility of their schedules, the intellectual challenge of their practice, and the recent breakthroughs in psychiatric research. Psychiatrists are less likely to be called to the hospital after hours and therefore usually have more time available to spend with family and friends. In addition, interests in art, music, and literature are not only compatible with psychiatry but encouraged through groups which explore psychiatric aspects of literature and culture. It is clear that psychiatry is a rewarding and satisfying branch of medicine for the student who has carefully considered his own interests and abilities in making this career decision.

External Readings: General Psychiatry

8.1-A-1 "Mental and Emotional Problems," In: The American Medical Association Medical Guide, (Kunz, JRM, ed.). New York: Random House, 1982. pp. 294-307.

8.1-A-2 Barsky, AJ & Brown, HN, "Psychiatric Teaching & Consulting in a Primary Care Clinic," Psychosomatics 23:908-21 (September 1982).

8.1-A-3   Reich, W, "Psychiatry's Second Coming," Psychiatry 45:189-96 (August 1982).

8.1-A-4   Robbins, LL & Herman, M, "Profiles of Famous American Psychiatrists, Karl Menninger, MD," Psychiatric Annals 12:153-64 (January 1982).

8.1-A-5   General Hospital Psychiatry 4:24-27 (April 1982).

8.1-A-6   Glass, RM & Freedman, DX, "Psychiatry," Journal American Medical Association 254:2280-83 (October 25, 1985).

8.1-A-7   "Outlook 1982: Prepare for Major Shifts in Psychiatry," Patient Care 16:167-223 (January 15, 1982).

8.1-B-1   Lipp, MR. The Bitter Pill: Doctors, Patients, and Failed Expectations. New York, Harper & Rowe, 1980. 204 pp.

8.1-B-2   Shepard, M, et al. Psychiatric Illness in General Practice. Oxford: Oxford University Press, 1981. 238 pp.

8.1-B-3   Neill, JR & Sandifer, MG. Practical Manual of Psychiatric Consultation. Baltimore: Williams & Wilkins, 1980. 256 pp.

8.1-B-4   Comfort, A. Practice of Geriatric Psychiatry. New York: Elsevier/North Holland, 1980. 110 pp.

8.1-B-5   Tomb, DA. Psychiatry for the House Officer. Baltimore: Williams & Wilkins, 1981. 213 pp.

8.1-B-6   Whitaker, CA & Malone, TP. The Roots of Psychotherapy. New York: Brunner/Mazel, 1981. 272 pp.

8.1-B-7   Glickman, LS. Psychiatric Consultation in the General Hospital. New York: Marcel Dekker, Inc., 1980. 273 pp.

8.1-B-8   Basch, MF. Doing Psychotherapy. New York: Basic Books, 1980. 188 pp.

External Readings: Child Psychiatry

8.2-A-1   Earls, F, "The Future of Child Psychiatry as a Medical Discipline," American Journal Psychiatry 139:1158-61 (September 1982).

8.2-A-2   Guze, SB, "Child Psychiatry: Taking Stock," Contemporary Psychiatry 24:1-5 (January-February 1983).

8.2-A-3   Copans, S & Racusin, R, "Rural Child Psychiatry," Journal American Academy Child Psychiatry 22:184-90 (March 1983).

8.2-A-4   Schetky, DH, "Corporate Family Lifestyles: A Child Psychiatrist's Perspective," Psychiatric Annals 12:862-71 (September 1982).

8.2-A-5   Benedek, EP, "The Role of the Child Psychiatrist in Court Cases Involving Child Victims of Sexual Assualt," Journal American Academy Child Psychiatry 21:519-20 (September 1982).

8.2-A-6   "Calvin Settlage, MD: Looking at Children," Journal American Medical Association 245:2147-49 (June 5, 1981).

8.2-A-7   Jellinek, MS, "The Present Status of Child Psychiatry in Pediatrics," New England Journal Medicine 306:1227-30 (May 29, 1982).

8.2-B-1   Simmons, JE. Psychiatric Examination of Children. Philadelphia: Lea & Febiger, 1981. 311 pp.

8.2-B-2   Rutter, M. Helping Troubled Children. New York: Plenum Press, 1975. 373 pp.

8.2-B-3   Towns, P. Educating Disturbed Adolescents: Theory & Practice. New York: Grune & Stratton, 1981. 225 pp.

8.2-B-4   American Medical Association. The Physician and The Mental Health of the Child. (3 vol.). Chicago: AMA, 1979, 111 pp.: 1980, 155 pp.: 1981, 121 pp.

8.2-B-5   Sherman, M (ed.). "Pediatric Consultation-Liaison," The Psychiatric Clinics of North America. 5:239-443 (August 1982).

8.2-B-6   Binder, BJ (ed.). "Child Psychiatry: Contributions to Diagnosis, Treatment & Research," The Psychiatric Clinics of North America. 3:367-631 (December 1980).

Section 9 - GENERAL SURGERY

William L. Smead and Patrick S. Vaccaro

William L. Smead, MD, is an Assistant Professor and Chief, Division of Peripheral Vascular Surgery, Department of Surgery, The Ohio State University College of Medicine. He is active in the practice of general and vascular surgery as well as numerous clinical and basic science research projects.

Patrick S. Vaccaro, MD, is an Assistant Professor and attending surgeon in the Division of Peripheral Vascular Surgery, Department of Surgery, The Ohio State University College of Medicine. He is active in both clinical practice and teaching.

General surgery has undergone a remarkable evolutionary process over the past century. Until recently, general surgery included operative procedures involving all anatomic parts of the body and physiologic systems. Every surgeon was trained to practice "general surgery" which encompassed "everything." Inevitably, as knowledge increased in specific problem areas, special interests developed within this larger framework. Specialty groups were formed and then accredited, fragmenting surgical practice and education.

Currently, the major surgical societies have expressed concern that further development of specialty certification will eventually decimate the field of general surgery by assigning all of its various parts to those with specialized training and leaving nothing behind for the surgeon with a broader perspective. Throughout this era of specialization, however, general surgery has remained a dynamic and energetic field.

Scope of General Surgery. General surgery almost defies definition as it offers such a remarkable range of options. The field is probably best described as the primary surgical care specialty involving clinical experience, education and research in such areas as wound healing, nutrition, fluid and electrolyte balance, and infection problems. This core knowledge is essential to the quality care of all surgical patients.

The extraordinary scope of this specialty is emphasized by the statement issued by the American Surgical Association, Committee on Issues:[1] "General Surgery includes the practice of surgery of the head

---

[1] American Surgical Association. Committee on Issues. Revision, February 1, 1982.

and neck, breast, vascular, thoracic, gastrointestinal tract, hernias, colon and rectum, oncology related to the GI anatomic areas, plastic and reconstructive, pediatric, endocrine, surgical emergency and critical care including trauma, hand, transplantation, and endoscopy." As few surgeons can maintain current state-of-the-art knowledge in all of these areas, most limit their practice to a portion of this broad spectrum based on specialized training or experience. Others, particularly in non-metropolitan areas, practice true "general" surgery, referring only the most complicated cases to larger specialty centers.

Perhaps the major domain of the general surgeon is the abdominal cavity where surgical management of benign and malignant diseases of the gastrointestinal tract and biliary system takes place. Operations on the gallbladder and bile duct exploration are the procedures most commonly performed by the general surgeon, usually for gallstones and their complications. Appendectomy still remains a common emergency procedure, most often performed in children.

Operations on the stomach for benign ulcer disease and its complications of bleeding, obstruction, and perforation are declining in frequency but are also commonly performed. Operations for inguinal, umbilical, and other abdominal wall hernias are also frequent in the average general surgeon's practice. Inflammatory diseases of the small and large intestine may require surgical management for their complications and often require close professional cooperation with gastroenterology colleagues. Cancers of the stomach, pancreas, colon, and liver are among the most common malignancies and typically require surgical management, perhaps in combination with radiotherapy and chemotherapy. Surgeons with particular interest and experience in these problems frequently acquire expertise in a multitude of endoscopic techniques. Hematologic diseases involving the spleen may require surgical extirpation of this organ in combination with medical therapy.

The head and neck has been a surgical territory staked out by a multitude of surgical specialties including general surgery. Otolaryngology, oral surgery, and plastic surgery have all professed a special expertise in this area and have brought about a decline in general surgical activity in this field. Endocrine surgery of the thyroid and parathyroid glands is generally excluded from this battlefield and remains a challenging area requiring the close cooperation of endocrinologists and the surgeon. General surgeons with a particular interest in surgical oncology continue to be very active in head and neck malignancies as well as those of the breast and other soft tissue.

A large group of general surgeons concentrate on the management of patients with peripheral vascular disease. Since there are few corresponding experts in medical practice, the vascular surgeon spends a considerable portion of practice time in the diagnosis and medical management of patients with arterial, venous, and lymphatic diseases. Atherosclerosis is one of the most common diseases afflicting the human race and frequently causes symptoms by the obstruction or aneurysmal dilation of major arteries. In the treatment of symptomatic occlusive disease, direct surgical removal of the atheromatous plaque (endarterectomy) or various bypass procedures may be required to restore function or prevent catastrophe. Aneurysmal degeneration of the arterial wall with subsequent dilation leading to eventual rupture is treated by surgical exclusion and graft interposition. Venous valvular insufficiency and varicose veins are common human afflictions and may require ligation and stropping of the involved venous systems. Less frequently, direct valve repair or replacement or bypass procedures may be indicated.

The general surgeon remains the single physician most appropriately prepared to manage the critically injured patient with multiple trauma and direct subsequent sub-specialty consultation. Critical care specialists in surgery have emerged, frequently working closely with anesthesia colleagues.

Organ transplantation is one of the new frontiers of medicine offering exciting opportunities for the young surgeon. Transplantation of the kidney is now an almost commonplace operation with success rates often exceeding 80 percent. Transplantation of the heart, lungs, liver, and pancreas have all be achieved in many medical centers, and further progress is occurring at an almost unbelievable rate. Treatment by general surgeons of lung and esophageal disease, plastic and reconstructive problems and hand surgery continue despite the development of distinct surgical sub-specialties involving the same areas.

It is precisely this extraordinarily wide range of diagnostic and surgical activities that attracts most general surgeons to their field. Although the current era of specialization threatens to shrink the boundaries of general surgical practice, content diversity should sustain the energy and vitality of the discipline.

General Surgical Practice. The most comprehensive reports on surgical practice have been provided by the Study of Surgical Services for the United States (SOSSUS) [1] and related reports.[2,3] In this national study, data were collected regarding virtually every aspect of surgical practice providing unique insights into the practice of surgery

---

[1] Zuidema, GD (ed.). Surgery in the United States: A Summary Report of the Study on Surgical Services in the United States. Baltimore: American College of Surgeons and the American Surgical Association, 1975.

[2] Bloom, BS, et al., "Surgeons in the United States: Opinions on Current Issues Related to Surgical Practice," Surgery 82:635 (November 1977).

[3] Bloom BS, et al., "Surgeons in the United States: Practice Characteristics," Archives Surgery 113:188 (February 1978).

across the country. The most striking conclusion is the wide variety in surgical activities reflecting the needs of the patients and the training of the surgeons involved.

Another clear conclusion is that general surgeons work hard. The average general surgeon labors 51.2 hours per week, a work load surpassed only by the cardiothoracic surgeon. Roughly 75 percent of this time is devoted to direct patient care (37.4 hours), divided between hospital and office care. The general surgeon spends more time in the operating room (12.0) hours than most other surgical specialists, but much of this time is spend in preparation and in assisting other surgeons. Time spent actually performing operations is much lower (4.4 hours), suggesting that many surgical skills may be underutilized.

The average surgeon performs three to four operations a week, each lasting around 80 minutes. The median annual work load is 170 operations. However, the mean work load of the top 25 percent is seven times that of the lowest quartile. While 10 percent of surgeons perform at least one procedure per day, nearly 20 percent perform less than one per week. Approximately 50 percent of general surgeons operate at least three times per week. Maximum operative work load is reached 18 years following graduation from medical school.

In addition to operative patient care, the general surgeon spends a significant amount of time in preoperative diagnosis of surgical disease and the postoperative management of patients. In addition, the average surgeon spends one and a half days per week in the office involved in the outpatient management of patients pre- and post-operatively. Many surgeons, particularly those in rural settings, spend large amounts of time in the general practice of medicine, delivering primary patient care. In one recent study, nearly half of the average general surgeon's practice income came from services provided outside the operating room.

The 25 percent of time spent outside direct patient care is generally devoted to administrative activities and professional education. Many surgeons, because of their compulsive work habits, are recruited for management responsibilites in hospitals, or local, national and international medical societies. Unless constant vigilance is exercised, the individual may get bogged down in time-consuming committee work to the exclusion of activities related to surgical care. On the other hand, involvement in the activities of various professional societies helps maintain knowledge and skills at the cutting edge of surgical science and offers the side benefits of friendship and intellectual kinship.

The scope and variety of general surgical practice was emphasized by the SOSSUS report. Only three operations, cholecystectomy (10.1 percent), hernia repair (9.4 percent), and appendectomy (5.0 percent) accounted for as much as five percent of the total surgical work load. Seventeen different procedures contributed one percent or more to the total work load while "other procedures" accounted for nearly half.

Such extraordinary variety in surgical procedures reflects an even greater spectrum of patient problems, diagnostic dilemmas, and therapeutic challenges. As a result, professional boredom and intellectual stagnation are more rare than other more specialized fields.

Many practice options are available. Roughly 40 percent of all surgeons engage in group or partnership practice. Multi-specialty groups, with a mean size of 33 physicians, are by far predominant. Single specialty groups and partnership practices, average three or four physicians per group. Group practice allows coverage during nights, weekends, and vacations, and hence improves lifestyle by promoting flexibility. The solo practitioner (46.9 percent) in exchange for more control of his practice, sacrifices convenience and must handle all emergency calls. Academic surgeons comprise nearly four percent of the total. Thus they add teaching and research responsibilities to those of patient care, significantly increasing their work load beyond the average.

Most general surgeons locate their office in a medical building, although a significant number work directly out of a hospital or clinic facility. In the SOSSUS study, 47 percent of general surgeons limited their surgical activity to one hospital, and only 10 percent found it necessary to work in more than four. Surgical practice in more than one hospital is often awkward as the surgeon must juggle operating schedules and patient care responsibilities amidst a variety of conflicting obligations. The more critical the requirement for postoperative care, the more important it is to consolidate surgical practice into a minimum number of hospitals. Itinerant surgery at widely separated facilities is specifically proscribed by the American College of Surgeons.

On average, surgical specialists earn nearly 40 percent more than other physicians. Despite working longer hours and a heavier patient load, the general surgeon's income falls below that of other surgical specialists. Surgeons consistently place in the upper five percent of all income earners in the United States.

From a staffing standpoint, general surgeons are well distributed across the country with few geographic or population centers lacking ready access to their expertise. Like all physicians, a preponderance are concentrated in metropolitan areas but over the past two decades there has been some shift to nonurban settings.[1]

General Surgical Training. The remarkable advances in surgery over the past 50 years have captured the imagination of many of our brightest students and stimulated an interest in pursuing surgical careers. Many

---

[1] Schwartz, WB, et al., "The Changing Geographic Distribution of Board-Certified Physicians," New England Journal Medicine. 303:1032 (October 30, 1980).

students, even at the undergraduate level, work formally or informally
with surgical clinicians or research scientists in an effort to explore
career possibilities. A broad academic background in both science and
the humanities provide the best framework on which to build a life in
surgery.

According to one study most surgeons choose their specialty during
the surgical clerkship required in medical school. "Gratification from
the type of practice" was mentioned as an almost equally high-ranking
reason, although the exact meaning of this phrase is open to
interpretation. An attraction to direct and definitive diagnosis and
therapy with generally unambiguous outcome probably influences the
majority of candidates. The satisfaction of fine craftmanship and
technical expertise may attract others. The wise student examines the
field from many angles and seeks out opinions from many practicing
surgeons before making a final decision.

The choice of a surgical residency depends largely upon career goals
and expectations. Large university-based programs generally provide the
broadest experience in all surgical disciplines and additional
opportunities to explore research interests. Many private community
hospitals, however, also provide strong clinical training programs.
Geographic and family considerations may also play an important role in
this decision.

Data from the National Resident Match Program provide a clear
picture of current surgical residency programs. Of 15,563 first year
residency positions available in 1982-83, 14.0 percent of medical
students elected general surgical residencies. Competition is
increasing though - for the first time since the Residency Match
Program has been in existence, more students sought surgical residencies
in 1983 than there were positions available.

Over the past several years, studies of graduating medical students
show that 18-20 percent choose some surgical career. Of these students,
one-third wish to include a research fellowship in their post-graduate
training, primarily to prepare for a career in academic surgery.
Although there has been a dramatic increase in the number of women
applying and being accepted for surgical residency positions, 88 percent
of the surgical residents in 1983 were men. Minority groups were also
underrepresented (6.4 percent), a statistic that parallels medical
school enrollment.

Because of the intensive level of clinical activity, residency
training in surgery is traditionally more rigorous and demanding than
most other specialty programs. Programs in general surgery currently
require five years of training with graduated levels of responsibility
depending upon individual performance and seniority. Most on-call
schedules require that the resident spend every second or third night in
the hospital in direct patient care. Research activities generally

require additional years in the laboratory without clinical responsibilities. Further sub-specialization in other general surgical disciplines, such as surgical oncology, transplantation and peripheral vascular surgery, mandate additional fellowships of one to two years.

Board certification requires satisfactory completion of an approved residency program and a passing performance on written and oral examinations administered by the American Board of Surgery. Recertification is required at ten-year intervals to assure continued quality control and stimulate continuing professional education.

Surgical Manpower Needs. The Graduate Medical Education National Advisory Committee (GMENAC) predicted a surplus of nearly 12,000 general surgeons by the year 1990 if current training levels are maintained. The Committee thus recommended: (1) decreasing by 17 percent the total number of medical students based on 1980-81 enrollment, (2) slashing the number of first-year residency positions in surgery by 20 percent, (3) restricting the number of foreign medical graduates entering the U.S. programs, and (4), encouraging primary care specialties by offering grants and reimbursement incentives. Only token response has been made to these recommendations. However, many observers contend that projected supply and requirement figures could be in error by as much as 20 percent.

Nevertheless, almost half of the general surgeons questioned in SOSSUS study felt that there was an oversupply of physicians in their specialty. Certainly the workload statistics quoted earlier suggest that there is room for additional operative activity in the average general surgeon's schedule. Further, the data in Table I-1 indicate that nearly one-half the surgeons were not certified in this discipline. Thus the surgical societies have recommended limitation of surgical privileges to those with certified specialty training.

Over the past decade, there has been a 35 percent growth in the surgeon/population ratio. The 18,475 board-certified general surgeons in 1983 represent a 8.1 surgeon/100,000 population ratio, excluding the large number of non-board certified surgeons who increase this figure by some 90 percent. Social and market forces can be expected to limit practice opportunities if this trend continues.

The Surgical Horizon. The science of general surgery has a nearly limitless potential for further growth and development. New diagnostic techniques will allow us to explore areas of the body previously inaccessible by noninvasive techniques and many diseases will be identified at a time when curative rather than palliative procedures can be performed. Contemporary surgery is distinctly different from the surgery of a decade ago while the surgical technology of a decade hence will undoubtedly exceed our current imagination.

Transplantation of major body organs constitutes a new frontier in medicine. With new techniques to control tissue rejection, large numbers of patients with end-stage cardiac, kidney, and liver diseases are being restored to active life. Future developments promise to expand the scope of this activity dramatically.

The technical frontier of microsurgery should explode during the next decade. Current techniques have allowed the reimplantation of fingers, the movement of large flaps of soft tissue from one location to another to cover large defects, and the revascularization of arteries on the surface of the brain. Further, laser technology promises to expand the surgeon's ability to resect tissue in a bloodless field.

The general surgeon will remain the primary physician caring for most patients with soft tissue malignancies and will be, therefore, in the forefront of the research efforts that ultimately result in the cure of cancer. Similarly, the general surgeon with an interest in the management of peripheral vascular disease will be a central figure in finding solutions to the management of atherosclerosis, the leading killer of adult Americans through heart attacks and strokes.

Despite the many evolutionary changes and increasing sub-specialization, general surgery will remain at the forefront of surgical progress. Heavy commitments in time and energy are rewarded many times over by the intense job satisfaction derived from good surgical results. The extraordinary variety of diagnostic and therapeutic problems attracts the interest of most general surgeons and stimulates their development throughout their careers. All things considered, few general surgeons would trade places with any other specialty in medicine.

External Readings

9-A-1   Baue, AE, "Surgery," Journal American Medical Association 254:2299-2300 (October 25, 1985).

9-A-2   "Young Surgeons Discuss Controversies Involved in Surgical Practice," Bulletin American College Surgery 67:27-29 (July 1982).

9-A-3   Crile, GJ, "How to Keep Down the Risk and Cost of Surgery," Inquiry 18:99-101 (Summer 1981).

9-A-4   Bunker, JP, et al., "Surgical Innovation and Its Evaluation," Science 200:937-41 (May 26, 1978).

9-A-5   Mannick, JA, "Presidential Address: Vascular Surgery - 'A Part of the Main'," Surgery 90:927:31 (December 1981).

9-A-6   Moore, WS, "What's New in Peripheral Vascular Surgery," Journal Cardiovascular Surgery 24:49-52 (Jan-Feb 1983).

9-B-1   Wind, GG & Rich NM. Principles of Surgical Technique: The Art of Surgery. Baltimore: Urban & Schwarzenberg, 1983. 227 pp.

9-B-2   Kra, SJ & Boltax, RS.   Is Surgery Necessary?   New York: Macmillan, 1981. 215 pp.

9-B-3   Kramer, M. Invasive Procedures. Hagerstown, MD: Harper & Row, 1983.

9-B-4   Eiseman, B. Prognosis of Surgical Disease. Philadelphia: WB Saunders, 1980. 530 pp.

9-B-5   Miller, DC. Diagnosis and Management of Peripheral Vascular Disease. Menlo Park, CA: Addison-Wesley, 1982. 314 pp.

9-B-6   Chassin, JL. Operative Strategy in General Surgery: An Expositive Atlas. New York: Springer-Verlag, 1980. 558 pp.

9-B-7   Schien, CJ. Introduction to Abdominal Surgery. Hagerstown, MD: Harper & Row, 1981. 521 pp.

9-B-8   Jirsch, DS (ed.). Frontiers in General Surgery. Philadelphia: FA Davis Co., 1982. 390 pp.

Ambulatory Surgery

the American College of Surgeons approves the practice of performing certain operative procedures in ambulatory surgical facilities, provided that the appropriate quality assurance measures are in force. Of prime concern is the patient's suitability for ambulatory surgery as well as the provision of proper standards for surgical privileges and for accreditation of the facility.

- Socio-Economic Factbook for Surgery 1986. Chicago: American College of Surgeons. p. 105.

Section 10 - CARDIOTHORACIC SURGERY

John L. Pennock and John A. Waldhausen

John L. Pennock, MD, is Assistant Professor of Cardiothoracic Surgery, Pennsylvania State University College of Medicine, Hershey, PA. He has completed post-doctoral research fellowships in mechanical circulatory assistance, the artificial heart, and cardiac transplantation. His clinical and research interests lie in adult cardiothoracic surgery and in cardiac replacement, mechanical and biological.

John A. Waldhausen, MD, is the John W. Oswald Professor of Surgery and Chairman, Department of Surgery, Pennsylvania State University College of Medicine, The Milton S. Hershey Medical Center. His clinical and research interests are in the fields of congenital heart surgery, myocardial preservation and surgical education.

Stephen Paget wrote in his 1896 edition of Surgery of the Chest:

Surgery of the heart has probably reached limits set by nature to all surgery. No new method and no new discovery can overcome the natural difficulties that attend a wound of the heart. It is true that 'heart suture' has been vaguely proposed as a possible procedure and has been done on animals; but I cannot find that it has ever been attempted in practice.

Yet a year later, Ludwig Rehn successfully closed a stab wound of the heart in a 22 year-old male. When Dr. Luther Hill similarly closed a stab wound of the heart successfully in 1902, this was the first reported cardiac surgical procedure ever performed in the United states.

Alex Carrel perfected the technique of anastomosing small blood vessels in 1902 and was awarded the Nobel prize in 1912 for his efforts. Cutler and Levine at the Peter Brigham Hospital in Boston performed the first mitral valvulotomy for mitral stenosis in 1923 utilizing a valvulotomy inserted into the left ventricle. Souttar, in 1925, pioneered the opening of a stenotic mitral valve by introducing his finger into the left atrial appendage and splitting the valve with finger pressure. These landmark contributions represent the beginnings of valvular heart surgery before the advent of cardiopulmonary bypass.

Robert Gross, in 1938, successfully closed a patent ductus arteriosus. This marked the beginning of congenital heart surgery. In a historic operation at The Johns Hopkins Hospital, Dr. Alfred Blalock successfully anastomosed the left subclavian artery to the left pulmonary artery to correct cyanosis due to Tetralogy of Fallot. This operation opened the door to the surgical management of true congenital cardiac anomalies, the famous blue baby operation, before the advent of cardiopulmonary bypass. It was also the beginning of the modern era of cardiac surgery.

In 1953, Dr. John Gibbon first successfully employed the heart-lung machine to close an atrial septal defect at the Jefferson Medical College. This event marked the threshold of the most significant advance in cardiac surgery which allowed cardiac surgeons to enter the chambers of the heart and correct almost all known cardiac lesions by some degree of surgical intervention. Utilizing this technique, holes between chambers of the heart could be closed, diseased valves could be replaced by artificial valves, and blood flow could be redirected in order to produce normal physiological flow.

Gordon Murray, in 1954, experimentally anastomosed an auxillary artery to the anterior descending coronary artery preempting the modern era of coronary artery surgery. A long list of surgical innovators including Michael DeBakey, Edward Garrett, George Green, Rene Favaloro, David Sabiston, and Frank Spencer perfected the techniques of coronary artery bypass surgery which are now routinely used in over 600 hospitals across the nation.

Transpleural, or open thoractomy surgical procedures, were not performed until the early 20th century because of the inability to manage respiratory function by means of tracheal intubation and positive pressure ventilation. The first transpleural esophagectomy with staged reconstruction was not performed until 1913 by Torek. In the United States, Marshall, in 1937, performed the first successful one-state esophagogastrectomy for carcinoma of the esophagus. In 1933, the first successful pneumonectomy for bronchogenic carcinoma, performed by Evarts Graham, represented a major milestone in thoracic surgery and established pulmonary resection as the primary method of treating carcinoma of the lung. In 1941, Dr. Cameron Haight performed the first successful correction of congenital tracheoesophageal fistula with closure of the fistula and primary anastomosis of the esophagus.

New developments in the field of cardiac surgery include the application of cardiac transplantation pioneered experimentally and clinically by Norman Shumway and the use of mechanical artificial cardiac devices to treat end-stage heart disease for which no lesser procedure can offer a realistic expectation of benefit. In addition, we have seen the successful application of combined heart and lung transplantation clinically in 1981 by Dr. Bruce Reitz at Stanford University. Finally, the first implantation of a total artificial heart for permanent use took place in 1982 by a team at the University of Utah.

What do physicians do in cardiothoracic surgery? The historical developments chronicled above give a good indication of the specialized nature of this field. Cardiothoracic surgeons operate on the heart, lungs, the esophagus, the chest wall, and the great vessels within the chest cavity. The specialty encompasses diseases related to the organs within the chest from newborns to senior citizens. This field of surgery is relatively young compared to other surgical disciplines. After all, the heart-lung machine was only first used in 1953.

In common practice, the cardiothoracic surgeon serves as an expert in diseases of the chest for the community. He evaluates patients with cardiac diseases; pulmonary surgical diseases, such as cancer of the lung and pulmonary infections; and diseases of the esophagus such as reflux esophagitis, motor disturbances of the esophagus and esophageal reflex. He provides the necessary surgical care to patients with chest trauma, adult and congenital heart disease, adult and congenital pulmonary disease, diseases of the esophagus, and aneurysms of the ascending and descending thoracic aorta.

In recent years, some members of the specialty have tried to divide the field into cardiac surgery and non-cardiac thoracic surgery. Although many cardiothoracic surgeons perform adult cardiac procedures exclusively, many of us believe that the field will remain "general thoracic surgery." The reason is that surgical training necessary to become a competent cardiothoracic surgeon includes proven competency in all aspects of adult and congenital esophageal, pulmonary, and cardiac surgery.

Certification by the American Board of Thoracic Surgery is achieved by fulfilling the following requirements: (1) certification by the American Board of Surgery (five years of approved general surgical training including 12 months as Chief Resident); (2) two years of approved training in thoracic and cardiovascular surgery including 12 months as Chief Resident; and (3), satisfactory performance on the American Board of Thoracic Surgery examination. Thus, training includes the surgical treatment of diseases of the lungs, pleura, chest wall, esophagus, mediastinum, diaphragm, congenital heart disease, and acquired heart disease.

As in all surgical disciplines, the surgeon, and only the surgeon, should make the all important final decisions as to whether a patient is a candidate for an operation and, if so, what procedure is most appropriate. Wisdom, good decision making, and sound judgement are qualities that must be innate to the prospective cardiothoracic surgeon. These qualities are polished and improved with appropriate surgical training. The potential for developing these qualities must be present in the individual before surgical training is undertaken. As Dr. Andrew Morrow stated:

> If an operation is advisable, this decision should be presented to the patient by the surgeon, and the basis for the decision explained in terms meaningful to him. Also if an operation proves inadvisable in a patient severely

ill with heart disease, it is the difficult duty of the surgeon and not any other physician taking care of the patient to present this judgement and the reasoning behind it to the patient.

Moreover, Dr. Alfred Blalock noted "the fact that a patient is going to die does not necessarily mean that he should be operated upon." The surgeon performing cardiac procedures should be a skilled cardiologist who happens to be able to perform operations upon the heart. The skilled thoracic surgeon is not just a technician, although cardiothoracic surgeons are among the most skilled technical surgeons of all the surgical disciplines. The good cardiothoracic surgeon conducts operations with deliberate facility and learns early to maintain poise and control when unexpected events occur. In the field of thoracic surgery, as in other surgical disciplines, the course of the patient after surgery is directly related to the manner in which the operation is conducted.

Several groups have attempted to reconstruct how a cardiothoracic surgeon spends his time. In a study by Bloom and colleagues, 7,298 physicians reported that the average thoracic surgeon worked 55.6 hours a week. He or she spends 35 hours in direct patient care, 13 hours in the operating room, 38 hours total in the hospital, seven hours in the office, and six hours in practice administration. The complexity of operating room procedures performed by thoracic surgeons was twice that of all other surgeons.

Thoracic surgeons, like other surgeons, require time to build up practices. For all surgical specialists, this peak was reached about 18 years after graduation from medical school. Operations on valves of the heart, cardiac revascularization, pulmonary resection, operations on atrium, septum, and ventricle with prosthetic devices, insertion of pacemakers, thoractomy and pleurotomy, and bronchoscopy comprised over 50 percent of the operative workload. Thoracic surgeons displayed an interesting generational effect where those aged 55 years or older performed mainly operations on the chest and lungs while those younger than 55 did mainly cardiac and vascular procedures.

In 1970, there was an average of one thoracic surgeon per 100,000 population. The cardiothoracic surgeons in 1970 performed approximately 56 major thoracic operations per year. In 1976, the average was similar but each surgeon performed approximately 87 major thoracic procedures. With the advent of coronary artery bypass surgery, it is estimated that the average cardiothoracic surgeon todays performs 100 major procedures a year and, indeed, coronary artery bypass for the past few years has strained our manpower capability.

Cardiothoracic surgeons tend to have inexhaustible drive, and well-directed aggression. Medical students usually choose the field of thoracic surgery as their future career after spending some time on the cardiothoracic service. Since cardiothoracic surgery is a sub-specialty of general surgery, principles of good surgery are learned only through first obtaining indepth experience and broad knowledge in the field of general surgery. Therefore, a potential thoracic surgeon should also enjoy general surgery because five years will be spent training to be a general surgeon before entering thoracic surgery training.

We adhere to the philosophy that a good liberal arts education is as important to a well-rounded physician as any other profession. However, the advent of mechanical assist devices for the heart, the development of artificial heart valves, and the new experimental field of total cardiac replacement by mechanical means, have created a need for more students with bioengineering backgrounds to become thoracic surgeons.

A study of thoracic surgeons was conducted in 1976 by Atkins and Orthner. They gathered responses from 2,240 thoracic surgeons between 34 and 54 years of age who performed nearly 200,000 major thoracic or cardiac operations. Fifty-four percent of active surgeons responding were in solo practice. Forty percent practiced in groups of two to four surgeons while the remaining six percent were in groups of six or more. Surgeons who did predominantly cardiac surgery were almost always in group practice. The Pacific region of the country led with 1.4 surgeons per 100,000 population while the Southeast Central region of the United States was lowest with 0.8 surgeons per 100,000 people. Five regions of the country, including the Pacific, Northeast, Central, South Atlantic, and Mid Atlantic accounted for two-thirds of all board certified thoracic surgeons.

Thoracic surgeons devoted an average of 57.9 percent of their professional activities to cardiothoracic work, 19.1 percent to peripheral vascular work, and 22.1 percent to other activities. At a national level, 29.3 percent of active thoracic surgeons reported that they essentially limited their practice to cardiac and thoracic surgery. Based on this survey, 87.4 major thoracic and cardiac operations were performed per surgeon per year.

An investigation of future health manpower requirements by Feldstein and Viets indicates that over the next 15 years average case loads for board certified thoracic surgeons will actually increase if the board certification rate remains approximately 160 physicians per year. There is no question that with the advent of coronary artery surgery the demand for thoracic surgery is continuing to expand. However, a manpower surplus for cardiothoracic surgery may occur after 1990.

Newer sub-specialties imply that unique individuals be trained by the year 2000. Congenital cardiac defects, even of the most complex type, are now being repaired. To perform these procedures, specialized training will become a requirement in the future. The congenital cardiac surgeon will have spent an additional year as a fellow in a center with a large volume of patients with congenital cardiac lesion. Cardiac transplantation has been shown to be therapeutic in terms of survival time and quality of life.

Although the actual number of cardiac transplants that can be performed in any given year is probably around 2,000, there are only about a dozen surgeons trained in the immunology, specialized patient care, and transplant techniques in the country. In addition, cardiac replacement by means of a mechanical heart may be a practical aspect of cardiac surgery by the end of this century. The demand for such a device is well into the tens of thousands. Thus, the frontiers of academic cardiothoracic surgery will remain fascinating.

External Readings

10-A-1   Annals Thoracic Surgery 28(5):403-422 (November 1979).

10-A-2   "Disorders of the Heart & Circulation," In: The American Medical Association Family Medical Guide, (Kunz, JRM, ed.). New York: Random House, 1982. pp. 370-417.

10-A-3   Bloom, BS, et al., "Thoracic Surgeons and Their Surgical Practice," Journal Thoracic Cardiovascular Surgery 78(2):167-74 (August 1979).

10-A-4   Morrow, AG, "What the Cardiac Surgeon Ought to Be," Surgery 72(6):819-26 (December 1972).

10-A-5   "Coronary Artery Bypass Surgery," Journal American Medical Association 246:1645-49 (October 9, 1981).

10-A-6   Loop, FD, "Cardiothoracic Surgery," "Journal American Medical Association 254:2305-07 (October 25, 1985).

10-A-7   "NIH   Consensus-Development   Conference   Statement: Coronary-Artery Bypass Surgery: Scientific and Clincial Aspects," New England Journal Medicine 304:680-84 (March 12, 1981).

10-B-1   Behrendt, DM & Austen, WG. Patient Care in Cardiac Surgery. Boston: Little, Brown & Co., 1980. 214 pp.

10-B-2   Harlan, BJ, et al., Manual of Cardiac Surgery. New York: Springer-Verlag, 1980. 204 pp.

10-B-3   Daughtry, DC (ed.). Thoracic Trauma. Boston: Little, Brown & Co., 1980. 284 pp.

10-B-4   Humprey, EW & Lawrence, D. Manual of Pulmonary Surgery. New York: Springer-Verlag, 1982. 259 pp.

Section 11 - COLON AND RECTAL SURGERY

William R. C. Stewart

William R. C. Stewart, MD, is Chief, Division of Colon & Rectal Surgery, and Director, Colon & Rectal Surgery Residency Program at Grant Hospital, Columbus, OH. He is also Chief, Division of Colon & Rectal Surgery at Mt. Carmel Medical Center, Columbus, OH. He is a diplomate of the American Board of Surgery and the American Board of Colon & Rectal Surgery.

Colon and rectal surgery is an extremely gratifying, and often neglected, field of medical endeavor. General surgery and technical advances in vascular, cardiovascular and thoracic surgery have resulted in many physicians pursuing these fields with subsequent over crowding of these specialties. Colon and rectal surgery, on the other hand, which may appear to be less glamorous, has not been flooded with applications for residency training. Hence this is one of the smallest recognized surgical specialties in the United States.

In order to be eligible for examination by the American Board of Colon and Rectal Surgery, the resident must complete (1) five years of an approved general surgery training program with a senior year of responsibility as Chief Resident, (2) one year's fellowship as Chief Resident, and (3) one year's fellowship training in one of the 25 approved residency programs in colon and rectal surgery. In addition, the candidate must sucessfully pass Part I of the American Board of Surgery.

As more specialties appeared in surgery, the general surgeon found his field becoming more fragmented. There are now approved fellowships or residency programs in pediatric surgery, vascular surgery, cardiovascular surgery, chest surgery, orthopedics, gynecology, oncology and head and neck surgery. With increasing fragmentation, the general surgeon's field often involves multiple trauma, breast and endocrine surgery, gastrointestinal surgery, and the treatment of hernias of the abdominal wall. Most of the gastrointestinal surgery, upon which the general surgeon focuses his attention, involves the liver, biliary tract and pancreas, small intestine and colon. Very few general surgeons are well trained in the field of anorectal surgery.

A colon and rectal surgeon not only is trained in the diagnosis and surgical treatment of diseases of the small and large intestine but also in the field of anorectal surgery. The diseases of the large and small intestine, which the colon and rectal surgeon confronts, are primarily inflammatory bowel disease (Crohn's disease, chronic ulcerative colitis, diverticulitis) and neoplasms (both benign and malignant) of the colon and rectum. In addition, this specialist may handle very sophiscated procedures such as operations involving sphincter preservation.

A large portion of the colon and rectal surgeon's practice involves diagnosis and treatment of neoplasms of the colon. This includes the diagnosis and extirpation of polyps (which are precursors of carcinoma) to the treatment of frank malignancies themselves. Adenocarcinoma of the colon and rectum, as a major medical problem, could be virtually eliminated were polyps detected and removed prior to becoming malignant or if carcinomas were recognized earlier and proper surgical treatment instituted.

Cancer of the colon is the leading cause of cancer death and accounts for approximately 50,000 deaths per year - yet 120,000 new cases of cancer of the colon and rectum are detected annually. Cancer of the colon may be detected not only radiographically but by direct visualization. Education of the general population and family practitioners in the screening and detection of neoplasms is one of the major responsibilities of the colon and rectal surgeon. Cancer of the colon offers one of the best chances of complete cure if detected early.

Anorectal surgery and colonoscopy comprise, by far, the largest portion of the colon and rectal surgeon's practice. It is this expertise which most widely separates the colon and rectal surgeon from the general surgeon. Most anorectal operations are done in community hospitals as compared with university centers so most colon and rectal residency programs are located in outlying hospitals.

The colon and rectal surgeon is the only physician with surgical expertise through the colonoscope. (Granted, some general surgeons are quite experienced in this procedure.) However, at the present, the medical gastroenterologist carries out most of the colonoscopy and colonoscopic surgical procedures in the United States.

In general, colon and rectal surgery offers the very desirable admixture of major operations, such as colon surgery, and small, less time-consuming but equally rewarding, procedures such as colonoscopy, hemorrhoidectomy, fissurectomy, and fistulectomy. The former fulfills the surgeon's ego need for more extensive and complicated major surgical procedures and represent an interesting challenge, not only in diagnosis but indications for surgery, medical treatment and preoperative and postoperative care. Although anorectal procedures and colonoscopy require much technical expertise to achieve the desired results, they are accompanied by very few life threatening complications. Thus preoperative and postoperative care are fairly routine.

The colon and rectal surgeon is often the "butt" of many jokes. (i.e., the colon and rectal surgeon - "The Rear Admiral;" the colon and rectal surgeon from Denver - "The mile-high pile guy;" "Keeping ahead by working behind," etc.).

One of the most grateful patients in the field of medicine is one who has had significant anorectal discomfort that has been eradicated either medically or surgically. In general, individuals place high value on their rectum and anus, and basic functions thereof. It is very gratifying to see such a patient who has suffered servere anorectal pain for some time to have this pain completely eliminated and bowel movements no longer presenting a fear or problem. It is this group of patients that praise surgeons the loudest.

It is because of "word of mouth" by grateful anorectal patients that the colon and rectal surgeon not only has a large physician referral practice but also a large patient-to-patient referral practice as well. Because of this large component, the colon and rectal surgeon is not as dependent on other physicians who refer patients and, therefore, tends to be more independent.

Our group practice consists of three colon and rectal surgeons. In reviewing our records over the past 12 months, we found the following statistics. Fourteen percent of our total operative procedures were abdominal operations, 60 percent were anorectal procedures, and 26 percent consisted of fiberoptic colonoscopy. Approximately 30 percent of our practice involves office procedures. This includes both the diagnosis and treatment of new patients, both medically and surgically, (i.e. excision of thrombosed external hemorrhoids, removal of small polyps, incision and drainage of abscesses) as well as postoperative follow up of surgical patients.

Frequently, the colon and rectal surgeon is referred a patient either by patients or other physicians for complete examinations because of some major symptom or because the family practitioner is too busy, or does not wish, to carry out rigid or flexible sigmoidoscopy in his office. As education of the family practitioner increases in techniques of rigid and fiberoptic sigmoidoscopy, one may expect an increased referral of patients with predetermined pathology.

Disadvantages of this speciality may include occasional cases of massive bleeding, bowel obstruction or perforated bowel. However very few night calls are likely. The colon and rectal surgeon's work is mostly elective and prescheduled which facilitates the use of valuable time.

In summary the speciality of colon and rectal surgery is not over crowded but does require a year of additional residency training following the five-year general surgical residency. This speciality offers a desirable admixture of major abdominal intestinal surgery with simpler, equally rewarding and relatively less major, procedures such as anorectal surgery and colonoscopy. The latter requires much technical expertise to achieve the desired result but is accompanied by very few life threatening complications, and preoperative and postoperative care is fairly routine.

External Readings

11-A-1   Hoexter, B, & Law, SB.   "Office Diagnosis of Common Anorectal Problems," Hospital Medicine 17:41:52 (February 1981).

11-A-2   "The Options in Rectal Trauma," Emergency Medicine 14:139-145 (June 10, 1982).

11-A-3   Wangensteen, OW, "The Early Diagnosis of Acute Intestinal Obstruction With Comments on Pathology and Treatment," Diseases Colon and Rectum 25:66-78 (January-February 1982)

11-A-4   The Practitioner 226:617-96 (April 1982).

11-B-1   MacLeod, JH. A Method of Proctology. Philadelphia: Harper & Row, 1979. 194 pp.

11-B-2   Goldberg, SM, et al. Essentials of Anorectal Surgery. Philadelphia: JB Lippincott Co., 1980. 389 pp.

11-B-3   Herberer, G & Deneke, H (ed.). Colo-Rectal Surgery. Berlin: Springer-Verlag, 1982. 204 pp.

11-B-4   Todd, IP (ed.). Operative Surgery: Colon, Rectum and Anus. London: Butterworth & Co., Ltd., 1977. 412 pp.

11-B-5   Rios, M. Color Atlas of Anorectal Diseases. Philadelphia: WB Saunders Co., 1980. 207 pp.

Section 12 - NEUROLOGICAL SURGERY

Russel H. Patterson, Jr.

Russel H. Patterson, Jr., MD, is Professor of Surgery (Neurosugery), Cornell University Medical College and Neurosurgeon-in-Chief at the New York Hospital and is director of a large clinical neurosurgical division. He has been President of a number of neurosurgical societies and is past Vice-Chairman, American Board of Neurological Surgery.

Neurosurgeons vary greatly in how they spend their time, with the result that there is no more an average neurosurgical practice than there is an average animal or a color. A typical student's conception of the speciality of neurosurgery springs not only from encounters in medical school but also from fancies energized by television, the press, and popular novels. Biographies recounting the exploits of the giants of the past round out the image. Predominant among these are the chronicles of Harvey Cushing, who at his peak operated upon more than 200 patients a year for brain tumor. Most of us have settled for a practice that differs from Cushing's and yet have found deep satisfaction from our work. It is true that there are neurosurgeons who do operate annually on well over 100 patients with brain tumors or 50 or more with aneurysms, but such practices are distinctly unusual. These men work in major medical centers and have taken years to develop a reputation for competent work, which has led to the referral of patients from long distance.

A more common practice is that of the neurosurgeon who serves as the expert in diseases of the nervous system for the community. In such a setting, serving as the primary care physician for nervous system diseases, he evaluates neurological patients, performs neuroradiological procedures, and provides necessary surgical care to patients with back trouble, head injuries, and the occasional brain tumor or aneurysm. However, the picture is changing. Even in the smaller communities, neurosurgeons find themselves doing progressively less neuroradiology. Computed tomography has made the air study almost obsolete. Arteriography is performed by catheter techniques, which require skills that radiologists are reluctant to share. Myelography still remains in the domain of many neurosurgeons, but even in the evaluation of spinal disorders computed tomography is gaining ground, and neuroradiologists continue to assume an increasing proportion of the diagnostic work.

Neurosurgeons have resisted this incursion into their practice, which has led to bitter battles among the staff in some hospitals about the privilege of performing and interpreting diagnostic radiological procedures. In addition to their loss of ground in diagnostic radiology, neurosurgeons practice less neurology than in former times because of the greatly increased number of neurologists completing neurology training programs. These changes can benefit the neurosurgeon if he choses to practice in an area with a suitable ratio of population to neurosurgeons. Neurologists and neuroradiologists free him for what he does best, which is the providing of surgical judgment and skills.

Office practice occupies a substantial proportion of most neurosurgeons' time. The relatively few neurosurgeons who somehow have established a practice with a large volume of major operations generally have an abbreviated office practice. Their new patients for the most part are referred from other neurosurgeons or neurologists and usually arrive with the diagnostic neuroradiological procedures already performed elsewhere. Most of the patients they see will require an operation or at least a sophisticated opinion about the need for an operation. These neurosurgeons see few patients in follow-up because this work is done by the referring physician or by willing neurologists in the neurosurgeon's institution.

A more typical neurosurgeon is likely to see 10 or more consultations for each operative patient. Most patients will have back disorders, and others will have conditions such as headache, chronic pain, and cerebrovascular insufficiency. A substantial amount of the neurosurgeon's practice may be derived from patients with head, spine, and peripheral nerve injuries brought to the hospital emergency room. Computed tomography has helped a great deal in unraveling the morphology of trauma, which puts the neurosurgeon in the satisfying position of making decisions concerning management based on a better knowledge of the pathological changes that are present. The wearying effects on the solo practitioner of having to care for injured patients at night has been one stimulus for the formation of neurosurgical partnerships. Spinal trauma is another area in which the neurosurgeon is likely to share the responsibilities for patient care with other physicians. In this case it is with the orthopedist in trying to restore a normal bony alignment to the spinal cord.

Trauma promotes lawsuits, and neurosurgeons may examine patients at the request of a lawyer to estimate the extent of an injury and the prognosis. Any neurosurgeon is likely to become a medicolegal expert not only as a result of caring for injured patients but also because of the serious problem of medical liability. The high cost of insurance to protect against suits of medical malpractice in states such as California and New York has altered patterns of practice, and not all of the changes are for the best.

A number of groups have attempted to reconstruct how a neurosurgeon spends his time. In a study of neurosurgeons by Mendenhall and associates, 426 neurosurgeons submitted a detailed diary of their activities for one week . . . During the week, the average neurosurgeon worked 57 hours and saw 84 inpatients and 22 outpatients. He spent 4.5 hours daily in the hospital, of which two hours were in the operating room. The total number of operations was projected to reach 134 annually. Patients with spinal disorders occupied approximately 40 percent of the neurosurgeon's professional time out of the hospital and 27 percent of his time in the hospital. Of the operations performed, 22 percent were on the head and 15 percent were on the spine . . .

Padberg reviewed the applications for membership in the American College of Surgeons received between 1977 and 1981 from 339 neurosurgical applicants. Their median age was 41 years, and they averaged three years since being certified by the American Board of Neurological Surgery. Their practice profiles revealed that the median number of brain tumors operated upon per year was nine, the median number of aneurysms was four, and the total number of operations averaged 106 per year. Seventy of these were either cranial or spinal. The number of major cases may not seem high, but age and experience bring increasing numbers of referrals.

Some young neurosurgeons would like to stay in academic practice, and to do this they must gain some training in research methodology. Their first several years after residency probably will be heavily weighted toward the laboratory rather than toward patient care. As time passes, research becomes a lesser part of their life and patient care becomes more important. Many neurosurgeons will develop special interests and some will restrict their practice to such areas as pain, epilepsy, or pediatric neurosurgery . . .

After a time, a neurosurgeon discovers that a big practice and high income do not necessarily mean financial security. Somehow living expenses, particularly if the neurosurgeon has a family, tend to keep pace with income. This leads many neurosurgeons who have sufficient spare time into complex ventures in real estate, oil and gas, and other schemes that may provide an income for retirement.

Whatever the style of practice, neurosurgery is quite time consuming, often at the expense of repose and the family. It also is a speciality from which there is almost no retreat. The field is so specialized that the neurosurgeon rarely will have an opportunity to make a midlife change in career . . .

On the other hand, neurosurgery is an exciting, challenging speciality that deals with serious illness and involves risky, complex operations. It also pioneers in the use of high technology. The last several years have seen the introduction of the laser and the ultrasonic aspirator. Neurosurgeons use sophisticated microscopes and depend on complex radiographic procedures. Present-day neurosurgery is distinctly different from the neurosurgery of five years ago, and no doubt the technology of neurosurgery five or ten years hence will be beyond what we now imagine.

- 113 -

All in all, neurosurgery is the queen of modern medicine, and few of us would exchange it for another speciality.

External Readings

12-A-1   Neurosurgery 11:101-02; 107-111 (July 1982).

12-A-2   Patterson, RH, "Neurosurgery," Journal American Medical Association 254:2310-11 (October 25, 1985).

12-A-3   Pasztor, E, "Some Aspects of Personality of the Neurosurgeon," Acta Neurochir 65:141-52 (1982).

12-A-4   Bucy, PC, "Neurosurgical Residency Training Programs," Surgical Neurology 18:149-50 (August 1982).

12-A-5   Watts, C, "Neurosurgical Manpower: What Are the Issues?" Surgical Neurology 18:241-245 (October 1982).

12-A-6   Miller, JD, "Neurosurgery - Where Is It Going" Surgical Neurology 20:79-81 (July 1983).

12-A-7   Louie, H, "Presidential Address to the Neurological Society of America," Neurosurgery 11:451-53 (September 1982).

12-A-8   King, RB, "Research, Research Training and Neurological Surgery," Neurosurgery 9:353-55 (October 1981).

12-B-1   Smith, RR. Essentials in Neurosurgery. Philadelphia: JB Lippincott, 1980. 319 pp.

12-B-2   Wilson, CB & Hoff, JT. Current Surgical Management of Neurological Disease. New York: Churchill Livingstone, 1980. 355 pp.

12-B-3   Walker, AE. Cerebral Death. Baltimore: Urban & Schwarzeberg, 1981. 212 pp.

Section 13 - OBSTETRICS AND GYNECOLOGY

J. Craig Strafford

J. Craig Strafford, MD, is in private practice at Holzer Clinic, Inc., Holzer Medical Center in Gallipolis, Ohio. He is a member of the Board of Directors, a Clinical Instructor at The Ohio State University, Division of Obstetrics & Gynecology, a Fellow of the American College of Obstetricians & Gynecologists and diplomate, American Board of Obstetrics & Gynecology.

Human sexuality, reproduction and birth comprise the most basic of human experiences. In order to treat the medical aspects of these topics, the uniquely multifaceted specialty of obstetrics and gynecology developed. Some 30 years ago, the disciplines of obstetrics and gynecological surgery were combined in order to offer the female patient complete reproductive health care from a single provider.

Since then, three major sub-specialties have emerged: (1) reproductive endocrinology and infertility, which deals with the problems of ovarian hormonal function and conception; (2) perinatology and high risk obstetrics, an area concerned primarily with intrapartum complications related to pregnancy, i.e., problems for both the fetus and mother during gestation; and (3), gynecologic oncology. This latter area involves the diagnosis and treatment - using chemotherapeutic, radiologic and surgical modalities - of cancers found in the female reproductive tract. These sub-specialists also repair congenital abnormalities that occur in such systems. The vast majority of obstetricians/gynecologists (OB/GYN), however, are generalists who refer patients to their sub-specialized colleagues as needs arise.

As an obstetrician, one delivers babies - sometimes at 3:00 a.m. and sometimes after a difficult prenatal course or a protracted period of labor. This process, though, is always accompanied by the attendant hopes and aspirations of a new beginning. The freshness of the birth experience, which reflects the renewal of life, never fades.

Recent figures show that over 29,000 physicians in the United States limit their practice to OB/GYN. Residency programs in this field turn out nearly 1,100 such specialists annually. Thus approximately 6.6 percent of the current medical school graduating class selects a residency in OB/GYN.

Students contemplating specialization in OB/GYN should be well grounded in the physical and social sciences. Further, they should read widely in and be knowledgeable about the humanities - literature, fine arts and music. These fields not only represent the essence of human experience but provide one basis for personal enjoyment when a change of pace from a hectic practice is needed.

The OB/GYN specialist serves in a variety of settings. The vast majority are found in private practice, either in solo or group arrangements. A nationwide trend toward the group practice of medicine generally has resulted in an increasing number of such specialists becoming affiliated with single or multi-specialty groups. In addition, some specialists in OB/GYN find careers in academia where diverse responsibilities include teaching, research, public service and practice. Others have been engaged by governmental agencies concerned with demographic trends or by hospitals/organizations concerned with the review of medical care.

The practice of OB/GYN includes the care of normal and high-risk pregnancy, contraception and guidance related to family planning, management of infertility, and acute and chronic gynecologic care. The latter often involves menstrual disorders and the treatment of cancerous tissues.

Preventive services also constitute an integral part of an OB/GYN practice. Regular routine gynecologic evaluations, including a Pap smear, breast and pelvic examinations, have been shown to be of great value in both the early diagnosis of disease and in maintaining the patient's general health. Prenatal care, of course, can be interpreted, in large part, as preventive medicine.

Many specialists in OB/GYN work 60 hours per week, have an office-based practice, and attend patients in labor and delivery. Since biologic systems seldom follow computer models, the specialty cannot be expected to exhibit all the characteristics of an exact science. One does, however, become accustomed to the irregularities of practice, and with certain lifestyle modifications, the constancy of interruptions tends to become routine.

To succeed as a specialist in this field requires patience, persistence and flexibility. A portion of one's time will be spent simply waiting for biologic events to unfold. One must also be comfortable with repetition as many of the same events repeat themselves in patient after patient. Efficient time management is essential in order to keep abreast of current developments in practice and science while simultaneously caring for a large volume of patients. Because of these pressures, the successful specialist needs to be able to organize multiple patient care activities including the office and emergency room. Flexibility is required in order to adjust to irregularity in office schedules, eating habits and rest periods.

The specialist in OB/GYN maintains a unique position in modern medicine. First, this practitioner is expected to be competent and current in both medical and surgical skills. Second, this individual serves as both primary and specialty physician for his or her patients.

In dealing with women and their reproductive potential, the specialist must also be conversant with related developments in cardiology, endocrinology, psychiatry, pulmonary medicine and renal medicine. Moreover, the obstetrician/gynecologist is highly trained in abdominal, obstetrical and urologic surgery. Finally, technological skills have been augmented by the adoption of ultrasound imagery and laser surgery to supplement the basic armamentarium of laparoscopy, hysteroscopy and colposcopy. Since new diagnostic and treatment modalities appear frequently, the practitioner is continually challenged to maintain the highest standards of care.

To ensure the public that this obligation has been satisfied, the American Board of Obstetrics and Gynecology certifies diplomates who successfully demonstrate their knowledge and skills via the examination process. Certification is limited to 10 years after which proficiency must be demonstrated again. Quality of care objectives are also supported by the American College of Obstetrics and Gynecology through publication of a journal, organization of post-graduate courses, and dissemination of information related to advances pertaining to this specialty.

Because of expectations regarding birth and reproduction, the practice of OB/GYN tends to be laden with more emotional characteristics than most other medical or surgical disciplines. The success or failure associated with a child's birth is commonly attributed to the obstetrician. Thus his or her role in delivery is sometimes the focus of malpractice litigation, a dark cloud that looms over the otherwise sunny landscape of OB/GYN.

Unfortunately, no social mechanism exists to cope with the reality that not all pregnancies, surgical procedures, or supervised recoveries can be successful. The OB/GYN specialist functions near the center of this controversy where the constant threat of a medical malpractice suit may bring financial obliteration for the clinician and his/her family. The resultant stress and frustration saps energy from worthwhile professional endeavors.

Pregnant women are generally healthy and usually deliver healthy infants. However, as highly technical electronic fetal monitoring threatens to displace the sympathetic role of a physician at the bedside, patient dissatisfaction seems to rise accordingly. When the physician's skill or performance is found lacking, society provides a mechanism that enables injured parties to pursue monetary retribution. This process not only raises the cost of insurance premiums (according to a California Medical Association survey, most specialists in OB/GYN have a premium that exceeds $25,000 per year) and legal fees, but it also induces physicians to practice "defensive medicine" (ordering tests or carrying out procedures whose real benefit may be marginal) which in turn raises the cost of health services even further.

Some controversial aspects of OB/GYN also pose questions of morality and ethics. Pregnancy termination, research utilizing fetal material, the extent of medical care for severe congenital malformations, and dissemination of information on contraception are all issues which require that clinicians in this field must first make a personal decision before rendering care. The obstetrician/ gynecologist is thus placed at a focal point of social concerns involving reproduction of the species and human sexuality. In this context, he or she becomes not only the provider but allocator of health care, a bio-ethics concern the pervasiveness of which is seldom reached in other specialties.

Elements of future developments in OB/GYN are already evident. Basic knowledge and new techniques are expanding rapidly even though the delivery function has occurred more than 20 billion times. For example, researchers are investigating prenatal fetal surgery, applied human genetics, artificial insemination, and embryo transfer. Social issues include teenage pregnancy, the expanding role of women in the workplace, the effect of environmental toxins and pollutants on pregnancy and lactation, and the persistent topic of the quantity vis-a-vis quality of life. Consequently, students should avoid OB/GYN if they are searching for a nice quiet corner in the field of medicine.

In summary, the obstetrician/gynecologist has an opportunity to provide nearly total medical and surgical care for one's patients. Further, the specialty can be practiced in virtually any health care setting. Despite the dynamics of our civilization and the health care delivery/financing system, the need for reproductive health care will continue. The specialty, for the most part, deals with happy, desired outcomes - the birth of a child. One whose skills reduce the pain associated with childbirth and preserves the reproductive function can derive considerable intrinsic satisfaction from this contribution.

External Readings

13-A-1   Kunz, (ed.). The American Medical Association Family Medical Guide. New York: Random House, 1982. pp 582-605;616-43.

13-A-2   Hill, EC, "Obstetrics and Gynecology." Journal American Medical Association 254:2308-09 (October 25, 1985).

13-A-3   "Here's Why Most Women Seek An OB-GYN for Primary Care," Patient Care 16:97-101 (October 30, 1982.

13-A-4   Fribourg, S, "Obstetrics and Gynecology in the 1980's," Journal OB/GYN 143:730-31 (July 15, 1982).

13-A-5 Keith, LG, et al., "Perspective on Vaginal Contraception: A Method for the 1980's," Contemporary OB/GYN 19:63-82 (May 1982).

13-A-6 Bates, GW, "When Puberty Begins, So Do Many of Its Disorders," Contemporary OB/GYN 16:165-76 (May 1982).

13-A-7 MacDonald, D, "Previous Obstetrical or Gynecological Surgery," Clinics in Obstetrics & Gynecology 9:147-63 (April 1982).

13-A-8 Wexler, P, "Natural Childbirth and Consumer-Oriented Obstetrical Care," Continuing Education for the Family Physician 16:29-35 (June 1982).

13-A-9 "Is This Cesarean Section Cost Effective?" Continuing Education for the Family Physician 19:161-73 (February 1982).

13-A-10 Harris, BA, "Indications for Cesarean Section," Continuing Education for the Family Physician 17:45-53 (September 1982).

13-A-11 Anderson, DG, "Ideas and Ideals: Presidential Address," American Journal of Obstetrics and Gynecology 143:239-42 (June 11, 1982).

13-A-12 Emans, SJ, "Gynecology and the Young," Emergency Medicine 14:93-140 (April 30, 1982).

13-B-1 Friedman, EA (ed.). Obstetrics Decision Making. Trenton, NJ: BC Decker, 1982. 222 pp.

13-B-2 Queenan, JT (ed.). Managing OB/GYN Emergencies. Oradell, NJ: Medical Economics Co., 1982. 157 pp.

13-B-3 Fadel, HE (ed.). Diagnosis and Management of Obstetric Emergencies. Menlo Park, CA: Addison-Wesley, 1982. 324 pp.

13-B-4 Kleinman, RL. Family Planning Handbook for Doctors. London: International Planned Parenthood Federation, 1980. 243 pp.

13-B-5 Scully, D. Men Who Control Women's Health: The Miseducation of Obstetrician-Gynecologists. Boston: Houghton Mifflin, 1980. 285 pp.

13-B-6 Glass, RH. Office Gynecology. Baltimore: Williams & Wilkins, 1981. 360 pp.

13-B-7 Ryan, GM (ed.). Ambulatory Care in Obstetrics Gynecology. New York: Grune and Stratton, 1980. 510 pp.

Section 14 - OPHTHALMOLOGY: A MEDICAL AND SURGICAL SPECIALTY

Robert N. Shaffer

Robert N. Shaffer, MD, is Clinical Professor, Emeritus, of Ophthalmology, the University of California School of Medicine, San Francisco, CA. He has been Co-Director of the Glaucoma Clinic and is also the Executive Secretary of the American Board of Ophthalmology.

It is relatively easy for the college student to choose medicine as a career. The choice of a specialty is much more difficult. Medical students have had a great deal of involvement in the major specialities but minimal involvement in the smaller ones. The decision to shrink from the study of the whole body to the eyeball cannot be taken lightly. Yet surveys show that ophthalmologists are among the most professionally satisfied of all physicians.

Ophthalmology represents a microcosm of medical practice. The ophthalmologist must be a family physician, an internist, a surgeon, a pediatrician, a psychologist and a neurologist. Yet he or she is a general practitioner in such a small area of the body that most of its intricacies can be mastered. There is little competition from other specialists who have a profound respect for the eye. Like other primary care physicians, the ophthalmologist has the opportunity to become well acquainted with the problems of patients and their families and can be of service from the cradle to the grave.

History of Ophthalmology. The value of vision has always been held close to that of life itself. In the "Code of Hammurabi", about 2250 B.C. in Babylon, it is written, "If a physician operates on a man and causes the man's death; or, with a bronze lancet, opens an abscess in the eye of a man and destroys the man's eye, they shall cut off his fingers." Such a law curbed the enthusiasm of over-eager surgeons. The malpractice attorney serves a somewhat similar purpose today.

It was not until the mid-19th century that the invention of the ophthalmoscope by Helmholtz prepared the way for the solid scientific base up which modern ophthalmology is founded. Modern ophthalmology is based upon studies by sophisticated eletrophysiology, microbiology, electron microscopy, CAT scans, ultrasonography and fluoroscein angiography. All of medicine has benefited by microsurgical techniques developed for ophthalmology. Corneal transplantation was the first successful use of homotransplants. Ultrasound is used diagnostically and in cataract surgery. The laser is being used in retinal and glaucoma surgery.

Who Should Become An Ophthalmologist? The student who likes heavy, large-scale surgery such as orthopedics or gastroenterology is unlikely to be attracted to ophthalmology. The potential ophthalmologist must value accuracy and be willing to take painstaking, meticulous care in his or her observations. The ability to note minor variations from the normal is essential in diagnosis. Fortunately, this precision is available because most areas of the eye can be examined under high magnification and an accurate diagnosis is usually possible. Therapy can then be chosen logically.

Competition for residencies in ophthalmology is sufficiently intense that the student with below-average grades will find acceptance difficult. Good vision is important since impairment of binocular vision, depth perception or color vision interfere with the effective use of ophthalmic instruments and interpretation of observations. Good hand-eye coordination is essential: The delicate precision of the watch-maker is needed in ocular surgery.

The average ophthalmologist will spend four or five days a week in the office, seeing approximately 25 patients a day. Much of the time, at first, will be spent in routine eye examinations and the prescribing of glasses and contact lenses. In cities it takes some time to establish a surgical practice. In smaller communities, a full-scale ophthalmologic practice is usually developed in one or two years. Emergency night calls are less common than in many of the specialities.

The practice is a mixture of medicine and surgery, ranging from refraction and the treatment of infections, allergies, injuries and crossed eyes to the most delicate of surgical procedures. The most common operation is cataract extraction. Patients tend to come directly to the ophthalmologist for eye problems, rather than by referral from another physician. The ophthalmologist must be a physician first and an ophthalmologist second by being constantly alert to detect general medical problems in his or her patients. These vary from the recognition of hypertension and endocrine problems such as hyperthyroidism and diabetes to tumors of the skin and central nervous system. The localization of hemorrhages and primary and metastatic neoplasms of the brain can often be accomplished by study of the visual fields and by motor and sensory abnormalities of the eye and extraocular muscles. Since sight is so precious to all, a vision-threatening disease can be terrifying to the patient. The understanding ophthalmologist must serve as a psychiatrist, carefully explaining the problems and treatment to the patient and family by offering compassionate understanding in addition to clinical expertise.

There are some disadvantages to ophthalmology. Like any job, the average practice has a degree of repetitiveness and tedium which is inevitable. A large percent of the practice comes from routine eye examinations and the prescribing of glasses. Contact lens fitting is interesting, but servicing a contact lens population can be a problem. Some busy doctors employ optometrists or office assistants to perform the routine work. Such technicians must be as dedicated and precise as the ophthalmologist and they are hard to find. Further, ophthalmic equipment is very expensive - the cost of setting up an office may reach $100,000.

The terms - ophthalmologist, oculist, optometrist, optician - confuse the public. Ophthalmologists and oculists are eye physicians who have successfully completed four years of medical school, a year of clinical internship, and at least three years of special training in the medical and surgical care of the eyes. The optometrist has had at least two years of college and four years of optometric school. This specialist is licensed to prescribe and dispense corrective lenses and to screen for eye diseases as well as serve as an optician. The optician's function is like a druggist; he or she fills an ophthalmologist's or an optometrist's prescription for glasses.

There are twice as many practicing optometrists as ophthalmologists, yet the latter perform about half of the nation's refractions. Confusion between ophthalmology and optometry is due to the fact that optometrists refer to themselves as "eye doctors." However, they have no medical degree and are expected to refer any patient with a disease process to an ophthalmologist.

Ophthalmologists have tended to congregate in the larger cities, leaving the smaller communities to the optometrists. Since most of cities have a full complement of ophthalmologists, career opportunities in this specialty are more likely to be found outside the large urban area.

The Graduate Medical Education National Advisory Committee projected that in 1990 ophthalmologists will be in over-supply by approximately 40 percent. Yet a report prepared by the American Academy of Ophthalmology predicts that by the year 2000, the number of ophthalmologists will barely meet the population's needs. Such disparate conclusions result from varying opinions as to the estimated future need and demand for ophthalmologists' services. At present there are approximately 14,300 ophthalmologists practicing in the United States. In a population of 230,000,000, this yields a ratio of one ophthalmologist for every 16,000 persons. An oversupply in the future is certainly possible and some effort is being expended to reduce the number of residencies. If the trend toward settling in smaller communities continues, though, an undersupply is also possible.

Unlike some other specialities, the American Board of Ophthalmology has not issued any certificates of special competence in sub-specialty areas. Nevertheless, the development of many highly sophisticated methods of diagnosis and treatment has resulted in the establishment of a number of training fellowships in sub-specialty fields. Residents who are considering an academic career or working in a multi-specialty ophthalmology group practice should probably plan to take an additional year of post-residency training. The most common sub-specialty programs are as follows:

Cornea and External Disease. This non-surgical sub-specialty stresses the diagnosis and treatment of diseases of the cornea, sclera, conjunctiva and eyelids. It is of particular interest to those interested in microbiology, pharmacology and autoimmune disease.

Glaucoma. Increased intraocular pressure can cause blindness by destroying the optic nerve. This specialty involves the diagnosis, medical and surgical treatment of the condition in both pediatric and adult populations. A large proportion of patients with glaucoma will be found in the older group.

Pediatric Ophthalmology. This sub-specialty deals with the medical and surgical management of genetic and developmental anomalies of the eye. It involves the treatment of strabismus and a wide range of inflammatory, genetic and neoplastic conditions occurring in the first 20 years of life.

Neuro-ophthalmology. The neuro-ophthalmologist is a diagnostician, particularly interested in the pathology of the intracranial nervous system as it affects the eye. Over 50 percent of all intracranial lesions involve the visual or the oculomotor pathways. This sub-specialty is often combined with surgery of the orbit.

Ophthalmic Pathology. Special training is needed in preparing and examining of ocular tissue. Some general pathology training is required. The sub-specialty is ordinarily practiced in relation to teaching programs in medical school hospitals.

Vitreo-retinal Disease. The vitreo-retinal specialist is an expert in diagnosis and the medical and surgical treatment of local, systemic and genetic diseases as they affect the retina and vitreous. The specialty deals with retinal detachments, diabetic retinopathy, macular degenerations, hemorrhage and infections of the vitreous body.

The general ophthalmologist must have some familiarity with all of these sub-specialty areas in order to recognize the disease entities and know when and to whom the referral of difficult problems should be made. This role is similar to the family physician who recognizes and treats the majority of the problems but refers serious diagnostic and surgical cases to an appropriate specialist.

Unfortunately, most students interested in ophthalmology have only limited access to an ophthalmology department and there is a dearth of elective courses. Efforts should be made to take at least one elective as well as observe the activity in the ophthalmology clinic and in surgery. If possible, an ophthalmologist's office should be visited to obtain a first-hand view of actual practice. Residents in the various specialities are glad to talk about their impressions and suggest a true picture of the trials and frustrations, and the joys and rewards which they are experiencing.

Medical students must begin investigating prospective residency programs by the spring of their third year of medical school. In 1978, the Ophthalmology Matching Program (OMP) was established to coordinate appointments for residency positions. A pamphlet prepared by OMP contains a current directory of residencies and includes a list of application instructions and pertinent dates.

Residency training programs in ophthalmology now require a first postgraduate clinical year (PGY-1) in a program approved by the Residency Review Committee and accredited by the Accreditation Council for Graduate Medical Education in the United States, or, by the Royal College of Physicians and Surgeons of Canada.

The American Board of Ophthalmology requires that this first year of training in patient care focus on general clinical medicine, such as family practice, internal medicine, surgery, pediatrics or neurology etc. The results from the Ophthalmology Matching Program are available before the National Residency Matching Programs forms are due. Therefore the candidate will know the location of the residency before having to make choices for the PGY-1 year. Choosing a postgraduate year away from one's medical school has the advantage of broadening one's exposure to new ideas.

There are approximately 155 residency training programs and around 545 first-year positions available in the United States each year. Each has its own special strengths and weaknesses. The more prestigious programs are usually associated with the most highly regarded medical schools. They will have a large corps of professors, instructors, interns, residents and fellows who can be of great help in teaching. There are usually good research facilities available. Such residencies should be sought particularly by those interested in a continuing academic career. Those interested in a family-type practice may prefer residencies associated with hospitals that service a large clinic population which provide greater responsibilities and more primary surgical experience but less didactic training.

One should look for balance between didactic instruction and clinical experience. Training programs should have regularly scheduled didactic instruction in the basic and clinical sciences. There should be enough full-time faculty members so that help will be available when needed. Usually a ratio of one faculty member to three residents is sufficient. In addition, a large staff of part-time or clinical faculty members can give added strength and diversity to the teaching program. The resident should have a graduated increase in primary responsibility for patient care. There should be good examination facilities with supervision. There should be sufficient surgical cases that the resident can include exposure to the entire range of the more common ocular operations both as the assistant and as a primary surgeon.

Because of the competition for residency positions, it is wise to apply to four or five programs. Most departments will require personal interviews. To avoid unnecessary travel expense, interviews in different geographic areas should be grouped if possible. Plan to spend sufficient time to look at the facilities and to talk to the residents.

Finally, in addition to the educational opportunities which are available, one must keep in mind that three years of one's life will be spent at this institution. Are the current residents happy in their work? Are they satisfied with the teaching and with their opportunities for medical and surgical care of patients? Are they pleased with the rest of the medical center? Is it located in a physically safe and desirable community? Are cultural and recreational opportunities available? If plus values can be assigned to all of these factors, one can probably be assured of a stimulating and happy residency.

After the successful completion of one year of clinical medicine in an approved program and three years of approved residency either in he United States or Canada, application can be made to the American Board of Ophthalmology to take its examinations.

This application should be completed in January or February of the year the residency is to be completed. The Written Qualifying Examination consists of a four-hour, two hundred multiple choice questions. Approximately 75 percent of the candidates will be successful and will then be assigned to another city for the two-day oral examinations six to twelve months later. Over 90 percent of the candidates pass this examination. The successful candidate is then certified as a diplomate of the American Board of Ophthalmology.

In summary, Ophthalmology represents a microcosm of medical practice. It presents challenges in diagnosis but provides exquisite scientific techniques which help to make those diagnoses more precise. It is a medical specialty which requires understanding of many general medical problems, the specific action, side effects and interaction of general and ocular drugs. It is also a surgical specialty in which microscopic visualization and sophisticated microsurgical equipment has permitted amazingly successful treatment of disorders in the delicate tissues of the eye. Continuing advances add to the challenge and stimulation so that ophthalmology will continue to be one of the most enjoyable and rewarding of the specialty fields in medicine.

External Readings

14-A-1   Trobe, JD & Kilpatrick, KE, "Future Requirements For and Supply of Ophthalmologists," Archives Ophthalmology 100:61-66 (January 1982)

14-A-2   The Practitioner 226:819-923 (May 1982).

14-A-3 Goldberg, MF & Sugar, J, "Ophthalmology," Journal American Medical Association 254:2301-03 (October 25, 1985).

14-A-4 Eliasoph, I, "Eyes Get Hurt Too," Bulletin American College Surgery 66:11-13 (October 1981).

14-A-5 Campbell, RK & Klein, OG, "Eye Care for the Diabetic Patient," Journal American Medical Association 245:2087-88 (May 22/29, 1981).

14-B-1 Chalkley, T. Your Eyes. Springfield, IL: Charles C. Thomas, 1982. 126 pp.

14-B-2 Vaughan, D & Asbury, T. General Ophthalmology. Los Angeles: Lange, 1980. 410 pp.

14-B-3 Sarax H & Chevaleraud, J. Techniques in Ophthalmologie. Paris: Masson Pub., 1982. 144 pp.

MDs Warned on Possibility of Rationing

. . . I am convinced that we could bring more health to Americans with a dollar-a-pack tax on cigarets than we could by adding another $100 billion to health care spending. You give me some of those empty hospital beds to lock up drunk drivers and I'll save more lives than the hospital will. Resources have a variety of possible uses, yet this society seldom asks about what are the most cost-effective alternatives . . .

- Governor Richard Lamm (CO), speaking at the AMA Forum for Medical Affairs. Quoted in American Medical News, December 20, 1985. p. 11.

Section 15 - ORTHOPAEDIC SURGERY

J. Paul Harvey, Jr.

J. Paul Harvey, Jr., MD, is Professor of Orthopaedics, University of Southern California Medical School and is past Chairman of the section. Dr. Harvey's basic interest has been the care and treatment of patients suffering from severe trauma and research into these problems.

An orthopaedic surgeon is usually a busy, interested person who sees many patients. This specialist deals with problems of the musculoskeletal system - the bones, joints, muscles, nerves and vessels that cause them to function or that provide them with nutriment. The field covers a wide anatomical range dealing with body mechanics, gait, and upper extremity function. It is less concerned with the cardiorespiratory, gastrointestinal, genitourinary or central nervous systems except as these systems areas affect a particular patient's problem.

Historically, orthopaedic surgeons dealt with chronic, unusual afflictions of the musculoskeletal system such as polio, congenital dislocation of the hip, avascular necrosis of the head of the femur, (Legges Calve Perthes disease), avascular necrosis of other bones, malunion and non-union following fractures. Orthopaedic surgeons took care of some fractures but shared these in great part with general surgeons. Today, however, orthopaedic surgeons treat most of the fractures that occur.

As in all branches of medicine, one individual practitioner, through special capabilities, may undertake a particular procedure in large numbers. There are a few surgeons who only do joint replacement operations, some only the hip. There are a few surgeons who primarily do arthroscopy - looking directly into a joint with an instrument with lenses and a light and perhaps doing some operative procedure with this and other apparatus. The typical orthopaedic surgeon in a community hospital, through, serves a wide variety of patients.

Most beginning orthopaedic surgeons often first see their patients lying uncomfortable and sometimes badly hurt in the emergency room at unusual hours. Under these circumstances, the orthopaedic surgeon must do a primary history and physical examination and be responsible for total care of the patient. He or she may seek help for specific problems by consultation with other physicians in other specialities. Trauma patients tend to be younger and initially healthy, but beware, this is not always true.

Although all orthopaedists handle some trauma and usually help cover the hospital emergency room, one tends to find after a while in practice the major role is that of a secondary physician who obtains patients by referral from other physicians for some specific musculoskeletal problem. If the patient has other problems such as heart disease or a multi-organ system disease like diabetes, the referring physician assists or even assumes primary management of the other problems besides the orthopaedic condition. However, any good physician should be knowledgeable about the patient's diagnosis, treatment(s) received, problems that might occur, and what affects these factors would have on the orthopaedic surgeon's involvement with the individual.

The sophisticated patient in a metropolitan area, and even the others, may well go directly to an orthopaedic surgeon for backache or fracture treatment, thus making the orthopaedic surgeon into a primary physician. However the orthopaedic surgeon prefers to have patients referred by others in order to obtain good historical information.

Orthopaedic problems occur in all ages. Those in children have always been an important aspect of orthopaedic practice. In years past the bulk of these patients were children suffering from the residuals of poliomyelitis Doctors would spend many days at the clinic examining polio and other symptoms. A few who needed surgery were referred to the hospital where the surgeon had his primary base. The other patients would receive follow-up care and management as needed. Now such clinics tend to be associated with large teaching hospitals. The cost for these services had usually been and still is underwritten by Crippled Children's Services funded by the state legislature. Those surgeons who manage such clinics usually run them for years, and the newcomer often has to wait to participate in the management of such a clinic.

Many private charities have funded specialty orthopaedic hospitals and clinics. The oldest such institution, founded in 1863 to care for ruptured and crippled children in New York City, is now known as the Hospital for Special Surgery. Similarly, Shriners hospitals founded early in the 20th century provide superb care for crippled children of all races, colors and creeds in various locations in the United States, Mexico and Canada, entirely gratis. These hospitals have also provided training in children's orthopaedics for many orthopaedic surgeons.

School nurses who are trained to recognize scoliosis (curvature of the spine) in school children often refer patients directly to orthopaedic surgeons. Also, obstetricians delivering babies or pediatricians will refer newborn children to orthopaedists. Thus, infants with recognizable musculoskeletal problems, such as club feet, congenital dislocation of the hip, absence or partial absence of the limbs and other such congenital anomolies, will be referred directly to the orthopaedist. Infections of bone, osteomyelitis, and joints are much less frequently seen now. Early use of antibiotics by pediatricians has prevented many or most of the infections that once caused severe difficulties and often death in children. Thus the musculoskeletal diseases of children under 17 today consist primarily of trauma, primary fractures or dislocations, congenital anomalies or generalized neuological diseases such as cerebral palsy. Certainly the severe problems of the past, poliomyelitis residuals and osteomyelitis, are very infrequently seen in the average practice of an orthopaedic surgeon today.

Congenital anomaly problems are often severe and may involve several different systems such as meningomyelocele which involves the central nervous system, genitourinary system and the musculoskeletal system. There is a tendency for the patient to be handled in a center where meningomyelocele clinics are often headed by a pediatrician interested in kidney disease. This specialist acts as the primary physician with urologists, neurosurgeons and orthopaedic surgeons participating in problems as appropriate. This coordinated management approach to problems has proven more successful than often existed in the past when each physician reigned supreme in his own office with his own patients.

The mature patient comes to the orthopaedic surgeon because he suffers back pain, trauma and other less common musculoskeletal problems. Some of these problems can be clearly diagnosed but many musculoskeletal pains are vague and with no well defined etiology. Back pain specifically still needs much investigation to determine all the causes. As it is difficult to be specific or necessarily successful in treatment of each complaint, there exists an area where other health faddists compete for the patient.

Also, trauma centers are developing specific hospitals geared to the treatment of the patient with multi-system trauma. With the use of helicopters, patients who have had sudden severe injury, as in an automobile accident, are brought directly to a center where several different specialists including orthopaedic surgeons are immediately available to treat the different systems injured. One begins, of course, with resuscitation, being sure the airway is clear and fluids are available to replace those lost. Concern about the cardiorespiratory system is paramount and usually the general surgeon interested in physiology is the primary physician responsible for the patient. In those centers which are functioning, remarkable work has been done to resuscitate and treat severely injured patients. Once again teamwork is essential with physicians of different disciplines working together for the good of the patient.

Finally, the elderly patient makes up a significant portion of the orthopaedist's practice. Fractures about the hip joint are more common in the elderly, but other fractures occur too. Originally these fractures were treated by traction and bed rest which was frought with difficulty since many patients suffered pulmonary problems and died. With the development of the Smith-Peterson nail in the early 1930's, internal fixation of these fractures was undertaken. The patients got up immediately and the mortality rate dropped.

Degenerative joint disease becomes more apparent with age. Joint replacement, particularly the hip and knee, have become quite successful since initiated by Sir John Charnley in the early 1960's who employed polymethyl methacrylate plastic cement to hold the components in place. Although 20 years later we are finding problems with the cement, and efforts are being made to provide replacements, the results in general are good and many people have been helped.

A whole new field, bioengineering, has developed which consists of engineers interested in biocompatible materials that can be inserted in the body. The materials must be capable of bearing loads repetitively and be designed to fit readily into the anatomical site involved. Students with an engineering background might find fulfillment as an orthopaedic surgeon, or as a scientist finding and studying material for use in the body, or as designer of structures to be implanted to replace joints or other body components.

Specialties have developed within the field of orthopaedics. Treatment of hand problems have long been a specialty with orthopaedists, plastic surgeons and even some general surgeons limiting themselves to this area. It is interesting, painstaking, and occasionally tedious work. In the past years clinicians have learned vascular surgery techniques involving replantation of severed limbs. This skill has led to the new field of grafting muscles and bones with intact vascular systems which can be anastomosed into vessels at new sites offering new possibilities for reconstruction of absent or damaged anatomical areas. Since World War II when the army organized specific hand centers, the hand has been recognized as a specific specialty with its own professional societies and meetings.

The treatment of scoliosis has also evolved into a specialty requiring extended follow-up both preoperatively and postoperatively. Operations on the spine are long and physically demanding and the casts or bracing are large and need much management. Thus teams tend to develop and the average orthopaedic surgeon finds that all the extra help and equipment needed is only worthwhile if many cases are seen. Therefore most orthopaedists refer their few scoliosis patients to the surgeon who specializes in this problem.

Childen's orthopaedics, including treatment of scoliosis, has become a specialty. Since most of the children's problems stem from severe congenital anomalies, one finds that concentration in a children's hospital is of value because patient's families are usually willing to go to a center where pediatricians and others are available for complete treatment of the patient.

A new field, sports medicine, has achieved prominence in the past several decades. The presence of highly paid athletes in baseball, football, basketball, hockey, tennis, track, ballet and modern dance demands knowledgeable physicians who care for problems and injuries often but not entirely specific for these activities. Everybody seems to enjoy dealing with people in the limelight and many orthopaedic surgeons seem pleased to be able to list well-publicized people as their patients. With this, of course, goes a demand for expertise and understanding of people whose response and feelings might be different from the average patient. Fellowships for training in sports medicine are popular. The orthopaedic surgeon interested in these aspects of medicine will find great opportunity, although more likely with a high school or college team than a major league sports team. There is a sports medicine association and a journal devoted to these problems.

A recent innovation in orthopaedics has been the performance of arthroscopy as mentioned before. Some operations can be performed either through this instrument or by inserting small instruments through other tiny incisions into the joint. Saline is run through the joint during the procedure to keep it distended. Urologists have long used a similar system to examine the bladder. Although a few specialists limit their practice to working only with the arthroscope, in the future it will simply be another portion of the armamentarium of the average orthopaedic surgeon.

Orthopaedics is dynamic, interesting, demanding much work, much patient contact and some heavy physical labor when operating. This field originally dealt with trauma, polio residual and infection. With the advent of antibiotics and polio vaccine, two of these areas have almost disappeared. However, improved methods of fixing fractures with internal fixation devices of great ingenuity, intramedullary rods fixed at either end, plates (even with the concept of plates which might be absorbed into the body after several months of use), auger well for the future. The use of an image intersifier and image holding mechanism with x-ray fluoroscopy greatly reduce radiation exposure and permits fracture fixation through small openings with decreasing morbidity. The use of joint replacement has opened up many new possibilities with most of the development still to be done.

Musculoskeletal problems are chronic and the doctor may follow patients for years. An orthopaedist sees some patients at intervals often for life (either his or her own life or the patient's life). As children grow, problems change; braces or other types of apparatus must be changed and often repaired. Many problems do not need operations but may be handled by exercise, bracing or good common sense. Thus, orthopaedists see many patients before finding one who may need an operation. Indeed, only two to ten percent of all patients seen in a general orthopaedic practice may need an operation. Patients who have had surgery require long term postoperative supervision. In the case of a fractured tibia or femur, one might expect a year's management before complete recovery and return to full function.

Orthopaedics at the present time and in the foreseeable future is and will be a developing, dynamic field. The modern orthopaedist should know some basic engineering, material science, and muscle physiology but will absolutely need to have a superb understanding of anatomy. If you have interests in the above mentioned topics and are willing to think and work hard, orthopaedics may provide a very rewarding life. But do leave time for your family, it is very easy to get caught up completely.

External Readings

15-A-1   "Disorders of the Muscles, Bone & Joints," In: The American Medical Association Family Medical Guide. (Kunz, JRM, ed.). New York: Random House, 1982. pp. 529-57

15-A-2   Mindell, ER, "Orthopedic Surgery," Journal American Medical Association 254:2313-15 (October 25, 1985).

15-A_3   Couk, D, "Blue Ridge Orthopedics," Journal American Medical Association 247:1261-65 (March 5, 1982).

15-A-4   Steinberg, ME, "What's New in Orthopaedic Surgery," Orthopaedic Review 11:29-32 (May 1982)

15-A-5   Kagen, LJ, "Musculoskeletal Syndromes of the Elderly," Drug Therapy 11:63-66 (September 1981).

15-A-6   "Bones and Joints in the ER," Emergency Medicine 14:114-60 (March 15, 1982).

15-A-7   Hage, P, "American College of Sports Medicine: New Growth, New Future," The Physician & Sports Medicine 10:123-127 (1982).

15-A-8   Mirking, G & Shangold, M, "Sports Medicine," Journal American Medical Association 254:2340-43 (October 25, 1985).

15-B-1   Monk CJE. Orthopaedics for Undergraduates. New York: Oxford University Press, 1981. 240 pp.

15-B-2   Ryan, JR. Orthopedic Surgery (Medical Outline Series). Garden City, New York: Medical Examination Pub. Co., 1981. 278 pp.

15-B-3   Katz, JF. Common Orthopedic Problems in Children. New York: Raven Press, 1981. 210 pp.

15-B-4   Debrunner, HU. Orthopaedic Diagnosis. Chicago: Year Book Medical Pub., 1982.

15-B-5   Heidertz, W. Sports Medicine. New York: Thieme Stutt-Gart, 1980. 169 pp.

15-B-6   Straub, LR. Clinical Trends in Orthopaedics. New York: Thieme-Stratton, Inc., 1982. 339 pp.

15-B-7   Bourdillon, JR. Spinal Manipulation (3rd ed.). New York: Appleton-Century-Crofts, 1982. 230 pp.

15-B-8   Cantu, RC. Sports Medicine in Primary Care. Lexington, MA: Collamore Press, 1982. 229 pp.

Section 16 - OTOLARYNGOLOGY-HEAD AND NECK SURGERY

Roger L. Crumley

Roger L. Crumley, MD, FACS, is Clinical Professor of Otolaryngology-Head & Neck Surgery at the University of California, San Francisco. He is currently the Treasurer, American Academy of Facial Plastic & Reconstructive Surgery, and Chairman, Public Relations Committee of the American Academy of Otolaryngology-Head & Neck Surgery.

Otolaryngology-head and neck surgery is the specialty that deals with problems of the ear, nose and throat. . . The modern otolaryngologist-head and neck surgeon is trained to deal with problems of the entire head and neck region, including trauma, tumors, infections, congenital anomalies, and the aging processes. Like the neurosurgeon, who confines his expertise to the structures in and around the central nervous system, the otolaryngologist-head and neck surgeon (O-HN surgeon) deals with virtually all diseases and lesions above the clavicle, except for visual and eye-related disorders (ophthalmology), and lesions of the brain (neurosurgery, neurology).

Some primary care physicians and other specialists (particularly if trained prior to 1970) may be unaccustomed to consulting their former "ENT" doctors for patients with thyroid tumors, cleft lip and palate deformities, skin cancer, parotid lumps, face lifts, jaw fractures, and facial lacerations; yet these are exactly the diseases and problems most modern otolaryngologist-head and neck surgeons are best trained to manage. It is the purpose of this report to reacquaint the reader with otolaryngology and to make him or her aware of the vast changes in the specialty . . . which prompted the name change.

This evolution has been a gradual one, with accelerating momentum in the 1970's and 1980's. Technological advances were responsible for some changes in the specialty, much as CT scanning revolutionized the practice of radiology. Other changes in otolaryngology grew out the gradually expanding familiarity with a surgical region . . . Some of the most important changes include the following:

1. Development and refinement of antibiotics. For example, the acute streptococcal otitis media which formerly progressed to coalescent mastoiditis, requiring the specialist to perform mastoidectomy, is now often controlled by antibiotics. This has resulted in ears which require ossicular reconstruction and other innovative hearing operations.

The antibiotic era has also greatly decreased the numbers of tonsillectomies and adenoidectomies performed. As a result the ENT surgeon has had more time for other regions of the head and neck.

2. The introduction of the flexible fiberoptic endoscope has revolutionized the diagnostic work-up of lesions of the esophagus, trachea, and bronchi. Many otolaryngologist-head and neck surgeons quickly perform these procedures in outpatient facilities (in their own office or at the hospital), thereby leaving time for more extensive surgical undertakings of the head and neck. In some localities, other specialists (gastroenterology, pulmonary medicine) have ventured into the field of fiberoptic endoscopy, while the head and neck surgeon has kept busy with other diseases of the head and neck. Those O-HN surgeons who have learned the newer fiberoptic techniques have retained the older rigid esophagoscopes and bronchoscopes as the rigid scopes . . . are more useful for removal of foreign bodies.

3. "Nasal" polyps, formerly snared and removed repeatedly in the ENT specialist's office, are now known to originate in the ethmoid and maxillary sinuses. The development of such polyps is related to allergy and/or infection. As a result, treatment of nasal polyps is now known to be most effective when antibiotics, allergic desensitization, and sinus surgery are employed. This is in contradistinction to the older ENT routine of office removal of the nasal portion of the polyps.

The expanded knowledge of and familiarity with paranasal sinus surgery has allowed the modern O-HN surgeon to participate in the treatment of problems not formerly thought to be within his province, such as surgery of the pituitary gland via the sphenoid sinus and orbital decompression for the exophthalmos of the hyperthyroidism performed via the maxillary and ethmoid sinuses.

4. In the first half of this century, the most "major" operation performed by the otorhinolaryngologist was laryngectomy, performed for removal of cancer of the larynx. Thyroid tumors, tongue cancer, and metastatic tumors to the cervical nodes were often managed by general surgeons or oncologic surgeons. Over the past thirty years, however, the increased interest in oncology among otolaryngologists, and the fact that most tumors of the tongue, tonsil, throat, and larynx are first discovered during a routine head and neck (ENT) examination, have thrust the modern otolaryngologist-head and neck surgeon into the primary role in the management of tumors of the head and neck region.

Expertise in dealing with the larynx and with laryngectomy has promoted familiarity with the thyroid glands, its anatomy and physiology, and its surgery. Most otolaryngologist-head and neck surgeons trained in the last ten years now perform thyroidectomies, finding their knowledge of the recurrent laryngeal nerve and its anatomy most helpful, as dissection and preservation of this nerve is the most important technical aspect of thyroid tumor surgery. The essential preoperative necessity of vocal cord assessment by mirror examination has resulted in an increased awareness of the recurrent nerve and an improved rate of its preservation, while emphasizing the importance of the the O-HN surgeon in treatment of disorders of the thyroid gland. Meanwhile, a routine technique performed by otolaryngologists, teflon injection, has benefited patients with vocal cord paralysis from prior thyroidectomies or neck injuries.

While . . . otolaryngology has gradually evolved to encompass the head and neck surgical aspects described, great advances have been made in the treatment of ear diseases and deafness. Whereas the otolaryngologist formerly performed stapedectomy, myringotomy, and mastoidectomy as the most common ear operations, the current otologist performs surgery in and around the entire temporal bone. The O-HN surgeon knows all the causes of vertigo and how the diagnostic work-up should proceed. In many cases referral of the vertiginous patient most appropriately is to the otologist (O-HN surgeon specializing in ear diseases only) or the O-HN surgeon for initial diagnostic work-up. In many cases, the O-HN surgeon will secondarily refer to a neurologist if the symptoms are not clearly inner ear in origin.

Some tumors of the skull base, internal auditory canal, or posterior cranial fossa are removed by modified "craniotomies" performed by otologists working with or without a neurosurgeon. (It should be mentioned that not all O-HN surgeons perform such operations of the skull base. Such skull base surgery is usually performed by those who have taken extra training and restrict their practices to otology and/or neuro-otology to supplement their residency training in otolaryngology-head and neck surgery.)

The development and refinement of electronystagmography (ENG) has enabled O-HN surgeons to diagnose more accurately the cause of vertigo and hearing loss. The introduction of computerized tomographic (CT) scanning has further streamlined the diagnostic work-up of dizziness and deafness to the extent that pneumoencephlography, angiography, and myelography are no longer necessary in each case . . .

Perhaps the most natural component of modern otolaryngology-head and neck surgery is head and neck "facial" plastic surgery. In many localities, a large proportion of facial cosmetic surgery is performed by O-HN surgeons, may of whom have received further training from older ENT specialists skilled in such surgery, or from general plastic surgeons. Most O-HN surgery residency programs provide residents with training in facial aesthetic surgery.

Continued interest and experience in maxillofacial injuries, as well as in reconstruction of major defects following cancer operations, has made it necessary for the O-HN surgeon to be well trained in plastic and reconstructive surgery of the head and neck. As a result, most O-HN surgeons are skilled at, and comfortable with, such techniques as skin grafting for skin or mucosal defects, local skin flaps, and bone grafting for mandibular defects.

These changes have been gradual, as mentioned above, and have not progressed at the same pace in all regions of the country. Some ENT practitioners, trained in the more traditional residency programs in the 1950's and 1960's, have been satisfied with the older concept of "ear, nose, and throat," and have consequently chosen not to involve themselves in these newer areas of head and neck surgery. Other O-HN surgeons may have finished comprehensive residency programs dealing with these newer areas and, entering practice, have been discouraged or thwarted in their desire to use their training in all these areas. In some localities, medical politics, or older established surgeons of other specialties, have hesitated to accept the newer O-HN surgeon. . .

The following is a partial list of clinical problems, diseases, injuries, and other afflictions which fall currently into the surgical jurisdiction of the otolaryngologist-head and neck surgeon. . . .

Thyroid Lumps. Tumors, cysts, and inflammatory processes in and around the thyroid gland necessitate a careful physical examination and I-131 or I-123 scan. Often a sonogram and needle biopsy are indicated . . . Frequently such masses are found to be thyroglossal duct cysts, branchial cleft cysts, or metastatic lymph nodes, and are not actually thyroid in origin.

Cleft Lip and Palate. These congenital anomalies require early consultation with an otolaryngologist-head and neck surgeon or a general plastic surgeon, depending on their training and experience and sometimes according to local tradition. The cleft lip deformity should be repaired at 2-3 months of age, while the palatal cleft is usually closed between one-two years. In any event, these children have a high incidence of nonsuppurative otitis media. The O-HN surgeon should be consulted in each case regarding management of this ear disease.

Facial and Jaw Fractures. Virtually all O-HN surgeons are experienced in the management of facial fractures. Frequently, fractures of the upper or lower jaw can be treated simply by the application of arch bars to the teeth. Patients complaining of diplopia after facial injuries should always have orbital floor tomograms and O-HN surgical consultation so that diagnosis and treatment of orbital blow-out fractures are not missed or deferred.

Facial Lacerations. Which consultant should be called? Both O-HN surgeons and general plastic surgeons repair facial lacerations. The techniques used are the same, so local tradition and availability of the consultants will determine who is summoned to the emergency room

Scar Revision of the Face and Neck. Unsightly scars from trauma, surgery, or childhood acne can often be revised and made less conspicuous. For the most part, the surgeon who is call to close facial lacerations is likely to be the best trained in scar revision. Patients with facial lacerations should be told that although their wounds will

heal nicely after primary suture repair, scar maturation takes as long
as 12 months. Any unanticipated scar which may be unsightly can be
revised by the O-HN surgeon following this interval.

Cosmetic Facial Surgery. Some O-HN surgeons have sub-specialties in
aesthetic surgery of the face and neck and restrict their practices to
such cosmetic surgery. Most O-H surgeons perform aesthetic surgery in
addition to other head and neck surgery . . . .

Skin Cancer. Small lesions of the facial skin, ears, eyelids, and
neck are often best removed for histopathologic examination. In
blue-eyed individuals with light complexions a high proportion of these
lesions will prove to be basal cell or squamous cell carcinomas.
Dermatologists, otolaryngologists, and general plastic surgeons are all
trained to manage these cutaneous cancers.

Allergy. The target organs for allergy are often the nose,
paranasal sinuses, pharynx, or laryns. It is also thought that allergy
may play a major role in nonsuppurative (serious, secretory) otitis
media.

Many O-HN surgeons perform standard allergy tests and administer
hyposensitization shots in their offices. Others refer allergic
patients to an internist or pediatrician who specializes in allergy . . .

External Readings

16-A-1   "Disorders of the Ear," In: The American Medical Association
         Family Medical Guide, (Kunz, JRM, ed.) New York: Random
         House, 1982. pp 328-29

16-A-2   Bowan, C, "The Many Facets of Otolaryngology," Journal American
         Medical Association 37:121-25 (May 1982).

16-A-3   Nalebuff, DJ, "The Many Faces of Otolaryngology," Medical
         Student 6:7-9 (April-May 1980).

16-A-4   Bailey, BJ, "Otolaryngology-Head and Neck Surgery," Journal
         American Medical Association 254:2303-05 (October 25, 1985).

16-A-5   Holliday, MJ, "Some Common Ear Problem," Hospital Medicine
         17:13-32 (May 1981)

16-A-6   Primary Care 9:261-437 (June 1982).

16-B-1 Morelock, M, & Vap, JB. Your Guide to Problems of the Nose & Throat. Philadelphia: GF Stickley, 1985. 160 pp.

16-B-2 Dayal, VS. Clinical Otolaryngology. Philadelphia: JB Lippincott, 1981. 355 pp.

16-B-3 Lesavoy, MA (ed.). Reconstruction of the Head and Neck. Baltimore: Williams & Wilkins, 1981. 319 pp.

16-B-4 Birrell, JR (ed.). Logan Turne's Disease of the Nose, Throat, and Ear. Littleton, MA: John Wright, PSG, 1982. 445 pp.

16-B-5 Cody, TR. Disease of the Ears, Nose, and Throat. Chicago: Year Book Medical Pub., 1981. 512 pp.

Health Care Financing

. . . the real action in our health care payment system right now isn't on the federal or state front, but on the private insurance front . . . where employers seem to have found the handles for influencing the cost behavior for their benefit plans . . . By 1985, roughly 26 percent of all health insurance dollars were either in self-funding or in health maintenance organizations . . . .

With these changes, with the economic leverage that insurers and employers have to seek economic concessions from providers, and the growing willingness of employers to question physician professional judgment, the era of provider dominated payment systems is coming to an end . . .

- Jeff Goldsmith, PhD, National Technical Advisor, Ernst & Whinney, Chicago. Quoted in Executive New Service, American Group Practice Association, October 15, 1985. p. 3.

Section 17 - PEDIATRIC SURGERY

Richard P. Harmel, Jr.

Richard P. Harmel, Jr., MD, is an Assistant Professor of Surgery, The Ohio State University in Columbus, OH and attending surgeon at Children's Hospital and The Ohio State University Hospitals. He is a pediatric surgeon whose investigations focus on intestinal transplantation.

Pediatric surgery is a relatively young surgical sub-specialty. Only within the last 20 years or so were the principal pediatric surgical societies established, residencies in the field accredited, certification offered by The American Board of Surgery, and divisions of pediatric surgery established in university departments of surgery.

It is a small specialty, with 400 pediatric surgeons practicing nationally. Perhaps because of this small size, there is a particular pride and spirit and friendliness among these specialists coupled with a real concern about the number, distribution, and education of pediatric surgeons necessary to provide optimal patient care. Several recent manpower studies have concluded that the present number and distribution of pediatric surgeons is about right and that the ratio of surgeons to population stable. Since 14 to 18 new pediatric surgeons graduate from residencies in the U.S. and Canada each year, this number seems unlikely to change very much in the future.

To become certified in pediatric surgery, a surgeon must first complete full training and become board certified in general surgery followed by two additional years of training in pediatric surgery before taking oral and written certifying examinations. Thus the total training time consist of six to seven years after medical school, excluding any additional time that many residents spend in a surgical laboratory to sharpen their investigative skills.

Once finished with training, pediatric surgeons can look forward to a fascinating professional life. Facilities such as neonatal intensive care units and specialists such as pediatric anesthesiologists, neonatologists, pediatric oncologists, and pediatric respiratory therapists that are essential to the care of many pediatric surgical patients cannot be provided anywhere other than regional centers. Most pediatric surgeons, therefore, are on the full-time or clinical faculty of medical schools and thus are involved in teaching medical students and residents, participate in clinical or laboratory research, and care for patients as well.

Pediatric surgery is unique among surgical sub-specialties in that age rather than anatomical boundaries circumscribe the field. Pediatric surgeons do head and neck surgery, non-cardiac thoracic surgery, abdominal surgery, vascular surgery and urologic surgery in various combinations; they have resisted the tendency of other specialties to increasingly narrow pigeonholing. For many pediatric surgeons, this diversity is one of the major attractions of the field. Aside from anotomic variety, pediatric surgeons also treat numerous medical problems such as congenital anomalies, trauma (including burns), cancer, as well as the standard inflammations and infection of general surgery. Premature and newborn infants have a variety of unique physiological problems, undergo very rapid changes in clinical status and have large nutritional requirements. Consequently, skills in the pre- and postoperative care of these patients are particularly important to the pediatric surgeon.

Pediatric surgeons spend much of their time seeing inpatients in the hospital and operating. Typically one or one and a half days per week are spent seeing new or follow-up patients in the office or clinic. Additional time may be spent teaching, formally or informally, or in the laboratory. Hours tend to be irregular, as much of this specialty involves emergency problems which must be dealt with when they occur, even in the middle of the night. Common surgical conditions seen by pediatric surgeons include inguinal hernia, undescended testes, appendicitis, intussusception, and hypertrophic pyloric steonsis. The more unusual, and more interesting, problems include congenital anomalies such as esophageal atresia, congenital diaphragmatic hernia, imperforate anus, and abdominal wall defects, and pediatric tumors such as neuroblastoma, Wilms' tumor and rhabdomyosarcoma.

Pediatric surgery differs from adult general surgery in the surgeon's relationship with his patient. The surgeon must deal with the parents as well as the patient, and must have a genuine liking for children, the patience and gentle manner necessary to gain the confidence of a child, and empathy and concern for parents and their worries and fears. He must also be an astute clinician who can make a diagnosis from nonverbal clues from an often uncooperative patient. The popular image of the brusque, decisive, aggressive surgeon just does not apply to pediatric surgeons.

There is no particular undergraduate background that might predict successful performance as a pediatric surgeon. Aside from the necessary grounding in basic sciences and mathematics, a broad general education is much more desirable than early undergraduate specialization at the expense of diverse liberal arts courses. There is plenty of time in medical school and after to develop the special skills and knowledge to facilitate a clinical or research career.

Pediatric surgery offers the considerable satisfaction of correcting otherwise fatal congenital anomalies in very young children who can then look forward to normal lives. Yet, there is also the intense sadness and frustration of watching an aggressive malignancy take the life of a young child or of being unable to reverse inexorable respiratory insuffiency after a technically successful repair of a diaphragmatic hernia in a baby who has no other defects. The satisfactions outweigh the frustrations, however, and it is fun to work with children, most of whom are spontaneous, happy, and amazingly resilient.

The field offers abundant challenges clinically and in the laboratory. Some of the questions being investigated are: How can combination therapy for childhood malignancies be improved? How can we reverse the respiratory failure of some diaphragmatic hernia patients? What causes biliary atresia? How can neonatal necrotizing enterocolitis be prevented? How can the survival of patients with short bowel be improved? Many trainees in the field are electing to spend time in pediatric surgical laboratories, in addition to their residency time, to better qualify themselves as future investigators.

Fetal surgery has received much publicity recently and represents a new area in which clinical work is just beginning and possibilities are largely unexplored. In the laboratory, diaphragmatic hernias have been repaired and obstructed urinary tracts have been drained, in utero. Along with this, new techniques in fetal diagnosis, such as real-time ultrasound, may revolutionize the way certain congenital defects are handled. Micro-vascular techniques now permit vascularized tissue transfer such as esophageal replacement with jejunum and placement of abdominal testes in the scrotum. The technique has many other potential applications. In all these areas, opportunities will exist for pediatric surgeons with additional training and experience.

External Readings

17-A-1   Hendren, WH, "What's New in Surgery: Pediatric Surgery," Bulletin American College Surgery 68:43-48 (January 1983).

17-A-2   Coran, AG, "What's New in Surgery: Pediatric Surgery," Bulletin American College Surgery 69:37-41 (January 1984).

17-A-3   O'Neill, JA & Vander Zwagg, R, "An Analysis of the Need for Pediatric Surgeons in the United States," Journal Pediatric Surgery 11:765-72 (October 1976).

17-A-4   Battaglia, JD, "Neonatal Surgery: Changing Patterns," Journal Pediatric Surgery 17:666-69 (1982).

17-B-1   Morse, TS. A Gift of Courage. Garden City, NY: Doubleday & Co., 1982. 326 pp.

17-B-2   Potts, WJ. The Surgeon and the Child. Philadelphia: WB Saunders, 1959. 255 pp.

Section 18 - PLASTIC SURGERY

Ronald B. Berggren and William P. Graham, III

Ronald B. Berggren, MD, is Professor of Surgery and Director, Division of Plastic Surgery at The Ohio State University College of Medicine. He is currently Chairman, Plastic Surgery Training Program Directors Group and a Director of the American Board of Plastic Surgery.

William P. Graham, MD, is Chief, Division of Plastic Surgery, Milton S. Hershey Medical Center in Hershey, PA. He is currently Secretary-Treasurer of the American Board of Plastic Surgery. His research interests cover nerve regeneration and medical history.

Plastic surgery is a specialty that is not limited to a region of the body, organ system, age group, or type of disease. It is best described as a specialty devoted to the solution of difficult problems in wound healing and has as its goal the restoration or creation of the best function of a part of the body with superior aesthetic appearance. Practitioners rarely participate in all areas of plastic surgery.

The breadth of the specialty and its ever changing content offer opportunities for individuals who have had varied educational backgrounds. Undergraduate majors from art to engineering would be useful in some area of plastic surgery. While it seems obvious that hand-eye coordination and manual skills are important prerequisites for a surgeon in any specialty, there are some traits that are of particular importance to the plastic surgeon. Curiosity, creativity and flexibility are important since the specialty has an ever changing scope. Some of the procedures are long and tedious with results that may be altered by small changes. The surgeon must be comfortable in these situations and patience and meticulous attention to detail is essential. The results of much of plastic surgery have an immense effect upon the patient's emotional and psychological makeup and the surgeon must be empathetic and understand human psychology.

The need for a broad education continues into medical school. The student should make the best use of elective time to acquire a broad base of medical knowledge in many areas. Experience in surgery and psychiatry are of particular value. Clinical rotations in surgical specialties, such as neurosurgery, orthopaedics, or pediatric surgery, might prove more valuable than general surgery since much of the residency experience will be in general surgery.

When the student has specific goals for his future in plastic surgery, the curriculum may be tailored with these in mind. If the goals are in the area of clinical surgery, experience in orthopaedics, otolaryngology, oral medicine, ophthalmology, neuroscience, pathology, anatomy, and psychodynamics would be useful. If the student sees non-clinical activities in his future, experience in wound healing, biochemistry, pharmacology, neuroscience, embryology, experimental pathology, or genetics would be helpful.

While there are several approved types of surgical residency training, most candidates for plastic surgical training programs have had three to five years of general surgery after graduating. Residency training in other surgical specialties (e.g., otolaryngology or orthopaedics) may be acceptable prerequisites. Most plastic surgical training programs are for a two year period but may physicians spend an additional six to twelve months in a particular area.

The plastic surgeon is trained to manage patients with congenital anomalies of the head and neck. The most common are clefts of the lip and palate but there are many other congenital deformities of this region including fractures of the bones of the jaws and face. Treatment of tumors of the face and neck, and reconstruction of these regions after removal of the tumors, also are within the specialty.

Hand surgery makes up a large amount of the practice of many plastic surgeons including the management of acute injuries, the correction of hand deformities and reconstruction of the hand. Some plastic surgeons devote their entire practice to the treatment of this appendage.

Plastic surgeons usually contribute to the care of the burned patient by carrying out reconstructive procedures after recovery from the initial injury. The plastic surgeon manages these patients during the acute phase following the burn and a few plastic surgeons devote all their professional time to the treatment of such individuals.

There is a broad range of problems of the body requiring reconstruction by the plastic surgeon. Although the plastic surgeon is not usually the individual who removes the woman's breast for disease, he is responsible for reconstruction after its removal. A great deal of progress has been made during the past decade in methods for reconstructing women's breasts that result in a more aesthetically pleasing appearance. Breasts may also be reduced in size, increased in size, or changed in shape by the plastic surgeon. Operations of this type are sometimes cosmetic in purpose, but in cases in which the patient has significant symptoms or has developed with severe asymmetry, the procedures may serve an important therapeutic function.

Defects of the body surface resulting from injury, previous surgical procedures, or congenital deformity may be treated by the plastic surgeon. This specialist often works closely with experts in other fields to bring the unique knowledge of reconstruction methods to a problem. A good example is the patient who has suffered a nerve injury to the leg where there is a significant loss of skin coverage and the fracture cannot be expected to heal without tissue to cover it. The plastic surgeon will use technical skills to close the wound.

Plastic surgeons have developed techniques that have been adopted by other specialities. Microvascular surgery allows the surgeon to connect blood vessels of one millimeter or less in diameter. This skill is used in reimplanting amputated parts or in moving large pieces of tissue from one part of the body to another. Craniofacial surgery is a discipline developed by plastic surgeons that makes it possible to reposition and reshape the bones of the face through incisions that will be hidden from easy view. Severe deformities of the head and neck can be corrected by these methods. Plastic surgeons, working in the laboratory and in the operating room, have controlled the blood supply to the muscles and the overlying skin so that it is possible to transfer these tissues more quickly and easily and to obtain better results.

The most visible area of plastic surgery is aesthetic or cosmetic surgery. In the United States today, this component makes up 40 percent of plastic surgical practice. Cosmetic surgery includes face lifts, breast enlargement, nose surgery, body sculpturing and similar procedures.

Although many patients are referred to plastic surgeons by other physicians, there are a large number of self-referred patients or patients sent by former patients. Traditionally the plastic surgeon has established his practice in a large urban community. There is a need for more plastic surgeons in the less populated areas of the country. When a plastic surgeon begins practice, a large portion of time is spent in repair of acute injuries. As a result, many patients are referred from the emergency rooms in local hospitals. As the practice becomes established, the surgeon may pursue a broad practice encompassing all of the general reconstructive plastic surgery or find a specific area and devote full time to that field.

There is an alternate route for beginning a practice; that is, to continue through a fellowship in a specific area and then find a group of physicians or an institution that is looking for a surgeon with these special skills and interest. When the clinician enters into this type of association, he or she is assured at the onset of a practice in a special area of plastic surgery. However, the possibility of future diversification may be restricted. The areas in which plastic surgeons may concentrate their efforts include: hand surgery, head and neck cancer surgery, craniofacial surgery, care of the burned patient, pediatric plastic surgery, or cosmetic surgery.

Over half of those currently certified by the American Board of Plastic Surgery received their credentials in the past ten years. Despite this rapid growth, there are still opportunities for plastic surgeons in community and academic practice. The plastic surgeon is an important participant on the faculty of the medical school. He teaches medical students, students in nursing and allied medical professions, residents in other specialty training programs and administers and coordinates the educational program for residents in plastic surgery.

Research activities are even more varied than the clinical interest in the specialty. This diversity is the main reason for the continued change in the scope of the specialty. Research interests of plastic surgeons include; microvascular surgery, the biochemistry of collagen and its relationship to wound healing, the embryology and growth and development to the skull, nutrition and the surgical patient, the psychology of the patient and body image, the anatomy and blood supply of the skin, the immunology of tissue and organ transplantation.

There are challenges for future investigators in numerous areas related to plastic surgery. More studies are needed concerning the nature of wound healing. It would be of great help to the patients of all surgeons if we understood the nature of scar tissue and the events that start and stop the production of this tissue. There is broad awareness of the need for more research into the causes, natural history, and the treatment of cancer and the plastic surgeon can contribute in this field of research. Many of the conditions treated by the plastic surgeon are the results of aging and research is appropriate here. Recent advances have allowed the plastic surgeon to transfer tissue more easily, more quickly and with better results; but there is room for improvement requiring additional study involving the anatomy, physiology, and pharmacology of transferred tissue.

The most troublesome aspect of the practice of plastic surgery is also the biggest asset - diversity. Since the specialty is not defined by anatomic region, organ system, age group or disease entity, there are other specialities that overlap every interest area of plastic surgery. Discussion may arise on the national or local level concerning the definition of the appropriate physician to carry out a particular procedure. Furthermore, techniques developed by plastic surgeons may gradually be absorbed into other specialities and disappear from plastic surgical practice. The face of plastic surgery is constantly changing. It has been augmented by developments from creative research by broadly trained and experienced investigators and is depleted by migration of certain areas of expertise to other specialities. Some find the uncertainty of this constant flux disquieting.

Plastic surgery is an old specialty with references in the literature that antedate the birth of Christ. It is a changing specialty built by imaginative surgeons who have a broad background and education and who are creative and artistic. The best results are achieved by the individual who understands the physiology of the healing processes of the body, can use anatomic characteristics creatively, and can apply surgical skills artistically.

External Readings

18-A-1   Mathes, SJ, "Plastic Surgery," Journal American Medical Association 254:2315-17 (October 25, 1985).

18-A-2   Romm, S, "Molding a Career," Journal American Medical Womens Association 37:69 (March 1982).

18-A-3   Hanna, DC, "Current Policies of the American Board of Plastic Surgery," Plastic & Reconstruction Surgery 69:714-16 (April 1982).

18-B-1   Goldwyn, RM The Patient and the Plastic Surgeon.   Boston: Little, Brown & Co., 1981. 246 pp.

18-B-2   McKinney, P & Cunningham, BL. A Handbook of Plastic Surgery. Baltimore: Williams & Wilkins, 1981. 252 pp.

18-B-3   McQueen, DV & Celentano, DD. Plastic Surgery Practice and Training, Baltimore: American Association of Plastic Surgeons, 1982. 193 pp.

18-B-4   Goin, JM & Goin, MK. Chaning the Body: Psychological Effects of Plastic Surgery. Baltimore: Williams & Wilkins, 1981. 225 pp.

18-B-5   Johnson, CL, et al. Burn Management. New York: Raven Press, 1981. 156 pp.

18-B-6   Miller, SH, et al. Practical Points in Plastic Surgery. Garden City, NY: Medical Exam. Pub. Co., 1980.

18-B-7   McGregor, I. Fundamental Techniques of Plastic Surgery and Their Surgical Application. London: Longmans, 1981. 336 pp.

18-B-8   Weatherley-White, RCA. Plastic Surgery of the Female Breast. Hagerstown, MD: Harper & Row, 1980. 224 pp.

Section 19 - UROLOGY

Howard M. Radwin

Howard M. Radwin, MD, is Professor and Chairman, Division of Urology, University of Texas Health Science Center in San Antonio. He is also Chairman, Undergraduate Education Committee of the American Urological Association and a member of its Education Council.

The choice of medical specialties cannot be made by the application of a set of algorithms. It should combine a visceral sense of suitability with accurate information about the field. Experience on the relevant clinical service and association with practitioners, teachers, and residents will provide much of the necessary information. It would be a mistake, however, not to recognize that there is a limit to the appropriateness of attempting to make this a purely intellectual effort. Factors such as life style, practice opportunities, diversity of the field, requirements for training and economics do not fit into formulae which are easily applied. There is a place for non-cognitive judgment or simply a recognition of what one feels comfortable with.

Nevertheless, this subjective component is facilitated by a context of realistic expectations based on as much information as is pertinent. It is well to realize that it is perfectly allowable to enjoy the practice of medicine.

This section provides information which may be helpful to those considering urology as a medical career. The application process for urologic residency has always been highly competitive and this situation is not abating. There is a high level of satisfaction among urologists with their field and this disposition seems to be communicated to those in the early stages of training.

The reasons for entering a career in urology are diverse since there are a variety of alternatives within the specialty. Needs exist in clinical practice, and research and teaching, thus accommodating differing personalities. The majority of urologists are engaged in private practice. They are in a clinical setting which most find attractive, partially because of the variety of their experiences. Urologic patients encompass all ages; indeed, because of the prevalence of both congenital urologic deformities as well as problems in the elderly, they present an unusual opportunity to deal with the extremes of the age spectrum or to sub-specialize in one.

Urologists also encounter a greater variety of disease types than is commonly thought by those unfamiliar with the field. This leads to an important balance between different levels of gravity among patient problems. Thus the setting is neither unrelievedly grim nor trivial, a factor contributing to the liveability of the field. In addition, the urologist's time is divided between the office and hospital which reflects the fact that this field involves both a medical and surgical specialty. Thus the urologist may emphasize the type of work with which he or she is most comfortable. Among applicants for residency training, this factor of balance is cited often as the major reason for choosing urology.

Typically, the applicant has a surgical bent but wishes to apply it in a field in which long term relationships can exist with their patients and in which the physician is also required for medical management. In short, there is a desire to be involved in complex surgery but not to be trapped in the role of a technician. Related to this is the ability of an urologist to conduct diagnostic studies, a role often not found in the so-called "surgical specialities." It is through the development of diagnostic tools, such as urodynamics, that much of the basic physiology of the urinary tract has been described

The scope of urologic practice is quite broad. Since urology is an "organ system" specialty, it encompasses a large variety of diseases. The subject which is most commonly associated with the field is the treatment of those conditions which interfere with the drainage of urine, thus compromising nephron function. Classically, this has usually involved the correction of many forms of obstructive uropathy such as prostatic disease in the older male, and at the other extreme of age, to congenital obstructions in the infant. However, through the effort primarily of urologists encountering previously unexplained entities in which urinary transport was abnormal without demonstrable anatomic abnormalities, a number of dysfunctional states have been described. These may result from neurological defects, dysplasia, inflammatory processes, or other causes.

Calculus disease has always been a major concern of the urologist. It can interfere with renal function, may be associated with infection as either cause or effect, may be related to neoplasms, and can be the instigator of severe discomfort. Management of the patient not only involves the surgical removal of stones, but also appropriate search for etiology to prevent further calculus formation. In addition, the medical management of patients with the identifiable metabolic defect will be accomplished by the urologist as will dealing with renal insufficiencies.

Congenital anomalies affect the genitourinary tract with greater frequency that any other organ system and account for a large portion of the fascinating sub-specialty of pediatric urology. Since not all congenital anomalies manifest themselves in childhood, the general urologist must be familiar both with them and with the embryology of the system as well. The gamut of problems seen in children includes psychological and developmental difficulties as well as organic disease.

The treatment of cancer is a large part of urologic practice. Some of the most challenging neoplasms encountered involve the genitourinary system. Radical surgery is accomplished in many instances with success but endocrine therapy, chemotherapy and immunotherapy have important roles. Recent striking improvements in results in both testis tumors and Wilms' tumor in children attest to progress in the incorporation of both surgical and non-surgical techniques.

The involvement of the urologist with severe renal insufficiency and end-stage renal disease is a growing responsibility made feasible by increased emphasis on the basics of nephrology during training. This development has led to improved communication between the urologist and nephrologist. In many centers, urologists are extensively involved in renal transplantation in recognition of the fact that it is their responsibility to deal with surgical problems of the urinary tract. This has increased their experience in vascular surgery, which has been incorporated beneficially into other areas of the urologist's surgical activities. Ex-vivo and micro-vascular surgery have been developing adjuncts of this process and more urologists are competent to deal with primary renovascular reconstruction in addition to performing diagnostic studies in hypertension.

Urinary tract infections comprise a major portion of urologic practice, affecting every age group and both sexes. There is considerable overlap among the areas being discussed as in the observation that while infection may be both the presenting and the definitive problem, it may also lead to discovery of other forms of disease such as obstruction or stones. Moreover, infection frequently involves not only the urinary tract but also the accessory sex organs such as the prostate and epididymis.

Male sexual dysfunction has become a sub-specialty in itself with both increasing knowledge and availability of effective therapy. Infertility is managed with increasing sophistication in conjunction with gynecological evaluation of the patient's partner. Reversal of vasectomy attacks the opposite problem and has offered a popular entry for urologists into the arena of microsurgery. Impotence also is evaluated and treated by urologists. This requires dealing with both psychological and organic abnormalities. Surgical management of organic impotence today often includes the use of prostheses, some of which are complex. The use of prostheses in urology includes not only the treatment of impotence but also the employment of artificial urinary sphincters. This last procedure is already applied clinically in many centers and promises to make a major contribution to the treatment of incontinence.

Minimum training required for accreditation in urology is five years, three of which must be in urology and two in a different discipline, usually surgery. The requirements of the American Board of Urology allow appropriate variation in training requirements to reflect the strengths of the participating institutions. Thus, while the general pattern and overall content of the residency must meet increasingly stringent standards, it is possible to seek training which emphasizes a particular interest.

Since the number of residents at each level in a urology program ranges from one to four, and averages only two, there is commonly a much closer relationship between residents and faculty than possible in larger areas such as surgery or medicine. This feature offers the program director an opportunity to mold educational offerings to the needs of specific trainees, to become familiar with their concerns on both a personal and professional level, and to be directly involved in their activities. It also allows considerably more personal attention to be given to applicants. The care with which the program director chooses new residents, beyond the simple ranking of academic performance, is a good gauge of the importance assigned to the program.

The candidate will encounter a variety of environments in which training is offered. There are advantages and limitations to large public hospitals, university hospitals, prestigious private clinics, Veterans Administration medical centers and general community hospitals. This admonition is not to deny relative advantages but to emphasize that with some ingenuity, a number of scenarios may lead to optimal professional development. This concept also extends to differing clinical emphasis such as the availability of an intensive experience in renal transplantation or adrenal surgery as well as research and elective time. Since most program directors have strong preferences, this diversity may enable applicants to capitalize on these rich opportunities.

Programs are evaluated for accreditation by individual Residency Review Committees every few years. In addition, the Office of Education of the American Urological Association makes in-service examinations available to all residency programs. In these comprehensive examinations, the resident's performance is rated against those at a comparable level at other institutions. The results are analyzed by subject matter and indicate areas in which residents may need assistance. In addition to an excellent and plentiful schedule of educational programs offered by the Office of Education, there is also an annual program reviewing basic sciences relevant to urology for those entering or in the early stages of urologic training.

There is increasing concern that the number of physicians being trained today exceeds the demand in almost all specialties. Whether or not this is true, certain facts seem clear. First, the supply of physicians cannot be evaluated by a simple measure consisting of the number of physicians per 100,000 population. Distribution is so irregular that both excess and inadequacy are disguised. It is apparent that it is not until geographic areas generally considered desirable are saturated that adequate servicing of less attractive sites begins. This pattern is not surprising in a free society and cannot be expected to change unless inducements are offered. Second, although for many years urologists considered their number "about right" even in attractive locations, opportunities today are less readily available. The concept that even though one is well-trained and willing to work does not necessarily guarantee immediate success is a premise that the medical profession is coming to grips with a bit later than the population at large. Opportunities are still present, but a busy practice obviously is going to develop earlier in a region where relative need is greater.

Third, the demographics of American society favor urology in that the aging population increases demand for services in a group that already represents a major segment of urologic practice. Fourth, although no attempt has been made to limit the number of urologists arbitrarily, standards of accreditation of training programs have risen to the point that a number of marginal ones have been absorbed or disappeared. The number of new urologists completing training each year has stabilized at approximately 300, a figure representing less than two percent of the graduates of American medical schools.

The future of urology will probably reflect not only the effects of external forces but also the imagination, insight and abilities of those entering the field. With the improved quality of training, the acceptance of the appropriate role of the urologist as an organ system specialist, and the technological advances which appear on the horizon, the urologist is presented with great opportunity for a rewarding career. That it may not always be there for the asking, but will require effort and innovation, does not make this specialty less attractive.

External Readings

19-A-1   Kunz, JRM (ed.). The American Medical Association Family Medical Guide. New York: Random House, 1982. pp. 500-13; 570-81.

19-A-2   Kendall, AR, "Urology: Combining Medicine and Surgery," Medical Student 8(3):7-9 (March/April 1982).

19-A-3   King, LR, "Urology," Journal American Medical Association 254:2311-13 (October 25, 1985).

19-A-4   Fraley, EE & Watkins, E, "Surgery and Urology Manpower," Journal Urology 127:218-23 (February 1982).

19-A-5   DePauw, AP, "Perspectives on Cancer of the Prostrate," Hospital Medicine 17:81-96 (April 1981).

19-A-6   Trump, DL, "Update on D_x and Management of Bladder Cancer," Geriatrics 37:87-91 (July 1982).

19-B-1   Saunders, CD.   Your Guide to Urology.   Philadelphia: GF
         Stickley, 1982. 144 pp.

19-B-2   Brown, RB. Clinical Urology. New York: ADIS Press (Littleton,
         MA: John Wright-PSG), 1982. 401 pp.

19-B-3   Smith, DR. General Urology. Los Altos, CA: Lange Medical
         Publishers, 1981. 598 pp.

19-B-4   Kaufman, JJ.   Current Urologic Therapy.   Philadelphia: WB
         Saunders Co. 1980. 517 pp.

Relationship of Research to Practice

. . . All that this profession is and has become is
based on investigation and research.   Someone,
somewhere, sometime had an inquiring mind and the
intelligence and stick-to-itiveness to labor long hours
with one goal in mind - discovery! And it is their
discoveries and their accomplishments that enable us to
treat our patients and practice our profession . . .

The clinician receives the gratitude, undying
affection, and applause of his patients, but his
colleagues know all too well that he has, technically,
put into 'practice' the fruits of someone else's 'labor'
. . . .

- Henry, JB, "Dean's Welcome Remarks to the Class of
  1986," Journal American Medical Association 249: 1590
  (March 25, 1983).

Section 20 - ANESTHESIOLOGY

Reuben C. Balagot

Reuben C. Balagot, MD, is Clinical Professor of Anesthesiology and Chairman, Department of Anesthesiology at Cook County Hospital in Chicago, IL. His primary research interest is pain therapy.

The facetious caricature of the anesthesiologist as a person who sits on a hard stool and passes gas has begun to fade. However, this perception still elicits a slight twinge of resentment among older members of a specialty that has suffered some form of denigration, imagined or otherwise, at the hands of their surgical colleagues. This view may have been deserved in some circumstances because the anesthesiologist failed to perform as a physician and functioned more as a technician.

If this attitude was prevalent in the '50s and early '60s, it had greatly diminished by the late '70s so that the specialty could be regarded as among the most respectable. There are several reasons for this turnabout. First, in academia, anesthesiology has established itself as a solid basic, clinical discipline. It has excelled in medical education and has contributed more than a few deans of medical schools and health-science administrators. Furthermore, it has helped lay the foundation for some sub-specialties such as critical care, pain management, and ambulatory surgery.

Anesthesiology has also contributed greatly to the development of "miracle" surgery such as open-heart surgery, organ transplant and other complex procedures like radical cancer surgery, microvascular surgery - ones that could not have been possible without advances in anesthesia to safeguard the patient's welfare through the ordeal. As the public began to appreciate the importance of safe anesthesia in lessening the odds against survival from surgery, the market place stamped its imprimatur upon the specialty with all its attendant benefits. These often include the movement of anesthesiology into the delirious realm of high finance.

But what does the anesthesiologist really do? He creates a painless state in the patient during surgery while providing the surgical team with excellent operating conditions. This objective may be achieved by general anesthesia (inhalation and intravenous) or regional (spinal, epidural, block) anesthesia. This specialist's foremost consideration during this combined physiologic trespass is the patient's safety. He achieves this through skillful utilization of drugs (clinical pharmacology) frequently bordering on toxicity (clinical toxicology) but remains acutely aware of the effect of the drugs on the patient's physiologic state as modified by patient diseases and the impact of the surgical procedure. (These may be of great magnitude, e.g., open-heart surgery, brain surgery, etc.).

With the use of sophisticated electronic monitoring devices, the anesthesiologist keeps track of cardiovascular function by direct (invasive) or indirect (Doppler and non-invasive) moment to moment and instantaneous measurement of blood pressure; frequently introduces a flow-directed cardiac output, and monitors the status of the heart chamber that propels oxygenated blood to all parts of the body. He or she checks blood/gas status by periodic sampling and analysis of arterial blood for oxygen and carbon dioxide levels and state of tissue acidity (metabolic acidosis). The function also involves taking continuous electrocardiograms throughout and after the surgical procedure to detect deadly arrhythmias and cardiac wall ischemias. The electroencephalogram or its most sophisticated form, the evoked potential, is employed to make sure the brain is alive and continues to function. Such services may be regarded as clinical physiology at its best.

Not only does the practitioner do all the foregoing, he or she also keeps a permanent record of these changes. Physics and computer-oriented anesthesiologists have achieved great progress towards converting all this record keeping to voice-activated computers.

In the process of setting up optimal operating conditions for the surgical team, the anesthesiologist will paralyze the patient under general anesthesia (with curare-like drugs) and attach him to a ventilator. By virtue of this experience, the anesthesiologist has become a respiratory physiologist - an expert in respiratory failure, endotracheal intubation, and blood/gas analysis. Many of the procedures used in cardio-pulmonary resuscitation today evolved from the experience of anesthesiologists.

Thus in the course of managing the patient undergoing surgery, the anesthesiologist controls the administration of fluids (glucose or normal salt solution) and blood or its components. The routes for administering these fluids are established by the anesthesiologist (anesthetist) and represent lifelines for the patient. Such expertise gives yet another dimension to the specialty.

The foregoing are not the only functions anesthesiologists seem to have in common with the surgical team. The specialty has branched into other phases of medicine that has taken it away from the operating theater. By virtue of intensive knowledge of neuroanatomy, nerve physiology and pain mechanisms, particular expertise in the use of block needles, local anesthetics and nerve destructive agents, the anesthesiologist has become involved in pain management and research into this fascinating aspect of neuro-pathophysiology.

Because of expertise in the care of ill patients in the operating rooms and in the post anesthesia recovery rooms, the anesthesiologist is in the forefront of development and management of critical care units. Moreover, anesthesiologists were the first to develop and establish ambulatory surgery units - thus reducing surgical costs.

Are there special traits or skills that may predispose to superior performance as a clinician? Because situations handled by the anesthesiologist are apt to change suddenly, and occasionally in an unpredictable fashion, quick decisions may have to be made. Even though the anesthesiologist may be able to temporize momentarily by supporting cardiovascular and respiratory functions, and hence eventually control nervous system viability, a diagnosis eventually must be made in order to correct or mitigate the condition. If this proves impossible, the process(es), including the ongoing surgery, should be stopped.

Being able to think quickly and make sound decisions, therefore, constitutes a positive and desirable characteristic. Another useful trait is dexterity and coordination. It enables a person to learn techniques fast and apply them. Further, a trainee (resident) must grasp such concepts quickly. These traits also are found in the surgeon and athlete. In addition, the specialty requires dealing with patients, surgeons, other members of the operating room team, a knack of handling people and an ability to bring calm to a pressure-cooker situation. In the early days of anesthesia, there was a common knowledge among anesthesiologists that despite your level of competence, if you could get along well with the surgeon and he thought highly of you, continuation of your practice could be assured provided, of course, that you not decimate too many of his patients.

If your interest in anesthesiology pertains to research, it is essential to have a curious, questioning mind, a desire to get at the root of things. This trait per se is not sufficient however; imagination, inventiveness and scholarship are necessary and are needed to attack a problem once it is defined. But scholarship is a requisite to prevent you from reinventing the wheel.

An important corollary to scholarship is resourcefulness - it enables you to utilize or apply seemingly unrelated bits and pieces of knowledge or objects to the resolution of a problem. In fact, resourcefulness is simply old Yankee ingenuity applied to anesthesiological (medical) problems. The most important attribute of the would-be researcher thus is an inner drive and energy to pursue established research objectives. Moreover, the successful investigator will manifest a combination of ambition, desire and optimism - elements needed to sustain progress in the face of failures which require that the process start all over again.

What undergraduate background might facilitate performance as a clinician? Much of clinical medicine might be described as problem solving. The undergraduate with a penchant for solving problems might do well in medicine, including anesthesiology where problem solving may have to be carried out at a faster rate than other branches of medicine. Certainly, in a specialty that has become very much electronically oriented - the use of monitors is almost sine qua non to good anesthesia management. Consequently, a good background in or a decent understanding of basic electronics could be of great value.

Today, the anesthesiologist monitors almost every physiological parameter that is significant and accessible, e.g., a teflon cannula into a radial artery for direct and continuous blood pressure readings; a balloon-tipped, flow-directed (Swan-Ganz) catheter into a branch of the pulmonary artery thru an internal jugular vein - a window to left ventricular function - to mention a few. These controls are all made possible thorough sophisticated electronic surveillance including computerized calculation of cardiac output and associated parametric values. Surely a good grounding in physics will provide an appreciation of the mechanics of peripheral sensors used to monitor organs.

A background in physical chemistry and organic chemistry helps one understand the effect of anesthesia on biological processes even at the molecular level. A little knowledge of math, especially differential calculus - any biological process may be expressed as differential equations - and intergral calculus to look at the total effect or change, may provide a better grasp of biological phenomena as affected by anesthetics. And finally, some knowledge of statistics provides a greater insight into many of the clinical and laboratory research papers that appear in anesthesiology today. Without it, appreciation of many scientific papers will remain superficial and the ability to incorporate appropriate findings in practice may be impaired.

The foregoing applies to non-clinical positions as well. Research and teaching in anesthesia go hand in hand. Some of the best teachers I have known were excellent researchers in academic medicine. To summarize, anesthesiology is essentially the application of basic sciences to clinical medicine.

What are the major challenges and unknowns in anesthesia? In a recent modification of the residency program by the American Boards of Anesthesiology, the optional year of PG-4 was made mandatory and the number of training years increased from three to four. It also specified eight sub-specialties that a resident has to complete after the first or internship year: Anesthesia for neurosurgery; cardio thoracic; O.B.; pain and regional anesthesia; ambulatory or one-day surgery; critical care; post-anesthesia recovery care; and research. A resident has to spend two months or more in each of the above rotations in the second and third years of the residency after anesthesia training. However, a fourth year resident must also choose six-month periods in two sub-specialties, a sub-specialty and research, or a sub-specialty and anesthesia for complex surgical care that require extensive and intensive monitoring, e.g., trauma, burn, etc.

Of these specialties, critical care is a natural field for the anesthesiologist because of the procedures utilized and the urgency generated by tremendous efforts to save a patient. Despite, a high "burnout" rate, critical care has started to attract surgeons, internists and even pediatricians. Nevertheless, intensive training in the management of respiratory and cardiovascular emergencies makes the anesthesiologist a perfect candidate for this field. Another sub-specialty which tends to utilize the anesthesiologist's propensity with a needle, e.g. nerve blocks both diagnostic and lytic, is pain management, especially chronic intractable pain. Not only is the anesthesiologist very knowledgeable in this aspect of pain care, he also develops extensive experience in the use of narcotic and other analgesic drugs.

For the academically inclined, the ultimate challenge is research because it is so varied and utilizes many disciplines, e.g., physiology, pharmacology, molecular biology. The anesthesiologist, however, should beware of getting bogged down in a narrow, superficial segment.

The search for the ideal general and local anesthetic continues. Dare we anticipate the discovery of an agent that provides extensive and profound analgesia, mild to moderate sedation, sufficient relaxation without interfering with respiration, and is completely reversible at the end of the surgical procedure as determined by the biding of the anesthesiologist? While this level of control may sound impossible, many of the great techniques now taken for granted were deemed unlikely just 15-20 years ago. But the thought provoking question remains - could such innovations eliminate the specialty?

External Readings

20-A-1   "Role of the Anesthesiologist," Journal American Medical Association 247:1938 (April 9, 1982); 246:2692-93 (December 11, 1981).

20-A-2   Pierce, EC, "Anesthesiology," Journal American Medical Association 254:2317-18 (October 25, 1985).

20-A-3   Brown, EM, "Anesthesiology," Journal American Medical Association 247:2941-42 (June 4, 1982).

20-A-4   Freeark, RJ, "Current Relations Between Surgery and Anesthesiology - A Look at the Other Side," Surgery 90:565-76 (October 1981).

20-A-5   Rogers, MC, "Alice Through the Looking Glass - Anesthesiology for the Surgeon," Surgery 90:919-21 (November 1981).

20-A-6   "Anesthesia Outside the OR," Emergency Medicine 14:98-129 (January 30, 1982).

20-A-7   Roller, FD, "Anesthesia Review for Small Hospitals," The Hospital Medical Staff 11:23-27 (March 1982).

20-B-1   Hirsch, RA (ed.).   Health Care Delivery in Anesthesia.
         Philadelphia: GF Stickley, 1980. 253 pp.

20-B-2   Levine, RD, Anesthesiology: A Manual for Medical Students.
         Philadelphia: JB Lippincott, 1984.

20-B-3   Vandam, LD, (ed.). To Make the Patient Ready for Anesthesia.
         Menlo Park, CA: Addison-Wesley Pub. Co., 1980. 245 pp.

20-B-4   Gravenstein, JS & Paulus, DA. Clinical Monitoring Practice in
         Anesthesia. Philadelphia: JB Lippincott, 1982. 386 pp.

20-B-5   Brown, BR. Contemporary Anesthesia Practice, Vol. 4: Anesthesia
         and the Patient with Liver Disease. Philadelphia: FA Davis, Co.,
         1981. 184 pp.

20-B-6   Mayer, B. Pediatric Anesthesia: A Guide to Its Administration.
         Philadelphia: JB Lippincott Co., 1981. 272 pp.

20-B-7   Bunker, JP. The Anesthesiologist and the Surgeon: Partners in
         the Operating Room. Boston: Little, Brown & Co. 1972.

Physician's Role

Hugh R.K. Barber, chief of OB/GYN at New York Medical College . . . believes that the only way the medical profession can survive and maintain control of its destiny is for doctors to radically change how they practice: 'Provide preventive programs to replace the old concept of curative ones' . . .

- Kotulak, R, "Doctor Glut Signals End of a Golden Era," Chicago Tribune, December 16, 1984, p. 16.

Section 21 - EMERGENCY MEDICINE

Douglas A. Rund

Douglas A. Rund, MD, is Associate Professor of Preventive Medicine and Director, Division of Emergency Medicine at The Ohio State University, and Medical Director, Columbus, OH Division of Fire Emergency Medical Services. He is currently President of the International Research Institute for Emergency Medicine. Dr. Rund has authored several textbooks including, <u>Essentials of Emergency Medicine</u> and <u>Emergency Psychiatry</u>.

Where do you go when you are in pain, frightened by odd signs and symptoms, at your wits end? In a statement issued by the American College of Emergency Physicians in 1978, emergency medicine was described as "the medical specialty created by popular demand." This statement goes to the very heart of emergency medicine, medical care on demand; occasionally for life-threatening conditions, often for conditions that demand prompt attention because of discomfort or potential harm if care is delayed, but perhaps most often for conditions for which care could safely be scheduled for later attention. The word "Emergency" displayed by a hospital means, to the public, that services are available seven days a week, 24 hours a day, for all who feel the need. It is rare indeed for such services to be offered around-the-clock by other providers of medical care.

Since the end of World War II, there has been a rapid development of community emergency services and hospital emergency departments. This was due in part to major advances in emergency medicine made during the war and in subsequent years. Medical insurance also offered the means to pay for these services and the American public demanded access to such care.

Recognition of these facts by physicians, insurance companies, government agencies, and the general public led eventually to the development of emergency medicine as the newest of the recognized medical specialities. Physicians who were interested in this specialty and who recognized this as a growing area of medical practice, organized the American College of Emergency Physicians in 1968. This step created a focus for the development of this specialty, an organization responsive to the interests of physicians already working in this area and to others who sought entry into the practice of emergency medicine. In 1970, the University Association for Emergency Medical Services was organized, giving an academic arm to this developing specialty.

At the same time, communities across the nation recognized the need for improvement of emergency medical services in the pre-hospital phase of emergency medical care. Military medical corpsmen had demonstrated their ability to deal with many serious cases of trauma and illness in the field. In many parts of the United States, training programs were developed by community emergency medical services and by vocational education programs. In 1970, the National Registry of Emergency Medical Technicians was organized, standards were set, and examinations for certification inaugurated. That year, the first emergency medicine residency was also begun. This was more than coincidence. With increase in the skills of paramedical personnel in pre-hospital emergency care, it was soon apparent that this was not always matched by equal skills in the hospital emergency departments to which the patients were transported. Clearly, there was an urgent need for educating physicians in emergency medicine

Since that time, the growth of the specialty has been very rapid and in 1976, the American Board of Emergency Medicine was organized. By 1985, 3,240 physicians had been certified by the American Board of Emergency Medicine. Approved residency programs in the United States numbered sixty-eight with 234 positions for first-year residents in emergency medicine. The American College of Emergency Physicians now numbers over 11,000 physicians. The demand for residency positions in emergency medicine is still increasing and studies of health manpower in the United States indicate that, in contrast with other specialties, there will continue to be an undersupply of emergency physicians by 1990.

Medical students are attracted to this specialty because of the opportunities for placement in many areas of the United States, comparatively good earnings and expectation of set hours and other benefits. They are often caught up in the excitement of emergency care, in the great variety of problems that are seen, and the need for quick thinking and rapid action. There are certain drawbacks that also must be considered. Emergency physicians are frequently disturbed by the lack of continuity of care. Without special efforts they never learn what happens to the patients they see. This also makes it more difficult to learn from experience. Making judgements quickly is often quite stressful and the risk of misdiagnosis and mistreatment is greater than may be the case in situations where longer association with the patient is possible.

In many emergency departments there are periods of relative inaction, punctuated by periods of feverish activity. Not everyone can adapt to these changes. Also at least half of the patients who come to emergency departments have problems that can and often should be taken care of by primary physicians rather than emergency physicians. For reasons of convenience, physician availability, misjudgment, and a variety of social and economic factors, such patients often end up in emergency departments and emergency physicians may feel inappropriately used. Emergency medicine is demand medicine in the view of the public.

For medical students and recent medical graduates, the pathway to specialty certification by the American Board of Emergency Medicine requires three years of residency training in an approved program. This allows the physician to apply for Board Certification. A written examination is taken at a minimum of one year after of the residency and an oral examination six to twelve months thereafter. Some programs do not offer a first-year residency, but will accept a year of general medicine, general surgery, or flexible residency for entry into the second-year emergency medicine residency. However, 36 months of emergency medicine residency are still required. Until 1988, the Board will allow some physicians who have not pursued an emergency medicine residency to sit for the examinations. They must have had at least 7,000 hours of emergency medicine practice in a five-year period and at least a recognized internship.

While emergency medicine residencies may differ somewhat in the scheduling of clinical services in education programs, they all generally fall into the pattern prescribed by the Residency Review Committee. A typical three year emergency medicine residency may utilize the following plan:

First Year

Internal Medicine: Five months; Surgery: One to two months; Ob/Gyn: One to two months; Emergency Department/Intensive Care Unit: Four months.

Second Year

Orthopedics/Hand Surgery: Three months; Anesthesiology: One to two months; Toxicology/Poison Control: One to two months; Emergency Medical Service Systems: One to two months; Emergency Department: Five months.

Third Year

Radiology: One to two months; ENT/Ophthalmology: One to two months; Emergency Department Administration: One to two months; Toxicology/Poison Control: One to two months; Emergency Department: Six months; Electives: Two to three months.

A number of emergency medicine residencies are already offering a fourth or fellowship year. Often this is particularly suitable for emergency physicians interested in research and academic programs.

The emergency physician can look forward to a considerable variety of career options. In addition to patient care in hospital emergency departments, there are many opportunities for careers in administration and emergency department management. Many hospitals contract with groups of emergency medicine specialists to manage their departments. There has also been a great increase in free-standing emergency medical clinics, often called "Urgent-Care" or "EmergiCenters."

Community emergency medical systems are increasingly employing medical directors to oversee the medical aspects of their systems, to train emergency medical technicians and paramedics, and to maintain liaison with the physicians and the hospitals in the community. In large systems, this may be a full-time position but it is frequently combined with service in an emergency department. In communities where the emergency medical technicians and paramedics have on-line communication with emergency departments, there is need for physicians expert in such communications and the control of field operations. Where the emergency medical technicians and paramedics are guided by protocols, rather than on-line communication, there is need for emergency physicians who are expert in the development and review of such protocols and the provision of in-service training and case review for the field personnel.

Poison control centers represent another development in emergency medicine. Specialists develop methods for guiding hospitals, physicians, and the general public in the proper treatment of various presumed poisonings. This work often combines the specialties of emergency medicine, toxicology, pharmacology, and medical communications.

Disaster medicine requires physicians trained in emergency medicine with special additional training and experience in the organization and management of disaster medical services. There are positions for such physicians at federal, state and local levels and the burgeoning area of international health as well. The North Atlantic Treaty Organization has a fellowship in the Health and Medical Aspects of Disaster Care. A rapidly growing area involves study of the organization and delivery of emergency care around the world. A variety of international organizations have been established to bring together specialists in many parts of the world to foster exchange of ideas, mutual aid, and joint planning of education, research, and service.

In the past, emergency medicine has primarily attracted clinicians. However, there is growing research activity in this field, extending from basic research, to clinical trials of new diagnostic and treatment methods, to the organization and management of emergency health care systems. Often, such research is collaborative with basic scientists and clinicians in other specialties. It is the emergency physician, however, who is most likely to have access to the patients and the data that are required for study of the rapid assessment and management of conditions that are life-threatening.

It is likely that the leadership in the field of emergency medicine, in the next decade, will be in the hands of well trained emergency physicians who concentrate on specific problems of pre-hospital emergency care, the organization and delivery of emergency care in hospitals, the refinement of educational programs for medical students and residents, and the conduct of research in many areas of importance to this specialty.

External Readings

21-A-1 Zaccardi, JA, "Emergency Medicine: A Newly Recognized Specialty," Medical Student 7(3):13-15 (April/May 1981).

21-A-2 Leitzell, JD, "Emergency Medicine. An Uncertain Future," New England Journal Medical 304:477-80 (February 19, 1981)

21-A-3 Riggs, Jr., LM, "Emergency Medicine: A Vigorous New Specialty," New England Journal Medical 304:480-82 (February 19, 1981).

21-A-4 Nowak, RM, "Emergency Medicine," Journal American Medical Association 254:2319-21 (October 25, 1985).

21-A-5 "Emergency Care Guidelines," Emergency Medicine 14:173-84 (June 15, 1982).

21-A-6 Patient Care 16:59-62; 109-15 (October 30, 1982).

21-A-7 Pachter, HL, "Some Tips on Trauma Care," Emergency Medicine 14:205-09 (February 15, 1982).

21-A-8 "Calming the Acute Psychotic," Emergency Medicine 14:182-94 (May 15, 1982.

21-A-9 Jeejeebhoy, K, "A Critical Type of Upper GI Bleeding," Emergency Medicine 14:47-57 (March 15, 1982).

21-A-10 "MD's Save Lives as Weekend Deputies," Medical World News 21:32-43 (August 18, 1980).

21-B-1 Sword, R. Emergency Room. New York: Charles Scribner's Sons, 1982. 224 pp.

21-B-2 Eisenberg, MS & Copass, MK. Emergency Medical Therapy. Philadelphia: WB Sauders, 1982. 407 pp.

21-B-3 Rutherford, WH, et al. Accident and Emergency Medicine. Philadelphia: JB Lippincott, 1980. 393 pp.

21-B-4 Hocutt, JE. Emergency Medicine: A Quick Reference for Primary Care. New York: Arco, 1982. 439 pp.

21-B-5 Caroline, NL. Emergency Care in the Streets. Boston: Little, Brown & Co., 1979. 524 pp.

21-B-6 Rund, D. Essentials of Emergency Medicine. New York: Appleton-Century-Crofts, 1982. 453 pp.

Section 22 - NUCLEAR MEDICINE

Thomas M. Anderson

Thomas M. Anderson, MD, is Chairman, Department of Radiology Mercy Hospital and Medical Center, Chicago, IL, and a Clinical Assistant Professor of Radiology at the University of Chicago. He is board certified in Diagnostic Radiology and Nuclear Medicine.

The physician involved in the diagnosis and treatment of disease through radiopharmaceuticals is working in a dynamic area with a fascinating history and a promising future. The development of diagnostic nuclear medicine has roughly followed two broad areas; the radioactive labeling of hormones or drugs coupled with their detection in laboratory tests to assess functions of the body from samples of body fluids or tissues, and, the diagnosis of disease processes within the living patient by the injection of organ-specific radiopharmaceutical compounds.

In its infancy, a variety of physicians - specialists trained in internal medicine, pathology, or radiology - developed techniques and expertise in nuclear medicine. As attempts were made to standardize postgraduate training in nuclear medicine, there were regular disagreements as to which group of physicians could best discharge the responsibilities of carrying out nuclear diagnostic procedures and training other physicians in these techniques. Such disorder led to the formation of a Conjoint Board of Nuclear Medicine which initially issued certifying examinations for all practitioners of nuclear medicine who were able to pass the tests. The Board also standardized what is now a two year residency requirement in an approved post graduate training program in nuclear medicine for certification.

The fascination of imaging techniques utilizing radiopharmaceuticals has always involved a basic concept. This is that one utilizes some aspect of the physiology of any organ system imaged and not simply its anatomy when using radionuclide techniques. In traditional radiology, a chest x-ray might provide images of the lungs by passing a diagnostic x-ray beam through those tissues and recording the image on an x-ray film. The nuclear medicine specialist's approach to pulmonary imaging, however, includes ventilation studies where lung function is tested by means of radioactive labels for gases localizing as air is breathed. He also uses perfusion studies that rely on radioactive tracers which are distributed by the blood flow to the lungs. A knowledge of pathophysiology of the pulmonary system can enable the nuclear medicine specialist to predict, with a high degree of accuracy, which of a variety of pathologic conditions cause shortness of breath in a patient sent for consultation.

Similarly, there are unique and specific approaches to cardiac imaging and the detection of a variety of conditions ranging from ischemic heart disease to myocardial infarction. In addition, there are specific tracer compounds that image the liver and biliary system in a variety of conditions ranging from hepatitis to metastatic tumor to gall bladder disease. Finally, there are several sophisticated approaches to imaging the kidneys and urinary bladder and the diseases that effect those organs.

A common misunderstanding of the nuclear medicine physician's approach is to insist that nuclear studies are "nonspecific." True, the radiographic approach to abdominal imaging through computerized tomographic apparatus can often provide more precise pictures to characterize specific areas of abnormality in the body. However, the sensitivity of an imaging technique based on the physiologic activity of the tissue studied is difficult to surpass. A radionuclide bone image study may reveal subtle conditions presenting as pain ranging from stress fracture in joggers to the early spread of metastatic tumor in bones while the standard x-ray evaluation of the areas in question shows no abnormalities.

In the laboratory, the diagnosis of a variety of metabolic conditions involving the thyroid gland, the adrenal glands, the blood tissues, including anemias, and the monitoring of a variety of therapeutic drugs are regularly studied. These problems are controlled by the use of radioisotope labels to detect and quantify minute amounts of hormone or chemical which would otherwise be unmeasurable in the patient's tissues.

The best candidates for specialized training in nuclear imaging should have a strong interest in physiologic processes in the body and the ways in which disease states alter the normal physiology. A comfortable control of radioactive materials requires a certain facility with mathematics and the physics of atomic interactions. This is not to say that an individual with great enthusiasm for English literature or music cannot effectively participate as a nuclear medicine specialist. One of the most important historical characteristics of physicians in nuclear medicine has been a lively imagination and willingness to utilize fresh approaches to old problems.

In general, the nuclear medicine specialist practices in a hospital setting. Many of the conditions referred for diagnosis are complications of serious illness in patients undergoing intensive medical or surgical therapies. This specialty requires an administrative talent for dealing with a host of regulations at the state and federal levels ranging from the proper transport and delivery of radioisotopic materials to radiation safety in the nuclear department and even matters of waste disposal. The nuclear medicine specialist is often the Radiation Safety Officer for a hospital. A certain amount of time and energy is spent in educational activities for hospital medical staffs to ensure that regulations are followed and that employee and patient concerns about radiation exposure are properly answered.

Depending on the traditions of the institution where a nuclear medicine physician is based, the practice may be primarily an imaging consultation service involving patients that need to be interviewed and examined, a laboratory consultation service with very little patient contact, or some combination of the two. It is no accident and a source of frustration to nuclear medicine physicians that practitioners of diagnostic radiology, clinical pathology, and endocrinology or cardiology regularly view isotope related procedures as a natural extension of their own practice activities.

The future development of nuclear medicine as a medical specialty most probably will revolve around two areas: one is the development of imaging devices; the other the continued growth and development of radioisotope labeled compounds not now in current use. Along the lines of technology, the Single Photon Emission Computerized Tomographic (SPECT) cameras now available in nuclear medicine utilize the same computer software as the CT scanners of diagnostic radiology to achieve ever more improved diagnostic accuracy of smaller lesions on the radioisotope images. The development of Positron Emission Tomography (PET) offers exciting potential for early diagnosis of cerebrovascular and even electrophysiologic abnormalities of the brain. Thus far, the common usage of PET scanners has been hampered by the requirements for a nearby cyclotron to generate the ultrashort half-lived radioisotopes used in its diagnostic procedures.

Nuclear medicine physicians are also active in the development of Magnetic Resonance Imaging (MRI), a technology that provides images of the body without use of any type of ionizing radiation. Of course, the continued development of new radiopharmaceutical compounds offers the promise that labeling tumor specific antibodies with radioisotope materials can in effect offer the "silver bullet" for the detection of cancers in a variety of organ systems. Such a capability does not exist at this time but its potential development seems tantilizingly close.

All in all, nuclear medicine offers an attractive field of practice for a physician with an inquiring mind. Present day practice is not without its "turf" squabbles and other irritations, but the future of the specialty, even in the face of a variety of competing imaging technologies and laboratory diagnostic techniques, has high promise for an interesting and rewarding career.

External Readings

22-A-1   A Patient's Guide to Nuclear Medicine.   New York: The Society
          of Nuclear Medicine, 1983. 16 pp.

22-A-2   Guidelines for Patients Receiving Radioiodine Therapy.   New
          York: The Society of Nuclear Medicine. 1983, 8 pp.

22-A-3   Silberstein, EB, "Nuclear Medicine," Journal American Medical
          Association 254:2325-27 (October 25, 1985).

22-A-4   "New Family of Radiolabeled Amimes Helps Assess Efficacy of
          Therapies," Radiology Today, pp. 4-17 (June 1984).

22-B-1   Press Kit from the 32nd Annual Meeting of The Society of
          Nuclear Medicine (Highlights of the latest developments in
          nuclear medicine). 1985. 60 pp.

22-B-2   Alazraki, NP & Mishkin, FS (eds.).   Fundamentals of Nuclear
          Medicine. New York: The Society of Nuclear Medicine, 1984.
          208 pp. (for medical students).

22-B-3   Ell, PJ & Williams, ES. Nuclear Medicine.   St.   Louis:
          Blackwell/Mosby Book Distr., 1981. 296 pp.

22-B-4   Spencer, RP (ed.).   Nuclear Medicine: Focus on Clinical
          Diagnosis. Garden City, NY: Medical Examination, 1980. 279
          pp.

22-B-5   Ryo, UT, et al. Atlas of Nuclear Medicine Artifacts &
          Variants. Chicago: Year Book Medical Publishers, 1985. 220 pp.

22-B-6   Quin, JL (ed.). The Year Book of Nuclear Medicine. Chicago:
          Year Book Medical Publishers, 1980. 325 pp.

Section 23 - PATHOLOGY

Donald A. Senhauser

Donald A. Senhauser, MD, is Professor and Chairman, Department of Pathology, The Ohio State University College of Medicine. He is a member of the Board of Governors of the College of American Pathologists. His area of research is thyroid disease.

The scientific discipline of pathology consists of the study of disease and disease mechanisms. It is one of the oldest of the medical sciences. Its modern origins extend back to the medieval anatomist, such as Veslius, and during the Renaissance it became know as "morbid anatomy." Pathology came to fruition as a distinct discipline and recognized branch of medicine with the publication of Morgagni's work in the 1770's. Autopsy, or gross pathology, and "morbid anatomy" made major contributions to our understanding of disease during the 18th and 19th centuries. During this time, the scientific method of the discipline was formalized; the correlation of changes in form with changes in function.

Understanding of disease processes was limited, however, until the work of Rudolph Virchow (1821-1902), who by combining gross and microscopic observations on diseased tissue, developed the concepts of cellular pathology which became the foundation of all modern medical practice and our understanding of disease processes. Today, pathology is a basic discipline common to all medical specialties. The student who enters pathology will find it a medical specialty with a long and distinguished history which retains its dynamic role in modern medical progress.

Pathology is both a basic and a clinical science which links biomedical science with the clinical practice of medicine. Thus the medical student is first introduced to pathology in the second preclinical year of his medical school education. The pathology course is usually arranged into two parts; general pathology or the study of effect of mechanisms of disease, and, systemic pathology or the study of the effect of these disease processes on the various organ systems of the body. The student learns to apply knowledge of normal anatomy, physiology and biochemistry to the understanding of the abnormal anatomy, physiology and biochemistry - areas termed together as "pathophysiology." The understanding of disease mechanisms is the foundation of all rational medical care.

The medical student will continue to interact and learn with the pathologist because, unlike many other basic scientists, pathologists play an active and vital role in hospital patient care. They are responsible for morphological and laboratory analyses which provide much of the data used in the diagnosis and treatment of the patient.

<u>Academic Pathology</u>. The purpose of the research in pathology is to reveal new understanding of the basic nature of the disease process as a first step toward devising better ways to identify, control and prevent illnesses. One of the rewards of performing research is that the pathologist uses the tools of modern biomedical investigation from many basic science disciplines in addition to those of morphology, including biochemistry, cellular biology, immunology and microbiology. The pathologist brings these analytical tools to bear on a problem which has its roots in a clinical disease by using research to meet concerns of patient care. Increasingly, investigations focus on the cellular, sub-cellular and molecular aspect of the disease process. Thus the experimental pathologist utilizes electron microscopy, cell culture (molecular biology), flow cytometry, immunological techniques, and computer modeling in the quest for new knowledge.

The other major activity of the academic pathologist is teaching. Principles of pathology are taught at the undergraduate level and to resident physicians who are training to be specialists not only in pathology, but also in other disciplines such as internal medicine, surgery and obstetrics and gynecology. In addition, he or she may advise graduate students who are working toward their PhD degree in experimental pathology. Because of this broad educational experience at all levels, many pathologists have become medical school deans or leaders in the academic health centers.

<u>The Practice of Pathology</u>. All pathologists, regardless of practice setting, engage in teaching, patient care, and research. Indeed, one of the attractions of the field is the broad opportunities that it offers to enjoy all of these activities throughout your professional career. Depending on the setting of one's practice, of course, the pathologist engages in these three basic activities to a greater or lesser extent.

The majority of physicians trained in pathology enter medical practice and the vast majority of specialists served in hospitals. As such they participate in the day-to-day care of hospital patients by providing and interpreting laboratory information to help solve diagnostic problems and to monitor the effects of therapy. The pathologist is responsible for professional management of the hospital diagnostic laboratories, which include surgical pathology and the autopsy service, as well as the blood bank and the chemistry, hematology, immunology and bacteriology laboratories.

Diagnosis and treatment frequently rests on the information revealed by tests from these laboratories as well as the knowledge and scientific skill of the pathologist consulting with the attending physician. The rapid application of new knowledge and tests to the bedside requires that the hospital pathologist be available for guidance and direction of the clinical laboratory.

The surgical pathologist plays a unique role in patient care through the rapid intraoperative diagnosis of tissue removed from the patient for frozen section examination prior to definitive surgical therapy. Each diagnosis is made in collaboration with the patient's physician after full consideration of the clinical history and the results of other laboratory tests. This activity places the pathologist in a central role in patient care, since his diagnosis often forms the underpinning for future therapy, especially in the treatment of cancer. The hospital pathologist has been defined as a physician who practices medicine armed with his laboratory rather than a stethoscope.

The amazing growth in the kinds of laboratory tests produced in a hospital laboratory necessitates that pathologists employ the most advanced data processing and computer science resources. Most hospital laboratories have computer capability to store, transmit, collate, and interpret laboratory data for the clinician and the patient. Thus many pathologists, in addition to their other skills, have become experts in computers.

The practicing pathologist must develop skills in many areas of medicine. In smaller hospitals, a single pathologist or a group of two or three are responsible for the broad general aspect of laboratory medicine. This is a challenging and demanding role, but for the physician who wants to remain interested in all aspects of medicine, it is a delightful way to practice pathology. In the large, more sophisticated hospitals, the pathology department may have six to 12 or more pathologists who practice as a group, and who generally gain special training in a sub-specialty area after their general pathology training. One or two may run the chemistry laboratory, others concentrate on immunology or the blood bank, and still others on microbiology or surgical pathology. In this fashion, the demands of difficult and complex medical problems can be met.

Regardless of the size of the hospital, a major role of the pathologist remains medical education. A good example of this activity is the autopsy. Although performing autopsies may occupy only a small percentage of their time, pathologists find them intellectually stimulating. The autopsy provides unique insights into the natural history of disease, and in the hospital setting, the influence of therapy on the disease process of the patient. The autopsy becomes the focus for the pathologist's role as an educator through sharing the findings of the "final diagnosis" with the patient's attending physician. Together they search for lessons from each case that will benefit instructional contributions, often presented at clinical-pathological conferences and other teaching sessions.

The pathologist is responsible for the laboratory information about the patient from admission to discharge or death and serves as an information resource to physicians on the medical staff. Hospital-based, he or she is available to the patients and their physicians as a consultant much of the time and frequently initiates consultations based on abnormal or unexpected laboratory results. Thus consultation and education go hand in hand in the hospital setting.

Specialty training in pathology begins after graduation from medical school. Pre-medical students who enjoy courses in biology and especially laboratory and/or research opportunities in biology or zoology are apt to be interested in a career in pathology. However, most persons do not make a decision about a career in pathology and laboratory medicine until after the general pathology course in the second year of medical school and after they have taken some electives in pathology and laboratory medicine during the third and fourth years of their medical education. Around half of the residency candidates take a postgraduate year in a clinical discipline prior to entering the specialty of pathology while the remainder enter the specialty directly from medical school.

While there is no sterotypic personality for the pathologists, the specialty appeals to students who develop a high degree of interest in the biology of disease and disease mechanisms during their medical school training but who also want an association with clinical medicine and patient care. Pathology allows the pathologist to remain a student of abnormal biology whether practicing in an academic department or a hospital setting.

Pathology is one of the smaller of the medical specialties with 15,000 active practitioners. The pathology societies provide the vehicle for communication and comradeship for the pathologist. Thus they represent a relatively close knit fraternity which has continuing medical education as its organizing focus. Medical school graduates need four to five years of post graduate training in a approved residency program to prepare for a career in pathology. About 80 percent of the residency positions are within university and affiliated hospitals. Generally, the educational programs are structured into periods alternately spent in anatomic pathology and clinical pathology (laboratory medicine). Nearly all residents will participate in some basic or clinical research project during their training.

After successful completion of the residency program, the physician becomes eligible to sit for the examination given by the American Board of Pathology to fulfill the requirements for certification in anatomic and/or clinical pathology. Increasingly, in response to the enormous growth of information and greater complexity of the discipline diplomates of the Board are interested in sub-specialization. Special competence examinations are now available in forensic pathology, neuropathology, dermatopathology, medical microbiology, radioisotopic pathology, chemical pathology, hematopathology, blood banking, immunohematology, and immunopathology. The basic certificate from the American Board of Pathology, and one or two years of additional training or appropriate experience, are prerequisites for taking the special competence examinations.

A career in pathology can provide a life-long opportunity to participate in patient care, teaching and research. Pathology offers unique opportunities for interaction with the many disciplines that make up modern medicine and provides the opportunity for continuing intellectual satisfaction and growth. This specialty also allows better control over one's time and a more orderly life style than available in fields where patient demands often interfere. However, the flip side of the coin is that, in general, the pathologist is once removed from a direct doctor-patient relationship as he or she fills the role of "the doctor's doctor."

In general, choosing a career in pathology means a commitment to the practice of medicine in a hospital setting, a complex and at times a frustrating environment. The pathologist serves the medical staff and the patients but also must meet the demands of the institution and its administrative structure. As head or a part of a major hospital department, the pathologist will be expected to develop certain administrative and management skills in addition to professional expertise. Since he is professionally responsible for the technicians and technologists in the laboratory who actually perform of the test procedures under his direction, the pathologist must learn many of the techniques of personnel management. This is necessary if he is to form an effective team which can produce accurate, reliable laboratory information in a timely fashion. This specialist will also be involved in many important hospital committees and so must develop considerable skill in interpersonal relations. Thus pathologists must develop the attributes of the team player to run an effective hospital department.

In general, the hospital-based pathologist does not have the opportunity to generate the very high incomes sometimes associated with the procedure-oriented specialties but can anticipate a comfortable living. This lowered economic expectation is balanced by the fact that he or she can better control and organize professional time and benefit from both the opportunity for a lifetime of learning and the satisfaction of a full and active intellectual lifestyle.

External Readings

23-A-1   McLendon, WW, "Pathology and Laboratory Medicine," Journal American Medical Association 254:2321-23 (October 25, 1985).

23-A-2   Goyer, RA, "Pathology," Journal American Medical Association 247:2973-75 (June 4, 1982).

23-A-3   Lundberg, DG, "Pathology," Journal American Medical Association 245:2212-13 (June 5, 1981).

23-A-4   "A Pathologist's Point of View," Journal American Medical Association 247:1935 (April 9, 1982).

23-A-5   "Doctor Sleuths," Medical World News 22:63-81 (May 11, 1982).

External Readings (continued)

23-A-6   Statland, BE, "A Strategy for Selecting Laboratory Tests," Contemporary OB/GYN 19:92-101 (May 1982).

23-A-7   Bartlett, RC, "Making Optimum Use of the Microbiology Laboratory," Journal American Medical Association 247:1336-38 (March 5, 1982).

23-A-8   "Laboratory Medicine: Putting Doctors to the Test," Medical World News 21:39-53 (September 29, 1980).

23-A-9   Legg, MA, "What Role for the Diagnostic Pathologist," New England Journal Medicine 305:950-51 (October 15, 1981).

23-B-1   AMA. Laboratory Tests in Medical Practice. Chicago: American Medical Association, 1980. 200 pp.

23-B-2   Schaeffer, M (ed.). Federal Legislation and the Clinical Laboratory. Boston: GK Hall Med Pub., 1981. 204 pp.

23-B-3   Roueche, B. The Medical Detective. New York: Times Books, 1980. 372 pp.

23-B-4   Stefanini, M & Benson, ES. Progress in Clinical Pathology. New York: Grune & Stratton, 1981. 324 pp.

Practice Productivity

. . . most docs spend as much as 70 percent of their workday in administrative chores, about one-half of which could be done by computer . . .

- attributed to a German medical instrument company. Quoted in the Wall Street Journal, February 5, 1982, p. 1.

Section 24 - PHYSICAL MEDICINE AND REHABILITATION

Miriam E. Lane and Gordon M. Martin

Miriam E. Lane, MD, is Professor of Clinical Rehabilitation Medicine at Mt. Sinai School of Medicine, CUNY, New York. A physiatrist, she is also Acting Director, Department of Rehabilitation Medicine, Hospital for Joint Diseases, Orthopaedic Institute. Dr. Lane chairs the joint committee on graduate education of the American Academy of Physical Medicine & Rehabilitation and the Association of Academic Physiatrists.

Gordon M. Martin, MD, FACP, is Emeritus Consultant and Chairman, Department of Physical Medicine & Rehabilitation, Mayo Clinic, Rochester, MN and Emeritus Professor of Physical Medicine & Rehabilitation at Mayo Medical School and Mayo Graduate School. He is Executive Secretary-Treasurer, American Board of Physical Medicine & Rehabilitation, a former President of the American Congress of Rehabilitation Medicine, and an active member of the American Board of Medical Specialties.

Physical medicine and rehabilitation (PM&R) is concerned with the evaluation and optimal functional restoration of patients with disabilities and limitation of physical activity, regardless of etiology. Limitation of activity is defined as a significant impairment of the ability for self care, usual daily activities, and ambulation.

According to the Bureau of Census, 26 million people 18-64 years of age have a work disability. Another 10 million persons outside the 18-64 age range are disabled. Two-thirds of all disabilities, as measured by limitation of activity, are due to conditions affecting the musculoskeletal and circulatory system as well as to diseases of the nervous system and the sense organs.

The traditional medical specialities such as internal medicine, orthopaedic surgery, neurology, etc., address the diagnosis and treatment of the specific disease or condition resulting in disability. The specialty of PM&R is concerned with the disabled patient and with the diagnostic, therapeutic and management procedures necessary to maximize the patient's residual functional abilities. The stated goal is the attainment of maximal physical functional capacity and psycho-social adjustment.

The complexity of these diagnostic and therapeutic procedures varies with the nature and extent of the given disability and the patient's circumstances. A relatively simple localized musculo-skeletal disability may require local therapeutic measures only; complicated disability with severe functional impairment (e.g. spinal cord injury or

cerebral palsy) requires comprehensive rehabilitation measures that
involve several other medical and allied health professional
disciplines. Thus the specialty of PM&R is patient oriented and
emphasizes the need for team care.

It is undoubtedly a measure of the success of this relatively young
medical specialty that, today, the concepts of multidisciplinary and
interdisciplinary team care, as well as the concept of functional
restoration toward optimal societal integration, have become an accepted
part of modern medical care. These concepts, when first pioneered by
Frank H. Krusen and Howard A. Rusk about 40 years ago, were considered
quite revolutionary. According to Rusk,[1] the basic philosophical
tenet of rehabilitation medicine is that the physician's responsibility
does not end when acute illness is over or surgery is completed; this
responsibility is fulfilled only when the individual patient is
retrained to live and work within the framework of his residual
capacities.

Scope of the Specialty. Physical medicine and rehabilitation is
broad in scope and deals with patients of all age groups.
Paradoxically, the medical progress over the past decades, such as the
discovery of antibiotics and the development of physiological support
systems, contributed to an increased number of disabled persons who
survive for many years. A further increase in chronic diseases is to be
expected in the future as the result of the marked shift toward an aging
population in which chronic "wear and tear" diseases lead to
disability. The basic rehabilitation goal of optimal function
performance in the home and the community throughout life thus acquires
greater importance for an increasing number of patients.

Disabilities in need of rehabilitative intervention vary from the
neurodevelopmental and musculoskeletal disabilities of childhood,
through the post-traumatic and work-related disabilities of adulthood,
to all disabilities resulting from degenerative and chronic diseases in
the later years of life. This variety requires specific evaluation and
therapeutic measures for specific disabilities. In depth specialty
development is ongoing and is occurring in the areas of pediatric
rehabilitation, spinal cord injury rehabilitation, cardiopulmonary
rehabilitation, orthopaedic rehabilitation and geriatric rehabilitation,
to name but a few.

Electrodiagnosis is a rapidly expanding component of the specialty
which includes clinical electromyography, nerve conduction studies,
sensory evoke potential studies and other techniques. Clinical
electrodiagnosis helps in the evaluation of neuromuscular diseases such
as myelopathies, radiculopathies, peripheral neuropathies and nerve
injuries, as well as myopathies.

[1] Rusk, HA, "Rehabilitation," Journal American Medical Association
140:286-92 (May 21, 1949)

Academic Content. The specialty of PM&R rests on a basic science infrastructure that includes anatomy, kinesiology, exercise and muscle physiology, neurophysiology and biomechanics. The clinical superstructure combines elements of internal medicine, cardiology, rheumatology, neurology, orthopaedics, pediatrics, geriatrics and behavioural sciences.

Special evaluation and therapeutic methods used extensively in rehabilitation medicine are physical, occupational and speech therapy procedures and modalities such as hydrotherapy, thermotherapy, ultrasound, electrical stimulation, therapeutic exercise and feedback techniques. These constitute the "physical medicine" component of the specialty. The therapuetic applications of physical agents have been utilized since antiquity and thus it is apparent that physical medicine, in various forms, has been part of health care throughout the centuries. The integration of these traditional therapeutic measures into the wider concepts of rehabilitation is of more recent origin. Modern physical medicine and rehabilitation was recognized as a medical specialty in 1947, with the creation of the American Board of PM&R. The name "physiatrist" was chosen to describe the specialist in this field of medicine.

Manpower Need and Supply. Today there are over 2200 Board certified physiatrists in the United States, the majority of whom are in active practice.[1] There is a recognized shortage and a recent GMENAC study projects a need for 4,060 physiatrists in 1990, based on a ratio of two physiatrists per 100,000 population.[2]

At the present, there are 68 approved residency programs in the United States, offering a total of 710 positions, 98 percent of which were filled in 1984. Two hundred thirty-five residents entered their first year of training in 1983-84.

Residency Training and Board Certification. An approved residency in PM&R for residents consists of four years of specialty training, including 12 months integrated internal medicine (or acceptable equivalent) plus 36 months of physical medicine and rehabilitation including pediatric rehabilitation, selected supplementary services and pertinent research experience.

Training is primarily clinical and includes a minimum of three months of electrodiagnosis. A guided research experience is encouraged

---

[1] American Board of PM&R, unpublished data. Figures from the AMA, however, report less than 1600.

[2] Garrison, LB, et al. Physician Requirements - 1990: Five Hospital Based Specialties; Anesthesiology, Nuclear Medicine, Pathology, Physical Medicine, and Radiology. Final Report. (June 1982). Battelle-Huran Research Center, 4000 NE 41st St., Seattle, WA 98105.

during the training period. Full Board certification is obtained by satisfactory performance in both the written (Part I) and oral (Part II) examination. While the former may be taken immediately upon satisfactory completion of an accredited residency training program, the latter requires an additional year of broadly based clinical experience in the practice of physical medicine and rehabilitation or a fourth year in a residency program with full clinical responsibilities plus teaching and/or research involvement.

Physiatric Practice and Career Development. Practice opportunities abound for both the certified specialist entering the field, as well as for the senior clinician with years of academic or clinical experience. A shortage of physiatrists also exists in the academic field. Out of a total of 616 full-time budgeted faculty positions in PM&R throughout the United States, 38 were unfilled in 1980 and the shortage has has increased since them.

Practice and career development are flexible and can be easily adapted to individual preferences and interests, both as to type and content of practice. While a full-time or part-time hospital or clinic based practice is frequently chosen, private group or solo practices are equally well represented.

The proportion of time devoted to clinical patient care, research, teaching and administration will vary with the type of practice, as well the categories of patients and their disabilities. The most complicated cases are encountered more frequently in a specialized rehabilitation hospital or in the rehabilitation department of a university hospital. This type of practice is also one where professional interactions are most prominent, both with colleagues from different specialties and with other members of the rehabilitation team (physical therapist, occupational therapist, speech therapist, rehabilitation nurse, social worker, psychologist, vocational counselor, etc.). Disabilities that appear commonly in the hospital setting include hemi-para- and quadriplegias or paresises of various etiologies, amputations, complicated fractures, advanced rheumatoid arthritis, and neurological disorders leading to limitation of activity such as multiple sclerosis, amyotrophic lateral sclerosis, and Parkinson's disease.

A primarily office-based practice will deal with a greater number of relatively short term disabilities. These include soft tissue injuries, localized joint inflammatory or degenerative disease, low back pain, myositis, tendinitis and bursitis. In both settings, electrodiagnosis will be an integral part of the clinical practice.

The clinical practice of PM&R is rewarding as most patients will improve through the efforts of the physician and the rehabilitation team. Because PM&R is relatively young, it is dynamic and open to new concept and methods. Opportunities for research are abundant in such laboratory areas as musculoskeletal anatomy and kinesiology, exercise physiology, biomechanics and bioengineering, gait analysis, and electrodiagnosis and neurophysiology as well as clinical research.

Economic and "Quality of Life" Considerations. The income from a practice in PM&R compares well with the income from other medical and even some surgical specialities. Starting incomes are often higher on the average, than in other fields. The practice usually permits some free time for family life and pursuit of other personal interests.

The relatively small size of the specialty has its advantages as well. While in the larger specialties there is strength in numbers, there is also anonymity and little opportunity to have a strong voice. In PM&R, on the other hand, the smaller number of Board certified specialists in active practice, provides better opportunities to meet personally with the leaders in the field. In addition to the regional specialty societies, there are three important national specialty organizations and several international specialty groups which provide ample opportunity for scientific presentations, continuing medical education, professional exchange of ideas and social interaction.

In summary, physical medicine and rehabilitation is a clinical, primarily, patient-oriented specialty, dealing with a broad spectrum of disabilities in patients of all age groups. There is a recognized shortage of physiatrists in the United States that is projected to last into the 1990's. Physiatric practice opportunities are available in both the hospital and office setting as well as in the academic environment. Research is encouraged. The field provides intellectual and emotional satisfaction, more than adequate income, as well as excellent professional and social contacts with other colleagues and leaders in the field.

External Readings

24-A-1   Lehmann, JF, "Rehabilitation Medicine: Past, Present and Future," Archives Physical Medicine Rehabilitation 63:291-97 (July 1982).

24-A-2   Fowler, WM, "Viability of Physical Medicine and Rehabilitation in the 1980's," Archives Physical Medicine Rehabilitation 63:1-5 (January 1982).

24-A-3   Porcelli, AV, "Physical Medicine & Rehabilitation: Growing Specialty With a Team Approach," Medical Student 9:8-13 (January/February 1983).

24-A-4   Fla, KJ, "Physiatry and the Physiatrist: A Personal Experience," Archives Physical Medicine Rehabilitation 63:41-43 (January 1982).

External Readings (continued)

24-A-5   Johnson, EW, "Physical Medicine and Rehabilitation," Journal American Medical Association 245:2215-16 (June 5, 1981)

24-A-6   "Glen Reynolds, MD: A Matter of Attitude," Journal American Medical Association 245:2217 (June 5, 1981).

24-B-1   Krusen, FH, et al. Handbook of Physical Medicine & Rehabilitation. Philadelphia: WB Saunders, 1982.

24-B-2   Washburn, KB. Physical Medicine & Rehabilitation: Essentials of Primary Care. Garden City, NY: Medical Examination Pub. Co., 1981. 225 pp.

24-B-3   Hirschberg, GG, et al. Rehabilitation (2nd ed.). Philadelphia: JB Lippincott Co., 1976. 474 pp.

24-B-4   Nichols, PJR (ed.). Rehabilitation Medicine: The Management of Physical Disabilities. London: Butterworth & Co., Ltd., 1980. 353 pp.

24-B-5   Prensky, AL & Palkes, HS. Care of the Neurologically Handicapped Child. New York: Oxford Univ. Press, 1982. 331 pp.

24-B-6   Stolov, WC & Clowers, MR (eds.). Handbook of Severe Disability. U.S. Department of Education, Rehabilitation Services Administration. GPO, 1981. 445 pp.

Section 25 - PREVENTIVE MEDICINE

Martin D. Keller

Martin D. Keller, MD, PhD, is Professor of Internal Medicine and Chairman, Department of Preventive Medicine, The Ohio State University College of Medicine in Columbus, OH. He is also Academic Director, the Department of Emergency Medicine at OSU.

Until recent years the patient who confronted his doctor with, "I am fine doctor, and I want help in staying well," provided somewhat of a shock to the clinician. While pediatricians and obstetricians deal with many healthy patients, only specialists in the growing field of preventive medicine are primarily concerned with health promotion and disease prevention. This specialty extends from the appraisal of health risk factors in an individual patient and the prescription of risk-mitigation strategies to broad programs aimed at protecting the health of the general population. It is the specialty that takes both a "macro" as well as "micro" view of human health - the community and the individual. Consequently, there is great occupational variety open to persons with specialization in this field. The American Board of Preventive Medicine, certifies competency in three broad areas: public health-general preventive medicine, occupational medicine, and aerospace medicine. Each area encompasses a great variety of career opportunities.

While many medical specialties have some concern for the prevention of disease, preventive medicine specialists spend most of their time in activities specifically aimed directly at this goal. They often work with large population groups, through a variety of health care delivery organizations, public agencies, and industries. They emphasize both personal and environmental protection against the biological, chemical, and physical agents that cause disease as well as establishing a personal life style to promote health and prevent illness. It is, thus, an optimistic specialty that focuses on health rather than morbidity. It is also a specialty in which a serious manpower shortage is expected throughout the next decade.

The American Board of Preventive Medicine was formally incorporated in 1948 and is one of 23 specialty Boards engaged in the certification of American medical specialists. Those who graduate from medical school in 1984 and thereafter must have completed training in an approved preventive medicine residency program to achieve Board eligibility.

In addition to the knowledge and skills required of all physicians, preventive medicine requires competence in a variety of subjects that are only sparsely included in other medical specialties:

Epidemiology is the broadest area in preventive medicine that serves as the key to the entire discipline.

Epidemiology deals with understanding the distribution of specific diseases in a population and the factors associated with their occurrence. It seeks to identify persons at highest risk and develop strategies for the prevention of the disease, early detection if the disease cannot be prevented, and prompt, effective treatment. This is also the area of the medical detective who pursues the causes of disease and investigates unusual outbreaks or epidemics in order to halt the spread of disease or recurrence.

In the United states, this work is exemplified by the preventive medicine specialists in the Epidemic Intelligence Service at the Centers for Disease Control in Atlanta, and by epidemiologists employed in various state and local health departments, businesses, and the armed forces. Internationally, epidemiology is one of the major disciplines in the control of epidemic and endemic diseases and prevention of the transport of disease throughout the world. This is also the specialty that frequently designs clinical trials for the evaluation of new diagnostic and treatment procedures and builds strategies for protecting and enhancing the health of the population.

Biostatistics ranges from the collection and evaluation of vital statistics (births, deaths, disease occurrence, etc.), to the design of research and analysis of data derived from investigations in every aspect of health and medicine. It is the key to gathering information in a way that allows fair analysis and conclusions that can be applied to practice.

Environmental Health is concerned with the biological, chemical and physical agents associated with the occurrence of human disease, methods of detecting and monitoring the presence of such agents in the environment, and methods of controlling environmental hazards. It also covers the laws and regulations relevant to potential hazards in the workplace and in the general community. In highly-developed technological societies, this is an area of great current and future emphasis.

Clinical Preventive Medicine involves the application of preventive measures, early detection of inapparent disease, and the development of systems to provide prompt and effective care for individual patients, occupational groups, and the general population. The growth of "wellness" programs for individuals and insurees in health care programs and other factors have brought clinical preventive medicine activities to the forefront of medical care.

Health Policy, Planning, and Implementation of Health
Programs covers a variety of activities, including the
organization, financing, administration/management, and
evaluation of effectiveness of health programs. All of
the disciplines listed above have a role in providing data
and recommendations for these purposes.

Specialists in preventive medicine apply their skills and knowledge
as clinicians, teachers in medical schools and schools of public health,
as researchers in various public and private agencies, and health
administrators and planners. They may work in government agencies at
local, state, national and international levels and in private
health-care organizations. There is particular growth in the demand for
programs among business firms, in health maintenance organizations, and
other organizations where clinical practice is aimed at the prevention
of illness and the promotion of health.

There are also a great many voluntary health agencies (Cancer
Society, Heart Association, Lung Association, etc.) and foundations that
have positions for specialists in preventive medicine. Pharmaceutical
firms and other marketers of health products and services have engaged
specialists in preventive medicine to assess the potential market for
new products and services. Moreover, special "fitness" programs are now
being established by hospitals, industries, and individual
entrepreneurs. These programs assess a patient's health status and
risk-profile in order to prepare tailor-made plans for specific
interventions such as immunization, diet, exercise, smoking-cessation,
and other lifestyle and protective changes to maximize health status and
minimize the risk of disease.

Specialists in preventive medicine also assess the over-all needs of
a group or community and help plan and implement measures to improve the
general health status of these populations. This specialty thus lends
itself to a global view as similarities and the differences among the
world's populations are examined with respect to morbidity and health.
The development of these programs require sensitivity to the political,
cultural, economic, and environmental factors that affect the health of
the community. Indeed, many academic preventive medicine units are
known as the community medicine department.

Preventive medicine specialists are also comfortable with numbers
and not frightened by statistics or computer methods. They acquire
basic skills in statistics and understand the principles of research
design and investigation. They are frequently called upon to
communicate ideas to the public in general, to boards of health,
industrial groups and various governmental agencies or serve as expert
witnesses and advisors in matters affecting the health of the public.

The relative confidence with which we drink our water and eat our
food is the result of pioneering efforts of epidemiologists and
specialists in water purification, sewage treatment, and food and milk

hygiene. Immunization programs for poliomyelitis, pertussis, and rubella have been major preventive medicine accomplishments. The virtual eradication of smallpox from the world has been one of the great achievements of the latter half of the twentieth century.

However, even in the most advanced societies, there are occasional breakdowns in the system leading to food poisoning outbreaks, environmental emergencies, and other unexpected occurrences that call upon the investigative skills of specialists in preventive medicine to determine their causes and institute controls to end them. With the increasing number and complexity of chemical substances put into our environment by automobile exhausts, industrial wastes, food additives, and pesticides and herbicides, there is continual need for specialists who can monitor and investigate their potentially harmful health effects. In a sense, the specialty of preventive medicine provides a corps of physicians who, together with a variety of allied medical professionals, are in the forefront of protecting society against serious breakdown in health safeguards and in restoring safety when incidents occur.

Residency. A residency in preventive medicine generally requires three years. The first year, usually the clinical year (PGY-I), is often taken in an approved program in internal medicine, family medicine, or pediatrics. Occasionally, this is part of the preventive medicine residency programs per se. The second is an academic year in which the resident takes courses in epidemiology, biostatistics, environmental health, and health services administration. This generally leads to a Master of Public Health or a Master of Science degree in preventive medicine. This third year is the practicum or field year providing experience in one of the specialty areas. In general preventive medicine or public health, the practicum is usually pursued in local, state or federal health agencies, ambulatory health-care settings, or hospitals. Those seeking specialization in occupational or aerospace medicine frequently work in the medical departments of business organizations or in aviation or aerospace programs. The residents gain skills in health promotion programs, epidemiology, and administrative methods. Specialized post-graduate programs in preventive medicine are offered by the Epidemic Intelligence Service of the Centers for Disease Control in Atlanta, by other specialized government agencies, and by the armed forces.

Medical students interested in careers in preventive medicine should start by discussing the field with faculty members of preventive (or community) medicine at their medical schools. They may also correspond with preventive medicine residency programs directors listed in the Directory of Preventive Medicine Residency Programs in the United States and Canada which is available from the American College of Preventive Medicine. This directory gives details about funding, degrees offered and areas of emphasis in over 70 accredited programs.

External Readings: Aerospace

25.1-A-1   Mohler, SR, "Aerospace Medicine," In: Last, JM (ed). Maxcy-Roseunau: Public Health & Preventive Medicine. (11th edition). New York: Appleton-Century-Crofts, 1980. pp: 846-63.

25.1-A-2   Berry, CA, "The Space Connection - and Health on Earth," Proceedings: Annual Meeting, Medical Section, American Council of Life Insurance. 1982. pp: 109-13.

25.1-A-3   Wehrly, DJ, "Some Ideas About Preventive Medicine & Health Promotion in Aviation Medicine," Aviation Space Environmental Medicine 52:168-70 (February 1983).

25.1-A-4   Dietlein, LF, "Spaceflight and the Telltale Heart," American Journal Surgery 145:703-06 (June 1983).

25.1-B-1   Deltant, R. (ed.). Aerospace Medicine. Philadelphia: Lea & Febiger, 1984.

25.1-B-2   Engle, E & Lott, A. Man in Flight: Biomedical Achievements in Aerospace. Washington: Aerospace Medical Assoc., 1979.

External Readings: Occupational Medicine

25.2-A-1   "So You Want To Be An Occupational Physician," Occupational Health & Safety 50:53-57 (September 1981).

25.2-A-2   Polokoff, PL, "Health Care in the 21st Century," Occupational Health & Safety 51:31-34 (September 1982).

25.2-A-3   Frank, AL, "Occupational Medicine," Journal American Medical Association 254:2333-34 (October 25, 1985).

25.2-A-4   Walker, B, "The Relevance of Occupational Medicine," Journal National Medical Association 74:367-72 (April 1982).

25.2-A-5   Harrington, JM, "Health and Safety in Medical Laboratories," Bulletin WHO 60(1):9-16 (1982).

25.2-A-6   Collins, TR, "The Occupational Examination: A Preventive Medicine Tool," Continuing Education for the Family Physician 16:77-82 (February 1982).

25.2-A-7   McCahan, JF, "Occupational Medicine," Journal American Medical Association 243:2201-02 (June 6, 1980).

25.2-A-8   Goldman, RH & Peters JM, "The Occupational and Environmental Health History," Journal American Medical Association 246:2831-36 (December 18, 1981).

25.2-A-9   Palokoff, PL, "Occupational Career: Avoidable Risk." Occupational Health & Safety 51:23-26 (August 1982).

25.2-B-1   Goldsmith, F & Kerr, LE. Occupational Safety and Health. New York: Human Science Press, 1982. 320 pp.

25.2-B-2   Monson, RR. Occupational Epidemiology. Boca Raton, FL: CRC Press, 1980. 219 pp.

External Readings: Public Health

25.3-A-1   Foege, WH, "Public Health and Preventive Medicine," Journal American Medical Association 254:2330-32 (October 25, 1985).

25.3-A-2   Relman, AS, "Encouraging the Practice of Preventive Medicine and Health Promotion," Public Health Reports 97:216-19 (May-June 1982).

25.3-A-3   Doege, TC, "Environmental and Public Health," Journal American Medical Association 243:2183-85 (June 6, 1981).

25.3-A-4   Peterson, DR, "Public Health and Preventive Medicine," Journal American Medical Association 245:2216-18 (June 5, 1981).

25.3-A-5   Berlin, NI, "Preventive Oncology, Today and Tomorrow," Preventive Medicine 11:368-72 (May 1982).

25.3-A-6   Public Health Reports 97:224-32 (May-June 1982).

25.3-A-7   Goldman, HH, "Mental Illness and Family Burden: A Public Health Perspective," Hospital and Community Psychiatry 33:557-59 (July 1982).

25.3-A-8   Bianco, NE, "Clinical Immunology As A New Specialty In Public Health," Bulletin Pan American Health Organization 16(1):65-69 (1982).

25.3-A-9   Wiesner, PJ & Parra, WC, "Sexually Transmitted Diseases: Meeting the 1990 Objectives...," Public Health Reports 97:409-16 (September-October 1982).

25.3-A-10   Chilton, LA, "Are Physicians Educable?," Journal School Health 52:479-82 (October 1982).

25.3-B-1   Public Health Personnel in the United States, 1980.
Washington: DHHS Pub. No. (HRA) 82-6. p. 7-48.

25.3-B-2   Arnold, CV, et al. (eds.). Advances in Disease Prevention.
New York: Springer Pub. Co., 1981. 306 pp.

25.3-B-3   Lynch, HT (ed.). Genetics and Breast Cancer. New York:
Nostrand Reinhold, 1981. 253 pp.

25.3-B-4   Schneiderman, LJ (ed.). The Practice of Preventive Health
Care. Menlo Park, CA: Addison-Wesley, 1981. 363 pp.

External Readings: Research

25.4-A-1   Rothman, KJ, "Epidemiology Today," Nutrition Today 17:20-21,
23 (May/June 1982).

25.4-A-2   Gittelsohn, AM, "On the Distribution of Underlying Causes of
Death," American Journal Public Health 72:133-40 (February
1982).

25.4-A-3   Muller, C, "Health Status and Survival Needs of the
Elderly," American Journal Public Health 72:789-90 (August
1980).

25.4-A-4   Rustine, DD, "Controlling the Communicable and Man-made
Diseases," New England Journal Medicine 304:1422-24 (June 4,
1981).

25.4-A-5   Kannel, WB, "Meaning of the Downward Trend in Cardiovascular
Mortality," Journal American Medical Association 247:877-80
(February 12, 1982).

25.4-A-6   Miller, RW, "Areawide Chemical Contamination," Journal
American Medical Association 245:1548-51 (April 17, 1981).

25.4-A-7   "Scientific Activities," Bulletin WHO 60(3):331-37 (1982).

25.4-B-1   Wechsler, H. et al. (eds.). Social Context of Medical
Research. Cambridge, MA: Ballinger Pub. Co., 1981. 334 pp.

25.4-B-2   Jelliffe, DB & Jelliffe, EFP. Advances in International
Maternal & Child Health. New York: Oxford University Press,
1981. 224 pp.

25.4-B-3   WHO: Towards a Better Future, Maternal and Child Health.
Geneva: World Health Organization, 1980. 42 pp.

25.4-B-4   Thomas, GS, et al. Exercise and Health. Cambridge, MA:
Oelgeschlager, Gunn & Hain, 1981. 228 pp.

Section 26 - RADIOLOGY

Stephen R. Baker

Stephen R. Baker, MD, is Associate Professor of Radiology and Co-Director, Department of Radiology at Albert Einstein College of Medicine, and Co-Director, Department of Radiology at Albert Einstein Hospital in New York City.

In the past two decades, probably no other medical specialty has changed as much as diagnostic radiology. Technological advances have enlarged the scope, broadened the challenges, and heightened its rewards. Many diseases, which until recently could only be recognized with assurance at operation or autopsy, can now be diagnosed, and in some cases treated, using techniques under the purview of the radiologist.

Until the early 1960s, diagnostic radiology consisted primarily of the interpretation of radiographs and the performance of relatively simple procedures including fluoroscopic examinations of the upper and lower gastrointestinal tract, intravenous urography for visualization of the kidneys, ureters and bladder and myelography to reveal abnormalities in the spinal column. By the mid 1960s it was possible to include imaging of organs with radioactive isotopes. Over the years, improvements in instrumentation and chemistry have made isotopic or nuclear medicine studies increasingly sophisticated, especially in the evaluation of heart disease. At about the same time, angiography was developed for clinical use which allows x-ray demonstration of blood vessels through administration of a dye placed into an artery via a catheter introduced through the skin. While angiography carries risks and requires skill, it allows the radiologist to measure the presence and extent of diseases in hitherto inaccessible parts of the body.

In the early 1970s, computed tomography (CT), which combines x-rays with electronic spatial reconstruction technology, quickly became an essential diagnostic tool. Computed tomography brought about a quantum leap important in the recognition of tumors, strokes, infections and deformities in the brain and spinal cord and has advanced understanding of the natural history of neurologic diseases. It also enabled the prompt, accurate and detailed elucidation of many chest and abdominal abnormalities. Untrasound, which appeared in the 1970s, has manifold uses. It is now the test of choice for the detection of many cardiac conditions and has become an important element of prenatal care. Recent refinements in mammography have enlarged the radiologists contribution to the early recognition of breast cancer.

In the late 1970s, radiology entered into the treatment realm. The marrying of angiography with the exquisite localizing facility of computed tomography and ultrasound permitted performing biopsies and draining abscesses through the placement of needles and catheters.

Interventional procedures which can be accomplished in the radiology department without the need for general anesthesia offer an alternative to surgery and its attendant complications and convalescence. Catheters are also being used to open up narrowed arteries in the heart, kidneys and extremeties.

Presently a new imaging device, nuclear magnetic resonance (NMR) which creates images of body parts by the interaction of radiowaves with magnetic fields, is undergoing extensive clinical appraisal. The ultimate role of NMR is uncertain but the information it provides promises to uncover new and exciting diagnostic possibilities.

The rapid enlargement of the radiologist's field of view has changed the specialty in profound ways. In the past, most practitioners were competent in radiation therapy as well as diagnosis. Today, practically no newly certified radiologist is also trained in radiation therapy. These two components of traditional radiologic practice have evolved into separate specialties. The well-equipped radiology facility of today is vastly different from that of even a few years ago. Radiology is capital intensive, new imaging devices are expensive, requiring additional space and personnel before becoming obsolescent in a few years. For example, C-T scanners cost about a million dollars. Nuclear magnetic resonance machine cost several times more and many must be housed in specially prepared sites to avoid inadvertent exposure to patients and electronic equipment.

In the past, more radiologists were office-based or combined a private practice with work in small hospitals. Now, the start-up costs of an office are beyond the reach of most young radiologists. Moreover, radiology departments in all but the smallest hospitals are too large for a single practitioner. Hence, group practice, consisting of two to perhaps twenty radiologists is the rule. Groups may provide service to one or several hospitals, often along with a least one separate office. Reimbursement may be on a fee for each case basis, or a group may receive a percentage of total radiology department income, or the hospital may pay each radiologist a salary.

With economics driving radiology toward a corporate enterprise, specialization exists in almost every group practice. In small groups which can not provide the full range of sophisticated and expensive imaging devices, each group member may have similar tasks. But as hospital size and range of services increase, radiologists tend to become experts in one sub-specialty. Sometimes, in addition to their special responsibilities, individual members participate in routine film interpretation. In other circumstances, each may confine himself exclusively to a specific area.

Some sub-specialties like pediatric radiology and neuroradiology require an additional one or two years of fellowship training beyond residency. Consequently, pediatric radiologists and neuroradiologists are found most often in larger hospitals where they can devote almost all their energies to their particular interest. With the growth of interventional techniques, angiographers may be fully occupied performing procedures. In small radiology associations, angiography and other catheter studies are usually shared among several radiologists.

Nuclear medicine is another domain where one or only a few radiologists spend most of their time. Sub-specialization in ultrasound or computed· tomography of the chest and abdomen (as distinct from computed tomography of the brain and spinal cord which are the territory of the neuroradiologist) is increasingly common and has been facilitated by post-residency fellowships that combine training in these two modalities. In some large departments, division of labor is by body region with one radiologist assigned to abdominal disease, another to imaging examinations of the chest, etc. Another form of organization is the separation of responsibility into body systems with gastrointestinal, genitourinary and musculoskeletal radiology as distinct categories.

Sub-specialization has many advantages. As radiology has grown, space for new instruments and devices is often found in far-flung places in the hospital. Efficiency is enhanced when radiologists can remain in one location rather than move around throughout the day. Concentrated attention in one section of radiology provides expertise that a generalist could not acquire. Even in office practice, there is a need to focus on specific activities. The typical office of today usually contains a restricted range of services (fluoroscopy, routine radiography, ultrasound and mammography is a frequent mix). Hence, young radiologists learn that they must become adept in a particular area. It is folly for a graduate to hope to know all of radiology.

And yet, there is still a need for the generalist for smaller practices. Even in larger groups, the radiologist who understands the capabilities, limitations, risks, advantages, disadvantages, and cost of procedures without necessarily knowing all their intricacies can best advise a referring physician about examinations to resolve a clinical problem. As the impulse towards cost-containment and the urge for accountability grows stronger, there is an emerging need for the general radiologist, interested in patient care as well as radiologic images, to function as a consultant. Interposing himself between referring physicians who may not be familiar with many new procedures in radiology, and sub-specialists who often have a vested interest in promoting the virtuosity of the machines they use, the radiology consultant can help rationalize case in a cost-effective way.

Radiology attracts physicians who like the intellectual challenge involved in reaching a diagnosis. It is an alluring field for those who seek to be related to all disciplines in medicine. Talented observers of visual images are apt to do well in this specialty. A drawback of radiology is a remoteness from direct patient care. For the most part, the radiologist's responsibilities end when the diagnosis is achieved. However, the need for more active and ongoing consultations with referring physicians and the clearly demonstrated benefits of intervention techniques will place some radiologists in a more intimate relationship with patients.

The training period in radiology is four years. In some teaching programs an internship is a prerequisite; in others, entrance into residency occurs directly after graduation from medical school. Many residents spend one or sometimes two years in a fellowship before entering private practice or academic radiology. In the future, the need for fellowships will depend on their availability and their importance in the job market. Radiology has become a popular choice for graduating medical students and the number of applicants to training programs goes up each year. Residency positions will probably remain at present levels, if not decrease slightly in the next few years. Admission to teaching programs, especially in academic centers, have become increasingly competitive.

In the near and medium terms, employment prospects for radiologists is subject to several uncertainties. In the larger cities of the Northwest and Midwest, population and hospital bed per capita will probably not rise significantly. Hence the availability of positions should remain limited. In smaller cities in the East and in much of the South and West there is still room for growth. The coming changes in reimbursement for medical care, ushered in by the mandated prospective payment scheme for Medicare patients, may constrain if not constrict the utilization of radiology services, although there no assurance of this eventuality. Enlargement of the range of services has in the past created jobs for radiologists. However, the cost of new devices such as the NMR, the regulations controlling the purchase of expensive equipment, and the impetus for consolidation of resources through regionalization argue against unrestricted expansion.

There are many issues concerning the relationship of radiology to other specialties. Nuclear medicine is a separate specialty, and while many nuclear physicians are also radiologists, others are internists with no other training in imaging interpretation. The control of isotopic studies has been wrested from radiologists in some institutions. Obstetrical examinations account for more than fifty percent of all ultrasound studies. The degree to which the monitoring and interpretation of ultrasound examinations will be under the direction of obstetricians instead of radiologists is a subject of debate in many hospitals. Computed tomography and nuclear magnetic resonance are of great interest to neurologists and neurosurgeons. The relationship between neuroradiologists and other neuro-physicians can be contentious in places where control of CT and NMR is an open question. The resolution of these and other turf skirmishes may determine how much work radiologists do with the new imaging devices.

A significant percentage of x-ray examinations are not done by radiologists but by gastroenterologists, general practitioners, internists and urologists. There is a growing consensus that all routine radiologic studies should be directed and evaluated by radiologists because they are best qualified to provide expert interpretation and ensure that standards of x-ray exposure and high image quality are met.

The future need for radiologists and the nature of their interaction with other specialties are unclear. However, there is one feature of radiology which will be just as pertinent a decade from now as today. Nearly every diagnostic radiologist enjoys his job immensely. In fact, in 15 years of practice I have never heard a colleague wish to do anything else in medicine. On the other hand, in discussions with non-radiologists about job satisfaction, many envy the radiologist's lot.

External Readings

26-A-1   Bengelsdorf, IS, "Radiology Changing as Technology Booms," American Medical News 25:12 (December 3, 1982).

26-A-2   "Role of Radiologist," Journal American Medical Association 247:2233 (April 23/30, 1982).

26-A-3   Jacobson, HG & Leeds, NE, "Diagnostic Radiology," Journal American Medical Association 254:2323-25 (October 25, 1985).

26-A-4   Heilman, RS, "What's Wrong with Radiology," New England Journal Medicine 306:477-79 (February 1982); 307:445-47 (August 12, 1982).

26-A-5   "CT Scanning: The Story Thus Far," Emergency Medicine 14:85-95 (May 30, 1982).

26-A-6   Young, P, "Using Tiny Trails to Outflank Disease," American Way 16:142-48 (March 1983).

26-B-1   Squire, LF. Fundamentals of Radiology. Cambridge, MA: Harvard Univ. Press, 1982. 324 pp.

26-B-2   Schreiber, MH (ed.). Introduction to Diagnostic Radiology. Springfield, IL: CC Thomas, 1980. 368 pp.

26-B-3   Germann, DR & Risher, JK. Practical Radiologic Diagnosis. Reston, VA: Reston Pub. Co., 1981. 307 pp.

26-B-4   Jones, B & Braver, JM. Essentials of Gastrointestinal Radiology. Philadelphia: WB Saunders Co., 1982. 224 pp.

26-B-5   Rosebaum, HD. Pearls in Diagnostic Radiology. New York: Churchill Livingstone, 1980. 241 pp.

Section 27 - CLINICAL NUTRITION

Steven B. Heymsfield, MD, et al.

A growing number of physicians are emerging from clinical training with expertise in nutrition. Underlying and providing impetus for this trend are major advances in the diagnosis and therapy of a wide variety of nutritional disorders.

Until recently little objective information was available on the nature of postgraduate training in clinical nutrition. With the long range plan of moving towards a uniformity of training and potential sub-specialty certification, the American Board of Nutrition and the American Society of Clinical Nutrition sponsored a survey of clinical nutrition training programs in the United States. . . The survey provides an in-depth analysis of program geographic distribution, departmental affiliations, funding sources, number of trainees, educational and clinical components, and the nature of subsequent positions held by trainees. . .

Of the 50 responding training sites, heterogeneity existed in the proportion of program time devoted to clinical nutrition. Therefore not all of the survey questions were answerable at some centers, and this is reflected in the varying number of respondents in the results that follow. . . While a high density of programs exists in the Northeast (24/50), large areas of the United States are without identifiable clinical nutrition training programs. Overall the geographic distribution of programs conforms to the regional localization of medical schools. . .

Of the 50 programs, the largest proportion were within the department of internal medicine (42 percent), followed by surgery (24 percent), pediatrics (18 percent), and nutrition (six percent). Five of the programs (10 percent) combined disciplines, such as internal medicine and surgery. The largest sub-specialty group was gastoenterology, with six divisions identified in internal medicine and two in pediatrics . . . The duration of each training program . . . ranges between one and three years. The majority of programs are two years in duration. . . The number of applicants, positions per year, and total trainees for the 50 centers in 1983 was 216, 72, and 103 respectively. . . . The admission requirements are highly variable, owing in part to the diverse sub-specialty backgrounds of the training programs. . . .

The two major sources of funding are federal grants and hospitals, which together account for nearly two thirds of the support for training programs. The remaining support is provided by universities, private foundations, industry, and other organizations. The later category includes foreign government support of their respective trainee and private donations. With respect to the level of financial support, . . . over half supplied trainees with a stipend that ranged from 20 to 25,000 dollars/year. . .

The survey also gathered data on the proportion of time spent with six sub-specialty patient groups. Taken collectively, internal medicine, pediatric, and surgical services accounted to 85-90 percent of the hypothetical average trainee's exposure to patients. In contrast, five percent or less of the trainee's time was spent with patients cared for by obstetrics and gynecology, family practice, and geriatric programs. . .

Specific details of the clinical curriculum were supplied by 31, 18, and seven centers in years one, two, and three respectively. The curriculum information was averaged in order to . . . depict the three major categories; clinical exposure via the nutrition support team, research, and teaching. The latter category represents teaching experience in addition to that supplied during nutrition support and other patient related activities. The data indicates that with each advancing year, the proportion of nutrition support activity declined; for years one, two, and three, the proportion of trainee time dedicated to this activity went from about one-third, to one-fifth, and in the last year to one-tenth. Contrastingly, there was a relative increase in the amount of research, with this activity representing one-third, one-half, and eight-tenths of the trainees' time in years one, two, and three respectively. Teaching activity remained reasonably constant at about five percent of trainee time for each of the three years. . . .

We also examined information regarding the remaining clinical exposure to specific patient groups and disease states not indicated under the nutrition support category. Again, the general decrease in clinical contact with each year is noted. The three largest groups of patients seen by trainees (each 5-10 percent of trainee time) were alimentary disease, cancer, and eating disorders/obesity; surgical patients, diabetics, and individuals with hyperlipidemia each constituted less than five percent of the trainees non-nutrition support clinical exposure/year . . .

Thirty-eight and forty-two trainees graduated in the years 1982 and 1983, respectively. . . Five potential trainee appointments following completion of the program were identified. Of these, the largest proportion over the two year period entered academic medicine (65/80), with 14 of the remaining 15 graduates electing to pursue private medical practice. One of the 80 trainees decided upon a position in government, and none selected careers in industry or public administration.

The primary aim of this survey was to provide an updated listing of clinical nutrition training programs. A major difficulty in preparing such a listing is that the clinical nutritionist represents a chimera: one or more sub-specialties are often blended to produce the final training program. The surveyed programs ranged from a minor to a major nutrition component, and an attempt was made to characterize each center . . . by adding brief comments to the tabular material. The listing should provide a starting point for prospective trainees, and should also facilitate communication between centers. The aim of the Society is to publish an updated listing on a biennial basis . . .

External Readings

27-A-1   White, PL & Selvey, M, "Nutrition in the 1970's" Journal American Medical Association 243:2220-22 (June 6, 1980).

27-A-2   Cheraskin, E, "Nutrition: A Basis for Holistic Health," Journal Holistic Health 5:49:55 (1980)

27-A-3   Michael, L, et al., "Nutritional Support of Hospitalized Patients," New England Journal Medicine 304:1147-52 (May 7, 1981).

27-A-4   Callaway, CW, "Nutrition," Journal American Medical Association 254:2338-40 (October 25, 1985).

27-A-5   Pitkin, RM, "Is She Eating for Two," Contemporary OB/GYN 19:130-40 (January 1982).

27-A-6   Lang, C, et al., "Nutritional Support: A Foundation for Critical Care," Critical Care Quarterly 5:47-55 (September 1982).

27-A-7   American Journal Clinical Nutrition 36 Supp:1095-1116 (May 1982).

27-A-8   Roe, DA, "Drug-Nutrient Interrelationships," Practical Gastroenterology 6:32-38 (January-February 1982).

27-A-9   Butterworths, CE, "The Advantages of a Nutrition Support Team," Resident & Staff Physician 27:76-83 (November 1981).

27-A-10 Biesel, WR, et al., "Single-Nutrient Effects on Immunological Functions," Journal American Medical Association 245:53-58 (January 2, 1981)

27-A-11 "Symposium of Assessing Therapeutic Dietary Claims," Bulletin New York Academy Medicine 58:219-340 (April 1982).

27-A-12 Primary Care 9:445-619 (September 1982).

External Readings (continued)

27-B-1   Weisner, RL & Butterworths, CE. Handbook of Clinical Nutrition. St. Louis: CV Mosby Co., 1981

27-B-2   Winick, M. Nutrition in Health and Disease. New York: John Wiley & Sons, 1980. 261 pp.

27-B-3   Cunningham, JJ (ed.). Comtemporary Clinical Nutrition Philadelphia: GF Stickley, 1985. 400 pp.

27-B-4   Gilchrist, A. Foodborne Disease and Food Safety. Chicago: American Medicine Association, 1981. 200 pp

27-B-5   Silberman, H. & Eisenberg, D. Parenteral and Enteral Nutrition for the Hospitalized Patient. Norwalk, CT: Appleton-Century-Crofts. 1982. 306 pp.

27-B-6   Lasewell, AB, Roe, DA & Hochheiser, L. Nutrition for Family and Primary Care Practitioners. Philadelphia: GF Stickley, 1985. 450 pp.

27-B-7   Guggenheim, KY. Nutrition and Nutritional Diseases: The Evolution of Concepts. Lexington, MA: Collamore Press, 1981. 378 pp.

27-B-8   Barness, LA, et al. Nutrition and Medical Practice. Westport, CT: AVI Pub., 1981. 408 pp.

Section 28 - CLINICAL PHARMACOLOGY

T. Donald Rucker

T. Donald Rucker, PhD, is Professor and Head, Department of Pharmacy Administration, University of Illinois at Chicago, and Adjunct Professor of Preventive Medicine, The Ohio State University. Dr. Rucker is a medical economist with major research interests in quality assurance pertaining to prescription drug therapy.

Clinical pharmacology is the medical specialty that combines proficiency in both medicine and the basic science of pharmacology. This field is concerned with the specific action of pharmaceutical preparations on living systems, how they interact with other drugs, and their complex role in contributing to patient health status. Since more than three billion prescription orders are written annually by American prescribers, it should be apparent that drug therapy represents the major treatment modality of modern medical care.

If drugs are to be used rationally, evidence must be gathered about a product's bioavailability, blood levels and pharmacokinetics, tolerated and effective dosages, metabolic disposal, and anticipated side effects. Such studies represent the province of the clinical pharmacologist. Clinical pharmacologists thus help to define the amount and duration of drug therapy appropriate for a patient's particular medical problem and determine valid methods for isolating drug effects from other factors.

A major responsibility of the clinical pharmacologist is to conduct scientific experiments that determine possible uses and toxic characteristics of new chemical substances as well as established products. Clinical pharmacologists also often serve as therapeutic consultants to doctors in training and attending physicians who have questions about probable drug results. Regardless of whether the focus is patient care or research, a noted expert, Dr. Louis Lasagna, has observed that "the ethical, psychological, social and economic aspects of human pharmacology constitute a quantum jump from studies in animals."

Preparation for the specialty requires that a student pursue a PhD in clinical pharmacology offered by a medical school or the MD degree with subsequent specialization in this area. The PhD route may be preferable for those seek a research position in the pharmaceutical manufacturing industry or clinical laboratories. The MD route is essential if you wish to be involved directly in patient care. While some residency training programs have identified graduates who entered private medical care practice, most pursue teaching or research. Among those with academic positions, graduates are found in the following departments in medical schools: anesthesiology, medicine (including clinical pharmacology units), pediatrics and psychiatry. Moreover, clinical pharmacologists also hold positions in divisions of cardiology, endocrinology, renal medicine, and surgery, as well as occupational & environmental medicine in a school of public health.

Many experts, perhaps more than 20 percent, have obtained both the MD and PhD degrees. Several medical schools offer joint programs which shorten the length of training required by independent programs. Regardless of interest in a single or dual degree, students should consult the invaluable reference sponsored by the Burroughs Wellcome Fund, Clinical Pharmacology which is published by Peterson's Guides. This publication provides important details about the 35 established and 23 new training programs available in this field.

As in other medical disciplines, sub-specialties have arisen in clinical pharmacology. Among those where MDs are employed are cardiovascular pharmacology, chemotherapy, neuropharmacology and pediatrics. Frontiers in clinical pharmacology include probing the complex behavioral/medical/social dimensions of substance abuse and addiction and the study of genetic differences affecting patient response to drug therapy and the field of immunopharmacology. The latter involves the ability of pharmaceutical agents to suppress the body's immunity mechanisms when organ transplants are carried out.

While clinical pharmacology is sufficiently broad to accommodate a variety of undergraduate backgrounds, all training at this level should include courses in differential and integral calculus, statistics, as well as organic and physical chemistry. Writing and speaking constitute the vehicles by which clinical pharmacologists communicate their findings and undergraduate programs should help support proficiency in these skills.

Clinical pharmacology manifests one attribute that distinguishes it from many others in medicine. Because of manpower shortages which seem likely to persist well beyond the end of this century, prospects for continued employment and satisfactory economic reward appear to be very favorable. Moreover, many training programs offer superior stipend support for qualified candidates. Individuals interested in the variety and challenges associated with joint careers comprising patient care, teaching and research, may find that clinical pharmacology warrants intensive consideration.

External Readings

28-A-1   "Drug Abuse Related to Prescribing Practices," Journal American Medical Association 247:864-66 (February 12, 1982).

28-A-2   "Prescribing for the Elderly," Patient Care 16:14-62 (June 30, 1982).

External Readings

28-A-3   Horwitz, RI & Feinstein, AR, "Improved Observational Method for Studying Therapeutic Efficacy," Journal American Medical Association 246:2455-59 (November 27, 1981).

28-A-4   Patterson, R & Anderson, J, "Allergic Reactions to Drugs and Biologic Agents," Journal American Medical Association 248-2637-45 (November 26, 1982)

28-A-5   Rosenbaum, JF, "Current Concepts in Psychiatry - The Drug Treatment of Anxiety," New England Journal Medicine 306:401-04 (February 18, 1982).

28-A-6   Done, AK, "The Trouble With Reducing Fever," Emergency Medicine 13:137-52 (December 15, 1982).

28-A-7   Werry JS, "An Overview of Pediatric Psychopharmacology," Journal Child Psychiatry 21:3-9 (January 1982).

28-A-8   LaPalio, LR, "The Stepwise Approach to Treating Hypertension," Contemporary OB/GYN 19:12-16 (May 1982).

28-A-9   Salzman, C, "A Primer on Geriatric Psychopharmacology," American Journal Psychiatry 139:67-73 (January 1982).

28-A-10 Frohlich, ED, "Clinical Considerations in the Patient Requiring Multidrug Management of Hypertension," Practical Cardiology 8:59-71 (May 1, 1982).

28-B-1   Conley, D (ed.). Clinical Pharmacology: A Guide to Training Programs. Princeton: Peterson's Guides, 1982.

28-B-2   Folb, PI. The Safety of Medicines: Evaluation & Prediction. New York: Springer-Verlag, 1980. 103 pp.

28-B-3   Wilkes, E (ed.). Long-Term Prescribing. Winchester, MA: Faber & Faber, 1982. 269 pp.

28-B-4   Bochner, F, et al. Handbook of Clinical Pharmacology. Boston: Little, Brown & Co, 1978. 313 pp.

28-B-5   Scherer, JC. Introductory Clinical Pharmacology. New York: JB Lippincott Co., 1982.

Section 29 - CRITICAL CARE

Harriet Page

Critical care specialists from 24 countries - anesthesiologists, surgeons, pediatricians, and nurses - met in Washington, DC, in the early 1980's to hear and see some 700 scientific papers and exhibits at the Third World Congress on Intensive and Critical Care Medicine. . .

Coma. Studies with the coma scale, . . . which . . . has some noteworthy advantages over the Glasgow Coma Scale, were described by Marialuisa Bozza-Marrubini, MD an anesthesiologist . . . . Any classification system . . . is useful for improving general understanding of coma, assessing initial severity, monitoring progress and response to treatment, separating cases into homogenous groups so treatments may be compared, and, finally, for predicting outcome. The Glasgow Coma Scale, which is really a scoring system, Bozza-Marrubini noted, assumes that various symptoms are independent of one another... When one category of signs cannot be evaluated, the total score becomes meaningless . . . and equal total scores may reflect very different clinical pictures.

The Bozza-Marrubini scale, she believes, is more "dynamic." Coma is classified by constellations of signs with progressive steps that correspond to the severity of brain failure, and it yields groups that can more readily be compared. It also includes assessments of brainstem function, which she believes are critical to the understanding of coma.

In her study, Bozza-Marrubini compared 200 cases of coma owing to traumatic brain injury, hypoxic-ischemic brain damage, or poisoning, scoring half of them by the Glasgow scale, half by her own. Besides providing correlated clinical patterns that define levels of brain dysfunction, her scale predicted the eventual outcome in 89 of 100 cases, she said. The Glasgow scale, even when a number of additional variables such as brainstem function were included, yielded this in only 61 cases. . .

Another approach to coma - a way to facilitate early recognition of intracranial hematoma - was described by neurosurgeon David J. Price, FRCS, of Pinderfields Hospital in Wakefield, England, who also expressed interest in the Bozza-Marrubini coma scale. Price found in a study of 200 patients with acute posttraumatic extracerebral hemorrhage that the most powerful indicators for presence of hematoma were a falling consciousness level and ultrasonograms demonstrating a shift of midline structures.

His approach is designed to solve "the dilemma of a young intern faced with a coma patient" and is a "triage measure" to see if computed tomgraphic (CT) scanning is needed. Ultrasound costs about $10 per procedure at his hospital, Price said, and, unlike a CT scan, can be performed on a patient who is "thrashing about." The more expensive CT scans must be performed at four-hour intervals, he added, and the patient must be still. His system, which combines ultrasound data with clinical data, is "reliable and sensitive," he said, and clearly defines risk of hematoma. . .

Malnutrition in Pediatric Patient. Protein-energy malnutrition is a common, and often unsuspected, problem in critically ill children, according to pediatric specialist Murray Pollack, MD, of Children's Hospital National Medical Center in Washington, DC. The problem often goes unrecognized . . . because the sick children are being fed.

In study of 73 young medical and surgical patients in intensive care units, Pollack and colleagues found acute protein-energy malnutrition in another 18 percent. Nutrient stores were also low in these patients, he said, with fat deficiency in 14 and protein deficiency in 21 percent.

Whether the patients were medical or surgical patients made no statistical difference. . . However, children younger than two years were more likely to be malnourished than those two years and older. He said the acute malnutrition appears to begin within 48 hours of admission but can be reversed, though with difficulty, while the illness persists.

Aspiration Pneumonitis. A high index of suspicion for aspiration pneumonitis, plus early, high-dose corticosteroid and antibiotic therapy and ventilatory support when needed, achieved a high survival rate in 70 patients, according to a report by anesthesiologist Joseph S. Redding, MD, of the Medical University of South Carolina.

He examined a series of patients with aspiration pneumonitis seen during a two-year period. . . Diagnosis was considered "probable" on the basis of history and physical examination and was confirmed by a shunt fraction (QS/QT) greater than 15 percent and x-ray changes consistent with aspiration. Forty-seven patients met both criteria, Redding said; another eight had elevated shunt fraction without x-ray changes, and 15 had x-ray changes without elevated shunt fraction. Sixty-two of the 70 patients received corticosteroids, and 64 received prophylactic antibiotics. Chest physical therapy was given to 39 of the 70 patients for atelectasis, and aspiration was the primary indication for mechanical ventilation in 27 patients.

While eight patients suffered complications of treatment, Redding said, only two died. He believes a randomized, multi-institutional study to ascertain the worth of high-dose corticosteroids and antibiotics in this condition is justified on the basis of these data.

The Hospice in the ICU. A plea that "the hospice concept" be incorporated into the daily environment of the ICU was voiced by Joseph M. Civetta, MD, President of the Society of Critical Care Medicine.

"The concept that embodies the alleviation of suffering because of the importance of the quality of life can . . . be expressed in an intensive care unit," he said. "Not only is this fundamentally good for the patient's family and the society, but I believe it can have an extremely salutary effect that the personnel who work in intensive care. No longer is death regarded as failure, but the dying process becomes an opportunity to help, and thus every patient can benefit from his intensive care stay. Some may get better while others may die better."

Civetta, who is medical director of the surgical ICU at the University of Miami Jackson Memorial Hospital Medical Center, said that in the hospice context, controversies over "pulling the plug" seem to vanish. "Withdrawing and withholding agressive treatment can be viewed more accurately as an appropriate change of focus.

"No longer do we fruitlessly and expensively prolong the dying process but, rather, freed from the burden of supplying technologically demanding but ineffective treatments, we can devote our efforts to caring for the dying patient and his family. . . Our skills as medical professionals . . . may be unable to deal with the devastating critical illness, but we must not view this with a sense of failure. Rather, it is an opportunity for the expression of those unique human resources that can, in fact help the patient and family to cope with the dying process."

External Readings

29-A-1   Grehvik, A, et al., "Critical Care Medicine Certification as Multidisciplinary Sub-specialty," Critical Care Medicine 9:117-25 (February 1981).

29-A-2   Parrillo, JE, "Critical Care Medicine," Journal American Medical Association 254:2288-90 (October 25, 1985).

29-A-3   Wallace-Barnhill, G. et al., "Medical, Legal and Ethical Issues In Critical Care," Critical Care Medicine 10:57-61 (January 1982).

29-A-4   Grerbaum, DM & Holbrook, PR, "Fellowship Programs in Critical Care Medicine," Critical Care Medicine 10:347-51 (May 1981).

29-A-5   Thompson, WL, "Critical Care Tomorrow: Economics and Challenges," Critical Care Medicine 10:561-68 (September 1982).

- 201 -

29-B-1   Weil, MH & Shubin, H.   Critical Care Medicine: Current Principles and Practices.   New York: Harper & Row, 1976.   176 pp.

29-B-2   Miller, HA. et al., (eds.).   ICU Medicine: The Fifty-Sixth Hahnemann Symposium.   New York: Grune & Stratton, 1983.   172 pp.

29-B-3   Weil, MH & DaLuz, PL (eds.).   Critical Care Medical Manual. New York: Springer-Verlag, 1978.   370 pp.

29-B-4   Findeiss,   JC   (ed.).   Emergency   Medical   Care   (Vol.   2): Emergency Management of the Critical Patient.   Miami: Symposia Specialists, 1975.   280 pp.

29-B-5   Davis, JE & Mason, CB.   Neurologic Critical Care.   New York: Van Nostrand Reinhold Co., 1979.   291 pp.

Medical Ethics

. . . Despite its current status as a standard procedure, cardiopulmonary resuscitation does not really work that well. Only seven to 14 percent of the patients who receive it leave a hospital alive. 'Your going for the long shot . . . So the ideal situation is to let the patient decide whether to do it. Most say no. They want to die peacefully when the time comes.'

- Green, L. "No Easy Answers," Chicago Tribune Magazine, June 2, 1985. p. 31.

Section 30 - FORENSIC MEDICINE

Samuel R. Gerber and Elizabeth K. Balraj

Samuel R. Gerber, MD, JD, is Coroner, Cuyahoga County, Cleveland, OH. He is also Assistant Clinical Professor, Emeritus, at Case Western Reserve University, Cleveland and is Co-Founder of The Law Medicine Center at this same institution.

Elizabeth K. Balraj, MD, is Deputy Coroner and Forensic Pathologist in Cuyahoga County, Cleveland, OH. She is also Assistant Professor of Forensic Pathology at Case Western Reserve University.

Forensic medicine, also called legal medicine, treats the application of medical knowledge and skills to problems of law, justice and public welfare. This discipline thus serves society by supplying facts and expert opinions utilized in legal decisions for the administration of justice.

The diversity of the discipline is reflected in the ten sections of the American Academy of Forensic Sciences. Some - crimilanistics, engineering, jurisprudence, questioned documents and general - focus on civil as well as criminal litigation. Others - odontology, psychiatry, pathology/biology, physical anthropology, and toxicology - are oriented toward the human organism.

Forensic medicine, except perhaps for several ad hoc lectures on malpractice, is largely neglected in medical school. Consequently, American physicians have almost no concept of proper procedures and records necessary as evidence in civil or criminal cases.

Law and medicine have a common objective - to establish facts upon which to base a proper decision that will yield an appropriate remedy. Thus information must be obtained and evaluated and then decisions made only on the relevancy of the data. Misinterpretation of medical testimony in court may result from lack of understanding of how a physician arrived at a conclusion and hence lead to a miscarriage of justice.

The role of the coroner/medical examiner, a public official, is established by laws enacted in the various states. Although these statutes are dynamic and vary significantly, the provisions promulgated by Ohio are illustrative - the coroner must be notified when any person dies as a result of criminal or other violent means, or by casualty, or by suicide, or suddenly when in apparent health, or in any suspicious or unusual manner. The coroner must determine the cause, mode and manner of death, complete and file a death certificate of all cases coming under his jurisdiction, keep full and complete records properly indexed, furnish the County Prosecutor copies of records and such other information as deemed necessary, and present evidence in any civil or criminal court. Thus death in all its forms constitutes the professional realm of the forensic pathologist. However, in Louisiana, the coroner's duties extend to the living victims of sexual assault.

A major task of the coroner/medical examiner is to direct the medicolegal autopsy. This is a specialized examination requiring recognition and preservation of non-medical as well as medical evidence that may provide useful clues concerning the circumstances related to the demise of the individual. While examination of the body per se rarely provides sufficient information to validate the cause of death, this goal is difficult to realize without such evidence.

In addition, the coroner/medical examiner must collaborate and cooperate with other officials, aware of the extent and limitations of his authority. Distinction between suicide and accident, and occasionally the recognition or exclusion of homicide, is dependent to a great extent upon information gained from investigation into the circumstances and events preceding death. Such investigations should be conducted by persons trained in investigative techniques. The coroner/medical examiner is a member of the law enforcement team but, if justice is to prevail, he must also remain independent and objective.

Approximately two-thirds of the deaths reported to the office of the coroner/medical examiner are found to result from disease and the residual from violence. Thorough examinations must be conducted on each body though to ensure that the cause does not escape detection.

Different kinds of death evoke varying combinations of emotional and intellectual responses. The coroner/medical examiner or forensic pathologist may be confronted with a combination of grief and anger ("How could he do this to me?" asks the widow of the suicide victim), grief and hate (the homicide victim's family vis-a-vis the assailant), or grief and horror (the parents of the child victim of rape-homicide).

The parents of the infant who fall prey to sudden death syndrome ask, "What really killed our baby? Shouldn't his pediatrician, who examined the child the day he died, have recognized that he was seriously ill - sick enough to die within a few hours? Could we have prevented the death? Did the baby suffer? Did he smother? Did he die from something that happened during pregnancy? If we have another baby, could the same thing happen again?"

Occasionally, the questions can be quickly and correctly answered, thanks to information readily available from a complete autopsy. "How many times was my son shot? Where did the bullets hit him?" "Was my husband drunk when he drove his car into the tree?" "My father thought he had cancer when he committed suicide with an overdose of drugs prescribed by his psychiatrist. Did you find cancer at autopsy?" "Our daughter was six months pregnant when she and her husband were killed in that automobile accident last week. Was the baby a boy or a girl?" "I just received a copy of my son's death certificate from City Hall, and I don't understand the long words." Thus run the questions.

Some inquiries are answered readily, some with difficulty and still others may be impossible to answer. "Which one of the three bullets struck my wife first?" The forensic pathologist should be candid and possess sufficient intellectual security to concede readily the limitations of his or her knowledge. Under no circumstances should the forensic pathologist resort to untruths of half-truths. Tact, compassion, patience, probity, sympathy and even a little empathy are essential elements in job performance.

The effectiveness of the coroner/medical examiner is influenced also by rapport with practicing physicians as well as by the attitude of the public at large. Since death is generally considered an unpleasant subject, there is often a tendency is to shun mundane duties and to focus on the sensational cases or those of personal interest. As a result the medicolegal officer may feel a sense of isolation. This is, perhaps, one of the many reasons that it is not a popular career.

Potential for the Field. In order to enhance the scientific role of the coroner/medical examiner, and help overcome the shortage of qualified applicants, Dr. J.S. Bell offered a four-point program:

1. Opportunities must be available. We must educate the public to the fact that forensic pathologist/medical examiner services are mandatory to the proper functioning of the American criminal justice system.

2. We must be selective in recruiting only bright, dedicated, eager physicians to this medical field.

3. Income must be commensurate with training, activity and responsibility.

4. We must educate medicine and academia to the opportunities, the new frontiers, the wonders and excitement and scientific method of forensic pathologist and medical examiner work. It is a science and is practiced as such - we know it but others don't.

Training Programs. Several accredited training program exist for physicians interested in forensic pathology. Certification requirements include:

1. Applicants who hold a certificate in anatomic and clinical pathology or anatomic pathology only, or in special instances, clinical pathology only - one year of supervised training in forensic pathology in an institution accredited for such training by the ACGME, or approved for such training by the American Board of Pathology (ABP).

2. For combined certification in anatomic pathology and forensic pathology - two years of approved training in anatomic pathology and two years of approved training in forensic pathology in an institution accredited for such training by the ACGME.

3. For candidates holding a certificate in anatomic and clinical pathology, in anatomic pathology only, or in exceptional instances, clinical pathology only - two years of full-time experience in forensic pathology in a situation comparable to that of an institution accredited for training in forensic pathology by the ACGME. (7)

The education, training and preparation needed to qualify for the posts of coroner/medical and forensic pathologist are as follows:

1) Coroner - licensed physician or a citizen of good standing in the community (requirement varies somewhat from state to state); administrative capability; may be elected or appointed.

2) Medical examiner - Board certified forensic pathologist; administrative capability; most are appointed.

3) Forensic pathologist - Board certified in forensic pathology; minimal administrative capability. May be appointed as deputy coroner or deputy medical examiner.

Practice Opportunities. Today there are less than 250 Board certified forensic pathologists in the United States. However, there are numerous coroner/medical examiner offices with vacant full-time or part-time positions. Thus most practice opportunities are found in state and local government positions concerned primarily with determining the cause, mode and manner of death. Remuneration varies widely from jurisdiction to jurisdiction.

For individuals willing to pursue dual careers in law and medicine (see Chapter IV), some employment positions may be located in insurance companies, pharmaceutical firms, large hospitals, public health agencies, and group practices of physicians and attorneys.

External Readings

30-A-1   Rosner, R, et al., "Forensic Psychiatric Evaluations of Women Accused of Felonies," Journal Forensic Sciences 30:721-740 (July 1985).

30-A-2   Weinstock, R, et al., "Physicians' Confusion Demonstrated by Competency Requests," Journal Forensic Sciences 30:37-43 (January 1985).

30-A-3   McConnell, TS, et al., "Investigation of Hot Air Balloon Fatalities," Journal Forensic Sciences 30:350-363 (April 1985).

External Readings (continued)

30-B-1   Gordon,   I.   Forensic   Medicine.   New   York: Churchill
         Livingstone, 1982. 451 pp.

30-B-2   Mason,   JK.   Forensic   Medicine   for   Laywers.   Boston:
         Butterworths, 1983. 419 pp.

30-B-3   Trick, KLK. Forensic Psychiatry. Marshfield, MA: Pitman,
         1981. 207 pp.

Graduate Training

. . . Today, there are just less than 75,000 residents on duty in the United States in accredited programs . . . housestaff stipends, which averaged, depending on the year of residency, between $20,000 and $27,000 in 1984-85 . . .

Physician training takes place in about 1,550 institutions, including mental health agencies, ambulatory care clinics, and medical examiner's offices. By far the largest majority of training programs - 1,350 - are in hospitals, however, and 125 hospitals train 50 percent of all residents . . .

- American Medical News, June 14, 1985. p. 18.

Section 31 - GENETICS

"Gene Therapy: An Idea Whose Time is Near"

Martin J. Cline, MD

The concept behind gene therapy is the replacement of an abnormal gene by its normal counterpart in somatic cells; for example, the replacement of the abnormal beta-globin gene of sickle cell disease by the normal beta-globin gene in bone marrow cells.

Patients whose marrow cells have been manipulated genetically still carry the abnormal sickle cell gene in their eggs or sperm and would transmit the defective genes to their children. In contrast, in true genetic engineering, genes are introduced into fertilized eggs in such a manner that they are carried by the germ line of the organism and may be transmitted from parent to progeny.

Gene therapy currently is possible conceptually for diseases caused by abnormal function of a major single gene. Genetic manipulation of disorders involving the interaction of many genes is too complex for current technology; thus, genetic manipulation for correction of low intelligence or susceptibility to heart disease is not possible now.

Gene therapy therefore will be applied first to the treatment of diseases caused by abnormal function of a single gene in a specialized tissue. In sickle cell anemia, a point mutation results in a clinical syndrome of anemia, painful destruction of many tissues, and early death. In thalassemia, a variety of globin gene abnormalities cause anemia, stunted growth, deformed bones, and early death. In theory, introduction of a normally functioning globin gene into the marrow of patients with either disorder should cure the illness.

Currently, the precise details for optimizing gene therapy in the hereditary anemias are unknown; however, the general strategy of the clinical studies necessary to define the correct approach is clear. The strategy can be illustrated by studies undertaken . . . to explore the possibilities of gene therapy in thalassemia major. These studies involved a young woman with severe bone deformities, anemia, and intermittent heart failure, and an adolescent girl with lifelong anemia and the recent onset of heart problems. Both patients had . . . a limited life expectancy.

In July, 1980, the first patient entered a hospital in Jerusalem. Bone marrow was collected and incubated with a mixture of two purified genes. One of the genes was a <u>selective</u> gene meant to provide a proliferative advantage to the recipient cells. The other gene was a cloned normal human beta-globin gene. The patient's thigh was irradiated to create "space" in the marrow, and the marrow cells were returned intravenously to the patient. The procedure without irradiation was repeated on the second day. The patient left the hospital on the second day and experienced no undesirable side effects either then or later.

Ten days later a similar procedure was performed with a young Italian patient in Naples. She, too, left the hospital within two days without untoward side effects.

Based on studies on several hundred mice and of dozens of samples of human marrow incubated under culture conditions, it was presumed that perhaps one marrow cell in 100,000 would incorporate the new genes. It was hoped that this cell, when injected into the bloodstream, would "home" to the available space in the marrow of the patients. The genetically manipulated bone marrow cell then would proliferate under the drive of the <u>selective</u> gene and would distribute to each of its daughter cells the normal globin gene. If these cells were to make normal hemoglobin, then clinical improvement could be anticipated.

These studies were envisioned as the first of a series that would span many years. At the time of their inception, it was realized that the successful accomplishment of gene therapy would require the acquisition of knowledge in many areas. It was presumed that the information would be acquired in a stepwise fashion over a period of time.

The strategy was to define and overcome a series of obstacles. First, the cells would need to survive the period of incubation with cloned genes. Then, when reinjected, they would need to "home" to the marrow space and proliferate. The treated cells would need to carry the newly inserted genes in a stable and functional form. Finally, the production of globin by the new genes would need to be modulated within the normal range. Neither too much nor too little production of globin would be useful. These defined problems were the projected milestones in the research protocol.

We already knew from previous experiments that we successfully could insert new genes into marrow cells, at least transiently . . . . Studies in these two individuals therefore were aimed at the question of whether cells carrying new genes could be returned successfully to the bone marrow and resume proliferation. All evidence indicated that the risks involved to the patients were minimal and that a clear-cut answer to the first question could be obtained. There was even a chance, albeit a small one, that the new globin genes would function in these patients.

No doubt, more efficient techniques of gene insertion will be devised in the years ahead. Other vehicles, such as engineered viruses, may be used to introduce genes; the new genes may be highly engineered so that their function can be modulated by administered drugs. Regardless of the ultimate strategy, there seems to be general agreement among scientists knowledgeable in this field that the problems involved in this type of gene therapy are ultimately solvable.

When should clinical trials in such cases begin? The conventional strategy for examining a new mode of therapy in an otherwise fatal disease, such as far-advanced malignancies, include a phase I study of toxicity as a function of dose, a phase II study of efficacy against appropriate target diseases, and a phase III study comparing the new treatment with conventional therapy. We conceived of our initial studies as a phase I trial in an otherwise lethal disease. Studies of very long duration will be necessary to determine the potentials of gene transfer in the treatment of lethal genetic diseases.

Thalassemia appears to be the most appropriate disorder for initial study. In its severe form it is not curable and leads to premature death. It is based on a defined genetic defect; replacement of the defective gene with a normal one should ameliorate the disease. Furthermore, sound experiments should provide information about gene insertion, adequacy of the delivery systems, and gene expression. Sickle cell disease is another target.

A new experimental approach to thalassemia is marrow transplantation. It is hoped that marrow cells transplanted from a normal sibling will proliferate and synthesize the normal hemoglobin lacking in the patient. Although there are high risks in this procedure, no special ethical arguments are raised against bone marrow transplantation except those that apply to all types of innovative experimentation in man. Conceptually, the transplantation of bone marrow cells containing new genes is no different from the direct transplantation of the genes themselves. Gene therapy thus would appear to be the next logical step in the treatment of hereditary anemias.

What are the ethical issues associated with gene therapy for rare hereditary diseases? Although in my judgment the use of DNA as a biologic reagent for treatment should pose no new special ethical problems, many concerns are associated with the introduction of any type of innovative therapy. Clearly, extensive animal experimentation is necessary to define the obstacles, to work out the technical details, and to assure the safety of the procedure.

The severity of a disease is an important factor in deciding when to introduce a new treatment. With mild conditions that do not shorten significantly or affect adversely the quality of life, one hesitates to introduce a completely new treatment that may have unanticipated side effects. On the other hand, in the case of life-threatening diseases, one is generally less hesitant to use new treatments, particularly when the patient is in the late stages of disease and no good alternative treatments are available. Under such conditions as a terminal malignancy, a new treatment that has not been defined in detail may be acceptable.

One of the main controversies relates to the time of application of a new treatment. The appropriate timing of the introduction of a new treatment is not always obvious, and observers from different scientific or medical backgrounds may see this issue differently. Clearly, I believe the time for perfecting gene therapy is now.

Our society is highly sensitive to the rights and privileges of patients as potential experimental subjects. Few experimental studies are done that escape the scrutiny of ethics committees. This was not always the case. Jenner and Pasteur carried out their studies on smallpox and rabies prevention on single human subjects without the ethical safeguards we require today. These experiments were successful and established immunization schemes that eliminated lethal diseases and saved many lives. There was no assurance at the time that the first vaccinated subjects would not suffer serious side effects.

Our current attitudes toward human experimentation are more mindful of the rights of the individual and his dignity as a human being. In certain cases, however, it should be noted that ethics committees - because of understandable conservatism and caution - delay the introduction of innovative treatments that may help patients who are alive today and caught in the grip of an overwhelming disease.

My own two patients are still alive and in the same state of health in which I first met them - they are neither better nor worse. I wish I could tell you the results of the experiment, but I do not know them. Within two months of the gene therapy studies, all work in the laboratory was disrupted and soon thereafter money to continue the research was withdrawn.

The technical obstacles to successful gene therapy are likely to be overcome within a few decades. The scientific strategies for identifying and solving the major problems already are well defined. In the next few years we sequentially shall accomplish:

- Increased efficiency of gene transfer into cells of living animals by the use of targeted vectors.

- Construction of control signals that will permit modulation of expression of introduced genes.

- Testing in animals of a wide range of engineered genes.

- Clinical trials of single-gene therapy.

- Widespread and perhaps even routine application of gene therapy to specific genetic diseases.

In my opinion, the investigation and application of this type of gene therapy requires little public or private regulation beyond that which already exists in relation to the introduction of any new therapeutic modality. Sufficient safeguards for experimental subjects already exist in our society. The inherent dangers of introducing DNA into marrow cells or liver cells are probably no greater than those of many of the new drugs that are introduced annually into clinical medicine. Since the new DNA is restricted to the recipient patient and is not passed on to children or added to the gene pool of man, there are no considerations in this type of gene therapy regarding the alteration of man's heredity. It is hoped that neither lack of understanding nor excessive regulatory constraints needlessly will delay the application of this form of therapy.

It is less easy to define the future development of genetic engineering as applied to embryos. This type of genetic manipulation impacts directly upon man's heredity. The technical problems are more difficult, and the social and ethical considerations are vastly more complex than in the case of gene therapy.

My own perspective is that genetic engineering of animal or even human embryos is almost within the grasp of modern biology. In vitro fertilization of eggs and embryo transfer to foster mothers already have been accomplished for many domestic animals and human beings. Techniques for modulating engineered genes have been developed in several laboratories. It would appear therefore, to be only a matter of time before man can alter his own heredity.

Suppose we could eliminate diabetes, cancer, and heart disease for all generations by appropriate genetic engineering. Would we grasp the opportunity? My own view is that despite any number of regulations and restraints imposed by contemporary society, man eventually will alter his own heredity and thereby increase his control over his environment and his destiny. The only questions are ones of timing and how we chart the course.

External Readings

31-A-1   "Genetic Counseling and Prevention of Birth Defects," Journal American Medical Association 248:221-24 (July 9, 1982).

31-A-2   Anderson, WF, "Gene Therapy," Journal American Medical Association 246:2737-39 (December 11, 1979)

31-A-3   Hall, JG, "Medical Genetics," Journal American Medical Association 254:2296-98 (October 25, 1985).

31-A-4   Sepe, SJ, et al., "Genetic Services in the United States," Journal American Medical Association 248:1733-35 (October 8, 1982).

External Readings (continued)

31-A-5   Scirver, CR, et al., "Genetics and Medicine: An Evolving Relationship," Science 200:946-51 (May 26, 1978).

31-A-6   Nevin, NC, "Genetic Disorders," Clinics in Ob/Gyn 9:3-25 (April 1982).

31-B-1   Encyclopedia of Bioethics (Vol. 2). New York: The Free Press, 1978. pp. 513-73.

31-B-2   Feingold, M & Pashayan, H. Genetics and Birth Defects in Clinical Practice. Boston: Little, Brown & Co., 1983. 265 pp.

31-B-3   Simpson, JL, et al. Genetics in Obstetrics & Gynecology. New York: Grune & Stratton, Inc., 1982. 322 pp.

31-B-4   Stine, GJ. Biosocial Genetics: Human Heredity and Social Issues. New York: MacMillan Pub. Co., 1977. 579 pp.

31-B-5   Fraser, FC & Nora, JJ. Genetics of Man. Philadelphia: Lea & Febiger, 1975. 270 pp.

Shifting Patterns of Illness

. . . America is turning into a chemical culture . . . I firmly believe that by 1990 alcoholism and drug addiction will have surpassed cancer and heart disease as the number one health problem . . .

- G. Douglas Talbott, MD, director of the alcohol and addiction treatment program, Medical Association of Georgia. Quoted in the Chicago Tribune, September 30, 1984. Section 6, p. 3.

Section 32 - HOLISTIC AND WELLNESS MEDICINE

Unit 32.1 - Holistic Medicine

Nelson H. Kraus

Nelson H. Kraus, MD, MBA, is the President and Chief Executive Officer of Preventive Concepts in Worthington, OH. He is actively involved in providing consulting services in the area of health promotion to business and industry as well as practicing preventive medicine.

The only constant in medicine in change! This process is becoming much more rapid for a variety of reasons. Cost and cost containment are dramatically altering the way many hospitals and practitioners offer services. Competition and consumer choice is now a major force in the health care market place. As future health care providers you must be aware of these changes and practice options. One such option is holistic health or the evolution of prevention medicine.

The concept of treating the whole person has been around since the time of Hippocrates but has been lost recently in the technological explosion of the last 70 years. Its rebirth developed in California during the sixties and has now spread to almost every area of the country. Several decades ago most physicians and health care providers considered holistic health to be unreliable quackery practiced mostly by poorly qualified pseudo-providers. This perception has and continues to change rapidly. Many traditional providers are integrating holistic philosophies into their services, realizing that any good practitioner interacts with the whole, not just fragments, of a human being. Each patient is unique and an inseparable blend of mind, body, spirit, emotional, social and physical aspects. Unless all components are effectively considered and dealt with, the clinician is probably providing inadequate care. Future health care providers must realize that good practitioners focus on much more than the physical aspects of human existence and disease.

Central to the concept of holistic health is the idea that the PATIENT is responsible for his or her own state of health and NOT the physician. This position makes sense since patients live every moment of a lifetime with themselves, while the provider only spends a few minutes with them on a sporatic basis. Patients know much more about themselves than any health care provider and they make most of the decisions about their own health. They decide (in non-emergent situations) when to see the doctor and which one to visit. They decide whether they will follow the physician's instructions, get the prescription filled, take the full course of the medication, return for a follow-up visit or change doctors.

The holistic concept involves the patient as the person central to health care. The health care provider then becomes a facilitator and less of an authority figure. One result is a significant improvement in patient compliance which benefits both the patient and the doctor and helps reduce malpractice suits which seldom help anyone except attorneys.

Another important theme is the idea that health is much more than the absence of disease. Conventional medicine emphasizes the study, understanding, diagnosis and treatment of disease based on the assumption that this approach will lead to a healthy population. The holistic model, on the other hand, stresses that health is not an inflexible state reached only by the elimination of disease, but a dynamic state which must be actively pursued. So the focus here is toward health promoting activities and services in addition to disease screening and intervention procedures. The holistic practitioner emphasizes preventive steps such as health audits, health profiling, disease risk appraisals and patient information. This strategy acquaints the patient with to the future risk of disease as well as the potential for health. Thus the individual becomes actively involved in attempts to attenuate those risks and maximize health potential.

The concept of holistic health is exciting and growing rapidly but some of its idealism is difficult to blend with the realities of the present crisis-intervention, fee-for-service delivery system. Little money has been available for preventive holistic programs and innovative demonstration projects. This situation seems to be changing slowly as major corporations and health insurance plans turn to alternative means of reducing health problems and controlling runaway costs. Holistic medicine would seem to merit more intensive exploration not only for future practitioners but their patients as well.

In addition to the information sources enumerated in Appendix A, Holistic Medicine is a useful newsletter published by the American Holistic Medical Association, 6932 Little River Turnpike, Annandale VA 22003.

Unit 32.2 - 'WELLNESS,' THE NEW CATCHWORD

Charles S. Bryan, MD

Sweeping across our land is what amounts to a wellness movement. Wellness programs are now the pride of many major companies. Employers may soon offer their employees not "sick days," but "well days," to reward health rather than illness. Employers may provide "exercise breaks," as the Japanese have been doing for years, rather than coffee or cigaret breaks. Persons bearing the title "wellness educator" now turn up in all sorts of places, from hospitals to health spas.

Central to the movement is the catchword, "wellness." Although "health" and "wellness" might seem to be synonymous, the wellness educator seek to go beyond the traditional definition of health.

Health usually has been defined as the absence of disease. The apostles of the new wellness movement, however, employ an expanded definition of health. They embrace the World Health Organization's recent definition of health as "a state of complete physical, mental, and social well-being and not merely the absence of disease or infirmity."

Wellness, then, denotes optimum functioning of the individual, not just a normal physical examination combined with some reassuring laboratory studies.

There appear to be three major reasons for the wellness movement. First, it is perceived that physicians have, to some extent, abdicated their roles as "wellness advisers" . . . as about 80 percent of premature death attributed to heart disease, cancer, and stroke are preventable. . . A major way to prevent these deaths is to modify lifestyles but traditional medical training does not prepare physicians to answer . . . questions pertaining to lifestyle.

Second, it is suggested that the growing popularity of the wellness movement may reflect, in part, public hostility toward traditional medicine. Such hostility is, of course, as old as medicine itself.

Finally, and probably most significantly, it is suggested that the popularity of the wellness movement reflects a growing dependency in our society for expertise. If one wishes to take any activity seriously nowadays, it seems necessary to join a club, pay an instructor, subscribe to a magazine, etc. Why should wellness be an exception?

All of the aims of the wellness movement appear to be quite consistent with the aims of traditional medicine. For years, we have advocated lifestyle modification based upon established cause-and-effect risk factors such as obesity, smoking, and dependence on alcohol and drugs. For years, we have conducted research into other risk factors, such as stress, which might be modified. Seen as a supplement to traditional medical examinations, wellness programs appear to be quite admirable. Three potential areas of conflict emerge, however.

First some of the leaders of the wellness movement seem to imply that traditional medicine may be anachronistic. The author of a leading book, for instance, subtitled his work "an alternative to doctors, drugs, and disease."

The second area of potential conflict concerns what is carried out in wellness programs. Are participants sufficiently informed about the trade-offs involved in this or that exercise program? We should remember that establishing the actual benefit from most "lifestyle modifications" may be extremely difficult. Jogging provides an excellent example. One wonders, for instance, how today's avid joggers will view their benefits 20 to 40 years hence as they nurse osteoarthritic knees.

Finally, most importantly, is the qualification of persons identified as wellness educators. . . A cadre of largely untrained persons may proclaim themselves to be wellness educators, advising the public about this or that new diet or exercise program with little appreciation of underlying issues. It does not require an Alvin Toffler to envision that such persons, equipped with a bookshelf of the latest manuals and some do-it-your-self laboratory tests, could replace physicians as the providers of the "annual check-up." . . .

A cherished friend who underwent resection of an early colon carcinoma, found by her internist on a routine physical examination, might still be out there doing her jogging and relaxation exercises under the enthusiastic supervision of a poorly qualified "wellness educator," blissfully unaware of a metastasizing malignancy.

A Mississippi physician wrote recently that "lifestyle is our generation's big medical fad" and argued against the trend toward lifestyle intervention. An increasingly large segment of the public would disagree. So, I believe, would many (perhaps most) of the leaders in our profession. We cannot ignore the basic thesis of the wellness movement; we should support it.

We should assist these persons in two ways. First, we should insist on some standard of certification for wellness educators. We should recognize the potential for the public to be served badly by a new band of self-proclaimed paraprofessionals who are poorly prepared to comprehend the limitations of their methods.

Second, we should work with qualified wellness educators toward sharper definition of those methods of intervention that are beneficial. One long-term follow-up study, for instance, indicated that the patterns of psychological defense mechanisms provide an excellent prediction of illness. But how can these be modified effectively? We should continue to emphasize that the data in many areas are simply too scanty to make dogmatic recommendations.

The wellness movement does not seem to be a novel concept. We have always known that health - in its broadest sense - meant more than the absence of disease. I am reminded especially of the words of Freud who, pressed for a definition of health, responded that health is "the ability to work and to love."

External Readings

32-A-1 Gordon, JS, "Holistic Health Centers," _Journal Holistic Medicine_ 3:72-85 (Spring/Summer 1982).

32-A-2 Dismuke, SE & Miller, ST, "Why Not Share the Secrets of Good Health?" _Journal Holistic Health_ 5:11-19 (1980).

32-A-3 Livingstone, RB, "Specialization in Medicine Need Not Exclude Holistic Health," _Journal Holistic Health_ 5:11-19 (1980).

32-A-4 Polakoff, PL, "Pathology vs Prevention: The Health Promotion Debate," _Occupational Health & Safety_ 51:13-15 (June 1982).

32-A-5 Gymour, C & Stalker, D, "Sounding Board: Engineers, Cranks, Physicians, Magicians," _New England Journal Medicine_ 308:960-63 (April 21, 1983).

32-B-1 Hastings, AC, _et al._ _Health for the Whole Person: The Complete Guide to Holistic Medicine._ Boulder: Westview Press, Inc., 1980. 525 pp.

32-B-2 Vickery, DM. _Life Plan for Your Health._ Menlo Park, CA: Addison-Wesley Pub. Co., 1978. 318 pp.

32-B-3 Weed, LL. _Your Health Care and How to Manage It._ Essex Junction, VT: Essex Publishing Co., 1978. 194 pp.

Section 33 - SEX EDUCATION COUNSELING, THERAPY AND RESEARCH

Meral G. Crane

Meral G. Crane, MA, is Clinical Instructor in Human Sexuality at the The Ohio State University, College of Medicine, Department of Psychiatry. She serves as therapist with sub-specialty in Sex, Marriage and the Family at the OSU Mental Health Clinic and in private practice. She has taught continuing medical education courses for the American College of Obstetricians & Gynecologists in the United States and Mexico. In 1973-75, Ms. Crane directed the Human Sexuality Center at the University of Massachusetts.

This is a specialty area in which a physician can devote full-time, part-time, or intermittent attention as required by patient needs in any practice. A clinician can count on greater success and appreciation if one's medical education and personal growth is expanded to include human sexuality. It is now widely accepted that the physician should be concerned with the whole person. No specialty exists though where sensitivity to sexual matters would not improve the physician's practice.

Consideration of problems of sexuality along with other concerns may also increase the accuracy of medical diagnoses. Dr. Robert Long, Associate Clinical Professor of OB/GYN at the University of Kentucky in Louisville, (author of a syndicated column, "It's OK to Talk About Sex") states that many vague complaints may have their origin in unsatisfactory sexual functioning. He goes on to criticize physician evasion of frank communication regarding sexuality. Physicians often run medical tests, and even when nothing shows up, may repeat the same tests again. Often in frustration they attempt to treat the patient with a tranquilizer, thus delaying accurate diagnosis and appropriate treatment.

Problems of sexuality also often develop secondary to an illness or hospitalization. Once sex is accepted as a natural function, as established by Masters and Johnson following their extensive research in the human sexual functioning, a surgeon, who is about to perform a colostomy will consider the patient's sexual functioning. After consultation with the patient, the surgeon will plan to place the stoma in as strategically proper a spot as possible. Similarily, an internist is required to discuss the possible side effects of hypertension medication, which may include some degree of impotence in the male patient. It is important to consider what sort of sexual activity is safe and feasible at each stage following a heart attack or procedure such as heart surgery. At the very least, such discussion with the physician will inform the patient and his/her partner of options that are available in sexual activity, rather than leaving them in the dark with negative assumptions and fears that produce additional stress. Clearly, with our current knowledge of the physiology of sex, physicians can respond effectively to patients' sexual complaints. Physicians are seldom justified in avoiding the issue with an empathetic sad smile or a pat on the back. Indeed, the uninformed physician, uncomfortable with the discussion of sexuality, can cause harm. The physician carries authority and many patients, who seldom go beyond the mention of their sexual concerns, will accept the physician's comments as fact.

Your involvement as a physician with the problems of sexuality may be at a number of levels. The most basic is that of simply including sexuality as one more variable to be considered in your practice whatever your specialty may be. Given some basic facts and a positive attitude, you may deal directly with such problems as you can and make referrals to someone trained more extensively in this area. When planning to treat a patient, it is important that a longer time period be set aside than is typical in a brief medical appointment. There must be an unhurried exchange of information. Some physicians set aside half a day or even one or two days a week for scheduling patients where sessions last from one-half to one full hour. This is particularly true of family medicine specialists and gynecologists who incorporate sex counseling in their practice.

Others, including some psychiatrists, work in clinics that are specially set up for the treatment of problems of sexuality. These are often located in teaching hospitals and medical schools. An example is the Sex Therapy & Education Program of the New York Hospital-Cornell Medical Center, headed by Dr. Helen Singer Kaplan. Another is the Center for the Study of Sex Education in Medicine at the University of Pennsylvania, founded by Dr. Harold Lief, Professor of Psychiatry and Director, Marriage Council of Philadelphia. Dr. Lief states that the major reward of willingly and competently coping with the problems of sexuality that occur in medical practice "is the knowledge that one has helped to relieve suffering and anguish in a critical and sensitive aspect of a person's life," and that "a person who has overcome a sexual problem is among the most grateful of patients."

Among the most common concerns regarding sexuality that physicians face in practice are the organsmic dysfunction, especially in women, lack of sexual desire in men and women, and impotence and premature ejaculation in men. Working with couples, you may encounter disagreements regarding various styles of pleasuring, coital positions, and frequency of sexual relations. There is often tension over the expression of affection, whether it is done at all, or that it "always" leads to a demand to perform. In addition, such issues as sexual orientation conflicts and the "coming out" of a gay person demand sensitivity to the unique stresses of such problems. Although less common, the physician occasionally encounters such problems as tranvestism, transsexualism, exhibitionism, voyeurism and fetishism.

While some physicians may devote full time or most of their time to sex therapy, the point is not to make sex therapists of all physicians but to ensure that all physicians are competent to identify sexual problems. Some of these are secondary to other illnesses. It is important to be able to distinguish sexual problems even when the patient comes in with complaints that appear to be entirely unrelated. Physicians must be able to discuss matters of sex comfortably so that they may inquire about the patient's sexuality as part of regular history taking.

To begin with, a carefully taken history will help one understand the dynamics of your patient's sexual concerns. First, it is important to obtain a description of the current problem. As much as possible, the physician should stay clear of labels such as "frigid" or "impotent." It is better to speak of "difficulties" in achieving erection or orgasm. Find out how and when it all started and the events that were associated with the beginning of the problem. How has it changed over time? How intense is the problem at the present time? What does the patient think caused and has maintained the problem? What has been done to alleviate the problem thus far and with what results?

I will share with you, in brief summary, a model for the behavioral treatment of sexual problems known as the PLISSIT model. This was developed by Dr. John Hannon, Psychologist at the University of Hawaii Medical School, Human Sexuality Program, in Honolulu. Each letter or pair of letters such as P LI SS IT stands for different levels of approach. P stands for permission, LI for limited information, SS for specific suggestions, and IT for intensive therapy. Simply giving "permission" to do a sexual act can be enough to comfort a patient troubled by guilt or by peer pressures. Giving "limited information" may include the sharing of statistical data regarding sexuality to help the patient to feel more normal and, thus, less anxious. This may include facts about conception, contraception, physical development and more subjective information regarding male and female desires. Making "specific suggestions," with the goal of remedying a sexual problem, may include suggestion of various techniques. For example, "stop-and-go" and the "squeeze" technique might be recommended to a male who is struggling with premature ejaculation. It may be necessary to discuss the importance of communication and preferences for sensate focus exercises with a couple. These three brief therapy modes do, indeed, respond to the majority of the needs of the people concerned.

The first two steps of "permission" and "limited information" may also be used preventively by clinicians. What better person than a pediatrician or a family physician to educate parents and young people, in a matter of fact way, about the facts of the natural unfolding of a young person's sexuality. Positive comments about the developing body, as well as further information about what to expect and the meaning of such developments, go a long way in helping the young person feel self-confident instead of confused, fearful, and anxious. A parent who may not feel comfortable with the topic may be influenced to look upon the child's sexual growth with positive wonder and become more receptive to obtaining further information.

Each level of the PLISSIT Model requires increasing professional training and experience. As a physician, one can select the level at which you wish to practice according to experience and time constraints. When the problem at hand appears to require a level of knowledge and experience for which you are not prepared, a referral must be made. You might consult the Physician's Guide to Sexual Dysfunction Clinics in Sexual Medicine Today, December 1982; or review the National Register of the American Association of Sex Educators, Counselors & Therapists (AASECT) in your area. The AASECT certification requirements are different for sex educators, sex counselors, and sex therapist. Certified members are periodically recertified and must have continuing education credits for renewal. Information regarding certification and program offerings may be obtained from AASECT, 11 Dupont Circle NW, Suite 220, Washington, DC 20036, (telephone: 202-462-1171).

Making a referral to a specialist in the field of human sexuality should be done in a matter-of-fact manner as any other referral. It is important to reassure the patient that his/her condition is not so hopeless that you cannot take care of it yourself, but that persons with special training may be able to help more effectively. When the patient is in a relationship with another person, it may be wise to refer to a specialist who also has training in the dynamics of relationships along with the specialty of human sexuality. Dr. Harold Lief only refers patients to sex therapists who are members of the American Association of Marriage & Family Therapists. This professional association has stringent requirements for training and supervision as a condition for membership. Dr. Lief feels that physicians can be sex educators and counselors but that they should not serve as sex therapists unless special training is acquired in marital therapy and psychotherapy.

General training in human sexuality can be obtained in special institutes and through personal commitment to keep up with the literature. In the past two decades, many excellent books and periodicals have appeared dealing with current research on human sexuality, treatment, and follow-up. To date, there is one degree-granting, professional graduate school concentrating on human sexuality, the Institute for Advanced Study of Human Sexuality in San Francisco. This Institute provides courses open to professionals interested in continuing education as well as a full graduate program for those seeking a degree. There are a few post-doctoral externships available, as well, at the Masters and Johnson Institute in St. Louis, MO. This facility also provides a series of basic and advanced courses for professionals who wish to develop a sub-specialty in the treatment of the problems of sexuality. In addition, AASECT as well as many of the district offices of this Association, provide basic and advanced courses that count toward certification.

There are few specialties, indeed, that can provide such rich and rewarding opportunities for clinical practice, teaching, and research as well as for personal growth. Human sexuality offers an opportunity for physicians to collaborate with educators, counselors, therapists and a variety of behavioral and health science specialties. Dr. Jon Meyer, Associate Professor of Psychiatry and Director, Sexual Behavior Consultation Unit at Johns Hopkins, says of human sexuality: "It is rare to have a sub-specialty in psychiatry and medicine which has such a diverse and interesting patient group, studies a problem so fundamental to human development, has such strong historical roots, and partakes so fully in the fundamental controversies of psychological medicine. It is a specialty in breadt' and depth."

External Readings

33-A-1   "Special Problems of Couples," In: The American Medical Association Family Medical Guide, (Kunz, JRM, ed.). New York: Random House, 1982. pp. 606-15.

33-A-2   Renshaw, DC, "Sexology," Journal American Medical Association 254: 2343-45 (October 25, 1985).

33-A-3   "Sexual Dysfunction: Sorting Out the Body-Mind Mix," Medical World News 22:56-71 (October 12, 1981).

33-A-4   Lewis, D. "The Gynecologic Consideration of the Sexual Act," Journal American Medicine Association 250:222-27 (July 8, 1983).

33-A-5   "When Sex is a Headache," Emergency Medicine. 14:17-80 (January 30, 1982).

33-A-6   Psychiatric Annals 12:670-95 (July 1982).

33-B-1   Kaplan, HS. The New Sex Therapy, Vol. II. New York: Brunner/Muzek, 1979. 237 pp.

33-B-2   Offit, AK. Night Thoughts: Reflections of a Sex Therapist. New York: Congdon & Lattes, 1981. 256 pp.

33-B-3   Szasz, T. Sex: Facts, Frauds and Follies. Oxford: Blackwell, 1981. 195 pp.

33-B-4   Glick, ID & Kessler, DR Marital & Family Therapy. New York: Grune & Stratton, 1980. 380 pp.

33-B-5   Lief, HI (ed.). Sexual Problems in Medical Practice. Chicago: American Medical Association, 1982. 400 pp.

Chapter IV

OPPORTUNITIES FOR DOCTORS IN NON-CLINICAL ROLES

This chapter furnishes unique information on career opportunities for medical school graduates where employment is significantly removed from the diagnosis and treatment of individual patients.

Physicians with a primary interest in patient care, however, may also benefit by reviewing this section carefully. During or after completing medical school, your views may change concerning the attractiveness of medical practice. Many non-clinicians apparently entered their current job after some prior experience in patient care. Indeed, a number of organizations, such as the U.S. Air Force, encourage physicians with administrative duties to maintain a practice on a regular but part-time basis. In addition, certain positions, especially those in occupational medicine and public health, may also involve clinical activities. Thus the material below can be examined to suggest opportunities for dual careers as well.

Although more than 50,000 physicians function in a variety of non-clinical roles, this single statistic provides an inadequate basis for guiding career planning efforts. The diversity of possible options is suggested in Table IV-1 which enumerates job titles currently or recently held by medical school graduates outside the clinical model. Thirteen major categories provide a framework for examining employment in areas such as the planning, management and evaluation of health care services, the production of pharmaceutical products, and the provision of supportive services in allied fields covering education,[1] publishing and research. By investigating career choices in several non-clinical areas, doctors may not only find a constructive outlet for their professional/personal goals but help to alleviate a possible social problem as well.

All job titles depict positions that differ significantly from those of traditional medical practice. There are few studies, however, that examine the roles of physicians as non-clinicians, their career pathways, and employment prospects for the future. One investigation,

---

[1] " . . . about 1,000 new faculty positions are available each year and about 2,000 additional positions from attrition and turnover." Wyngaarden, JB, "Careers in Academic Medicine," In: Academic Medicine: Present and Future. Bowers, JZ and King, EE (eds.). North Tarrytown, NY: Rockefeller Archive Center, 1983. p. 136.

(Editors note: The number of new positions may be expected to fall sharply.)

conducted in 1979, estimated that 12,000 physicians were employed as administrators (the largest being government where some 6,000 were employed at the state/local level and 1,200 at the federal level); 15,000 as researchers, 8,000 as faculty members at colleges and universities; and another 2,000 as staff for insurance companies and legal firms.

In order to compile information on medical school graduates functioning as non-clinicians, numerous periodicals, newsletters, directories and related references were examined. The search generated more than 900 job titles where at least 80 percent of the physician's time was probably devoted to duties other than direct patient care. Since the source material did not cover the entire universe, or purport to be representative, our examples should be approached as guideposts for career exploration and not as a road map that specifies every choice that may appear on your journey. Moreover, additional career options may be found as doctors create their own businesses and assume positions never held previously by a physician.

Specific limitations of your resource should be kept in mind. First, certain segments manifest a bias toward executive positions. In such instances, additional inquiry will be required to determine whether other physicians may be employed at subordinated levels within the same orgainzation. Further, job titles were compiled according to the nomenclature employed most frequently. Thus, in several instances, an actual title may differ slightly from the one listed. Despite editorial effort to control redundancy, duplication of titles with similar responsibilities also may be found.

While a majority of titles usually signify a single employment possibility, some such as "Director, State Hospital" may represent multiple positions. In cases where minimum numbers could be established, a figure is reported as a suffix to the entry, viz., "Publishing, Editor (33)." Moreover, classification decisions were made to facilitate identification of primary areas related to conducting a job search. Some job titles, however, may apply to areas other than the one actually assigned.

Finally, certain positions may require special experience and/or additional training beyond the standard medical residency program. For example, a master's degree in Public Health or Business Administration may be mandated by some employers. In addition, a dual doctorate (MD/PhD) may be preferred if one expects to compete effectively for some posts in teaching or research.

With the above background in mind, Table IV-1 can be approached as a foundation for identifying alternatives to clinical practice and even seeking interesting frontiers. While assessing such options, your undergraduate major may provide one guideline to aid in the selection process.

TABLE IV-1

Non-Practitioner Positions Held by Medical School Graduates

BUSINESS/INDUSTRY

Advertising & Communications

Chairman, Medicine Department
Director of Medical Affairs
Director of Medical & Legal Affairs
Exec. VP
Exec. VP for Medical Affairs, HSN
Medical Director (8)
President
Project Director
Sr. VP, Director of Medical & Scientific
  Affairs
Sr. VP, Group Medical Doctor
Sr. VP & Director of Medical Services
Sr. VP & Medical Director
VP & Associate Medical Director
VP, Director of Medical Affairs
VP for Medical Affairs, Lifetime

Pharmaceutical Manufacturing[1]

Assistant VP & Director of Professional &
  Marketing Services
Associate Director of Medical Research
Associate Director of Medical Services
Associate Medical Director
Chairman of the Board
Chairman of the Board and President
Clinical Monitor, Research & Development
  Division, Corporate VP
Director
  Clinical Pharmacology
  Government Medical Affairs
  Medical & Clinical Investigation
  Medical Research, Marketed Products,
    Clinical Investigation Division
  New Product Planning (or Development)
  Product Development
  Professional Communications

Pharmaceutical Manufacturing (continued)

  Professional Services
  Regulatory Affairs
Director of CNS Clinical Research
Director of Clinical Research
Director of Development
Director of Field Sales Administration
Director of Medical Affairs (or Services)
Exec. Director, Biology Research
Exec. Director, Clinical Pharmacology
Exec. Director, Medical Division
Exec. Director, Virus & Cell Biology
Exec. VP
Exec. VP of Pharmaceutical R & D,
  Quality Control and Medical Activities
Exec. VP Research & Development
Group Manager, Clinical, Epidemiology &
  Biostatistics
Group Product Manager
Group Research Manager, Medical Affairs
Group VP
Head, Department of Clinical Research
Head, Department of Product Surveillance &
  Epidemiology
International Medical Liaison
Manager, Business Development, Surgical
  Products Division
Manager, Medical Investigation & Field
  Surveillance
Medical Director, Corporate Regulatory
  Affairs
Medical Director, Hospital Products
  Division
President (10)
President, Health Care Group
President, Research Laboratories
Research Director
Scientific Director
Sr. Director, Clinical Pharmacology
  - Domestic

---

[1] Also see: Jefferis, JE, "The Pharmaceutical Industry: A Physician's Role," Medical Student 9:16-18 (May 1983).

Pharmaceutical Manufacturing (continued)

Sr. Director, Clinical Pharmacology, Int.
Sr. Exec. VP
Sr. Vice President
Sr. VP, Researching & Development
Sr. VP, Scientific Affairs
VP & Medical Director, Corporate
  Regulatory Affairs
VP & Head, Molecular Biology Department
VP & Medical Director
VP & Medical Director - Worldwide
Vice President
  Anti-Cancer Research
  Clinical Affairs (or, Clinical Research)
  Corporation Medical & Scientific Affairs
  Dermatology, Pharmaceutical R & D Div.
  External Affairs
  Medical (or Medical Affairs)
  Medical and Research & Development
  Medical & Scientific Affairs
  Medical Research
  Medical Services
  New Product Development
  Regulatory Affairs
  Regulatory & Technical Affairs
  Research
  Research & Scientific Affairs

Publishing

Chairman, Editorial Board
Chairman and Chief Exec. Officer, Times
  Mirror Corp.
Chairman and Publisher
Director, Scientific Publication Division
Editor (33). Also Assistant; Book Review;
  Co-editor; Corresponding; Cover; Deputy;
  Managing; Medical; Senior
Editorial Director (11)
Editor-in-Chief; Chief Editor (30)
Editorial Writer
Exec. Director
International Editor
International Publisher
Medical Correspondent, NY Times
President
President (publishers' representative)
Publisher (newsletter on investment advice)
Publisher
Publishing Director & Editor

Other

Consultant (unspecified)
Consultant, Drug Regulatory Affairs
Corporate Manager of Environmental Health,
  IBM Corp.
Director, Employee Health & Safety (large
  textile manufacturer)
Director, Health Care Development
  (diversified conglomerate)
Director, Health Care Practice (large
  accounting firm)
Director, Medical Affairs (large chemical
  company)
Exec. Director, Institute for Health
  Planning
Exec. President & Medical Director,
  International Medical Services, Inc.
Medical Admin. (large manufacturing firm)
Medical Director (many manufacturing firms)
Medical Director (life insur. co.) (700)
Medical Director, Legislative & Regulatory
  Health Affairs (natural resources co.)

President, Hospital Corporation of America
President, LA Medical Mutual Ins.
President (major oil company)
President (many life insurance companies)
President, Medical Coding Systems, Inc.
President, Oxford Research International
President, Simborg Systems Corp.
President, (personnel search firm)
Regional Director, Life Extension Institute
Sr. VP, Hyatt Medical Management Services
Specialist, Health Services Evaluation
  (systems consulting company)
VP, Advanced Business Development (large
  medical equipment & supply company)
VP, R & D (computer software firm)

CERTIFICATION AND ACCREDITATION

Joint Commission on Accreditation of Healthcare Organizations

Assistant VP
President
VP for Accreditation
VP for Education
VP for External Affairs

CERTIFICATION AND ACCREDITATION (continued)

National Board of Medical Examiners

President and Director
Sr. Medical Evaluation Officer (3)
VP for Evaluation Programs

Chief Exec. Officer, American Board ....(10)
VP, Federation of State Medical Boards

CHARITABLE FOUNDATION/VOLUNTARY HEALTH ORG.

Deputy Director, Division of Health
  Sciences, Rockefeller Foundation
Director of Medical Services, National
  Foundation for Infantile Paralysis
Exec. Director, National Interagency
  Council on Smoking & Health (NYC)
Exec. VP (2)
President (charitable foundation) (3)
President (voluntary health organization)

Project Director, Inter-Society Commission
  for Heart Disease Resources
Scientific Director, The National
  Foundation for Cancer Research

CHARITABLE FOUNDATION/VOLUNTARY HEALTH ORG.
(continued)

Sr. VP for Research, Am. Cancer Society
Special Advisor to the President
  (charitable foundation)
VP, The Commonwealth Fund

EDUCATION

Medical School - Officials & Administrative Staff (by functional area)[1]

Academic Affairs
  Association Dean (35)
  Dean
  Vice-Chancellor
Academic & Research Affairs - Assoc. Dean
Administration - Asst/Assoc Dean for (9)
Admissions - Asst./Assoc. Dean; Chairman
  or Director (32)
Admissions & Curriculum - Associate Dean
Affiliated Programs - Associate Dean (3)
Allied Health Professional Training -
  Assistant/Associate Dean/Director (5)
Alumni Affairs - Asst. Dean/VP, or Director
Alumni Affairs & CME Coordinator

---

[1] Invaluable insights about an administrative career in academia are provided by:

Petersdorf, RG & Wilson MP, "The Four Horsemen of the Apocalypse: Study of Academic Medical Center Governance," Journal American Medical Association 247:1153-61 (February 26, 1982).

Geyman JP, "Career Tracks in Academic Family Medicine: Issues and Approaches," Journal Family Practice 14:911-17 (May 1982).

Petersdorf, RG, "Academic Medicine: No Longer Threadbare or Genteel," New England Journal Medicine 304:841-43 (April 2, 1981).

"Symposim on the Academic Physician: An Endangered Species," Bulletin New York Academy Medicine 57:415-502 (July-August 1981).

Mattern, WD, et al., "The Attending Physician as Teacher," New England Journal Medicine 308:1129-32 (May 12, 1983).

"Medical Education in the United States," Journal American Medicine Association (final issue in September each year).

Medical School - Officials & Administrative Staff (by functional area) (continued)

Ambulatory Affairs - Associate Dean (2)
Area Health Education Center - Assoc. Dean
Basic Sciences - Assistant/Associate
    Dean/Coordinator (9)
B.A.-M.D. Programs - Assistant Dean
Biomedical Graduate Studies - Assoc. Dean
Brookhaven National Lab. - Clinical Dean
CEO (Dean, President, etc.) (113)
Clinical Affairs - Asst. Dean; or Dean (47)
Continuing Medical Education - Assistant
    or Associate Dean (74); Coordinator or
    Director (4)
Council on Health Programs - Chairman
Curriculum - Asst./Assoc. Dean (17)
Development - Associate Dean
Education - Assistant Dean
Extended Medical Programs - Assoc. Dean (2)
Extramural Affairs - Asst./Assoc. Dean (3)
Faculty Affairs - Associate Dean
Faculty Council - Chairman

Geriatric Medicine - Associate Dean
Gerontology & Community Med./Assoc. Dean
Government Affairs - Assistant Dean
Graduate Medical Education - Asst./Assoc.
    Dean (11)
Graduate & Continuing Medical Education -
    Associate Dean
Health Affairs - Associate Provost & Dean
Hospital Affairs (Program) - Asst./Assoc.
    Dean (52)
Human Subjects Protection - Asst. Dean (2)
Interinstitutional Programs - Associate
    Dean (3)
International Programs - Associate Dean or
    Chairman (3)
Local Med. Center - Asst./Assoc. Dean (22)
Medical Director of Faculty Practice Plan
    - Associate Dean
Medical Education - Associate Dean
Medical Education & Curr. - Assoc. Dean
Minority Affairs - Assistant/Associate
    Dean/Coordinator (7)
Naval Regional Medical Center - Assoc. Dean
Patient Care - Associate Dean
Planning - Assistant Dean
Planning & Development - Assist. to the VP/
    Associate Dean (2)

Medical School - Officials & Administrative Staff (by functional area) (continued)

Planning & Operations - Associate Dean
Postdoctoral Programs - Assoc.
    Dean/Director
Postdoctoral Programs & Faculty Development
    - Assistant Dean
Preprofessional Education - Associate Dean
Public Health - Associate Dean
Publications - Head, Section on
Research - Assistant or Associate Dean (11)
Research Development (Neuroscience) -
    Associate Dean
Residency Affairs - Coordinator
Rural Health - Assistant Dean
Rural Health Education - Associate Dean
Scientific Affairs - Associate Dean
Special Projects - Asst/Assoc. Dean (5)
Student Affairs - Asst/Assoc. Dean (71)
Student Affairs & Admin. - Assoc. Dean
Student Affairs & Alumni Affairs -
    Associate (2)
Student & Curriculum Affairs - Associate
    Dean (11)
Student & Graduate Medical Affairs - Senior
    Associate Dean
Surgical Sciences & Services - Assoc. Dean
Undergraduate Medical Education -
    Assistant/Deputy Dean
VA Medical Center - Asst./Assoc. Dean (30)
VA Research - Assistant Dean
Veterans Affairs - Asst./Assoc. Dean (13)

Medical School - Officials & Administrative Staff (by title)

Academic Adv .or
Assistant Dean (2)
    Area Health Education Center (5)
    for Air Force Affairs
    for Ed. Programs, University Hospital (2)
    for a given class in Medical School (3)
    for Research, Budget, & Fiscal Affairs
Assistant to the Dean
Assistant to the Vice-Chancellor for
    Medical Affairs
Associate/Executive/Deputy Dean (53)
Associate Dean - Community Services
Associate Dean - Health Services
Assoc Dean/Coord. - Satellite Campuses (8)

Medical School - Officials & Administrative Staff (by title) (continued)

Associate Director
  Internal Director
  Medical & Laboratory Specialization
  Research Training & Degree Programs
Dean for Medical Services
Dean, School of Basic Medical Science
Director
  Ambulatory Education Programs
  Cancer Center (2)
  Center for Educational Resources
  Center for Health Services & Policy Res.
  Community Health Centers
  CME & Audio-Visual Coordinator
  Health Policy & Management, Division of
    Environmental Sciences Laboratory
  Institute for Health Policy Studies
  Institute for Medical Humanities
  Medical Center
  Medical Scientist Training Program
  Program in Behavioral Science, School
    of Biomedical Education
  Program in Health Services Evaluation
  Program in History of Medicine
  Research in Medical Education, Division
  Respiratory Studies, Division of
  Sports Medicine Center
  The Marine Biomedical Institute
  University (Student) Health Services (4)
President of the Medical Center &
  Vice-Chancellor for Medical Affairs
Special Assistant to the Dean
Special Assistant to the Dean, Binational
  Health Programs (2)
Vice-Chancellor, Health Sciences & Dean

Medical School - Basic Science Unit

(Department/Division/Section with Chair held by M.D. In many of these units, other faculty positions are also held by M.D.'s.)[1]

Anatomy
Biological Chemistry
Biomedical Engineering

Medical School - Basic Science Unit (cont.)

Biometry
Blood Bank Transfusion
Cell Biology
Center for Brain Research
Clinical Chemistry
Community Medicine

Diagnostic Nuclear Medicine
Environmental Health
Epidemiology & International Health
Genetics (Human Genetics)
Health Computer Sciences
History of Medicine (Health Sciences)
Immunology/Microbiology
Laboratory Hematology

Medical Biology
Medical Biophysics & Computing
Medical Physics (Professor of)
Medical Statistics & Epidemiology
Microbiology
Molecular Biophysics & Biochemistry
Neuroanatomy
Neurobiology
Neuroscience

Pathology
  Autopsy Service
  Clinical
  Cytopathology
  Experimental Pathology
  Forensic Medicine
  Immunopathology
  Laboratory Medicine
  Medical Technology
  Neuro-pathology
  Surgical Pathology

Pharmacology
  Clinical Pharmacology
  Laboratory of Applied Pharmacokinetics
  Molecular Pharmacology
  Pharmacology & Nutrition
  Pharmacology & Therapeutics
  Psychopharmacology

---

[1] Faculty in some basic sciences, as well as the clinical sciences, follow dual careers when they teach students and treat patients. Moreover, many often engage in research.

Medical School - Basic Science Unit (cont.)

Physiology
Physiology & Biophysics
Preventive Medicine & Biometrics
Public Health
Radiation Biology & Biophysics
Regional Laboratory Services
Social Medicine & Health Policy
Tropical Medicine & Medical
  Microbiology

Positions in Health Sciences but External to the Medical School

College of Chiropractic

Asst. Prof. Basic & Clinical Science
Assistant Professor of Clinical Science
Associate Professor of Basic Science &
  Clinical Science

School of Pharmacy

Asst. Clinical Prof. of Medical Science
Associate Prof. of Clinical Pharmacy (15)
Associate Prof. of Human Pathology (2)
Dean and Professor of Physiology
Research Assist. Professor of Pharmacology

School of Public Health

Assoc. Prof., Health Policy & Admin.
Dean (or Associate, or Assistant)
Dir., Ctr. for Analysis of Health Practices
Director, Community Health Sciences
Director, Inst. for Health Research
Professor of Health Administration
Professor of Medical Care Organization
Res. Prof. of Public Health Administration
  & Chairman, Dept. of Field Training

Faculty Positions External to the Health Sciences[1]

Associate Professor of Psychiatry &
  Religion, Yale Divinity School

Faculty Positions External to the Health Sciences (continued)

Director of Sport Medicine, U.S. Sport
  Academy
Professor, J.F. Kennedy School of
  Government, Harvard University
Research Associate, Conservation of Human
  Resources Program, Columbia University
Visit. Assoc. Prof. of Law, NYU Law School

University Officer

Act. Coordinator, Minority Student Affairs
Assistant Dean for Long-Range Planning
Assistant Vice Chancellor for VA Affairs
Asst/Assoc. VP for Health (or Med.) Affairs
Assistant VP for Interinstitutional Affairs
Assistant VP for Affiliated Institutions

Chairman, Board of Governors, Mayo Clinic
Chancellor (8)
Consultant - to Provost or Chancellor (2)

Director, Center for Human Growth &
  Development
Director, Continuing Health Professional
  Education, Medical Center
Director of the Medical Center
Dean

Health Program Advisor
President (6)
Senior Vice President (2)
Special Assistant to the President

Vice Chancellor for Academic Affairs
Vice Chancellor for Health Affairs (2)
Vice Chancellor for Health Affairs, Ohio
  Board of Regents
Vice President (3)
  for Academic Affairs
  for Clinical Affairs
  for Health Affairs (Health Sciences/
    Medical Affairs/Medical Center) (34)
  for Hospital Affairs
  for Interinstitutional Affairs

---

[1] One study covering the period 1980-81 found more than 100 physicians employed in academia outside the medical school.

GOVERNMENT - FEDERAL

Congress

Asst. Dir., Office of Technology Assessment
Congressional Science Fellow (sponsored by
  Federation of American Societies for
  Experimental Biology)
Counsel, Subcommittee on Health &
  Enviroment, Committee on Energy &
  Commerce, U.S. House of Representatives
Exec. Director, Prospective Assessment
  Commission, OTA
Manager of Health Program Analysis, OTA
Member, U.S. House of Representatives

Professional Staff Member
  Committee on Energy & Commerce, House
  Committee on Interstate & Foreign
    Commerce, House
Project Director, Gentics, OTA
Staff Director, Sub-Committee on Health &
  Science Research, Senate

Department of Defense - Staff

Assistant Secretary of Defense (Health
  Affairs)
Dean, School of Medicine, United States
  University of the Health Sciences
Deputy Assistant Secretary of Defense for
  Health Resources & Programs
Director, Office of Civilian Health &
  Medical Programs Uniformed Services
Special Assistant for Medical Readiness
Special Asst. for Professional Activities

Department of Defense - US Air Force

Administrative Positions

Aerospace Medical Division Commander
Aerospace Medical Research Laboratory
Air Force Med. Service Center Commander
Air Force Inspection & Safety Command (7)
Major Command Surgeons (13)
Military Enlistment Processing Command
OCHAMPUS (Civilian Health Program)
Office of Secretary of Defense (Health
  Affairs)
Office of the Surgeon General (6)

Administrative Positions (continued)

Tri-Service Medical Information Systems
  Program Office
USAF School of Aerospace Med. Commander

Consultant Positions

Air Force Medical Service Center (10)
Major Command Surgeon Offices (21)

Research & Development Positions

Aerospace Medical Research Laboratory (7)
Aeronautical Systems Division
Armed Forces Radiological Research
Armed Forces Institute of Pathology

Teaching Positions

School of Health Care Sciences (4)
Uniformed Services University of Health
  Sciences (8)
USAF School of Aerospace Medicine (5)

Other Positions

Air Force Manpower & Personnel Center
  Physical Evaluation Board (8)
Air Force Board for Correction of Military
  Records (2)
Aerospace Medical Division (AMD), Clinical
  Sciences Division (22)
AMD Epidemiology Division (2)
AMD Crew Technology Division (2)
AMD Hyperbaric Medicine Division (3)
AMD Occupational & Envir. Health Lab.
DoD Medical Examination Review Board (2)

Department of Defense - US Army

Chief of Training & Education, Aeromedical
  Activity, Ft. Rucker, AL

Department of Defense - US Navy

Commanding Officer
  National Naval Medical Center
  Naval Hospital (3)
  Naval Aerospace Medical Institute
  Naval Aerospace Medical Research Lab

Department of Defense - US Navy (continued)

Naval Air Regional Medical Center
Naval Biodynamics Laboratory
Naval Environmental Health Center
Naval Regional Medical Center (21)
Naval Medical Research Institute
Naval Medical Research Unit, Cairo, EG
Naval Submarine Medical Research Lab

Bureau of Medicine & Surgery

Assistant Chief for Health Care Programs
Assistant Chief for Planning & Resources
Assist. Chief for Professional Development
Deputy Director, Medical Corps Division
Deputy Surgeon General, Deputy Chief
Director, Contingency Planning Division
Director, Education & Training Division
Director, Medical Corps Division
Director, Program Operations Division
Officer-in-charge, Naval Undersea Medical
  Institute
Inspector General, Medical
Surgeon General/Chief

Other Staff Positions[1]

Assistant for Medical Corps Officer,
  Distribution/Placement, Naval Military
  Personnel Command
Assistant for Medical Corps Officer/Warrant
  Officer Distribution/Placement, Naval
  Military Personnel Command
Director, Med. Programs, Headquarters, USMC
Director, Professional Activities, Office
  of the Secretary of Defense
Fleet Med. Officer, Comd., Train. Command
Force Surgeon, Headquarters, Fleet Marine
  Force (2)
Head, Prof. Div., Chief of Naval Operations
Primary Care Medical Officer, Headquarters
  Fleet Marine Force
Staff Dir., Defense Medical Material Board
Staff Medical Officer/Medical Advisor,
  Headquarters, USMC

Other Staff Positions (continued)

Staff Medical Officer/Fleet Surgeon,
  Commander in Chief, Pacific Fleet
Staff Medical Officer, London, England

Department of Health & Human Services

Secretary

Office of Assistant Secretary for Planning & Evaluation

Assistant Sec. for Planning & Evaluation
Deputy Asst. Sec. for Planning & Evaluation

Office of Assistant Secretary for Health: Public Health Service

Assistant Secretary for Health
Deputy Asst. Sec. Disease Prevention
Deputy Assistant Secretary for Health
Deputy Asst. Sec. for International Health
Deputy Asst. Sec. for Population Affairs
Director
  Health Planning
  National Immunication Initiative Program
  Office of Adolescent Pregancy Program
  Office of Child Health Affairs
  Office of Health Info. & Health Promotion
  Office of Health Practice Assessment
  Office of Health Technology
  Office of International Health
  Office of Smoking and Health
  Special Health Initiatives
Science, Advisor, Deputy Asst. Sec. for
  Health Policy, Research & Statistics
Special Assistant for External Affairs
Special Assistant for the Asst. Sec. (3)
Surgeon General

National Center for Health Services Research

Director
Associate Deputy Director for Medical &
  Scientific Affairs
Associate Director, Professional Services

---

[1] Other billets, such as in Health Sciences Education & Training, or Medical Research, may be filled by physicians or any qualified Medical Department Officer.

National Center for HSR (continued)

Director, Division of Extramural Research
Director, Division of Intramural Research
Executive Secretary, Health Care Technology
  Study Section
Exec. Sec., Health Services Research Review

National Center for Health Statistics

Director
Director, Health Examination Statistics
Medical Advisor
Nutrition Advisor

Alcohol, Drug Abuse & Mental Health Administration

Administrator
Assistant Administrator for Agency Goals

National Institute of Mental Health

Director
Director, The Staff College
Deputy Director, NIMH
Special Assistant to the Director

Director, of Extramural Project Review
Deputy, Extramural Project Review
Chief, Applied & Social Project Review
  Branch
Chief, Basic Research Review Branch
Chief, Clin. & Ser. Develop. Review Branch
Chief, Clin. Manpower Develop. Review Br.
Chief, Research Development Review Branch
Director, Div. of Biometry & Epidemiology
Chief, Demography & Epidemiology Branch

Director, Div. of Extramural Res. Programs
Deputy Director, Division of Extramural
  Research Programs
Chief, Research Scientist Develop. Section
Chief, Small Grants Section
Chief, Clinical Research Branch
Chief, Center for Studies of Schizophrenia
Chief, Psychopharmacology Research Branch
Director, Div. of Manpower & Training
Associate Director of Research Training,
  Division of Manpower & Training
Chief, Psychiatry Education Branch

National Institute of Mental Health (cont.)

Chief, Center for State Mental Health
  Manpower Development
Training Specialist

Director, Div. Mental Health Programs
  Deputy Director
  Associate Director
  Chief, Community Mental Health Services
    Support
  Chief, Mental Health Services Support
  Chief, Mental Health Study Center
Director, Div. Sp. Mental Health Programs
  Deputy Director
  Chief, Center for Minority Group Mental
    Health Programs
  Chief, Center for Studies of Mental
    Health of the Aging
  Chief, Disaster Assistance & Emergency
    Mental Health Section
  Chief, National Center Prevention &
    Control of Rape

Centers for Disease Control (Alanta, GA)

Director
Assistant Director for International Health
Asst. Director for Public Health Practice
Assistant Director for Science
Assistant Director, Interagency Affairs
Assistant Director/Washington

Director, Bureau of Epidemiology
Director, Bureau of Laboratories
Director, Bureau of Smallpox Eradication
Director, Bureau of Training
Director, Bureau of Tropical Diseases
  Chief, Vector Biology & Control Division

Director, National Institute of
  Occupational Safety & Health

  Assistant to the Director
  Director, Office of Extramural
    Coordination & Special Projects
  Director, Division of Respiratory Disease
    Studies
  Director, Division of Safety Research
  Director, Division of Criteria
    Documentation & Standards Development

Centers for Disease Control (continued)

Director, Division of Surveillance Hazard
Evaluations & Field Studies
Director, Division of Biomedical and
Behavioral Sciences
Director, Division of Training & Manpower
Development
Medical Officer, Office of Program
Planning & Evaluation

Director, Nutrition Division, Center for
Health Promotion & Education

Food & Drug Administration

Commissioner
Deputy Commissioner

Associate Commissioner for Health Affairs
Director, Medical Review Staff
Associate Commissioner for Medical Affairs
Deputy Associate Commissioner for Medical
Affairs
Associate Commissioner for Science
Assistant Commissioner for Professional &
Consumer Programs
Director, Orphan Products Development
Medical Officer, International Affairs

Center for Drugs & Biologics

Director
Scientific Director

Office of Drug Standards

Director

Deputy Director-Medical Affairs
Deputy Assoc. Director for Drug Monographs

Director, Anti-Infective Products Divsion
Director, Cardio-Renal Products Division
Director, Surgical-Dental Products Division
Director, Metabolism and Endocrine Division
Director, Neuropharmacological Products
Division
Director, Oncology & Radiopharmaceutical
Products Division

Office of Drugs

Deputy Director
Director, Division of Drug Use Experience

Office of Drug Review & Investigation

Director, Div. of Scientific Investigations
Chief, Clinical Investigation Branch
Chief, Non-Clinical Labs. Studies Branch

Center for Devices & Radiological Health

Director, Office of Health Affairs

Office of Biologics

Director
Director, Division of Bacterial Products
Director, Division of Biologics Evaluation
Director, Div. of Blood & Blood Products
Director, Div. of Product Quality Control
Director, Division of Virology

Office of Medical Devices

Assoc. Director for Health Affairs

Office of Radiological Health

Director, Office of Health Affairs

Bureau of Foods

Associate Director for Sciences, Division
of Pathology
Associate Director for Nutrition & Consumer
Sciences
Special Assistant for Medical Affairs

Health Resources & Services Administration

Director, Office of Graduate Medical Ed.

Bureau of Health Professions

Deputy Director
Deputy Director, Division of Associated
Health Professions

Bureau of Health Professions (continued)

Deputy Director, Division of Health
Professions Training Support
Deputy Director, Division of Health
Professions Analysis
Director, Division of Medicine

Bureau of Health Planning

Medical Advisor

Health Services Administration

Administrator
Special Assistant to the Administrator

Bureau of Health Care Delivery

Director

Associate Bureau Director, Program for
Maternal & Child Health
Chief, Rehabilitative Services Branch
Chief, Genetic Disease Services Branch
Chief, Research & Training Services Branch
Associate Bureau Director, Program Office
for Community Health Centers
Associate Bureau Director, Program Office
for National Health Service Corps
Chief, Professional Affairs Branch
Director, National Health Service Corps

Indian Health Service

Director
Deputy Director

Bureau of Medical Services

Director
Deputy Director
Director, Bureau Prisons Medical Programs
Deputy Director
Director, Division of Hospitals & Clinics
Medical Director, Office of Workers'
Compensation Programs
Director, Division of Federal Employee
Occupational Health
Director, Division of Coast Guard Medical
Services

National Institutes of Health

Director
Deputy Director
Special Assistant to the Director

Director
Division of Computer Research & Tech.
Division of Research Grants
Division of Research Resources
Division of Research Services
Ethics Advisory Board
Fogarty International Center
NIH Clinical Center
Office of Medical Application of Research
Office for Protection from Research Risks
Director
Lister Hill National Center for
Biomedical Communications
National Cancer Institute
National Eye Institute
National Heart, Lung and Blood Institute
National Institute of Allergy &
Infectious Diseases
National Institute of Arthritis,
Metabolism & Digestive Diseases
National Institute of Child Health &
Human Development
National Institute of Environmental
Health Sciences
National Institute of General Medical
Sciences
National Institute of Neurological &
Communicative Disorders & Stroke
National Institute on Aging
National Library of Medicine

Health Care Financing Administration

Associate Administrator for Management &
Support Services
Deputy Director, Office of PSRO, Bureau of
Health Stds. & Quality
Director, Office of Professional &
Scientific Affairs, Office of the
Administrator
Director, Office of Child Health, Office of
Special Programs Deputy Director
Director, Bureau of Health Standards &
Quality
Senior Health Analyst, Office of Research

Rehabilitation Services Administation

Director, Medical Affairs

Social Security Administration

Special Assistant, Office of Program Policy
& Analysis

Regional Offices

Director, Service Delivery Assessment
Director, US Public Health Service Hospital
PSRO Representative
Regional Health Administrator, PHS (10)
Associate Director, Professional Services,
NCHSR

Department of State

Deputy Asst. Secretary, Medical Services
Deputy Medical Director
Asst. Medical Director, Environ. Health
Asst. Medical Director, Health Care Program
Asst. Medical Dir., Mental Health Program
Chairman, Tropical Medicine
Director, Domes Medical Program
Director, Overseas Medical Program
Medical Director, US Foreign Service

Agency for International Development[1]

Acting Director, Office of Health, Bureau
for Science & Technology
Chief, Health/Nutrition Division, Bureau of
Africa
Health Officer, USAID
Health & Nutrition Officer, USAID
Medical Officer
Chief, Health, Population and Nutrition
Division, Bureau for Asia
Chief, Health/Population/Nutrition, USAID
Mission
Chief, Health & Family Planning Division,
Chief, Office of Health & Nutrition, USAID

Agency for International Development (cont.)

Health Development Officer, USAID Mission
Population Officer
Deputy Director, Office of Health, Bureau
for Science & Technology

Tropical Disease Office
Chief, Health Services Division
Deputy Director, Office of Population,
Bureau for Science & Epidemiology

Medical Officer
Public Health Physician
Director for Health & Population, Bureau
for Science & Technology

Veterans Administration - Central Office

Administrator

Chief Medical Director
Assistant Chairman, Medical Director
Assistant Deputy, Chief Medical Director
Associate Deputy, Chief Medical Director

Assistant Chief Medical Director for
Academic Affairs
Clinical Services
Extended Care
Planning & Program Development
Professional Services
Research & Development

Director
Affiliated Educational Program Service
CE & Staff Development Service
Health Information Systems
Associate Director

Health Serivces R & D Service
Medical Research Service
Deputy Director

[1] Physicians interested in primary health care where they served as a training advisor, management systems specialist or planning advisor may wish to contact: MEDEX, Health Manpower Development Staff, University of Hawaii School of Medicine, 1833 Kalakaua Avenue, Suite 700, Honolulu, HI 96815.

VA - Central Office (continued)

Director, Mental Health & Behavioral
  Sciences Services
    Deputy Director
    Associate Director, Alcohol & Drug
      Dependence
    Associate Director, Psychiatry
    Associate Director, Treatment Services
Director
  Neurology Service
  Nuclear Medicine Service
  Pathology Service
  Radiology Service
  Rehabilitation Service
  Spinal Cord Injury Service
Medical Inspector

Veterans Administration - Field Stations

Associate Chief of Staff for Education
Associate Chief of Staff for Research &
  Development
Chief, Medical/Dental Division
Director, Education Services

Other Federal Government Departments and Agencies

Assistant Secretary, Occupational Safety
  and Health Administration, Dept. of Labor
Astronaut, NASA
Chairman, Aeromedical Standards Division,
  FAA, Dept. of Transportation
Chairman, Occupational Health Division, FAA
Chairman, Program in Scientific Medical
  Standards, FAA
Chief, Aviation Safety Research Office,
  NASA Ames Research Center
Chief, Aviation Toxicology Laboratory,
  Civil Aeromedical Institute, FAA
Chief, FAA Civil Aeromedical Institute
Chief, Medical Operations, Johnson Space
  Center, NASA
Chief, Medical Operations, Peace Corps
Deputy Director, Office of Sciences &
  Technology, Exec. Office of the President
Director of Gorgas Memorial Laboratory
Director of Life Sciences, NASA
Director of Medical Recruitment, Bureau of
  Prisons, Dept. of Justice

Other Federal Government Departments and Agencies (continued)

Director of the Woodrow Wilson Int. Center,
  Smithsonian Institution
Exec. Director, National Advisory
  Commission on Health Manpower
Federal Air Surgeon, FAA
Manager, Operational Medicine, NASA
Medical Director, Dept. of Justice
Medical Officer, Division of Disability
  Benefits, Railroad Retirement Board
Mission Specialist, Space Shuttle Program,
  NASA
President, Gorgas Memorial Institute of
  Tropical & Preventive Medicine, Inc.
President, Institute of Medicine
Principle Investigator, Skylab Biomedical
  Experiments NASA
Regional Medical Director, US Postal
  Service (4)
Scientist-Astronaut, NASA
Special Assistant to the President for
  Health Policy

GOVERNMENT - STATE

Department of Health (or Equivalent)

Administrator, Division of Health & Medical
  Services, Dept. of Health & Social
  Services (WY)
Assistant Comm., Health Care Programs (VA)
Assistant Director Division of Local Health
  Services
Assistant Director, Public Health Lab.
Assistant Director, State Hygienic Labs.
Case Control Reviewer, Receiving Hospital
Chief, Bureau of Maternal & Child Care,
  Dept. of Health & Envir. & Control (SC)
Chief Medical Office & Deputy Director,
  Health Facilities & Standards & Control,
  Office of Health Systems Mgt. (NY)
Chief Medical Examiner (NC)
Chief Physician, Bureau of Hospital
  Services, Offices of Health Systems
  Management (NY)
Chief, Office of Medical Services (SD)
Chief, Research & Statistics Office (HI)
Commissioner (NY, VA, VI)

Department of Health (or Equivalent) (cont.)

Commissioner, Dept. of Health &
Environmental Control (SC)
Commissioner, Dept. of Human Resources (GA)
Commissioner of Health (CT, NY, OK, TX, VI)
Commissioner of Public Health (TN)
Commissioner & State Registrar, Dept. of
Health & Environmental Control (SC)

Deputy Commissioner for Special Health
Services (TX)
Deputy Secretary, Dept. of Health & Mental
Hygiene (MD)
Deputy Secretary for Community Health
Services (PA)

Director - Unspecified
Director
Crippled Children's Division (SC)
Dept. of Health Services and State
Registrar of Vital Records (AZ)
Dept. of Health & Envir. Sciences (MT)
Division of Epidemiology, Bureau of
Health Services (KY)
Division of Health (MO)
Division of Health Services (NC)
Division of Planning (PR)
Division of Physical Health, Dept. of
Human Resources (GA)
Division of Public Health (NH)
Division of Public Health, Dept. of
Health & Social Services (DE)
Interdisciplinary Research Team,
Epidemiology Studies Section (CA)
of Health, Dept. of Health & Environment
(KS, MT)
of Public Health, Dept. of Human
Resources (DC)
of Public Health, Dept. of Public Health
(IL, MI)
of Health Services Division, Dept. of
Social & Health Services (WA)
of Office of Health Director (Canal Zone)
of Office of Statistics (MA)

Executive Director (CO, UT)
Exec. Officer, State Board of Health &
State Registrar of Vital Statistics (MS)
Physician Consultant, Dept. of Health &
Social Services (WI)

Department of Health (or Equivalent) (cont.)

Secretary of Health (PA, PR)
Secretary of Health & Mental Hygiene (MD)
Secretary & State Health Commissioner,
State Board of Health (IN)
Secretary & State Health Officer, Dept. of
Health & Human Resources (LA)
State Commissioner of Health (NJ)
State Director of Health (WV)
State Health Commissioner (VA, VT)
State Health Officer (AL, NV, ND)
State Med. Exam., Division of Health, (UT)

Insurance Program Administration (Medicaid, Workmen's Compensation)

Administrator, Division of Health & Medical
Services Dept. of Health & Social
Services (WY)
Associate Medical Director, Dept. of Income
Maintenance, (CN)
Chief Medical Director, Dept. of Public
Welfare, (IN)
Deputy Director, Medicaid Agency, (AL)
Medical Consultant, Dept. of Public
Welfare, (NE)
Medical Consultant, Division of Medical
Assistance, (CO)
Medical Consultant (county level), Dept.
of Social & Health Services (WA)
Medical Director, Dept. of Public Welfare,
(MA, NE)
Medical Director, Office of Medical Policy
& Procedures, Dept. of Social & Health
Services, (WA)
Member, Medical Review Team, Dept. of
Public Welfare, (IN)

Mental Health Agency

Administrative Asst., Mental Health Center
Assoc. Com., Office of Mental Health
Chief Exec. Officer (Administrator;
Director) Department
Commissioner, Dept. of Mental Health &
Mental Retardation (VA)
Director, the Nathan S. Kline Institute for
Psychiatric Research
Director, Rockland Research Institute
Director, State Hospital

Mental Health Agency (continued)

Director, Research, NY Psychiatric Inst.
Equal Employment Opportunity Officer,
  Central Office
Hospital Aide, Mental Health Psychiatric
  Center
Hospital Aide Supervisor, Mental
  Retardation Development Center
Mental Health Administrator
  Dept. in Mental Health Central Office
  Local Mental Health & Develop. Center (2)
  Mental Health Receiving Hospital
Social Program Coordinator, Mental Health
  Psychiatric Center
Social Service Worker, Mental Retardation
  Development Center

Other

Administrative Assistant, Supervisor,
  Med. Units, Dept. of Human Services, (OK)
Administrative Asst., Employment Services
Assemblyman, 9th District, (CA)
Chaplain, R & C Correctional Institution
CEO, Medical Board of Regents
Chairman, Exec. Committee, Statewide PSR
  Council, Inc. (NY)
Commissioner of Public Health, Dept. of
  Human Services, (DC)

Coordinator of Medical Services, Dept. of
  Social & Rehabilitiation Services, (KS)
Deputy Commissioner for Programs, Dept. of
  Human Resources, (TX)
Director, State Health Planning Comm., (NW)
Majority Leader, House of Representatives
  (FL)
Medical Consultant, Dept. of Social
  Services & Housing, (HA)
Medical Consultant, Dept. of Social
  Rehabilitation Services (RI)
Member, governing board of various
  departments such as Education, Health
  Licensure, Workers Compensation and
  Administrative Services
Psychiatrist Consultant, Dept. of Welfare,
  (WV)
Sec., Dept. of Human Resources, (KY, NC)
Social Program Coordinator, Dept. of
  Economic & Commercial Development

Other (continued)

Utilization Review Administrator, Dept. of
  Social & Rehabilitation Services, (KS)
Vocal Rehabilitation Counselor,
  Rehabilitation Services Commission
Youth Ldr. Super., Veteran's Children Home

GOVERNMENT - LOCAL

Alcohol/Drug Abuse Coordinator, county
Air Pollution Control Officer, county
Assistant Comm. for Biostatistics, city
Assistant Health Director for Disease
  Control, county
Assistant Health Officer, county
Assistant Medical Examiner, city
Chief, Acute Communicable Disease, city
Chief Medical Officer, The Fire Dept., city
Chief, Preventive Med. Servces Div., county
Commissioner (or, Commission of Health),
  Dept. of Health, city and county
Coroner (or, Medical Exam.), city & county
Deputy Commissioner, Health Dept. county
Deputy Director of Health for Personal
  Health Services
Director
  Community Mental Health Services, county
  Epidemiology, Health Dept., county
  Maternal & Child Health Program, city
  Medical Services, city
Director of Public Health (county health
  officer)
Director, Dept. of Public Health & Welfare
District Health Officer, city; state
Exec. Director, Health & Hospitals
  Governing Commissioner, Cook County
Family Planning Officer, county
Head, Communicable Disease Program, county
Health Commissioner, Health Division, city
Health Officer, county
Medical Health Officer, county
Medical Services Officer, city
Mental Health Officer, county
Program Chief, Substance Abuse Service,
  county
Public Health Director, city
Supervisor, District Health Program, county
Tuberculosis Controller/VD Controller,
  county

HEALTH CARE PROVIDER

(hospital, nursing home, health maintenance organization, etc.)

Assistant (or Associate) Director or
   Administrator
Associate Medical Director, Hospitals &
   Clinics, Health Sciences Center
Associate Medical Director, Southern
   California Permanente Medical Group
Chairman & CEO, National Medical Care, Inc.
CEO. (Administrator; Director; President)
Corporate Planning Advisor, Kaiser
   Foundation Health Plan
Director, Frontier Nursing Service
Director, Laboratory Computer Science,
   Massachusetts General Hospital
Director, Northwest Kidney Center
Director, Program Development, Health
   Development, Inc.
Director, Research Administration
Director of Medical Education & Director of
   Quality Assurance
Dept. of Medical Methods Research,
   Permanente Medical Group, CA
      Director
      Director, Technology Assessment
      Assistant Director, Epidemiology &
         Biostatistics
      Assistant Director, Health Services
         Research
Executive Director, Development & Public
   Affairs, The New York Hospital
Exec. Director, Planned Parenthood Clinic
Exec. VP & Dir., Johns Hopkins Hospitals
General Director
Medical Director [1]
Medical Director, HMO

HEALTH CARE PROVIDER (continued)

Medical Director, Ohio Masonic Home
Medical Director, Planned Parenthood Clinic
Medical Dir., Reg. Perinatal Center (NJ)
President
President Geriatric Care Associates
President, Health Activation Systems
   (Minneapolis)
Regional Dir. of Education & Research, So.
   CA Region, Kaiser Permanente Medical Gr.

Vice President
   General Manager, Kaiser Foundation
      Hospital Health Plan
   New & Emerging Technology, Hummana Corp.
   Professional & Academic Affairs
   for Education & Research
   for Medical Affairs (many hospitals)
   for Operations, American Health Systems
      (nursing home group)
   for Strategic Planning, American Medical
      International

HEALTH INSURANCE PROGRAM (Private)

Not-for-profit[2]

Medical Director, Blue Shield Plan
Medical Director - HMO operations, Blue
   Shield Plan
President, Blue Cross Plan
President, Blue Shield Plan
Sr. VP, Blue Cross Plan
Sr. VP & Medical Director, Blue Shield Plan
Sr. VP, Medical & Professional Affairs,
   Blue Shield Plan

---

[1] For one discussion, see: Lloyd, JS, "Hiring a Medical Director," The Hospital Medical Staff 11:17-22 (March 1982).

Also; American Medical Association. Medical Director in the Long-Term Care Facility. Chicago: AMA, 1977.

For a position description, see; Williams, KJ and Donnelly, PR. Medical Care Quality and the Public Trust. Chicago: Pluribus Press, 1982. pp. 346-66.

[2] Blue Cross and Blue Shield plans throughout the United States employ approximately 125 physicians on a full-time salaried basis and a similar number on a part-time basis.

Not-for-profit (continued)

VP, Medical Affairs & Medical Director, BS
VP, Professional Programs
VP, and Medical Director

Commercial

Asst. Assoc. or Chief (Medical) Director of
  Accident & Health Claims
  Claims
  Employee Benefits
  Group Claims
  Medical Policy and Program
Senior Medical Consultant
VP and Medical Director

LAW[1]

(Note: several positions duplicate listings elsewhere in this Table and inadvertently may include some where clinical practice still represents a majority of the individual's time.)

Associate Professor of Emergency Medicine
Associate Professor of Surgery
Attorney, (private firm specializing in
  aviation law)
Chairman, Four Sect. Committees, National
  Fire Protection Association & President,
  American College of Legal Medicine
Chief, Division of Medical Legal Research,
  Dept. of Legal Medicine, Armed Forces
  Institute of Pathology
Commissioner, Allegheny County
Coroner
Director/Associate Director;
  Division of Medical-Legal Affairs, VA
Head, Washington Office, American College
  of Physicians
Mayor of Kansas City
Member/Partner/Owner (law firm)
Professorial Lecturer, The National Law
  Center, GW University
Senior VP, Medical & Scientific Affairs
  (large drug firm)
Staff Associate, Division of Forensic
  Programs, National Int. Mental Health
Trial Attorney

PROFESSIONAL/TRADE ASSOCIATION

American Medical Association

Executive Vice President
VP - Scientific Information
VP - Medical Information & Scient. Policy
Director, Department of Physician
  Credentials & Qualifications
Assistant Director, Department of Physician
  Credentials & Qualifications

Director, Department of Undergraduate
  Medical Evaluation
Assistant Director, Department of
  Undergraduate Medical Evaluation

Field Rep., Graduate Medical Evaluation
Director, Division of Medical Education
Director, Division of Scientific Analysis &
  Technology
Assistant Director, Division of Scientific
  Analysis & Technology
Director, Department of Environmental,
  Public & Occupational Health
Assistant Director, Department of
  Environmental, Public & Occupational
  Health

Director, Division of Drugs
Assistant Director, Division of Drugs
Senior Scientist, Division of Drugs
Director, Dept. of Speciality Journals
Director, Dept. of JAMA Editorial Staff
Director, Dept. of JAMA Science
Senior Editor - JAMA

Association of American Medical Colleges

President

Director, Department of Academic Affairs
Director, Department of Health Services
Director, Department of Planning & Policy
  Development

Director, Division of Accreditation
Director, Division of Eduational Resources
  & Programs
Special Staff Consultant

---

[1] More than 85 percent of the nearly 2,000 physicians who have obtained a law degree still allocate a very high proportion of their time to medical practice. Thus a stong majority of physicians never use their legal background in any direct way to argument their income from practice, confront the malpractice issue or fight government regulations. Thus qualifications derived from legal training are employed primarily to help manage the doctor's business affairs more prudently or "clarify issues in their medical practice."

For individuals with the dual MD/JD degrees who stress the legal component in their professional career, major job opportunities are likely to be found in the following areas: (1) Federal government with positions often involving the development and interpretation of regulations covering environmental and toxicologic problems. (2) Selected colleges of medicine which offer a formal program in forensic medicine. (3) Large industrial companies where the doctor-lawyer serves as medical director with responsibilities for health benefits and workmen's compensation. (4) Pharmaceutical manufacturing firms and selected chemical companies where the production process or output may result in enhanced toxicologic effects. (5) Finally, an increased demand for the dual professional speciality may arise from organizations in the health insurance and health care delivery fields where unique expertise pertaining to the quality of care is required. In considering posts where the legal background is emphasized, the lack of managerial training and experience may preclude advancement to the executive level and hence restrict the physician-lawyer's role to one of technical expertise.

The majority of physicians with law degrees who apply this additional background, however, are affiliated with a college of medicine. This primary source of income is used as a base to conduct research, publish findings, and provide the foundation for serving as a part-time or intermittent consultant. This latter function is usually rendered to the same types of organizations cited above where a limited number of full-time employment opportunities exist. While the diversity of experience associated with this college-based model may constitute its primary appeal, the possibility of fluctuating income could prove to be a leading disadvantage for some.

Two universities, Duke and Illinois, offer an joint law medical program whch requires six years of training. Both, however, have been characterized by low enrollment. Further information can be obtained from the references below:

Curran, WJ & Shapiro, ED (eds.). Law, Medicine and Forensic Science. Boston: Little, Brown & Co., 1982.

Hirsh, HL. "Educational Opportunities in 'Law and Medicine' in Law Schools," Journal Legal Education 27:347-52, 1975.

Wecht, CH. Legal Medicine 1982. Philadelphia: WB Saunders Co., 1982. 291 pp.

Legal Aspects of Medical Practice. (Monthly published by Pharmaceutical Communications, Inc.)

The Journal of Legal Medicine. (Quarterly published by the American College of Legal Medicine).

Other

Associate Director, American Hospital
  Association
Associate Executive Director, Int. Health,
  American Public Health Association
Associate Exec. VP, Membership
Associate Exec. VP for Health & Public
  Policy, American College of Physicians

Chief Exec. VP (speciality medical society)
Deputy Exec. VP (state medical society)
Deputy Medical Director, American
  Psychiatric Association (4)
Director, Medical Services Division, NY
  State Medical Society
Director, The New York Academy of Medicine
Director, Office of International Medicine,
  American College of Surgeons
Director, Scientific Publications Division,
  NY State Medical Society

Executive Director
  American Association of Immunology
  American Fertility Association
  American Osteopathic Association
  American Public Health Association
  Educational Commission for Foreign
    Medical Graduates

  Federation of State Medical Boards, Inc.
  International Council of Societies of
    Pathology
  Private Doctors of America
  Society for Epidemiology & Voluntary
    Assistance
  World Society for Sterotractic &
    Functional Neurosurgery

Executive Officer
  American Health Care Association
  American Society for Pharmacology &
    Experimental Therapeutics, Inc.

  International Association of Coroners &
    Medical Examiners

Other (continued)

Executive Secretary/Executive VP
  American Society of Internal Medicine
  Council of Medical Speciality Societies
  Federation of State Medical Boards of the
    United States
  International College of Surgeons
  Undersea Medical Society

President, Association of Academic Health
  Centers
President, Greater NY Hospital Association
Project Manager, International Health,
  American Public Health Association
Scientific Program Coordinator, American
  Public Health Association

VP, Division of Science & Technology,
  Pharmaceutical Manufacturers Association
VP for Medical & Scientific Affairs,
  Propietary Association

RESEARCH (non-government)[1]

Associate Director for Clinical Research,
  Institute for Cancer Research

Director

  Arthur V. Davis Center for Behavior
    Neurobiology, Salk Institute
  Graduate Pain Research Foundation
  New American Research Institute (Chicago)
  Palm Beach Institute for Medical Research
  Quincy Research Center (Kansas City)
  Research & Development, InterQual (Chicago)
  Res. Institute of Lab. Medicine, Pacific
    Med., Center, Institute of Med. Sciences

Director & Resident Fellow, Salk Institute
Director for Education, Mayo Foundation
Director of Research, Mayo Foundation
Director of Research, San Diego Zoo

---

[1] Active research programs are also likely to be carried out by many faculty members enumerated in "EDUCATION: Medical School - Basic Science Unit" and by clinical professors as well.

RESEARCH (non-government) (continued)

Executive Director, Philadelphia Association
  for Clinical Trails
Investigator, International Fertility
  (Research Triangle Park, NC)
Medical Associate, International Program,
  The Population Council (NYC)
Medical Consultant, The Institute for
  Aerobics Research (Dallas)
Medical Manager, Cardiovascular Research
President
  Beneficial Plant Research Associate
  Biometric Testing, (Englewood Cliffs, NJ)
President
  Drug Abuse Council
  International Institute of Stress,
    University of Montreal
  Memorial Sloan-Kettering Cancer Ctr. (NYC)
  Rockburn Institute, (Elkridge, MD)
  Sidney Farber Cancer Institute

Research Associate, Harvard Botanical Museum
Research Associate, MIT Arteriosclerosis
  Center
Research Associate, Medical Research Center,
  Brookhaven National Laboratory
Research Fellow, Infectious Disease, Dept.
  of Medicine (New England Medical Center
  Hospital)
Research Scientist, Health Service Research
  Center (Univ. of Michigan)
Senior Fellow, The Population Council,
  (NYC) (2)
Senior Health Services Researcher (The RAND
  Corp.)
Team Member, Health & Nutrition Examination
  Survey (private consulting firm)
VP & CEO, Chicago Technology Park

MISCELLANEOUS

Author[1]
Chairman, Cable Health Network (television)

Director, Drug Standards Division, United
  States Pharmacopeia
Director, Occupational Health, United Mine
  Workers of America
Dir., Public Citizen, Inc. (Washington, DC)

Exec. Dir., Institute for Health Planning
Exec. Direction, Nutrition Foundation

Homesteader

Investment Counselor

Medical Consultant, The

President
  American Health Care Institute
  American League (baseball)
  Center for Corporate Health Promotion
    Reston, VA
  Commission on Prof & Hospital Activities
  Employment Agency
  Institute for Generic Drugs
  Management Sciences for Health, Boston

Producer & Director of Films for Television

Secretary-Treasurer, International Health
  Society (Englewood, CO)

Senior Professional Associate, Institute of
  Medicine, National Research Council
Senior Research Associate, Health Policy
  Program, Urban Institute

---

[1] For an outstanding survey, see: Peschel, ER (ed.). <u>Medicine and Literature</u>, New York:
Neale Watson, 1980. 204 pp.

PART-TIME ACTIVITES[1]

(compensation received but doctor still spends 80 percent or more time as a clinician or non-clinician)

Athletic Team Physician
Author
Chairman, National Digestive Diseases
    Advisory Board, U.S. Dept. of HHS
Chairman, Princeton Institute for Health
    Policy
Clinical Professor of Medicine or Surgery
Commissioner, Dept. of Health Services
    (county)
Chief Exec. Officer (speciality medical
    society)
Concert Pianist
Consultant, U.S. Secret Police
Consultant, Fire or Police Dept.; Workmen's
    Compensation Commission
Coroner/Medical Exam., (county or city)

PART-TIME ACTIVITES (continued)

Designer (contemporary women's fashions)
Editor (national/state/county medical
    journal)
Editorial Consultant/Editorial Review Board
Expert Witness
Foreign Language Interpreter
Magician
Mayor, Coos Bay, OR
Medical Director, World Boxing Hall of Fame
Medical Illustrator
Member, Board of Directors, (manufacturing
    firms)
Member, State Legislature

Photographer
President, Flying Physicians Association
President, National Council on Marijuana
President, National Society to Prevent
    Blindness
School Physician.

---

[1] For one discusson of four role models, see: "Doctors Plus: Practicing More Than Medicine," Medical World News 21:57-69 (December 8, 1980).

Physicians seeking part-time clinical positions may wish to participate in State Disability Determination Services. Under this program, two option are possible: (a) Medical Claims Reviewer: This consultant, working with a disability examiner, evaluates medical evidence in the file of a claimant to determine the nature and severity of the alleged physical and/or mental impairment. (b) Special Examiner: The consultant physician in this instance administers general and specific examinations and tests to claimants when prior medical evidence proved to be inadequate.

For further details, write: Director, Professional Relations Staff, Social Security Administration, Room 13-A-13 Operations Building, 6401 Security Blvd. Baltimore, MD, 21235. Alternatively, telephone (301) 597-1548.

The Dynamic Health Care Delivery System

There has been a blurring and breakdown of conventional boundaries . . . doctors are getting into a lot of areas that used to be reserved for hospitals; hospitals are setting up clinics to draw in patients . . . insurers are getting into medical practice . . .

The health care industry is experiencing a tremendous amount of corporate ferment . . . including a shift in patterns of ownership and control (from non-profit to for-profit), a shift from locally-controlled institutions to chains (the process of consolidation), vertical integration connecting various phases and levels of care in a single organization (such as an HMO), and diversification and corporate restructuring . . .

- Paul Starr, PhD; author of The Social Transformation of American Medicine. Quoted in Executive News Service, American Group Practice Association, November 16, 1983.

Chapter V

MEDICINE AND MEDICAL PRACTICE: EXPANDING YOUR HORIZON

This chapter introduces another perspective to help corroborate or possibly initiate your interest in medicine. In compiling this material, we have endeavored to stimulate your thinking about various forces that may influence and challenge the talents of physicians who enter medical practice.

The first four articles provide background information about physician automony from a historic perspective, suggest the close relationship between medicine and technology, and outline the concerns of blacks and women who enter the profession. The remaining selections cover a variety of topics germane to the contemporary practice of medicine. The contents of this chapter, therefore, may not only be useful but essential for those willing to look beyond the important step of determining the "best" medical specialty.

While space/resource constraints dictate that our examples be more arbitrary than comprehensive, judicious pursuit of the external readings can be employed to gain a broader understanding of the complex factors affecting practice options. Indeed, career and possibly job opportunities may be perceived if your survey is approached with these goals in mind.

Doctors and Their Autonomy:
Past Events and Future Prospects

Carleton B. Chapman, MD

The author is president of The Commonwealth Fund, New York 10021. This article is a revision of the second Walter B. McDaniel Memorial Lecture delivered at The College of Physicians of Philadelphia on 4 January 1978.

The doctor in American society plays a role that must be played; and the importance of that role is, if anything, increasing as our society grows more complex and our population larger. In addition, and closely related, is the fact that the doctor is still accorded special status within American society, something that is not likely to change substantively, despite the increasingly critical comments about the medical profession in the American press. The most obvious manifestation of the profession's special status is, of course, economic . . .

There are other manifestations of the doctor's special status. For example, doctors are required to serve on juries only very rarely, and are seldom penalized for parking violations while on professional missions. These are admittedly small things, the analogues of which were known even to the Romans; but they are collectively quite significant. It will not do, however, to press the modern case on the basis of evidence from the ancient literature, legal or otherwise. The reason is that the medical profession as we know it today did not begin to emerge until much later. Our real argument begins in 14th-century England, and the story from that date can be built around several more or less continuous themes of which professional autonomy and its near relative, maintenance of monopoly, are but two. They are, however, the most appropriate themes to follow for present purposes, and, as we shall see, the legal record tells us as much as or more than the medical. The story is one of intermittent and progressive limitation of autonomy and, somewhat later, modification of the right to create and maintain monopoly. But through it all, the special social position of the doctor is visible and, to an extent, determinant.

The First Step: Malpractice Law. The position of the medical profession in Britain in the several centuries following the Norman Conquest is difficult to pin down because, at the start, medicine and the priesthood were not easily distinguishable. The common law in its early stages is not known to have had anything to say about the medical profession since most doctors, if in conflict with the law, were probably dealt with under canon law or in local courts, from whose decisions English common law derives. There is however, a suggestion in the legal record of the early 14th century that a doctor was not liable for injury to patients unless he inflicted it with evil or criminal intent. There was no mention of culpability for ignorance or negligence, and it seems that if a patient of that time placed himself or his horse in the care of a bona fide doctor, human or horse, he had to bear his own loss if there were injury unintentionally inflicted. It may not have been as simple as that, since there are very few records of proceedings in England's numerous local or customary courts.

In contrast, actions of the King's courts have been recorded since the latter part of the 13th century, the chief sources of information about the earlier part of the record being known collectively as the Yearbooks. Several cases in the Yearbook record for the 14th century suggest that the position of the healing professions in the eye of the law changed dramatically before the century was out. In 1373 Justice Cavendish decided Stratton v. Swanlond, a case brought against a surgeon, in which the Justice said that if the patient is harmed as a result of the doctor's negligence, the doctor should be held liable. But, said Cavendish,

> . . . if he does all he can and applies himself with all
> due diligence to the cure, it is not right that he should
> be guilty therefore, (even) though there is no cure . . .

The importance of this case is that it contains most of the significant elements of 20th-century common law of malpractice and represents the first official invasion of the medical profession's autonomy. In addition, it seems to be the true origin of the common law doctrine called fault, or "no liability without fault" as it is sometimes phrased. The language of the court is quite explicit: unless the doctor were somehow negligent or careless, he was not liable even if he failed to produce a cure. This stands in sharp contrast to the principle of strict liability, which requires that he who causes the injury must compensate the injured party regardless of intent, negligence, or any other consideration.

It is significant that the fault principle makes its first appearance in a malpractice case and it may indeed have been devised to protect the doctor, in an age when malpractice insurance did not exist, from the full rigors of strict liability. It may have represented a sort of quid pro quo, recognizing the doctor's special social status but limiting his autonomy ever so slightly in the public interest. In any event, after Stratton v. Swanlond the doctor was no longer totally autonomous, as he seems to have been earlier in the 14th century, barring activity that we in our own time would term criminal.

The Second Step: Due Process. In the two centuries following Stratton v. Swanlond, the medical profession in London became highly stratified, and the physicians, who were at the top of the heap, consolidated their position by adopting the methods of the craft guild. Precisely how London's physicians managed to prevail over their chief rivals is not altogether clear, but the surgeons were beneath them in the hierarchy and the apothecaries were beneath the surgeons. It may, however, be relevant that the physician's patients were the high and the mighty, while the poor, if they received any medical care at all, were treated mostly by apothecaries and various folk healers. In any case, the physicians prevailed on Henry VIII to charter their professional guild in 1518 as London's Royal College of Physicians, and some time later Parliament gave it extraordinary powers by law. Not only was it the licensing authority for London, but it could also imprison or fine offenders, dividing the fines it received with the Crown. Those whom it imprisoned had to remain in prison until the College agreed to their release. Common criminals could sometimes be released on bail, but not those offenders who were convicted and imprisoned by the Board of Censors of the Royal College of Physicians.

Thus it was that the Royal College, accountable to no public authority, received by parliamentary delegation extraordinary legal powers, and it is a matter of record that the College used these extraordinary powers to maintain and to strengthen its monopoly. Its numbers were very few and the demand for the members' services was therefore such that their incomes were kept at at high level. There is, however, a suggestion of a social contract in the arrangements: the College undertook to protect and to serve the public expertly in return for which it received high social station and economic advantage. The caveat emptor imperative might apply to ordinary marketplace transactions, but not to the doctor-patient relationship. These general concepts have to some extent characterized the relations between the medical profession and the public ever since.

But predictably the College over reached itself, and it sustained a rude jolt when in 1606 it sent one Dr. Thomas Bonham to Fleet Street prison for practicing without its license. Bonham, who had a medical degree from Cambridge, denied with some justice that the College had any authority over him and was released from prison on a writ of habeas corpus. But the College, undaunted, relentlessly followed up its earlier actions with the ultimate result that Bonham brought a civil action for damages for false imprisonment. This time the matter came before the Court of Common Pleas, of which the irrascible and combative Sir Edward Coke was chief justice. The decision was against the College on the ground of conflict of interest. The College, said Coke, could not legally summon a man, try him in its own court, fine him, then put a part of the proceeds into owns coffers. Coke also indicated that the power to imprison without trial is a limited one in law and does not confer "any irregular or absolute power to correct or punish any of the subjects of the kingdom at their (the College's Board of Censors') pleasure." It was unlawful for the accused to have been imprisoned "without bail or main-prize, till he should be by the commandment of the President and Censors . . . delivered."

Bonham's is one of the most famous cases in English legal annals, not only because it limited the right of a private organization, responsible only to its own members, to take away an individual's liberty or property. Even more important, it involved certain fundamental constitutional issues including the right of the judiciary to overrule the legislature.

What Coke actually said in this connection was that " . . . when an Act of Parliament is against common right and reason, or repugnant, or impossible to be performed, the common law will control it and adjudge the Act to be void." This, in Coke's time and still in our own, was political dynamite and it got Coke into a great deal of trouble. It seemed reasonable within the context of Bonham's case, but it carried with it certain fundamental constitutional implications, some of which were later acceptable to American jurists but totally unacceptable in England. In Britain the legislature has, since 1688, remained unmistakably sovereign, answerable only to the electorate.

The whole issue of the supremacy of the legislature and its relation to the judiciary, along with the question of a Bill of Rights for England, is today being given new impetus by the debate on devolution. One can expect to hear Coke's arguments in Bonham's case cited again and again in the next few years. But for present purposes, the importance of the case is that it represented a second step in limiting the autonomy of the medical profession. The court, in effect, told the College that it could not, in the course of its pursuit of monopoly, infringe certain basic rights of the individual or use its own court arbitrarily as a means of enriching itself.

Step Three: Licensure. The College continued to use its parliamentary authority, but with much greater caution. It had, for years, tried charges of malpractice in its own court as well as inflicting punishment for practicing without a license. But, from the later 17th century onward, it tended to bring charges of both sorts into the regular courts. It remained, however, a licensing body until 1858 when the Medical Act created the General Medical Council and public authority took over licensure of medical practitioners. At the same time, public authority took control over medical education to a limited extent. Provision was made for professional influence and input, but the ultimate licensing authority was now quite firmly in the public sector.

In the United States, there were parallel events, but of special significance in both countries was the unification of the medical profession by the creation of national, guildlike professional organizations that were strong enough and coherent enough to influence public policy and legislation.

The American Medical Association (AMA) was created in 1847 and the British Medical Association (BMA), building on a prior regional organization, a few years later. Both organizations conceded quite early that licensure was a proper concern of government and to that extent accepted the loss of another component of their autonomy. In the United States it was not a serious loss since in most states membership on boards of registration was directly or indirectly under the control of state medical societies which themselves were constituent members of the AMA. Both of these great medical guilds promptly set about protecting the remaining autonomy of the medical profession chiefly by defending the profession's monopoly and the fee-for-service principle. In the United States, the AMA staked out the medical profession's territory in 1872 when it acknowledged that the protection of the health of the millions was the obligation of government but that private or curative medicine belonged to the doctors. Nearly 40 years later, it strongly reaffirmed its opposition to government intervention in the provision of personal health services, a view that had earlier been adopted in different form by the BMA. It was an emphasis that would one day bring the organized professions once again into conflict with the law.

The Fourth Step: Restraint of Trade. In Britain the trouble begin in 1915 when the Coventry Provident Association began to hire physicians and surgeons to provide medical care to its subscribers. It was a straightforward prepayment scheme but it ran counter to the fee-for-service principle. The BMA, through its Coventry division, informed three of the doctors employed by the Provident Association that they must immediately resign. When they refused, the doctors were promptly expelled from the BMA, which also informed its constituent members of the action and urged that the three be ostracized and boycotted. This meant that the three doctors were virtually excluded from hospital privileges and from consultation practice and, as a consequence, they took the only action available to them: they filed civil suit for damages against the BMA and its Coventry division.

The verdict went resoundingly against the BMA. Among many other things, the judge had this to say:

> The coercive force of the defendant Association rests primarily upon what are called the ethical rules. . . . (A physician) may be exposed to degradation and dishonor at the whim of a body which is void of the slightest statutory sanction in that behalf. . . . Such sanction belongs to the General Medical Council.

He went on to say that he could not " . . . ignore the deliberate and relentless vigor with which the defendants sought to achieve the infliction of complete ruin." He awarded the claimants 2400 pounds in compensatory and punitive damages, strongly intimating by his action (and statements) that the offense was clearly intentional and therefore had criminal overtones. After that time, the question of contract, which the BMA had called unethical, was settled; and it became moot with the establishment of the National Health Service in 1948.

The corresponding legal event in the United States did not occur until 1940, but it was remarkably similar to the earlier British case. It arose when the AMA tried to ostracize several doctors who practiced on salary with a group health association in the nation's capital. Prepayment for health services was considered unethical by the AMA, and the association left no stone unturned to punish doctors who worked under such arrangements. The federal government finally brought suit against the AMA under the Sherman Antitrust Act for conspiring to restrain legitimate business and professional activity. The AMA was found guilty, and the U.S. Supreme Court refused to review the verdict of the court below. That ended the AMA's practice of conspiring against group health and prepayment plans, many of which operate successfully today in the United States.

It is astonishing in retrospect that the BMA and AMA allowed themselves to fall into such legal traps. No doubt each had adequate legal counsel and they probably regarded their conspiracies as calculated risks. However that may be, both medical associations got clear and unmistakable answers from the courts: organized medicine could not give its own guild rules the force of law by conspiring to the detriment of its members or against anyone else. The American case is especially interesting in that the AMA claimed that it did not come under the Sherman Antitrust Act because it is a professional society, not a trade organization. But the court was unimpressed and, by inference, made it clear that the AMA had conducted itself after the manner of a trade association seeking to maintain monopoly. Whether or not the leadership of the AMA was carrying out the will of its members in this instance cannot be known, since no poll was taken then or later. To the extent, however, that the AMA's House of Delegates represented the membership, the leaders of the organization were unquestionably acting in accordance with the majority opinion of its individual members. Indeed, the leaders of both organizations probably had very little choice. It is axiomatic that when such guildlike associations begin to fail to represent the interests and views of their members, they are in serious trouble as organizations.

Unfortunately, court battles like these unmistakably obscure the numerous actions organized medicine takes that are clearly in the public interest. All the public can see is a giant, wealthy organization acting solely in its own interests. Lost from sight, in the case of the AMA, were its vigorous and public support of quarantine legislation, the pure food and drug movement, the establishment of state departments of public health, and the refinement of medical education. But the legal actions of 1915 in Britain and 1940 in the United States redefined and further limited the autonomy of the British and American medical professions. They could no longer force adherence to a preferred scheme for remuneration, one that kept the fees charged by physicians out of the public view as much as possible.

Step Five: Quality Control. My thesis so far is that the medical profession has been required to surrender its autonomy step by step since the late Middle Ages. It began with the evolution of the common law of malpractice based on fault and ultimately on negligence as the law now defines it. Next came the decision of the Court of Common Pleas which set limits on the lengths to which London's Royal College of Physicians might go in enforcing its own monopoly. Then came legislation in the 19th century that placed licensure, and to an extent medical education, under public authority. In the 20th century came legal limitation of the right of the medical profession to control the means by which doctors are paid for their professional services.

So what is left? In answer, it may be permissible to draw on the thought and creativity of a society that has long since disappeared, but that has left us a powerful intellectual legacy. Plato, in one of his dialogues, explored the consequences of destroying the autonomy of the medical profession altogether. In The Statesman, one of the spokesmen, in making a point that is now germane, used the medical profession as an example. The doctor abuses his autonomy, said the spokesman, and saves us or lets us die according to his own interests. "He cuts us up, burns us, and orders us to bring him money . . . as if he were exacting tribute." He is sometimes receptive to bribes from our enemies or from hostile relatives who wish us dead. He should, therefore, be placed under rigid state control.

To accomplish this, said the spokesman, we should call an assembly of all the people and invite opinions about

> disease, and how drugs and surgical or medical instruments should be applied to patients. We should take a vote on all these things and whatever the majority decides about each of them should be inscribed in stone and possess the force of law. We should then elect our physicians from among our number for one year terms, and severely penalize them if they fail to carry out the letter of the law.

What is more, said the spokesman, we should forbid all research, since the truth would already be laid down. Those doing research anyway should pay a grievous penalty "for corrupting the young and persuading them to practice the art of . . . medicine in opposition to the laws. . . . (For) nothing and no one . . . ought to be wiser than the laws."

The second spokesman, replying to all this, draws the conclusion that by such means all art (and all science) would be utterly ruined and, research being forbidden, could never rise again. He added: "and so life, which is hard enough now, would then become absolutely unendurable."

In our own time, Plato's fantasy has a familiar ring to it, what with the increasing paperwork imposed on today's practicing physicians, the increasing threat of penalty through malpractice actions, and the rigid restrictions placed by third-party carriers on how much they will pay for what. Can all this fail to lead to total subjugation of the profession along the lines laid down in Plato's dialogue? May not government, or the threat of malpractice actions, one day tell the doctor precisely what he may or may not do, even unto the patient's bedside?

The answer is in the negative for the simple reason that the peer judgment principle and application of technical expertise are indispensable no matter who pays the physician and no matter what the courts have to say about professional standards. Even in the Soviet Union and Great Britain, the medical profession maintains a considerable degree of what Freidson calls technologic autonomy, something he says ". . . is at the core of what is unique about the profession."

But what the American medical profession is now facing is not really further loss of professional autonomy, unless we define the term as the right of the individual physician to do precisely as he will, once he is legally licensed, without fear of judgment of any kind. What lies ahead is the prospect of routine, and one hopes judicious, peer judgment on the basis of properly defined standards of professional performance systematically applied. The signs of change in this direction are overwhelming. Professional meetings and the medical literature are filled with discussion of utilization review, medical audit, and mediation and arbitration panels, all designed to monitor one or more phases of the doctor's professional performance. None of this is really new, the need for outcome appraisal having been recognized soon after the turn of the century.

But it was the passage of Medicare and Medicaid laws, the rise of the so-called malpractice crisis, and the passage of the Professional Standards Review Organization (PSRO) law that brought matters to a head. Space does not permit detailed consideration of each of these complex matters, but they are all of a piece in one very critical sense: all focus sharply on the definition of standards and the creation of guidelines governing the application of those standards.

Where Malpractice Fits In. Looking at the malpractice problem first, if only because it is probably the least important in a relative sense, we find that the most prominent of the proposed remedies all embody some form of definition of compensable injury, and many others do so at least by inference. The need for such information, although denied by some trial lawyers, was firmly recognized and expressed by one of our greatest legal authorities, Oliver Wendell Holmes, in 1881. Holmes put it this way:

> Any legal standard must, in theory, be capable of being known. When a man has to pay damages . . . he is . . . supposed to have known what the law was. If now, the ordinary liabilities in tort arise from failure to comply with fixed and uniform standards of external conduct . . . it is obvious that it ought to be possible, sooner or later, to formulate these standards at least to some extent and that to do so must at last be the business of the court. It is equally clear that the featureless generality, that the defendant was bound to use such care as a prudent man would do under the circumstances, ought to be continually giving place to the specific one. . . .

But today, nearly a century later, the featureless generality still prevails where medical malpractice is concerned. It is still not possible even for the most knowledgeable and conscientious physician to know whether or not he has broken the law until a court says what it thinks the law is. There are discernible principles in the law of medical malpractice, but a wide variation in the application of those principles from court to court and case to case forces writers of legal textbooks to equate the exceptions with the rule. It may indeed be the ultimate business of the courts to define compensable injury, but it does not follow that the process must take place countless times, over and over again, in the adversary climate of the courtroom. Such definitions primarily require the application of medical expertise, before the fact of injury, by appropriate expert panels outside the courtroom for the eventual use of the courts. And quite predictably this is one way - perhaps the most appropriate way - the malpractice problem will be eased if not altogether solved.

The General Monitoring of Quality. But the definition of compensable injury is not, in itself, enough. Much more fundamental is the creation of standards of professional performance without specific reference to malpractice, an activity to which the medical profession even today is no stranger. The Medicare law made hospital-based utilization review mandatory, a requirement that was later extended to Medicaid (Title XIX) as well. The focus was primarily on cost control and only tangentially on control of quality. Experience with the utilization review mechanism has been largely unsatisfactory, a fact that has led to experiments with various forms of medical audit. But it was the PSRO law of 1972 that put peer review firmly and probably permanently on the American medical scene. It is not appropriate to attempt to summarize this complex and clumsy piece of legislation beyond pointing out that it contains within it the seeds of its own failure, and will require substantive revision in the future. Nor is it possible to subscribe fully to the expectations set out by Simmons and Ball when they say that "as PSRO becomes operational nationwide, the system will prove an efficient and effective system of control over the quality of outcomes of medical care." More likely, it will be a successor to the PSRO mechanism that will do so. But the principle of routine peer review that is incorporated within the PSRO law is here to stay and will undoubtedly alter the climate within which medicine is practiced in the United States.

Ultimate Mechanisms. For a number of reasons, we have not yet faced the fundamental fact that the two basic ingredients in the peer review principle are separate and distinct: the first is the creation of standards; the second is the monitoring process by which standards are applied. The two entities differ significantly in that one is properly a national activity, the other a local one. Fortunately, we have familiar mechanisms on which to build the peer review system of the future.

For the setting of standards, of which definitions of compensable events is merely one component, national mechanisms have existed and operated in a limited way for a very long time. These are the specialty societies and boards, including those representing generalists and family physicians, all of which have been setting professional standards for many years. Every time these organizations prepare an examination question and every time they arrange programs for national meetings or for continuing education requirements, they are recognizing, and sometimes setting, professional standards. Although they have set standards primarily to determine qualifications for certification and, in some cases, for preventing professional obsolescence, they act tangentially very much in the public interest. Many hospital governing bodies are guided by training standards set by specialty groups; in establishing the credentials of medical defendants and expert witnesses, the courts quite regularly take notice of certification by specialty boards according to standards that are applied nationally. And in the establishment of the fact of negligence, expert witnesses who are themselves certified specialists not infrequently draw on standards developed by their specialty societies, a trend that may confidently be expected to become more widespread.

The objection that standards set by specialty societies and boards are unfair to doctors who are not board-certified loses its relevance when the national trend toward certification as a specialist is taken into account, especially since general and family medicine have taken their place among the specialties. What is now needed is joint action by specialty boards and societies, to set professional standards, define compensable injury, and prescribe equitable guidelines for the application of standards and definitions. Standards, definitions, and guidelines must, in addition, be reviewed and revised at suitable intervals in order that they may be kept current, and every practicing doctor should have ready access to them through continuing education activities. The process should have both educational and preventive functions, and should provide services to the courts reliably but secondarily. The setting of standards, however, is inescapably a professional matter, involving the systematic assembling of a vast amount of existing experience into a new body of knowledge, designed more for practical than for theoretical purposes.

Standards and definitions are useless unless they can be consistently and regularly applied, and deviations from them promptly identified. This requires a local monitoring mechanism, examples of which have been in use in many hospitals and group practices for decades. What is now needed is a screening process the mesh of which is of such size as to retain instances of clearly questionable professional performances so that they may receive evaluation by peers on an individual basis. The design must be such as to render the process effective and fair but not be so cumbersome that it is self-defeating. It must also be able to extend beyond the reaches and the requirements of the law, in the expectation that by such means the incidence of both compensable events and substandard practice may ultimately approach an irreducible minimum.

What is needed is an integrated system of peer review which will not only protect the patient from substandard medical care but will, when necessary, serve the legitimate and proper needs of the courts while, at the same time, relating effectively to the state authority charged with professional discipline. Such an integrated system cannot replace either the courts or the disciplinary authority, but it must have the potential of reducing the incidence of compensable medical injury by identifying and controlling inadequate or unnecessary medical services, and by identifying members of the profession who, for one reason or another, are not rendering acceptable care.

But, one must ask, may not such a system - in view of the great difficulty of creating workable standards and of the possibilities of abuse that are inherent in it - actually represent precisely the sort of thing Plato described in The Statesman? May it not represent the final stage in the destruction of the medical profession's autonomy?

I think not. But the system would indeed represent the end of the tradition that each doctor is, within himself, totally autonomous and all but exempt from criticism or from penalty for incompetence, ineptitude, or venality. But more significant is the fact that actual and proper standards and definitions can only be worked out by the profession itself, acting on the basis of its own expertise and knowledge, but not primarily to enhance its autonomy and monopoly. One might add that the vast and difficult activities that lie ahead for the medical profession are, for the most part, no more than its basic professional ethic requires. Public and legal counsel, as the labor goes forward, are essential; but the action and the obligation are still fundamentally matters assignable to the medical profession.

In this connection, the group of able sociologists who have in recent years concerned themselves with theories of profession and especially with the working of the medical profession, have usually posed the primary question quite well. "How," asks Bledstein, "does society make professional behavior accountable to the public without curtailing the independence upon which creative skills and the imaginative use of knowledge depend?" And Berlant, in a book dealing indignantly with the antisocial aspects of professional monopoly, wisely declines "to make specific policy recommendations with respect to the organization of the medical profession . . . in either Britain or the United States." Freidson is a bit more courageous, and to some doctors, alarming, in his view that social control of the medical profession requires bureaucratization, "an indirect, external control system." However, the control system Freidson has in mind is not really non-medical or antimedical. He acknowledges the obvious necessity for professional expertise in any such system, but denies the right of the profession to design and control the system in its own interests, financial and otherwise. But the retention of legitimate, and even obligatory, autonomy actually has nothing to do with the maintenance of monopoly and special privilege as, for example, the Royal College of Physicians saw it in the 16th century.

The difficulty, as the profession goes about the taxing business of determining standards and guidelines, will not arise because it wishes to maintain and enhance monopoly. The chief difficulty will probably be of an altogether different sort. For decades the profession has been viewed as a monolithic giant, its members always speaking with a single voice. It is actually no such thing, and the primary question now is: Can the profession, working when appropriate with public authority, bring the strength and expertise of its many segments to bear, in good faith and to unassailable purpose, on the problems at hand?

The question must go unanswered largely because there is no relevant precedent. But there is surely no reason to believe that American society now wishes to destroy the medical profession by removing all traces of its autonomy. On the contrary, the special status, both social and economic, of the profession is under no massive and immediate threat. But the obvious message of the times is that the profession should retain the most fundamental aspect of its autonomy in order that it may apply it, in the public interest and in its own, to the setting of expert and ethically defensible standards, and to the creation of effective monitoring mechanisms.

This is a far cry from total destruction of the profession's autonomy as in Plato's fantasy. It is, in fact, something the medical profession has already done for specific and limited purposes. The pace is now accelerating. And if the future system for setting standards, prescribing guidelines, and creating monitoring mechanisms turns out to be judicious, effective, and fair both to patient and to doctor, it will because the medical profession has mobilized and unified itself to genuinely professional purpose.

External Readings: Historic/Ethics Perspective

Pernik, MS, "Medical Professionalism," In: Encyclopedia of Bioethics. (Vol. 3) New York: The Free Press, 1978. pp. 1028-33

Walters, L, "Biomedical Ethics," Journal American Medical Association 254:2345-48 (October 25, 1985).

Bryan, JE, "View from the Hill," American Family Physician 18:243-47 (August 1983).

Burnham, JC, "American Medicine's Golden Age: What Happened to It?" Science 215:1474-79 (March 19, 1982).

Council Report, "Guidelines for Ethics Committees in Health Care Institutions," Journal American Medical Association 253:2698-99 (May 17, 1985).

Gladston, I. Social & Historical Foundations of Modern Medicine. New York: Brunner/Mazel, 1981. 147 pp.

Kepler, MO. Medical Stewardship: Fulfilling the Hippocratic Legacy. Westport, CT: Greenwood Press, 1981. 299 pp.

King, LS. Medical Thinking: A Historical Preface. Princeton, NJ: Princeton University Press, 1982. 336 pp.

Aaron, HJ & Schwartz, WB. The Painful Prescription: Rationing Hospital Care. Washington: Brookings Institution, 1984. 161 pp.

Johsen, AR, et al. Clinical Ethics. New York: MacMillan, 1982. 187 pp.

TECHNOLOGIC ADVANCES IN MEDICINE
The good news and the bad

John. H. Budd, MD

A lot of exciting "good news" about health is circulating these days. For instance, 12,000 Americans (that we know of) have reached 100 years of age or more, and one of every four babies born in this country this year will reach the age of 85.

Of the about 50 heart transplants done in the world each year, 50 percent are done in the United States, and 50 percent of the recipients live at least five years.

More than 25,000 people in this country are wearing cardiac pacemakers, without which they might be disabled or dead. One hundred thousand of the devices were installed in 1978 alone, the latest year for which I found statistics. Sixty-four thousand Americans with otherwise fatal kidney disease are alive and functioning as beneficiaries of renal dialysis.

The new PETT (position emission transaxial tomographic) scanner can detect and also measure abnormality or injury in body tissues quite accurately, safely, and comfortably for the patient - an important break-through. When used in investigating for coronary heart disease, myocardial infarction, or brain tumor, for example, it can largely obviate the need for high-risk exploratory procedures such as cardiac catheterization, pneumoencephalography and ventriculography, cerebral angiography, and balloon catheterization. . .

One might say after perusing these commendable achievements that we in medicine are doing pretty well in guarding and improving the nation's health. But despite the good news, it is clear that the increased access to care, extension of life expectancy, and fantastic developments in technology have brought along problems. Technologic advances, especially, have created multiple consequences, some of them as fascinating and perplexing as the medical situations with which they deal. I'll omit such social, moral, legal, and philosophic issues as gene splicing, cloning, surrogate motherhood, and civil rights of the unborn and confine my focus here to the economic dilemmas created.

Cost is the main problem facing health care today, as both physicians and public agree. This was confirmed again in two recent public and physician polls sponsored by the American Medical Association. The 1980 health care bill is estimated at . . . about six times what it was in 1965 (the year Medicare was implemented, incidentally). At the present rate of acceleration, one authority has forecast the tab will rise to $758 billion by the end of this decade. We might ask whether our scientific discoveries are about to exceed our ability, or our willingness, to pay for them.

Longevity, to begin with, has its "good news-bad news" implications . . . However, it is already evident that a larger part of the Social Security solvency problem is due to this increase in life expectancy. Those who devised the program never imagined that so many of us would live beyond 65. They must feel today a bit like the planners who put together the Edsel.

There is also a direct health cost consequence - outside of retirement benefits - of the growing number of oldsters. Older people usually get diseases that are chronic, but many of these are no longer rapidly fatal; modern victims are kept alive longer, often at high cost. It is a fairly trustworthy rule of thumb that the longer we live, the more protracted and expensive our terminal illness, if any, is likely to be. Victor Fuchs has pointed out that a lot of the cost of health care is incurred in the last year of life, and all of us are destined at some point for that final year.

Consider these statistics. Medicare began in 1972 to pay for renal dialysis or transplant, regardless of patient age; in that year there were 11,000 cases costing $283 million. By 1979 the number had risen to 56,000 cases costing one billion dollars and in 1980 to 64,000 cases consuming about $1.5 billion. By 1990, the cost is anticipated to be six billion - for just this one bit of technology.

The CAT (computed axial tomographic) scanner, for a long time a prime target in health cost debates, is now becoming more appreciated as a diagnostic tool and ultimate cost saver. It is rather startling to think that the CAT may be approaching obsolescence as the PETT, mentioned earlier, comes on the scene. The cost of this new machine approaches two million, bringing, as you might guess, proportional cost problems in tow. To begin with, if the roughly 1,500 CATS in the country are replaced by 1,500 PETTs, a bill of three billion in today's dollars will ensue. Of additional significance is the fact that the replaced CATs will probably not be just discarded but sold to smaller, less affluent hospitals, generating for them an add-on expenditure. . .

Of more consequence is the PETT's great ability to detect defects previously unrecognizable or discovered only by procedures often omitted because of high risk. This is a great benefit, but also a potential problem. Suppose the current passion for preventive medicine, annual physicals, and early discovery of disease extends to routine PETT scanning of the coronary arteries for everyone. Even limiting such exams to those between ages 45 and 64, which would, according to recent census figures, still leave some 43 million candidates, would - at $300 per scan - cost about $13 billion per year. Extend the testing to other organs and systems and it is easy to project a cost figure of $75 billion or so. And this is just for testing. Now, if we choose to apply treatment to the defects discovered . . .

These days, about 100,000 coronary bypass operations are done in the United States per year at an average cost of $15,000 per case: total cost $1.5 billion. I heard one of our most respected cardiovascular surgeons state that about 25 percent of individuals over 45 have significant coronary arteriosclerosis. If the 40 million or so persons in this age-group can be screened safely, accurately, and comfortably by the PETT, it means we can identify more than 10 million potential candidates for bypass. If the cost of the operation were to remain at $15,000 and each candidate were to undergo such surgery, the total bill would be $150 billion.

The ultimate in organ replacement is the heart (the brain not yet having qualified as a feasible organ). The principal reasons for the small number of heart transplants to date are shortage of donors and the problem of tissue rejection. If the artificial heart becomes fact, the donor shortage will be overcome and tissue rejection eliminated. We are told that the number of patients who could use a heart transplant is 32,000. At $100,000 per case, this amounts to $3.2 billion per year.

One of our hospitals, lauding its capabilities and facilities, informed those reading its brochure that "Our lab provides over 570 different tests and other services, and we do one million tests a year," a testimonial to the fantastic proliferation of diagnostic technology. There is no doubt that data previously unavailable can now be obtained by tests. Franz Ingelfinger, the late great editor of New England Journal of Medicine, one day said, "If all available procedures are used, doctors can now diagnose illness with close to 100 percent accuracy. In major teaching centers," he went on, "patients still die but they rarely die undiagnosed." He raised the point that if conventional diagnostic methods achieve 95 percent accuracy, the addition of another series of tests increases accuracy only fractions of a percent per test, and the question of benefit outweighing costs and risk becomes applicable.

There is an ever-increasing tendency to rely on x-ray, laboratory, and other auxiliary reports to make a diagnosis. Tests are extremely valuable, but they should only supplement as necessary, not supplant, clinical acumen.

The increased reliance on technical procedures is encouraged by several factors. Patients are often more impressed by doctor action than by doctor thinking, by the number of tests ordered than by the questions asked in the history, by the medications prescribed than by the advice given, by the number of x-rays films taken than by the amount of thought behind their requisition. In today's litigious climate, the quality and completeness of patient care is often convincingly verified by ordering a multitude of tests, while failure to do so may become grounds for a malpractice suit.

A physician confronted by a diagnostic problem while his or her appointment schedule is running late is easily tempted to substitute a battery of tests for a careful history and physical examination and thus shorten a 30- to 40-minute consultation to a five to 10-minute brief encounter. Also, the third parties who pay for the majority of physicians' services reimburse thinking and decision making at a lower rate than they do tests and procedures. As pointed out by Donald Seldin, an all-night vigil managing a case of diabetic acidosis or hepatic coma is rewarded at a disproportionately low figure compared with a ten-minute endoscopy.

The American Society of Internal Medicine has fittingly called thinking and decision making cognitive services. Lonnie Bristow, the group's president, has observed: "It is easier to order a dozen tests than to sit down and have a discussion with your patients so they can understand and participate in their care."

Although it is difficult to appraise and devise reimbursement formulas for counseling and other cognitive services, a narrowing of the discrepancy in fees would seem to be a possible help in staying the rise in the physician component of health care costs. Uwe Reinhardt, professor of economics at Princeton University, remarked on the dilemma of containing costs, saying there is little incentive because "an insurance carrier is powerless to introduce economy, a health care provider has no incentive to reduce income, and a patient is indifferent to the high cost of getting well." We physicians are used to the familiar exhortation from patient and family. "Don't worry about the cost doctor; do everything you can. I have insurance."

It seems clear that rationing in some form is necessary as mounting costs consume resources needed for other essential goods and services - national defense, education, highway construction, not to mention interest on the national debt! Formal rationing is already being imposed to a degree. For example, Medicare declared a moratorium on paying for heart transplants, and Massachusetts General Hospital decided not to do the procedures, saying their responsibility is to evaluate new procedures in terms of the greatest good for the greatest number. Sweden prohibits kidney transplants in patients past a certain age. Call it priority evaluation, allocation of scare resources, distribution control; these are merely gentler synonyms for rationing.

The utilization of health care is best regulated by the physician, the one who knows most and best what is really necessary and the one who in many instances is the only one legally permitted to order the services and supplies used by patients. It is a difficult responsibility, especially when the doctor-patient relationship makes us instinctively focus on the patient's getting well and exclude thoughts about cost. Unfortunately, accepting such responsibility is necessary today, for failure to accept it allows it to go to others who may be strongly motivated but are certainly less knowledgeable in the comparative importance and value of cost and quality of care.

The obligation is not limited to physicians. It is a many-sided problem. The insurer who insures the almost uninsurable; the labor leader who insists on first-dollar coverage; the industrialist who yields to demand, complains about premium cost, and then passes the cost on to customers; the patient who asks for every possible test; and the government which tolerates an intolerable inflation all have similar responsibility. I believe we in the medical profession are realizing the need to include cost considerations in our decisions on patient care. It is up to us to continue assuming our share of this responsibility and to set the example that the others should follow.

External Readings: Research/Technology

"Meeting the Challenge of Research in Family Medicine..," Journal Family Practice 14:105-13 (January 1982).

Chesney, AP & Gentry, WD, "Psychosocial Factors Mediating Health Risk: A Balanced Perspective," Preventive Medicine 11:612-17 (September 1982).

"Interest in Sleep Disorders Awakening," American Medical News 25:17 (September 3, 1982).

Hayden, GF, et al., "The Case-Control Study: A Practical Review for the Clinician," Journal American Medical Association 247:326-31 (January 15, 1982).

Comroe, JH, "The Road from Research to New Diagnosis & Therapy," Science 200:931-37 (May 26, 1978).

Culliton, BJ, "Biomedical Research Enters the Market Place," New England Journal Medicine 304: 1195-1201 (May 14, 1981).

Griner, PF & Huth, E, "Research in General Internal Medicine," Annals Internal Medicine 96:518-19 (April 1982).

Fuhrer, MJ, "Medical Rehabilitation Research: Distortions, Deflections & Detractions," Archives Physical Medicine Rehabilitation 63:49-54 (February 1982).

Scherer, WF, "From Whence the Next Generation?" American Journal Tropical Medicine & Hygiene 31:423-28 (May 1982).

Davis, WK & Kelley, WN, "Factors Influencing Decisions to Enter Careers in Clinical Investigation," Journal Medical Education 57:275-81 (April 1982).

"Manmade Internal Organs," Medical World News 22:34-48 (June 22, 1981).

Kleinert, HE, "Microsurgery in Trauma: Its Evolution and Future," Bulletin American College Surgeons 67:10-19 (June 1982).

Weed, LL, "Problem-Knowledge Coupling," Journal Holistic Health 8:79-87 (1983).

Dykes, MHM, "Beating the Knowledge & Technology Explosion," Journal American Medical Association 246:1924-25 (October 23/30, 1981).

Bralow, SP (ed.). Basic Research & Clinical Medicine. Washington: Hemisphere Pub. Co., 1981. 280 pp.

Reiser, SJ. Medicine & The Reign of Technology. New York: Cambridge Univ. Press, 1978. 341 pp.

McNeil, BJ & Cravalho, EG (eds.). Critical Issues in Medical Technology. Boston: Auburn House Pub. Co., 1982. 432 pp.

Levine, RJ. Ethics & Regulation of Clinical Research. Baltimore: Urban & Schwarzenbert, 1981. 324 pp.

COMING HEALTH CUTS WORRY BLACK PHYSICIAN GROUP

Winning a place for blacks in medicine is a goal the National Medical Association (NMA) has pursued relentlessly for 88 years, despite changing economic and political fortunes.

Forty-five years ago the battle of the nation's first black physicians association was all uphill: There were fewer than 5,000 black physicians in the United States and all but 45 of the 350 black medical students in the nation were attending two predominantly black institutions, Howard University in Washington, DC, and Meharry Medical College in Nashville, TN.

Segregation was so pervasive that it affected decisions about who obtained health care and the physicians who rendered it, said Phillip Smith, MD, the NMA's current board chairman.

Many black neighborhoods had no physicians, Dr. Smith said, and few black physicians were able to obtain residency training or hospital privileges. Only 87 blacks in the whole country were board-certified. So many hospitals were closed to blacks, the records of the U.S. Public

---

Health Service show that in 1946 as few as one in every thousand hospital beds was open to a black.

This two-class medical system slowly disintegrated after the enactment of the 1964 Civil Rights Act, Medicaid, and health training programs, but some NMA officials now say they fear that blacks may be returning to charity wards and second-class care. Sherril Lynn Walker of Duke University, president of the Student National Medical Association. (SNMA), said she "dreads" the possibilities that variable interest student loan programs may discourage low-income blacks from entering medicine in the future and that government loan cutbacks could foster a system of medical training that caters to the rich and the powerful.

NMA Executive Director Al Fisher admitted that the association of black physicians was "waiting to see which way Congress moves to resolve national health policies and what impact there will be on physicians."

At stake in current political battles are the gains that black physicians and their patients have made during the past two decades. Health facilities have been desegregated, government loan and scholarship programs have wooed some 3,800 blacks to U.S. medical schools each year, nearly 12,00 black physicians now are in practice, and government-financed health care significantly has improved the health status and the life expectancy of American blacks.

Federal insured health programs also have increased the average income of black physicians. Black physicians now earn an average income of $66,000 a year, Fisher said, although he contends they must work twice as hard as their white counterparts to achieve their income level because their patients often live in economically depressed areas, are poorer, and pay physicians less.

Today's black physicians primarily are concerned about how the federal government will address the issues of indigent patients' access to care, the distribution and the supply of physicians, and "the kinds of medical services that will be available to the growing numbers of elderly blacks in the U.S.," Fisher said.

Some NMA members already are expressing concern about the indirect effects of shifting federal policies on black physicians and their patients, but both Dr. Smith and Frank Royal, MD, a former NMA president, made it clear that it was too early to tell what the full impact of these changes would be.

Dr. Smith, who practices obstetrics and gynecology among urban blacks in Los Angeles, said that a federal cap on Medicaid had triggered reductions in public health care spending for unemployed and uninsured low-income workers that eventually could affect the supply of physicians in West Coast minority communities. California's Medicaid program,

Medi-Cal, once offered liberal benefits to people of some means who had no way to pay for medical care. Unemployed or medically indigent Californians even had the option of obtaining care from private physicians who treated Medi-Cal patients, Dr. Smith explained. Many uninsured persons turned to inner-city black physicians whom the federal government had encouraged to establish practices in areas where there were few, if any, physicians.

Beginning in January, however, medically indigent adults in California were required to obtain care at public hospitals or facilities that had contracted to provide low-cost care, Dr. Smith said. The change in state policy prompted a third of Dr. Smith's own patients to abandon his practice.

New rules also have meant a cut in income for Dr. Smith and other Los Angeles minority physicians whose practices primarily comprise Medi-Cal patients. Presumably, they also have affected adversely other black physicians in California.

Additional California policy shifts, which now are in effect, are "making a business of health care," Dr. Smith said, and they threaten to reinstitute a "two-tiered system of medicine" in which "people of means can be treated with one level of care and people who are poor receive a reduced type of care."

Those changes involve contracting out Medi-Cal services to the lowest-bidding hospitals in California, Dr. Smith said. A new law . . . would prevent California's poor patients from choosing their own physicians by waiving so-called freedom of choice provisions in Medicaid programs, a policy change that Dr. Royal said had the "potential of destroying the whole Medicaid concept because it immediately institutionalizes Medicaid."

The Richmond, VA., practitioner predicted that freedom of choice waivers would lead back to a "two-tiered delivery system" of charity wards and clinics "wherever they occur." The waivers also would be "totally disastrous" for physicians who relied on Medicaid to establish their offices in inner cities, Dr. Royal said, because "the population they committed themselves to serve would no longer be there."

The effects of state Medicaid reversals already may be being felt by some minority physicians, Dr. Royal said. He claims that three black physicians from California recently moved their practices to Richmond, where Medicaid policy shifts have been much less severe.

Another knotty issue for the NMA is the so-called corporatization of medicine, and physicians' ranks appear to be split over its risks and its benefits. Fisher said NMA members were concerned about "whether we'll have a pluralistic health care system, whether we'll have one which the health professions will dominate, or whether we'll go to a system that gives corporations a much greater role."

Interviews with black physicians turned up serious conflicts of opinion about the effects of corporate-owned hospitals and health maintenance organizations (HMOs) in minority communities. There are differences about whether corporate enterprises will improve or lower the quality of care for underserved black patients in urban ghettos, and whether free enterprise medicine would shut out black private practitioners altogether or enable new black physicians to stabilize their incomes rapidly, pay off educational loans, and work fewer hours than their predecessors.

Dr. Royal, who sits on the board of the Hospital Corp. of America, called hospital conglomerates the "saviors" for independent practitioners in underserved minority neighborhoods. The money saved by large corporate enterprises will let black communities support "a viable health care system," he said.

"If we are going to preserve what is called the free enterprise system in medicine (private practice)," Dr. Royal said, "it is my opinion that these companies will be the only saviors for me. We will either work with them or work for the government."

Another black physician, however, said he was worried about health care in minority communities becoming "controlled by outside interests who deal in volume" and may put more emphasis on profits than on Hippocratic ideals.

Minority medical students and residents have expressed similar reservations in the past, but their ideals apparently are beginning to give way under economic realities. More and more physicians are emerging from training programs with high debts, Fisher explained, and many of them are opting to "immediately begin to discharge their debts" by working in corporate situations as company employees.

Evangeline Franklin, MD, a minority internal medical resident completing her PGY-1 year at the University of Rochester, explained that the pressures of the anticipated physician glut and large loans, and the desire for more personal time and more reasonable working conditions also were influencing minority residents to consider working in HMOs, especially in instances in which physicians have married each other.

If the move to HMOs becomes a trend, the pattern could have far-reaching implications for minority communities, Fisher warned, because most minority physicians do not think that HMOs can survive in ghetto areas, where patients traditionally have been sicker and less able to pay for health care.

"If we're not careful, we'll end up with a split system that has some minority doctors employed in ideal corporate settings," Fisher said, and other black physicians located in government or philanthropic clinics where it may be difficult "to attract the kind of people that will be able to provide the quality of service that should be available to all people, regardless of what source pays for it."

Fortunately, internal issues facing the NMA are considerably less complex than external challenges. Operations, Fisher said, are more tranquil than they were seven years ago, when the association was recovering from near bankruptcy and was forced to sell a large Washington, D.C., headquarters building across from the State Dept. The organization apparently has rebounded from the draining series of projects than overextended its financial resources in the 1970s, Fisher said.

"Since 1975, the NMA has done a number of things of stabilize the financial base of the organization," he said. "We think that in terms of assets we're significantly better off than we were eight or nine year ago." Next month, the NMA plans to move out of the rented offices it currently occupies in northwest Washington, D.C., and into its own two million dollar office building near a new downtown convention center.

The NMA has not accomplished everything it set out to do, however. The percentage of black physicians who belong to the organization has not changed in the last eight years . . . Even though the total number of black physicians has grown from 6,600 to 11,970 since the 1970's Fisher admitted that the NMA was fighting for members "just like everybody else."

Black enrollment in medical school currently is 5.8 percent, far below the 12 percent goal the NMA set in 1975. This year's total enrollment is 3,869, 176 more than last year, and most black graduates are emerging from predominately white medical schools.

Increasing educational costs and declining numbers of low-interest government loans are threatening to erode the enrollment of blacks, Dr. Franklin said, because minority college students now "want to go into fields that are high pay, but not high risk."

Younger students are well aware that their predecessors are having problems repaying the educational debts they incurred in the days that government-insured loans were plentiful and cheap. They also know that government assistance to medical students is much harder to come by.

Several months ago, Howard University led the nation's medical schools with a 61 percent default rate on a low-interest national medical student loan program known as HPSL. The school's default rate since has been reduced to 44 percent through collection activities . . . but unless it is reduced to five percent by the end of March, there are proposals to drop Howard from the federally insured program.

That could have a significant adverse effect on Howard's approximately 500 medical students, who have been feeling the domino effect of cutbacks in federal assistance to health professions students. Until last year, as many as 125 medical students at the predominantly black school obtained financial aid in the form of National Health Service Crops scholarships that were repayable with work in underserved areas of the nation. That assistance since has been curtailed and is not expected to be renewed . . . Fewer than five scholarships were given to Howard students during the 1981-82 school year, so students increasingly turned to nine percent HPSL and variable rate Health Education Assistance Loans (HEAL) to finance their educations. By the end of the school year, 175 Howard students had taken out HPSL loans and 42 had obtained HEAL money. A year earlier when federal money was more abundant, only 119 students had HPSL loans . . . and none had HEAL loans.

This year . . . as many as 25 percent of the school's students will borrow through the HEAL program, although it is not yet clear how many will be able to obtain HPSL money. These borrowing patterns . . . indicate that "minority medical students are willing to do whatever it takes to get through medical school."

SNMA President Walker, however, questioned whether minority students in the future would be willing to continue to assume the financial risks of today's students. Costs of borrowing could be higher and will not be likely to be offset in the first few years of medical school by low-interest financing.

Her fellow minority students once were discouraged from borrowing HEAL money because its varying interest rate had the potential to escalate a $10,000 loan into a $115,000 debt over 25 years. Last year, however, they had begun to turn to the loan, figuring they could afford higher borrowing costs now because of low costs earlier in their education. Fortunately, improvements in the economy have driven down interest of the HEAL loan, she said. Rates had been as high as 18 percent in the last year, but have dropped to 11 3/4 percent in recent months. Government loan charts indicate that a $10,000 25-year loan now will cost students less than $60,000, provided that interest rates do not begin to rise again.

That has brightened the picture for minority students significantly. Their battle, however, like that of the NMA, continues to be uphill. - Phyllis Gapen

External Readings: Black Physicians

Lloyd, SM & Johnson, DC, "Practice Patterns of Black Physicians..," Journal National Medical Association 74:129-41 (February 1982).

Haynes, MA, "Blacks in Medicine," In: Academic Medicine (Bowers, JZ and King EE, eds.). North Tarrytown, NY: Rockefeller Archive Center, 1983. pp. 139-152.

Bowman, MA, "Specialty Choice of Black Physicians," Journal National Medical Association 78:13-15 (January 1986).

WOMEN IN MEDICINE: BEYOND PREJUDICE

Marcia Angel, MD

Women in medicine trend to evoke extreme views. On the one hand it is argued that women in medicine are simply more trouble than they're worth, that they ask too many special favors, are somehow not quite serious, and probably should be home with the children anyway. Opposed is the belief that women should be in medicine to the same extent as men, but are not because of discrimination based on prejudice. According to this view, once the barriers of prejudice are removed, all we need to do is encourage women to take their place alongside men, not only as practicing physicians but also in the higher echelons of academic and organized medicine. . . There is the suggestion that if we could but search out women more avidly we would have our female deans, department heads, and professors. Is it that simple? In an earlier editorial Relman focused on the impact of women on medicine; here I will concentrate instead on the impact of medicine on women doctors - and the families - and suggest that it is in this area that difficult problems remain, problems that go beyond prejudice.

Whatever our viewpoint, I think we can agree on one thing about women in medicine; the average women physician, that is, the woman who has children, must make major compromises in her profession, in her home, or in both. During her 30s, the period of life when career advancement is most rapid, she carries two sets of serious and time-consuming responsibilities - one to her profession and one to her children. That both are serious and time-consuming is attested to by the fact that so many men devote themselves exclusively to the first and so many of their wives exclusively to the second. The heart of the dilemma for the women physician lies in her responsibility to oversee the development of her children. If this is important - and few parents think that it isn't - then she inevitably has doubts about the course she has chosen and the priorities it implies. In doing one job well, may she not be doing another, possibly more important job, poorly? A solution is to forfeit professional advancement in return for time - that is, to enter "soft" specialties, look for relatively leisurely or part-time residencies, take salaried positions in clinics of health-maintenance organizations, and stay in the lower echelons of academic and organized medicine. How do her male colleagues see this? Incredibly, many of them choose to see this rather grim and highly responsible series of tradeoffs as frivolous or as evidence of incompetence.

Does the husband of a woman physician - who is almost always in a

- 272 -

profession himself, often medicine - have similar experiences? After all, he too is a parent in a dual-career marriage. I think he rarely does, for several reasons. Social custom dictates strongly that a man not be a "househusband" (the word doesn't even sound real). Furthermore, it is even more difficult for him to pace himself in his career than it is for a woman. He must have a career and he must commit himself fully to it; there is very little choice and therefore very little guilt. It is his wife who makes the choice to enter a consuming profession, for reasons that may be construed as largely selfish, and it is therefore she who feels responsible for the consequences of that choice and the compromises that have to be made.

How, then, can women reach the upper echelons of medicine, as Braslow and Heins urge, when it is so difficult just standing still? Clearly, it is not only a matter of equal opportunity and plenty of role models. As long as medicine retains its present character, most women will still not have the time and energy that it takes to match men in the upper echelons of medicine. They will still tend to be instructors and assistant professors rather than deans, department heads, and professors. Understanding this is an important first step in finding solutions to the problems of women in medicine. It is simplistic to assume that if we put more women on the lower rungs of various ladders, they will climb at the same rate as men. As Braslow and Heins point out, even in specialties, such as pediatrics, that traditionally have a large pool of qualified women, only a handful of department heads are women. It may be wise to accept the likelihood that even with the best will in the world, women will continue to be under-represented at the upper levels of medicine. Still, there will be some women who do have the desire and ability to reach the top. Certainly, women without children are in position to compete with men, as to a lesser extent, are women who are content with a decision to leave the childrearing to others.

For those women (and men) who wish to play an active part in raising their children, I believe that there should be a restructuring of medicine in ways that recognize the special needs of the family and the extraordinary efforts that women physicians now make. It is often argued that since the demanding nature of medicine is well known, women should either stay out of it or go into it wholeheartedly, without complaints. This argument, which can be used to justify nearly any long-standing inequity or impropriety, suggests that the structure of medicine is immutable. It isn't. Part-time work, time out for having and raising a family, and a smooth reentry into medicine could, with only modest ingenuity, be incorporated into the structure of medical training and academic medicine. Choosing such pathways should be not only possible, but respectable. The present practice of requiring each woman to blaze her own trail is, at best, clumsy and wasteful of effort. It is also demoralizing.

What are the arguments against making such accommodations? The more serious is that medicine is a calling so exacting that nothing short of ceaseless dedication is required to maintain the necessary skills. According to this view, any compromise in the time devoted to it means a lessening of quality. This argument is based on a rather remorseless - and unsubstantiated - view of what medicine should be. There is no evidence that women physicians are less competent than men, even though they work on average fewer hours. Indeed, women physicians are less likely than men to be sued for malpractice in proportion to their numbers. The truth is that nobody knows how much time it takes to be a good doctor. I think its quite possible that the average physician has gone beyond a point of diminishing returns. Doctors have traditionally been proud of their single-mindedness, of the long hours they devoted to their profession, of the nights without sleep during their training. Has this led to a sense of exaltedness that creates an empathy gap with their patients, most of whom lead quite different lives? Could this be a basis for the alleged arrogance of doctors?

A less serious argument made against accommodation to part-time work or leaves of absence is that it would be inefficient. Why should we set up a system that allows some physicians to work part-time while other work full-time? There would be merit to this argument only if there were a severe shortage of physicians in our society. Most experts, however, foresee a doctor glut rather than a shortage. Moreover, when we remember that women physicians earn considerably less per hour than their male colleagues, that they are more likely to enter primary-care specialties and that they manage without househusbands, it is clear that they are highly cost-effective members of society.

Women are in medicine to stay. When we force them to choose between their profession and raising their children, rather than providing part-time positions and reentry programs, we run two risks. The first, and I think the greater, is that they will choose their profession (such is the status of medicine). Many authorities see the weakening of the family as a serious threat to our society, and I share their view. Certainly a strong case can be made that we suffer more from lack of parenting than from lack of doctoring. To the extent that women physicians work part-time in order to raise their children, then, they are performing a highly useful function - for all of us.

The other risk is that professional compromises will become a way of life for women even when such compromises are no longer necessary. Women can expect to have about 25 years of professional life after their children are in school. If they have taken time to raise their children, they may find it prohibitively difficult to reenter medicine fully. They may instead continue in a type of practice that doesn't stretch their talents. This is the real inefficiency of women in medicine; talented physicians reluctantly spending their entire professional lives on the fringes. Our challenge is to adjust to the reality of women's lives instead of denying it, so that they can be better mothers and better doctors.

External Readings: Women in Medicine

"Women in Medicine: Two points of View," Journal American Medical Association 249:207-10 (January 14, 1983).

Romm, S, "Woman Doctor in Search of a Job," Journal American Medical Womens Association 37:11-15 (January 1982).

Rinke, CM, "The Professional Identities of Women Physicians," Journal American Medical Association 245:2419-21 (June 19, 1981).

New England Journal Medicine 305:705-06 (September 17, 1981).

"Betty Gilson, MD: Keeping the Faith," Journal American Medical Association 245:2139-42 (June 5, 1981).

American Medical News 25:11-13 (April 23/30, 1982).

Journal American Medical Womens Association 36:33-88 (February 1981); 36:95-108 (March 1981).

"The Economic & Academic Status of Women Physicians," Journal American Medical Association 245:2305-06 (June 12, 1981); 247:173 (January 8, 1982).

Brown, SL, & Klein, RH, "Woman-Power in the Medical Hierarchy," Journal American Medical Womens Association 37:155-64 (June 1982).

Harrison, M. A Woman in Residence. New York: Random House, 1982.

Campbell, M. Why Would a Girl Go Into Medicine. Old Westbury, NY: The Feminist Press, 1977.

American Medical Womens Association. Career Choices for Women in Medicine. AMWA, 465 Grand St., New York, 10002. 1983.

Morantz, RM, et al., (eds.). In Her Own Words: Oral Histories of Women Physicians. Westport, CT: Greenwood Press, 1982. 284 pp.

Morgan, E. Solo Practice: A Woman Surgeon's Story. New York: Little, Brown & Co., 1982.

Mandelbaum, DR. Work, Marriage and Motherhood. New York: Praeger, 1981. 303 pp.

PHYSICIANS' COMPETITORS: UPSTAGING THE STAR

In the long-running drama of health care, the physician has always played the lead. But his right to that role is being challenged, with growing effectiveness, by many of his fellow performers.

Trying to rewrite the script to gain wider scope for their talents - as well as the higher status that goes with the billing of a co-star or at least a featured player - are a growing number of pharmacists, nurse-midwives, podiatrists, optometrists, psychotherapists, nurse practitioners, and physician's assistants. Some physicians feel they're surrounded by other health workers nibbling away at their practices.

Such encroachments are by no means new, notes University of Maryland clinical professor of psychiatry Nathan Schnaper, whose specialty has perhaps been nibbled most and longest. Partly because of a widespread feeling among legislators that physicians "make too much money and shouldn't have the whole pie," he believes the trend can't be stopped. And as more non-physicians gain a place on hospital staffs, "pretty soon consumers will be part of the admitting team, too," adds Dr. Schnaper, who's president of the Maryland Psychiatric Society and chief psychiatrist for the Baltimore Cancer Research Program.

Speaking from one of the hotter battle zones, in which MDs have lost a long series of struggles with optometrists, Dr. James H. Allen of New Orleans, retired chairman of ophthalmology at Tulane, nevertheless rejects Dr. Schnaper's conviction that the nibbling is unstoppable. "I'll admit frankly, ophthalmology was asleep at the switch. But now we're awake and fighting back," says Dr. Allen. "The issue," he emphasizes, "isn't whether or not optometrists should use drugs in making a diagnosis. It's that they don't know how to make a diagnosis, because they're not trained to. Only a person with a medical degree should be permitted to use drugs on a patient."

The newest nibbling is by pharmacists, some of whom are now writing prescriptions as well as filling them. Nurse-midwives and podiatrists are expanding their clinical domains in ways some claim will jeopardize patients' health. Many nurse practitioners and even some physician's assistants - whose training was aided, abetted, and applauded by physicians - are striving for varying degrees of independence from their medical mentors.

Even so, AAFP's national president, Dr. John S. Derryberry of Shelbyville, TN, feels "doctors generally don't feel threatened, and have no need to." Most non-physician professionals "know their limitations and are willing to abide by them," he believes.

But here are reports from the various fronts.

Pharmacists: monitoring doctor's prescriptions - and writing their own. Registered pharmacists back their knowledge of drugs with the strength of numbers - 120,000 to 130,000 - and their presence in almost every community. They've been pushing for recognition as the professionals most capable of riding herd on prescriptions and OTC drugs, and some are now winning a role even in primary care.

"Pharmacists are as well educated as any mid-level practitioner in the rational use of drugs," says Fred M. Eckel, professor of hospital pharmacy at the University of North Carolina. A member of a committee rewriting the state's pharmacy-practice act, he admits the issue is turf. "If society is going to give non-physicians the right to use drugs" - as his state has given optometrists, nurse practitioners, and physician's assistants - "the same right should be extended to pharmacists, the most widely distributed and readily available health professionals."

In the Indian Health Service, pharmacists are being trained to provide care for patients with chronic or self-limiting illnesses. In some rural group practices in the South and Midwest, they're sharing triage duty with nurses as well as handling the follow-up of patients taking drugs.

One of the most extensive programs is at the Phoenix Indian Medical Center, where 50 pharmacists in the past four years have taken 12 weeks of classroom and clinical training, followed by a 12-week preceptorship, to become certified as primary-care pharmacist practitioners. One graduate described his subsequent job as "50 percent patient care and 50 percent pharmacy . . ."

The most wide-ranging study now under way is in California under a law authorizing a test of how well pharmacists, nurse practitioners, and physician's assistants can prescribe drugs under a doctor's supervision - and whether it's cost-effective to have them do it. In the three-year study, some 45 experienced pharmacists working in institutions took a physician-taught course on physical-assessment skills. They're being tested by the pharmacy schools of the University of Southern California and the University of California at San Francisco.

"The physician makes the diagnosis, but the pharmacist is responsible for monitoring drug therapy and does the prescribing for certain acute conditions," says USC pharmacy professor William F. McGhan, project co-director there. A state-appointed committee of pharmacists and physicians approved a broad formulary, excluding Schedule II and III drugs.

In April the American Pharmaceutical Association's House of Delegates declared that "the pharmacist is the expert on drugs and drug therapy on the health-care team." It endorsed "a prescribing role for the pharmacist, based on the specific diagnosis of a qualified health practitioner."

Nurse-midwives: practicing in hospitals - and 'away from mass medicine'. Since 1970, the American College of Obstetricians and Gynecologists has supported including nurse-midwives on an obstetrician's team. It says they may be allowed to "assume responsibility for the complete care and management of uncomplicated" deliveries. But births should be in hospitals, ACOG holds - not in "childbirth centers," and never in the home.

Many certified nurse-midwives (CNMs), with credentials from the American College of Nurse-Midwives, don't debate the issue. Most of these professionals, whose modern style of practice is far removed from the old-style "granny" midwives who once delivered many American babies, work under close - or not so close - supervision in obstetricians' offices or hospitals. But others prefer greater independence.

Marilynn Schmidt, a spokeswoman for ACNM in Washington, D.C., estimates about half her 1,700 fellow CNMs work in hospitals. ACNM's most recent survey found 97 percent practice there or in "alternative settings," with only three percent attending home deliveries. It certifies about 200 nurse-midwives a year.

There are few interprofessional problems in physician-scarce areas, Schmidt says. "But obstetricians feel nurse-midwives belong only where there aren't enough physicians - that they're fine in the hills of Kentucky but not in metropolitan areas."

ACOG's executive director, Dr. Warren H. Pearse, says geography isn't the issue. "Our feelings are very clear," he declares. "Neither freestanding maternity centers separate from hospital facilities, nor the home, represent safety for mother and baby."

Dr. Pearse rejects the nurse-midwives' claim that they attend only normal, "non-high risk" patients. He says New York City's Maternity Center Association - "the prime example of the freestanding, nurse-midwife-run center" - transfers up to 27 percent of its patients to a backup hospital through heavy Manhattan traffic during labor or immediately after the birth - "and that's after having screened out all of the so-called high-risk patients."

Gene Cranch, a CNM who is the center's assistant director, says only 18 percent to 20 percent are transferred during labor. Only six of the 700 women who've given birth there were taken to a hospital postpartum, she adds.

She believes some obstetricians are opposed "because we show good, safe maternity care can be given outside the hospital" at reasonable cost. "I'm not sure whether they're more concerned with safety or with economics. They consider births their turf," she says.

Obstetrician Alvin M. Donnenfeld, the center's senior medical officer - one of three OBs who help screen patients and treat them when needed - admits being closer to a hospital would be better. But he rejects hospital deliveries for everyone.

"The whole idea of the alternative birth center is to be away from the hospital, from 'mass medicine,' from the routine IV, from the 'high risk' attitude prevalent from the doorman to the nurse," he maintains. But Dr. Donnenfeld also opposes at-home births as "potentially too risky."

Obstetrician Robert M. Livingston of Englewood Cliffs, NJ, who has worked with CNMS at a child-birth center there for five years, concedes that many obstetricians "believe there's no such thing as a low-risk delivery, that every patient is potentially at high risk," he says. "I just don't buy that."

Dr. Livingston believes "a very large element" of the opposition is economic. "There's a lot of competition for OB patients, so there's a lot of jealousy when obstetricians see a midwife attracting 18 to 20 deliveries a month . ."

The key factor behind growth of alternative child-birth centers is consumer preference, Dr. Livingston adds. Possible explanations of the distrust of physicians, he suggests, are bad experiences with previous births and a feeling that obstetricians - female as well as male - give too little emotional support.

"Women today see nurse-midwives as being more sympathetic than obstetricians," he says. "Many of them are heading toward at-home delivery. They don't want to go to a hospital, and some nurse-midwives are attending them at home. But many women will deliver under more medical circumstances at a childbirth center with a nurse-midwife, and I think this trend will continue."

In the long run, "The belief that anyone who reads a book on the subject or takes a two-day course can become an expert in attending childbirth in the home" is a bigger issue, ACOG's Dr. Pearse believes.

Podiatrists: cooperation in sports, competition in surgery. Doctors of podiatric medicine have long held staff positions (mainly for treatment of diabetics and other patients with circulatory problems) at some hospitals. They won prominence from the fitness boom, which brought legions of runners and joggers limping and hobbling into their offices. But when it comes to curing bunions surgically, many orthopedists are quietly (for fear of lawsuits, they say) crying foul.

"Correcting a bunion is more than removing a little bit of bone," says a New Jersey orthopedist. "You have to correct the metarsal malignment. That can be done safely only in a hospital OR. Podiatrists who don't have hospital privileges try to do it in the office, which is a disaster, or just take off part of the bone - so of course the condition recurs."

New York City podiatrist Edwin J. Rosenblatt says he treats several hundred bunion patients a year, in his office if the problem is minor but otherwise in an OR. Especially in smaller hospitals, where they "get to know each other well," orthopedists and podiatrists often work together happily, he says.

Most of Dr. Rosenblatt's referrals are from GPs and FPs, he reports. "But one orthopod sends me his bunions and hammertoes. He says I do a better job than he can."

"The relationship between podiatry and medicine is more cooperative than competitive," asserts Gilbert Hollander, executive director of the Podiatry Society of the State of New York. "Diabetologists and gerontologists routinely refer patients to podiatrists."

Dr. Richard H. Kiene, acting chairman of orthopedics at Truman Medical Center in Kansas City, MO, and president of the American Orthopedic Foot Society, feels friction, where it exists, results from a change within podiatry from a "fairly conservative" approach to foot care to a more activist stance. "They operate fairly rapidly now," he says.

"There's no question that some animosity does exist," concedes podiatrist Arthur E. Helfand, chairman of community health at the Pennsylvania College of Podiatric Medicine in Philadelphia. "But it's conflict between individuals, not a widespread feeling."

If conflict is not widespread, at least part of the reason is geographical. About half the country's 8,500 podiatrists practice in the states where the five colleges of podiatry are located: New York, California, Illinois, Ohio, and Pennsylvania. Most of the rest are in a handful of other states.

Cardiologist-runner George A. Sheehan of Red Bank, NJ, is among physicians lauding podiatrists' efforts on joggers's behalf . . . Podiatrist Steven I. Subotnick of Hayward, CA, the "running foot doctor" who's on the editorial board of The Physician and Sportsmedicine, says podiatrists "filled a void." They "ended up functioning as triage officers and primary-care physicians for runners" who are outside medicine's mainstream, he adds.

"There's no conflict between orthopedists and podiatrists in sports medicine," believes orthopedic surgeon William G. Hamilton, official doctor for the New York City Ballet. Experienced podiatrists "do a fantastic job," he says.

But he adds: "We orthopedists see a lot of work done by podiatrists who have gotten in over their heads. And lately I've been seeing a lot of people asking for a second opinion after a podiatrist recommended surgery. It's difficult to generalize, but I've felt they were too aggressive."

Dr. Joseph E. Milgram, emeritus director of orthopedic surgery at the Hospital for Joint Diseases in New York City, feels the issue is mainly a matter of training. "There are many diseases that require knowledge of the body's reaction to the disease," he says. "It's not right to operate on one part of the body without knowing about the rest. Surgery isn't done on the foot but on the patient."

Optometrists: using drugs for diagnosis - and now for treatment. Conceding that well-organized and politically effective doctors of optometry have beaten them badly in state after state . . . some ophthalmologists, such as New Orleans' Dr. Allen, now see signs suggesting they can still stop the trend. Optometrists have gained diagnostic-drug rights in 25 states since 1971, and eight others had no prohibition to start with. In North Carolina and West Virginia, ODs have won the right to use drugs for treatment.

Dr. Allen is a founder and board chairman of P.E.N. Inc. (Physicians Education Network), a 2,000-member organization based in St. Petersburg, FL. "We're not against optometry," he insists. "We're for the eye health of the public."

Optometrist Stephen Miller, director of the primary-care division of the American Optometric Association in St. Louis, claims the steady growth in the number of states giving ODs drug-use rights "results from the experience that optometrists can and do use diagnostic agents safely and effectively. We've reached the point now where it's obvious our use of these agents hasn't created a hazard."

Among the eye experts to whom it's not obvious at all is the Ophthalmological Society of South Carolina's president, Dr. Charles B. Bobo of Greenwood. He's compiled a file of 70 cases of "problems" resulting from optometrists' use of diagnostic drugs - which he calls "automatic licensure for practicing medicine without proper education, by legislative fiat."

Another is Dr. Richard C. Rashid, ophthalmology professor at West Virginia University in Charleston, who says he knows of "many cases" of potential and actual eye damage caused by optometrists' drugs. In one, he says, an optometrist "undertook to treat a serious eye condition, an ulcer on the eye. The ulcer ruptured, with the patient losing vision in the eye."

Compiling a registry of eye damage among optometrists' patients in his state is ophthalmologist David W. White of Greenville, N.C. "It's ironic that just as government is leaning more and more toward consumer protection, non-medical practitioners are getting more and more latitude in areas where they're not qualified," he says.

Perhaps the sharpest criticism of optometric drug use comes from ophthalmologist Irving T. Staley of Marietta, GA, who was a practicing optometrist before going to medical school. He says he "questions the moral principles" of those who treat people without the proper training. "Optometrists aren't equipped by their training to use drugs," he believes.

Psychotherapists: old rivals becoming allies against new ones? It used to be just the clinical psychologists who offered psychiatrists stiff competition for patients needing mental help. Then came the psychiatric social workers and lay analysts, followed by marathon encounters, primal-scream therapists, games-people-play transactional analysts, and such eclectic activities as Erhard Seminars Training (est).

But in the psychology-versus-psychiatry competition, "We're still the little guys, and they're the big buys," says psychologist Anne Marie O'Keefe, special-projects director of the Association for the Advancement of Psychology, political arm of the American Psychological Association. In 23 states, the law lets psychologists join hospital staffs, and in one - California - it requires hospitals to consider their applications, even though such membership in any state is against the rules of the Joint Commission on Accreditation of Hospitals. "I haven't come across a single case" in which JCAH enforced its rule with disaccreditation, Dr. O'Keefe says, though she adds that hospitals have often dropped psychologists when the commission told them to.

And just as psychiatrists object to invasion of their turf by psychologists, psychologists are unhappy about other groups moving in on them. AAP favors antitrust actions against JCAH - but has to watch out for similar suits from non-PhD therapists.

Yale clinical psychologist Helen Block Lewis finds it "very unfortunate" that nearly anyone can hang out a shingle and claim to be a therapist. But she admits there's no reason why social workers with training in psychiatry, for example, can't do a lot of good.

Instead of continued conflict, Dr. Robert J. Campbell, American Psychiatric Association vice president and executive director of New York City's Gracie Square Hospital, believes psychiatrists and psychologists "will probably team up together in a stronger affinity." And beyond that, he envisions the four "mental-health core disciplines" - psychiatry, psychology, psychiatric nursing, and psychiatric social work - eventually settling into their own "most comfortable" turfs.

"Psychotherapy is not necessarily done best by the person who has a medical degree," he says. "It's a skill and a tool many specialties use." He thinks the ideal approach would find physicians "doing the triage, making the differential diagnosis, and formulating the treatment plan," then referring the patient to a practitioner of the proper level. A physician's bill could be considered an "unnecessary" health-care cost, Dr. Campbell concedes, if he merely refers a depressed patient to a marriage counselor, for example.

"But I don't know how to solve the problem of the brain tumor that presents as depression," he says. "Who but a physician would recognize that?"

Nurse practitioners: still debating how much independence they want. Some 38 states have amended their nurse-practice acts to permit medically trained nurses to diagnose, prescribed drugs, and do other things previously forbidden by medical-practice acts.

The nursing profession is far from united on whether it should move into primary care, and in what role . . . But nurses, especially nurse practitioners (NPs), have moved a long way toward independence.

There now are some 16,000 nurse practitioners in the U.S., with 2,000 more being added each year. Though many work in hospitals, doctors' offices, schools, or community-health facilities, some have solo practices - especially in rural areas - and others are establishing joint practices with physicians.

A recent Rand Corporation study for the U.S. Air Force . . . found nurse practitioners as well as physician's assistants (PAs) "performed as well as or better than physicians" in delivering primary-care services. After evaluating 14,000 patient visits, Rand found both NPs and PAs capable of handling all but complex medical problems, and noted they greatly increased physician productivity.

But the president of AAFP's California chapter, Dr. Hubert M. Upton of Mountain View, questions the wisdom of training increasing numbers of mid-level practitioners "when we have a surplus of physicians on the horizon." His organization, which supported the creation of NPs and PAs, is now reconsidering its position.

"The basic idea was to provide NPs and PAs for physician-scarce areas," Dr. Upton points out. "We agreed with the principle of physician extenders provided there was a need, that they would work in underserved areas and be adequately supervised, and that their services would be billed through the physician. That's not happening. They're being used in other capacities."

Studies show such health workers give "quality care, but of a limited quality," he says. The public is better served by turning out medical professionals with broad training, he maintains.

"Of course physicians are unhappy that some nurse practitioners are taking over the role of primary physician," retorts Dr. Katherine Nuckolls, head of the primary-care and nurse-practitioner programs at the University of North Carolina School of Nursing. "It gets into their pocketbooks."

Physician's assistants: officially they don't even think about independence. Leaders of the nation's 14,000 PAs insist they are serving - and want to continue serving - as physician extenders, following the doctor's orders and hewing to set protocol. But the independent role, forced on those who are geographically isolated, is tempting, especially for some of the older ones who served at military bases in places like Alaska or Greenland before becoming PAs in civilian life.

"There are some medically underserved area - in Appalachia and Alaska, for example - where the community cannot support a physician," notes Donald W. Fisher, executive director of the Association of Physician Assistant Programs, in Alexandria, Va. "But the doctor under whom the PA works is totally responsible for the care rendered."

That's the way PAs prefer it, Fisher insists. "We want physician supervision. It's absolutely essential. Every year, our House of Delegates passes a resolution reaffirming our commitment to dependent practice. I don't know a responsible person in this profession who even thinks about independent practice," he emphasizes.

PAs are most heavily represented in the Northwest (especially California, Oregon, and Washington) and Northeast, though they're still barred in New Jersey, where some physicians' and nurses groups vigorously oppose them . . . According go the most recent studies, about a fourth of the PAs practice in areas with few physicians, Fisher notes.

About 3,000 people, half of them women and most of those from nursing, are in 55 PA-training programs. Twelve states have given PAs the right to prescribe drugs from a specially screened list.

Some 15 PAs, along with 65 nurse practitioners and 45 pharmacists, are taking part in California's state-run but physician-supervised study of their ability to prescribed drugs. They're based in hospitals, nursing homes, public-health clinics, satellite facilities, and doctors' offices.

The California Medical Association didn't welcome the study but has been cooperating. CMA is watching it closely through a special task force headed by FP Wilfred Snodgrass, a UCLA assistant clinical professor of medicine and associate director of Santa Monica Hospital's family-practice-residency program.

Dr. Snodgrass says it's too early to draw conclusions from the study and notes that many people feel it won't ever be possible to make a fair evaluation because of the many differences in participants' backgrounds, in the training they were given, in the closeness of their supervision, and in the way they're asked to work. Other problems, he says, include a lack of adequate controls and the difficulty of judging care's quality and cost. Dr. Snodgrass doubts the study will come up with strong proof for either side.

And the future? With or without proof, Dr. Snodgrass believes "this whole movement of permitting parprofessionals to prescribe" will increase. One reason for such changes, as Baltimore's Dr. Schnaper points out, is that many lawmakers "feel physicians have a closed society" that should be opened by legislation.

"I'm not being pejorative about this," Dr. Schnaper adds. "I'm not making a value judgment. In the long run, it might turn out to be good."

The government threw its support behind the new non-physician-training programs, North Carolina's nurse Nuckolls notes, as one way of meeting an anticipated physician shortage. Even though predictions have changed, there will still be a need for more providers of primary care, she maintains.

"The issue that must be faced is, how much will society pay for it?" Dr. Nuckolls adds. "You can always try to met this need with primary-care physicians, but that's a very expensive way to go."

But for both individuals and institutions, saving money can be costly in ways dollars don't measure. "The issue is quality control," maintains Harvard pediatrician Philip J. Porter.

"Everybody wants to get into the act," he adds. "Some of them are tremendous assets, but others don't want to pay the price of becoming competent enough to do what they're doing." - Malcolm M. Manber

External Readings: Autonomy/Turf - Internal Issues

"An Anesthesiologist's Plea," Journal American Medical Association 246:2692-93 (December 11, 1981); 248:648-49 (August 13, 1982).

"A Radiologist's Point of View," Journal American Medical Association 246:2581-82 (December 4, 1981).

Kra, SJ & Boltax, RS. Is Surgery Necessary? New York: MacMillan Pub. Co., 1981. 215 pp. (This volume, which is also available in paperback from the New American Library, provides a lucid discussion of how medical and surgical approaches complement each other in patient care. For the purposes of career planning, Is Surgery Necessary? may be nominated as a fundamental reference for all students with an interest in medicine.)

- 285 -

MDs FACE A CHANGING WORLD

> HELP WANTED: Professional to join fast-growing personal services conglomerate. Must have strong organizational skills, solid financial background, good interpersonal abilities. Seeking risk-taker, open to new ideas, willing to move to new locale. MD degree required.

This could be the advertisement for the physician of tomorrow, if the predictions of a long-time interpreter of the medical scene are on the mark.

For more than 26 years, Tom Zirkle of Boulder, CO, has been a consultant to individual physicians, medical groups, hospitals, and health organizations, working from coast to coast.

His scenario for medicine's next 25 years may be unsetting to some physicians, intriguing to others. Since the original mandate of American Medical News was to "inform, stimulate, and challenge" its physician-readers, a look at what may lie ahead follows:

Accelerated change. Tremendous change reshaped medicine in the past 25 years and even greater change will mark the next few years, says the president of Zirkle, Lee, and Associates Ltd. Growing competition in medicine, an increasing abundance of physicians, and national emphasis on health care cost cutting are precipitating these changes.

"The pace of change is accelerating as competition evokes many different responses from physicians and health care institutions today," Zirkle says. "We will see the same degree of change that occurred in the last 25 years in a much more condensed time frame - perhaps in the next five to eight years."

Zirkle cites two examples of just how fast things are changing. A year ago the term preferred provider organization (PPO) was unknown to many physicians; today it is a professional buzzword. Nor was the idea of a state contracting with physicians or hospitals to provide services for certain types of patients familiar. California began negotiating such contracts for its Medi-Cal patients, and the concept is spreading.

"In five years every state in the union will be negotiating such contracts for Medicaid and maybe for other kinds of patients," Zirkle predicts.

New clinical "growth industries." Developments in the field of human genetics, immunology, pharmacology, and biomedicine will change medicine, reducing the need for and number of surgical procedures and increasing the need for more attention to the field of gerontology, Zirkle contends.

"Genetics, immunology, pharmacology, and biomedicine are the growth industries in clinical medicine," Zirkle explains, "all extending the normal life span. These developments will emerge from the large medical centers and teaching institutions, but the traditional technology transfer will not take place."

For example, when polio vaccine was developed, it moved from the research centers into the individual physician's offices where it was administered. But the "new medicine" largely will be dispensed in big medical centers.

"The changes on the scientific side of medicine will lead more physicians into these highly specialized fields and consequently into large medical groups or into the academic environment. As a result, many patients will be seen in these settings rather than in the primary care physician's office," Zirkle speculates.

Some specialties will be in greater demand; others will diminish in importance. For example, as non-interventional radiological procedures supplant the need for surgery, and become more widely used for therapeutic as well as diagnostic purposes, radiology will grow.

Longer life spans - as the U.S. population becomes increasingly older - will require more medical care and absorb an increasing share of national health care expenditures. The big question is, who will pay for it as the tax burden becomes heavier?

"As medical science extends life, there are projections for an average life span of 120 or 150 years instead of 75," Zirkle says. "Think about it. People will be retired for more years of their lives than they were productive. Sociologically, as well as medically, the implications are frightening and the financial considerations are mind-boggling."

An anti-technology, pro-regulatory climate. As the government foots more and more of the bill for health care, the clamor for reduced costs has risen, and attempts to clamp down the lid on use of some technologies are increasing. Now business and industry have joined the cost-cutting campaign. Most of the arguments against expansion of technology, in Zirkle's view, have been generated by economists and politicians, but there is some validity to high-cost criticisms.

"The health care industry hasn't really had to worry about costs in the past. Hospitals have taken a lot of abuse because their rates have run ahead of inflation. A big part of the hospital cost rise isn't inflationary, it's the result of increased intensity of services and the fact that unlike other industry, new medical technology generates higher, not lower, labor costs. The government is asking, 'Is all of this necessary?' but the bottom line is the value of a human life," the consultant points out.

Ultimately, this continuing clash between costs and care will affect every physician.

Shifting population and reduced MD mobility. In recent years Americans have been moving south and west, with the nation's "center of gravity" tilting heavily toward the Sun Belt. There's nothing really startling about this trend, Zirkle says, but the trend is important for physicians, particularly those not yet situated, in light of the fact that the number of physicians in proportion to the population is rising steadily.

Twenty-five years ago, selecting a place to practice was mainly a matter of personal preference. Now it is a matter of economics.

"It's a supplier's market, not a seller's market today," Zirkle emphasizes. The situation arises from both the operation of supply and demand forces and from pressures to be cost-competitive.

In his opinion, the most attractive practice opportunities are in the West - the fastest growing area of the country - with Texas the best immediate market.

"Texas is conservative and still has room for the independent physician, Zirkle says, adding that Mountain states also look good. He advises physicians seeking a new practice location to look at growth percentages in states.

More prepayment and "negotiated" fees. Prepayment programs have been coming on strong for several years now promoted by those most interested in cutting medical and hospital costs. That trend, Zirkle says, will continue, with some new and not necessarily desirable embellishments.

"The diagnostic-related group (DRG) approach coming to hospitals will come fairly quickly to outpatient medicine," Zirkle predicts, with insurance companies determining the module of service, reimbursing only up to a certain point regardless of level of service.

"Its inevitable," the consultant says, "The insurer will pay so much for certain procedures and no more."

He sees the threat that the insurance industry eventually will control medicine as very real, since the third-party payers will call the shots about reimbursement. Already some insurers are quietly developing fee schedules modeled on the DRG approach, and physicians must be prepared to deal with this possibility Zirkle warns.

It will be tempting for group of physicians to sign on with a big prepayment plan underwritten by a major insurer. The marketing will be professional, the supply of patients assured, cash flow problems will be solved, and at first, the fees will be adequate. But, Zirkle warns, chances are that a few years down the line, the insurer will say, "Let's renegotiate." The fees will be reduced and the approach will be "take-it-or-leave-it," since there will be other physicians standing in the wings ready to pick up the slack.

There will be occasions where a group of physicians can form their own prepaid plan to complete, but that won't always be economically feasible. At the same time, there will be great pressure from business and industry for physicians and hospitals to devise plans that will provide care to employees at lower-than-current rates. More cost-conscious patients will be searching for similar packages they can buy. So, not only will physicians be competing against each other, but various prepared plans also will be vying for patients' and employers' acceptance.

More and bigger medical groups. As the costs of launching a new practice and developing it to the profitable point increase, more physicians will align themselves with medical groups, at least for the initial years of practice, Zirkle says. Groups will get bigger and bigger, and the "megagroup" isn't far down the road, in his opinion.

The Colorado consultant says that there are now probably only 15 to 20 groups in country with more than 100 physicians, but by 1995 he expects that there will be 200 to 250.

"Some of the middle-size groups of 50 or so will grow just through natural processes. But there also will be mergers to gain market dominance and expanded market capacity, and strong central management will characterize these new joint ventures. We are beginning to see some of these mergers taking place today."

Groups will merge to gain bargaining power - to expand their sphere of influence, just as industry does.

Diversification of services. Hospitals, which are undergoing the first wave of cost-cutting attacks, are recognizing the changing medical environment and taking action to adapt to it. Zirkle notes that many are involved in corporate restructuring and are taking advantage of their resources to branch out into other income-producing activities, such as nursing homes, alcohol detoxification centers, wellness programs (which are probably not profitable but present a good image to the community), and consulting. It won't be long before the larger medical groups link up with some of these hospitals to capture significant market shares in their areas, Zirkle says.

"One way to diversify is to ally with others rather than expand horizontally. I think we will see the bigger medical groups entering into contracts with hospitals to provide certain kinds of services, maybe even joint ventures in such fields as radiology, for example," Zirkle says.

"Let's say that a freestanding ambulatory care center seems like a good idea in a town. A hospital and a group of physicians might get together to build it, with the hospital putting up 50 percent of the capital and the physicians the other 50 percent. And the profits would be divided on a 50/50 basis."

Health care conglomerates. Out of these initial alliances of hospitals and physicians will emerge new combinations of services and facilities, Zirkle says.

"The era of the health care conglomerate is dawning and it will cast a shadow over every doctor in the country," he stresses. "These conglomerates will be composed of large medical groups, hospitals, and insurance companies - and who knows what the financial connections may be? Prices for health care services are going to be established by these conglomerates and they will determine who does and does not get certain kinds of work.

"These conglomerates will develop for cost reasons, for access reasons, because of needs for specialized labor, such as certain types of technicians required to operate new medical technologies, and for market domination," he adds.

Publicly owned medical entities. "Some people think I'm crazy, but I think we will see the equivalent of publicly owned medical groups within 10 years," Zirkle says, as a response to growing competition from hospital-based physician groups.

"Hospitals, not-for-profit ones as well as for-profits, are coming to realize that they must compete with physicians, especially with strong medical groups in their communities. And they are using a variety of techniques, such as ambulatory care centers, to do it. So medical groups must respond. But to compete effectively with these hospitals, physicians are going to need a lot of money."

Basically, there are only three ways a medical groups can obtain capital for expansion, Zirkle explains. It can be generated from within the medical group, something that physicians have not done in the past; it can be borrowed at high rates; or it can be brought in through public stock offerings.

"Doctor don't like to leave 20 percent of their income in the group for capital expansion. Their lifestyles are geared to taking 100 percent of the pie, not 80 percent or 85 percent. Such accumulated capital would be taxed, and physicians would rather shelter this money instead," he says.

It's unwise to borrow large sums of money with no equity at today's high interest rates. So the logical thing for a group to do is to team up with somebody who has money - a hospital, an insurance company, perhaps an investment syndicate of some type, and make a public offering. Though professional corporations can't "go public," physicians in these groups can set up a separate corporation and contract to provide the services for such an entity.

Control - the big question. The problem is that "going public" could cost physicians control, Zirkle says. If a hospital puts up the bulk of the front money for expanded services in a joint effort, it is going to want some perks in return - some kind of contractual commitment that physicians will funnel patients to it. If a deal is made with a insurance company, there will be some similar trading of control for capital.

Where does this put the non-participating physicians and smaller hospitals? On the outside, looking in, Zirkle suggests. Since hospitals and insurance companies most likely will enter joint ventures with larger medical groups, the smaller hospitals and smaller medical groups could be squeezed out.

"The small guys will have to get together to pick up the pieces. But that will be a problem," Zirkle says. "They will have to organize in some fashion, but it will be difficult to do much on their own. Traditionally, there has been a lack of good management, effective leadership, and planning in the small provider setting. They will have to act fast to stay in the game, but without the necessary organization, they won't be able to make quick responses." One factor working against the smaller medical entrepreneurs is that controls and systems for building in the efficiency enabling them to be cost effective are poorly integrated or non-existent.

Over the long term, Zirkle says, the health care conglomerates and megagroups should do well, because they ultimately determine where patients get care and they can negotiate price, services, or whatever.

Marketing becomes essential. "As soon as a group of physicians loses its ability to catch and hold onto patients, it is in trouble," Zirkle warns. That's why marketing has assumed increasing importance in medicine. Though Zirkle wasn't talking about marketing in depth, he did say that it must be "more than just willingness to spend money. It must stem from a sincere desire to provide real service. You can use the slick devices to get people in the office door once, but the trick is getting them to come back."

The shifting terrain in the medical environment today has a number of negative aspects for many physicians, Zirkle points out. As the trend toward bigger combination of physicians, facilities, and payment programs develops, he thinks the smaller medical offices will begin to disappear.

"Certainly there will always be successful solo practitioners and small teams of physicians working together," Zirkle hastens to say, "but there will be fewer of these in the years to come."

Clout, MD mobility will diminish. As "big" becomes the byword, physicians will lose the clout that traditionally has been theirs in hospitals and in the organizations with various stakes in medicine and health care.

Physicians' mobility will be somewhat reduced as the physician supply expands, and the metropolitan and suburban areas of the nation, and indeed some areas of the country, become surfeited with MDs.

Cost constraints will reduce the extent of some health care benefit programs offered by employers to their employees, shifting more of the cost to the workers themselves. That development in itself will have ripple effects on consumers' medical purchasing patterns.

Reduced financial expectations. For some physicians, the bottom line will be lower incomes. For younger physicians, future financial prospects will be somewhat reduced, Zirkle believes.

"There is no question about it. A physician coming out of medical school today should have much lower expectations than one who graduated 15 or 20 years ago. Some specialties still in short supply, such as psychiatrists and anesthesiologists, may be exceptions here," Zirkle says.

Already, he says, the medical groups that a few years ago were courting new physicians zealously have reduced their offers. Some are no longer picking up the travel expenses of a physician who comes to visit, although most reimburse him if he decides to join the group.

Competitive pressures across the whole medical spectrum to keep costs down ultimately will compress some physicians' incomes. All the signs point to more "negotiated" fees, Zirkle says, with less freedom on the part of physicians to set their own prices.

"Price competition in medicine is coming along fast," he warns. "For the first time, physicians are beginning to look at their practices from a cost accounting standpoint to see which areas are making or losing money. Formerly, to offset a loser in one area, a doctor merely raised his fees a certain percentage across the board. Now fee increases are being made selectively with an eye toward what the competition is charging and more modest increases are the rule.

Income from capital investment.   As physicians begin to apply
cost-accounting approaches to medical practices to stay competitive,
something very significant may happen, Zirkle says.   They may begin to
shift their orientation from earning income by producing personal
services to one that depends more heavily on return on capital.

"Physicians have traditionally made money by providing personal
services - seeing patients, performing surgery, delivering babies.
Occasionally they have augmented these services by providing laboratory
tests, x-rays, etc., which for the most part did not require direct
personal involvement.   In the years to come, physicians will look for
ways to get return on capital without investing much personal time in
the activities," Zirkle suggests.

Investment in a freestanding outpatient surgery center is a good
example, the consultant says.   "You can get an excellent return, over
and above any individual procedures you as a physician might do.   The
profit comes from the facility charge, which can be lower than a
hospital's because it must allocate other costs to its surgical areas."

Non-physicians have been quick to pick up on the investment
potential in such facilities as surgical centers or minor emergency care
centers, he says.   Some are blanketing the country with notices of
intent to file certificates of need (CON) for construction of such
facilities.

A key to competing successfully is to keep tabs on what is in the
wind, he advises.   In states that still require CON approval to build a
health facility of any sort, physicians would be well advised to get
their names on the lists published by the state agency granting such
approvals.

In states where CONs aren't required, "keep your mouth closed and
your ear to the ground," Zirkle says.   "Watch for things like building
permits, public bids for contracts, hearings to rezone land.   That's how
the information gets out.   And people talk."

He also advises physicians to follow what hospitals are doing.

A change in earnings basis.   A major change for physicians is that
where once they were rewarded for productively, now they are being
rewarded for producing less services at a reduced cost.   The real
danger, in Zirkle's view, is how to maintain quality medical care while
providing services cost effectively.

"The problem here for medical groups is how to measure and reward
efficiency," Zirkle points out.   "The goal is to establish yardsticks,
then measure plus or minus against the yardstick.   But that means
physicians are doing the government's work for them.   Sooner or later,
they'll get their hands on these yardsticks and say, 'This is great!
Let's use them'."

In specialties in which physicians live by referrals and do not generate their own work, Zirkle says incentives don't mean much - it's volume of work and how much staff is needed to do it that counts. As a result, he contends, there will be more supply and demand, salary-type arrangements for such physicians in years to come.

"Ultimately, hospitals and medical groups that these specialists serve may say that instead of working on an incentive basis, they will be paid a salary. And if the salary isn't acceptable, there will be enough doctors out there so that somebody will be glad to come in and do the work at that figure," he warns.

"Staying Alive" professionally. The future isn't necessarily rosy, but there isn't any reason for all physicians to despair, Zirkle says.

"The future won't be relentlessly negative. There will always be some outstanding opportunities for physicians who are both perceptive and prepared, and who are willing to adapt and accept some levels of risk. The main point is that the nature of the opportunities will be different than physicians traditionally have experienced and so most MDs won't successfully adapt to the new circumstances. For a few, however, the opportunities may be greater than ever."

Historically, economic rewards in medicine centered on individual opportunity, stemming mainly from performance of personal professional services. Now and in the future, the new wave of opportunity will be almost exclusively available to organizations rather than to individuals, with rewards to be increasingly derived from investments of capital and leverage obtained from the services of others or the application of technology, Zirkle says.

"This means that doctors are going to have to learn the art of organization - how to join together and manage an organization for purposes of raising capital, exercising control, diversifying - in short, to make an organization a productive vehicle in many dimensions, rather than a single, isolated dimension, such as the use of professional corporations almost exclusively as a tax deferral mechanism," he says.

The new opportunities will be "windows of opportunity," available for only short periods, or as Zirkle says, "slit windows, not picture windows," that will offer only a fleeting glimpse of developing situations. "The reason is that many existing organizations - hospitals, the for-profit chains, and insurance organizations - will quickly perceive and act upon the same opportunities."

For this reason, Zirkle concludes, physicians must not only be alert and perceptive, but also must organize in anticipation of these events so they can act or react quickly. In the years ahead, "timing will be absolutely critical for those who compete in the same markets." - Carol Brierly Golin

MEDICAL INFORMATION SYSTEM, HEALTH RECORDS, AND KNOWLEDGE BANKS

Elmer R. Gabrieli

Elmer R. Gabrieli, MD, is a fellow of the College of American Pathologists and Director of Research for Gabrieli Medical Information Systems. He is also editor-in-chief of the Journal of Clinical Computing and the author of books and articles in the field of medical computing.

Perhaps the most complex and, at the same time, the most important act in clinical medicine is rational decision-making. Usually, decisions include identification of clinical problems; selection of the best-fitting diagnoses; judicious choice of therapy; prediction of the clinical course; and advice to patients concerning lifestyle, occupation, or how to cope with social/environmental problems. Information scientists equate medical decision-making with complex, but rational, information-processing amenable to analysis and simulation with various mathematical models.

Information Crisis in Medicine. The quality of a medical decision depends on many factors. One major decision-limiting factor is the accuracy and comprehensiveness of the collected patient data base; another is the physician's own medical knowledge and recall of data pertinent to the particular decision. Today, medicine in the United States is in grave difficulties on both accounts.

Only 40 to 50 years ago, the family physician - able to recall the family background, past medical history, previous surgeries and pregnancies, allergies, and general response to disease of his patient - was the guardian of the patient's past medical background. Today, with our mobile society and specialization in medicine, fragments of the patient's records are scattered, kept at hospitals, clinics, insurance companies, and X-ray departments; and, by default, the patient has become the carrier of his own medical history. It is a necessary, but expensive, time-consuming effort to reconstruct the past medical history every time the patient changes hospitals or visits a different doctor. More important, the quality of the medical history as given by the patient is often unsatisfactory. The average patient cannot remember the names of drugs he's used, or the exact name of surgery performed years ago.

The physician's own knowledge data base causes even more problems. Owing to intensive biomedical research, formal medical knowledge has been growing at a rate of about five percent per year, compounded. Several decades ago, this spectacular growth rate had already outstripped the ability of the physician to keep up with new knowledge. As a consequence, in the 1940s, specialization was formally accepted, and by the 1960s, more than 100 specialties were listed by the American Medical Association, each with a different body of scientific knowledge, language, technique, educational curriculum, and professional organization. Despite this already excessive specialization, a medical knowledge deficit (i.e., a difference between existing published knowledge and actual use of this knowledge in bedside decisions) is growing at an alarming rate. Due to this growing deficit medical decisions are rapidly declining in quality.

Educators and medical leaders are genuinely concerned about this growing medical knowledge deficit. Mandatory continuing medical education, periodic reexamination of certain specialists, and wholesale monitoring of the quality of medical decisions (peer review) are some of the major measures recently instituted to close the gap between existing knowledge and its clinical use. These efforts endorse the traditional rule that medicine is to be practiced from memory. Actually, clinical medicine is the last profession still relying on memory alone. An alternative is to complement the physician's failing memory with an automated medical information system to provide, instantly and selectively, the pertinent data required to optimizing the medical decision.

The purpose of this paper is to briefly describe, in functional terms, the blueprint of a computer-based medical information system, present the state-of-the-art, and list those factors still impeding rapid progress on a national medical information network.

Four Components of a Medical Information System. Although to the user the system in an integrated, single information source, there are actually four discrete modules within the medical information system.

The first module is the regional clinical case history bank. This is an organized body of patient files. Each file consists of the header (social and fiscal descriptors) and chronologically ordered clinical records kept as they have been recorded by the physicians and their teams. At the end of each file, a case summary is added. Carefully designed medical algorithms generate this automated synopsis, a high-density information-listing of those data that have long-range medical significance. The properly authorized physician can retrieve either the synopsis or the original records.

In order to protect the patient's right to privacy, all access to the fully identified patient files must be effectively controlled. The first module of the medical information system, the clinical case history bank, should evolve as a community-controlled data center, dedicated to support the local health care delivery system. Prompt and effective case history retrieval and protection of the confidentiality of the stored medical data should be the two primary responsibilities of such regional data centers.

The second module is the pooled clinical experience bank. This is essentially a statistical analysis of accumulated numerous regional clinical case history banks throughout the country. After adequate disidentification of the files (i.e., removal of the headers), the accumulated clinical data are transferred to a central bank where similar data or groups of data are exposed to statistical tests for variance, correlations, and patterns. Diagnostic procedures, clinical signs and symptoms, and therapeutic measures are analyzed for patterns, success rate, diagnostic, and/or prognostic significance. The results of these analyses should support public health and preventive medicine measures and will also be available to all practitioners using the information system. For example, the untoward effects of a new drug versus its therapeutic value, as accumulated in the pooled clinical experience module, should guide the physician in his practice.

The third module of the medical information system is the clinical knowledge bank. This is essentially a systematic representation of factual knowledge currently kept in printed form in textbooks of the various specialties. Analysis of a few such standard textbooks indicates that the amount of hard factual information in a textbook is relatively small. For example, a textbook on obstetrics, covering the physiology and pathology of reproduction, pregnancy, labor, delivery and puerperium, could be adequately represented by 3500 statements. A statement is a single proposition, representing one established fact. This corpus of 3500 statements is the clinical material usually covered by the medical school curriculum in obstetrics. Representation of the physiology and pathology of the liver requires 10,000 statements.

One experience with limited clinical areas such as hereditary blood-clotting disorders, hepatology, and obstetrics indicates that creating a comprehensive medical knowledge bank is a large, but manageable, medical task. That is, it does not represent a great technical challenge.

The fourth module of the medical information system is the biomedical research bank, a system of well-organized and extensively indexed blocks. Each block represents one research publication. Each block contains the findings of the report, the methods used and the credibility rating of the study provided by the expert reviewing the publication for the research bank.

User Benefits. With his office terminal or via the hospital's terminal, the physician can request any of the four types of services provided by the medical information system: (a) retrieval of a patient's synopsis, or recent records, or all past records; (b) retrieval of pertinent data from the pooled national clinical experience; (c) retrieval of pertinent established knowledge from the didactically organized knowledge bank; and (d) browsing in related areas of research, when clinically indicated, to consider what is currently experimental or speculative.

Present Impediments. The individual components of the briefly outlined medical information system have been tested, and both the medical and technical feasibility have been fully explored. There are, however, still several social, cultural, and organizational problems to be resolved before a full-scale national system can be installed.

The first problem is to enter human expressions into the computer. Medical communication is somewhat disciplined but essentially remains as an unrestricted linguistic representation of human thoughts. This medical communication in natural language must be transformed into machine-compatible codes. We have studied extensively this interface problem.

From the point of view of epistemology, medical communication contains medical expressions and commonly used words in conventional syntax according to accepted English grammar.

In the past, most of us believe that the medical record must be extensively structured in order to make these records computer-compatible. Prestructured forms may improve the uniformity of medical records, but forms may also decrease the accuracy of the physician's notes. Today, any medical communication whether it be prestructured or free text, can be made machine-compatible. An automated semantic transformation is needed at the interface to encode and to decode. The automatic encoder must be able to handle all medical expressions as well as common words used in medical texts. Thus a medical lexicon is needed which contains all medical terms, and a vocabulary is needed to code all common words. In the machine, the medical communication should be represented by its semantic equivalent, a coded mirror image.

The automated encoder is, therefore, a combination of a medical lexicon and a vocabulary with a program which degrades the input medical text, matches the components against the lexicon/vocabulary, and transforms natural language English into a string of codes. We have constructed such an automated encoder for obstetric and hematologic patient records. This system is now expanded to accept and process any medical text.

In the medical lexicon of the automatic encoder, a unique, randomly chosen, 4-character code is assigned to each medical term. In addition, a semantic hierarchy is imposed upon the medical lexicon in the form of a cognitive network, so that medical terms can be used as semantic guides, directing the retrieval of pooled medical experience, medical knowledge, or related biomedical research. As a result, a logical taxonomic system is required for classification of medical systems. This has been designed and used effectively. In this cognitive network, sematic relationships are represented by nodes as medical terms and by pointers as semantic arcs. This cognitive network attached to the medical lexicon directs retrieval of information along the semantic paths.

Another present impediment is the bias of many medical educators trained in the Gutenberg culture on the principle that memorizing is the only way to eliminate a medical information deficit. The task is to persuade the policymakers of medicine within government, organized medicine, and academia to consider the computer-based medical information system as a viable alternative to more forced memorization via continuing education, reexamination, peer reviews, and other human-memory oriented measures. Once the new concept is accepted, it will greatly affect the value system of our entire medical education process. Instead of selecting memory giants for admittance to medical schools, the ability for rational thinking and compassionate and humanitarian qualities will receive greater attention.

All four modules of the medical and technical aspects of a medical information system have been tested on a limited scale as small demonstration models. However, the transformation of these bench models into a national information network is a large bioengineering and medical multidisciplinary task. Full development and maintenance of the automated encoder call for a national committee. Referees will control the content of the biomedical bank, a role somewhat analogous to that of current editors of scientific journals. Organizing such a team of referees for the biomedical data bank may lead to a profound reorganization of our present scientific hierarchy.

The cost of developing and maintaining a national medical information system deserves comment. The cost of the present manual record system and the "cost" of medical decisions of declining quality are staggering and rapidly growing. Automation of medical data and information may close the gap between existing knowledge and clinical decisions and eliminate the need for peer review. Actually, the cost of memory-limited medicine with its information deficit and manual information recording, copying, and screening will be substantially reduced by information automation. The cost of peripatetic medical education will also be strengthened by the medical information network. Multidisciplinary teams will be needed for extensive orientation of all users within the medical educational and clinical communities. Perhaps the medical informationist will be a new discipline.

Privacy Aspects. Because paying for medical care is no longer a private matter in the United States, the right-to-know concept has caused an apparent conflict with the right-to-privacy concept. Actually, this conflict is more apparent than real; but to resolve this critical sociocultural matter, both an extensive public education campaign and an explicit national medical information policy are urgently needed. The evolving models sponsored by the Medical Society of the State of New York, a program for voluntary accreditation of medical data centers, may be a workable national solution. In bona fide clinical care, the content of the automated identified patient files should be properly and readily available to authorized clinical users. For all secondary uses - such as peer review, fiscal processing, managing, compiling biostatistics, epidemiologic surveys or research/teaching purposes - disidentified clinical data would be equally usable. Regional medical centers should be patient-care-oriented, and effective data protection should be a primary concern; however, national data centers, processing only pooled clinical experience data, should be free from the burden of protecting personal data.

Reorientation of Clinical Medicine and Medical Education. Transition from the memory-based clinical medicine of the Gutenberg culture to the electronic information system may be closer to revolution than evolution. Values cherished for centuries such as rapid memorization and effective recall will be replaced by judicious evaluation, rational decisions, and crisp logic. As high technology begins to assist memory, emphasis should be redirected to the human component of the traditionally humanitarian clinical medicine. To realize the benefits of the new while at the same time retaining from the past what is still valuable, is a true challenge to the health field.

External Readings: Information Systems

Journal American Medical Association 249:607-12 (February 4, 1983).

"Computer-Assisted Medical Decision-Making: Interest Growing," Journal American Medical Association 248:913-18 (August 27, 1982).

Schoolman, HM & Bernstein, LM, "Computer Use in Diagnosis, Prognosis, and Therapy," Science 200:926-31 (May 26, 1978).

Krieg, AF, "Computers in the Clinical Laboratory," Journal American Medical Association 245:2242-44 (June 5, 1981).

"Computers in Medicine," Journal American Medical Association 247:173-74 (January 8, 1982).

Miller, RA, et al., "INTERNIST-I, An Experimental Computer Based Diagnostic Consultant for General Internal Medicine," New England Journal Medical 307:468-76 (August 19, 1982).

Lindberg, DAB. The Growth of Medical Information Systems in the U.S. Lexington, MA: Lexington Books, 1979. 195 pp.

Blum, BI (ed.). Information Systems for Patient Care. New York: Springer-Verlag, 1984. 426 pp.

EVALUATION OF MEDICAL PRACTICES

Howard S. Frazier and Howard H. Hiatt

H.S. Frazier is director of the Center for the Analysis of Health Practices, Harvard School of Public Health, and H.H. Hiatt is dean of the Harvard School of Public Health, Boston, Massachusetts 02115. Both are professors of medicine at the Harvard Medical School.

Dacron grafts have saved the lives of thousands of people with potentially lethal defects in atherosclerotic blood vessels. Antibiotics have spared millions more the catastrophic outcomes of deep-seated bacterial infections. At the other end of the spectrum of medical interventions are those that are carried out exclusively for monetary gain in, for example, a few "Medicaid mills." If medical measures were always directed against acute disease that is lethal in the absence of intervention, the problem of evaluation would be a relatively simple one. Similarly, if the only, or principal, interventions in question were those prescribed by unethical doctors, we could construct corrective measures with reasonable dispatch. Evaluation of medical procedures, however, is a complicated undertaking that defies simplistic or rapid solution. Although the thesis of this article is that we can do better, we believe that our problems do not result from greed, stupidity, or sloth. Rather they can be ascribed largely to pervasive characteristics of our medical care system and to complexities in the meanings and measurement of risks and benefits.

We shall use the term efficacy to describe the net benefits and risks of an intervention. Its measurement requires the ordered collection of information about the natural history of the disease for which the intervention is proposed, and the short- and long-term risks and benefits that result from the intervention. Both society and the individual have a stake in the measurement of efficacy. Society is also concerned with the fair representation of the available information on risks and benefits to the individual that result from medical interventions. Further, it has a stake in aggregate risk and benefit, at least along that part of the spectrum that includes death and change in level of disability. Finally, as the largest single source of financial support for health care, society has a growing interest in the cost per unit of net benefit, or the cost-effectiveness of medical interventions.

Empirical information about risk and benefit is probabilistic in form. Because outcomes are value-laden, their measurement often is subject to unconscious bias or other forms of implicit selection. Since these difficulties are common to many other forms of scientific inquiry, we shall refer only briefly to them and consider in more detail some features of our present system of health care which inhibit seriously our ability to develop the kind of information upon which the measurements of efficacy and cost-effectiveness depend. Finally, we shall offer some suggestion designed to palliate, if not to cure.

Examples of the Problem. The evolution of medical practice requires, one might assume, the continual replacement of diagnostic, therapeutic, and preventive measures with ones of greater efficacy. However, the history of medical practice is replete with descriptions of procedures that have been widely employed, only to be discarded when they have been shown to be seriously flawed rather than after the introduction of a more effective measure. For example, Barnes describes many "therapeutic" measures that were ultimately abandoned because they were proved completely worthless, including dangerous surgical procedures carried out for such conditions as constipation and dysmenorrhea.

As one example of a diagnostic measure of considerable efficacy but with limitations that were inadequately appreciated for a long period, McDermott cites the Wassermann diagnostic test for syphilis. Only after almost 50 years of widespread use was it generally appreciated that half the patients with positive tests did not have syphilis. As a result, many thousands of people were incorrectly diagnosed as having the disease and thereby subjected not only to humiliation, but to the very considerable dangers that then accompanied antisyphilitic treatment.

Many examples can be cited of diagnostic procedures now in widespread use that have not been adequately validated. Fineberg has described the proliferating laboratory tests that last year accounted for in excess of $11 billion of our health resource expenditures. He pointed out that there is evidence that much laboratory usage, which is increasing at a rate of 14 percent annually, has little or no beneficial effect on patient care.

Many current therapeutic practices, both medical and surgical, have not been adequately evaluated. For example, over the last 25 years controlled studies have led to a progressive reduction in hospital stay for convalescence from myocardial infarction from six weeks to four weeks to three weeks to two weeks and recently to one week. Indeed, some English physicians maintain that patients with uncomplicated myocardial infarctions can be cared for at home with no greater mortality than in the hospital. Radical mastectomy remains the most widely practiced operation for breast cancer, but much evidence suggests that it is no more effective than simpler procedures. Tonsillectomy may be less frequently carried out now than previously, but one can question the justification for most of the almost one million operations still performed annually.

Limitations in Our Knowledge of the Natural History of Disease. Many factors contribute to the complexity of evaluation, but none is more prominent than deficiencies in our understanding of the natural history of most of the chronic illnesses treated in our health care system. McDermott cites as a prime example the evolution of our understanding of the late effects of syphilis. Until 20 years ago it was almost universally assumed that a patient with untreated syphilis was doomed to a disastrous outcome as a result of such infection-induced complications as severe mental disease, debilitating neurological problems, serious cardiovascular disease, or a combination of these and others.

Therefore, even though treatment in the pre-antibiotic era carried considerable risk, it was considered essential. Not until 1955 did a prolonged follow-up study of untreated patients by Gjestland show that 85 percent of people with untreated syphilis had a normal life span and that more than 70 percent died without any evidence of the disease. With the advent of antibiotics the risks and benefits of treating syphilis have changed dramatically, and treatment is now appropriately regarded as mandatory for all patients in whom a diagnosis of active disease is made. However, many other illnesses for which risk-laden interventions are now assumed essential probably have a similar natural history that is presently unappreciated. In the absence of baseline data of untreated illness, conclusions are necessarily uncertain concerning the effectiveness of intervention.

Imperfect understanding of the course of both untreated and treated disease, however, is but one of the difficulties confronting those who would attempt evaluation of medical interventions. We shall cite several others.

The Structure of Our Health Care System. Medical care for many Americans is discontinuous. In the absence of a primary care physician, comprehensive medical record keeping is very difficult. We are unable to follow adequately the effects of tonsillectomy on, for example, the frequency of sore throats in the five or 10 years following the operation. We cannot even assess the accuracy of the patient's impression of their frequency in the years before the tonsillectomy that is often carried out in response to that impression. [The problem is made more complex by a limited appreciation that tonsil and ear infections occur less often in unoperated children as they grow older]. The tendency of many Americans to choose the specialist to whom they take a self-diagnosed problem and to use multiple hospitals accentuates the lack of follow-up. Record systems, even for those patients with primary care physicians, do not begin to have the sophistication of which our technology is capable and that adequate data collection and interpretation demand.

Recent developments in the technology of computers have made possible experiments in the development of specialized data banks for the storage and study of large, standardized data sets concerning patients with a restricted group of medical problems who can be followed over prolonged periods. Appropriate safeguards of privacy appear feasible, and the aggregated experience may well make important contributions to efficacy questions in the foreseeable future.

Physicians function as largely autonomous decision-makers. Drugs must, of course, be approved by the Food and Drug Administration before they can be adopted for general use. However, the same is not true of other measures employed for diagnosis and treatment. For example, although there is widespread agreement that the coronary artery bypass graft surgical procedure has not been adequately validated, it is estimated that in excess of 80,000 Americans will be subjected to this operation this year. While some people derive major benefit from the operation, many others now operated on have characteristics that most experts agree should exclude them as candidates for the procedure. The independence of what must now be hundreds of surgeons carrying out the procedure makes it impossible to pool their experience in such a way as to maximize the learning experience for them and for society. Thus, a recently published report of a randomized trial of this operation involved about 600 patients studied over a period of up to three years. The conclusions reached from this limited experience have led to great controversy in the medical literature. We might know more if it were possible to summarize and analyze the experience of the estimated 250,000 patients who have simultaneously been subjected to the procedure under non-experimental conditions. We would surely know more if all patients had been operated on under experimental conditions.

Reimbursement mechanisms in our present health care system often provide incentives that interfere with proper evaluation. For example, most medical insurance plans cover hospitalization but not home care. Thus, a surgeon wishing to examine experimentally the effects of early discharge of patients subjected to, for example, herniorrhaphy, varicose vein surgery, or gallbladder surgery could do so only by increasing the cost to the patient, if such a measure as home nursing were judged important for adequate follow-up care and were not covered by insurance. Similarly, a group of doctors wishing to pursue the conclusion that home care is equivalent to hospital care for the patient with the uncomplicated myocardial infarction could do so in most instances only at great expense to the patient.

In addition, the process by which medical interventions move from "experimental" - and hence not reimbursable - status to that of "accepted practice" depends on criteria that are both insufficiently explicit and variably applied. The collection of appropriate and credible information on efficacy of new procedures prior to their widespread dissemination could be enhanced by the selective reimbursement of investigators contingent on their use of peer-reviewed protocols during clinical trials of new or controversial interventions. Upon completion of the trials, a well-supported judgment of the relative merit of the therapy could be made, and more general reimbursement begun if appropriate.

The present preoccupation of some in our society with legal action against physicians also militates against adequate evaluation. For example, a large fraction of all patients operated on for breast cancer ultimately die of their disease. Will the surgeon who carries out a simple mastectomy be liable to criticism or even legal suit if the patient unhappily is not cured, and if most surgeons in the community are still recommending radical surgery? Similarly, many physicians order skull x-rays for patients even with minimal head trauma despite studies that indicate the efficacy is very low. Today's imperative is a skull film; tomorrow's may be a computerized tomographic scan, at roughly ten time the cost.

Evaluation Is Not Exclusively a Medical Undertaking. As a result of the interactions of biology and medicine we have seen major progress in recent years in the diagnosis and treatment of disease. However, there has been much less success in combining the activities of physicians and members of other disciplines. Closer interactions with statisticians, for example, might have accelerated the development of clinical trials sophisticated in design and evaluation. Even more difficult is the measurement of quality of life. Most studies describing the results of surgical and medical procedures are couched in terms of survival rates after a certain number of years and recurrence of the problem for which the procedure was applied. The quality of life that follows the intervention seldom receives attention. In part, this reflects the fact that the physicians are not trained to seek ways of assessing quality of life any more than they are trained in the mathematical techniques required for the development of clinical trial methodology. The inability of medical people to deal optimally with such problems and the diffidence of many non-medical professionals with the requisite skills to enter the medical arena have had adverse effects not only on the needed assessments, but also on the development of important methodology.

Disappointment often follows the completion of even a well-planned and executed trial because of unrealistic expectations. Many people believe that real advances in medicine take place only in dramatic fashion, such as when a trial with polio vaccine demonstrated virtually complete control of a condition that was previously unmanageable. However, this is clearly the exception. Most innovations in surgery and anesthesia, as described by Gilbert et al., and probably in other medical spheres as well, occur in much less dramatic fashion. These authors conclude that:

> Since relatively small, though important, numerical gains or losses are to be expected from most innovations, clinical trials must regularly be designed to detect these differences accurately and reliably. When a systematic trial of a new therapy is being considered initially, it is frequently subject to great optimism. The advocate for a new therapy may believe, for a number of specific reasons, that it will prove to be greatly superior to the standard and, indeed, preliminary informal experience may

seem to provide good evidence for this. As our data show, this initial optimism, though frequently warranted, is often not justified.

Evaluation is not generally perceived as a continuing process. The results may be provider-sensitive; for example, the physicians conducting a trial based in multiple academic centers may be more highly skilled than community-based physicians who have less opportunity to practice these skills. As a possible case in point, in an early series of studies starting in 1964, thermography was first reported to have about 90 percent sensitivity for detection of breast cancer. By September 1977 the First National Institutes of Health Consensus Development Conference recommended abandoning general use of the procedure because sensitivity as measured in 27 centers involving 258,000 women was only 50 percent, and the false positive rate was high.

Finally, evaluation must take into account the subjective value systems of physicians and patients. Neutra has compared the indications for appendectomy in a variety of countries. In some, surgeons are willing to operate more frequently in an effort to minimize the number of patients with appendicitis whose atypical symptoms might lead to their not being recognized and, therefore, to increased mortality rates. As a result, these surgeons carry out a larger proportion of operations for what ultimately prove to be non-surgical causes of abdominal pain. Mosteller cites this situation as an example of what he terms "the safe surgery dilemma" - in this instance, the incompatible goals shared by both doctor and patient that nobody die of undiagnosed appendicitis, on the one hand, and that nobody with a normal appendix be subjected to appendectomy, on the other hand. Our skills in recognizing atypical appendicitis are imperfect, and Neutra's data suggest that, at one extreme, saving one additional life may involve so much additional surgery as to result in postsurgical convalescence equivalent to many lifetimes. Such considerations underscore the complexity of the problem of evaluation; a pathology report that a surgically removed appendix was normal does not by itself justify a conclusion that the surgery was unnecessary.

The issue of hysterectomy in postmenopausal women without uterine pathology also heavily involves value systems. There are those who argue that the removal of a normal uterus is justified in order, for example, to spare the woman the continuing anxiety that the organ may become cancerous. On the other hand, most doctors maintain that such surgery would be in lesser demand if attention were given to periodic examination and if there were more general understanding of both the prevalence and the epidemiology of uterine cancer, on the one hand, and the risks and costs of surgery, on the other.

Ethical Problems. Physicians' primary consideration is the care of the patients for whom they are responsible. Therefore, they can, in good conscience, recommend participation in a randomized trial only if they feel the prospects for benefit are equivalent with the two or more treatments being randomized. When one of the approaches proposed is no treatment, the problem is compounded by the previously described defects in our knowledge of the natural history of the illness being treated.

Premature dissemination of data on unproved intervention may lead subsequently to even greater ethical problems. We have already described the dilemma that may confront surgeons who recommend simple mastectomy for breast cancer, when most of their colleagues use the more radical approach, even though the latter has not been shown to be of greater efficacy. The fact that many other interventions in common practice remain to be fully validated puts into focus the magnitude of the tasks confronting medicine and society.

The Costs of Evaluation. Randomized clinical trials are extremely expensive. At present many are supported by the National Institutes of Health, and there is justifiable concern in the biomedical community that their costs diminish the amount of money available for essential basic biological research and other forms of applied clinical research. It is unfortunate that present arrangements dictate such choices for, as Gilbert et al. point out, "The cost of trials is part of the development cost of therapy." These authors make two additional points that are also relevant. First,

> Sometimes costs of trials are inflated by large factors by including the cost of the therapies that would in any case have been delivered, rather than the marginal cost of the management of the trial. In addition, the costs of trials assume much more realistic proportions when they are compared with the losses that will be sustained by a process that is more likely to choose a less desirable therapy and continue to administer it for years . . . The one sure loser . . . is a society whose patients and physicians fail to submit new therapies to careful unbiased trial and thus fail to exploit the compounding effect over time of the systematic retention of gains and the avoidance of losses.

Conclusions and Recommendations. Uncertainty surrounds the question of safety and effectiveness of a broad range of medical and surgical procedures. The costs in terms of lives, suffering and dollars are incalculable. The causes are many and complex, and there will be resistance to rapid change. A popular conception of a venal physician willfully prescribing unnecessary interventions is clearly incorrect; such people do exist, but undoubtedly account for only a small fraction of the problem. Much of the difficulty rests in our imperfect understanding of the natural history of the chronic illnesses that lead to the major demands on the resources of the health care system in Western countries. Most interventions for these conditions are designed to improve the quality of life. Since our measures for assessing quality of life are poorly developed, the problem of evaluation is further complicated.

Although no single reform will produce a great improvement in a short period, several reforms could bring about significant progress. Many changes will be difficult to implement, and their benefits will be visible only after several years or decades. However, if we neglect to identify and implement such changes, we doom ourselves and those who follow us to a continuation of the uncertainties, needless risks, and the escalating costs that characterize our present health care system. We shall summarize a few steps that could be constructive.

Medical services should be organized so that primary care and comprehensive health data collection are available to all citizens. Record systems should be kept in uniform or compatible fashion. New procedures should be regarded by physicians and patients as new drugs - not to be used except on an experimental basis and their usefulness has been validated. Methods should be developed so that all physicians and patients involved in a new intervention are enlisted in organized trials. Bunker et al. have suggested approaches to this problem.

Medical education should be broadened to give much greater emphasis to quantitative analytic methods, including epidemiology and biostatistics. Increased attention also should be given to the social sciences that could help provide approaches to such problems as measurements of quality of life, of costs and benefits, and of the diffusion of medical practices. Simultaneously, physician-investigators should encourage the participation of statisticians, epidemiologists, sociologists, lawyers, and others in research and patient care programs. Courses on health-related topics should be offered to graduate students in other programs besides those in medical school.

Society must understand that a major investment is desirable in the development of methods for the collection, analysis, and storage of medical data. In no other way will we accumulate the required information concerning the natural history of the health problems that afflict our citizens and the effects of intervention. This will be expensive and must be undertaken with an understanding that most payoffs will be deferred for many years. The investment should be made not at the expense of fundamental biological research or applied clinical research. Rather, it must be considered an integral part of medical care.

Many now look to regulation as a means of controlling the use of "unnecessary" or inefficacious procedures. As pointed out elsewhere . . . the protection afforded by the regulatory approach must be balanced against possible social costs resulting from the consequent inhibition of innovation, or the retardation of its spread. More important for the present discussion, credible regulations depend on the existence of adequate evaluations of efficacy. Regulation more commonly intensifies the need for information rather than substitutes for it. The regulatory approach is likely to offer only small advantages to the society that succeeds in making available to its people medical care of demonstrated benefit. To achieve such advantages regulation must be employed only when its benefits outweigh its drawbacks, and when its form is appropriate to the particular need.

External Readings: Quality Assurance

Donabedian, A, "The Quality of Medical Care," Science 200: 856-864 (May 26, 1978).

"Use of Quality Assurance to Bar Malpractice Claims," Patient Care 16:135,174,226 (May 15, 1982).

"Where the Real Roadblocks to Self-Policing Lie," Medical Economics pp. 85-88 (April 12, 1982).

Lawson, DH, "Pharmacoepidemiology: A New Discipline," British Medical Journal 289:940 (1984).

Komaroff, AL, "Algorithms and the 'Art' of Medicine," American Journal Public Health 72:10-12 (January 1982).

Williamson, JW, et al. Principles of Quality Assurance and Cost Containment in Health Care. San Francisco: Jossey-Bass, 1982.

Greene, RC. Medical Overkill: Diseases of Medical Progress. Philadelphia: GF Stickley, 1983. 310 pp.

AN HMO MEDICAL DIRECTOR LEARNS SOME LESSONS ABOUT COSTS AND PEOPLE

D. Bonta Hiscoe with Helen B. Hiscoe

D. Bonta Hiscoe, MD, is medical director of Health Central, a 27,000-member staff model HMO in East Lansing, MI. He wrote the article below with his wife, Helen B. Hiscoe, PhD, a professor of natural science at Michigan State University.

Our local health maintenance organization (HMO) has become an accepted part of the medical community. After three years it has earned the respect, if not the affection, of fee-for-service practitioners.

I am glad that I accepted the challenge of becoming its medical
director after 21 years in private practice as a general and thoracic
surgeon. I wanted to find out if it were possible to blend all of the
ingredients in a combined group-practice/small insurance company, and
come up with a balanced budget, medical care we would be proud to offer,
content and highly motivated providers, and satisfied subscribers. My
experience has served to reinforce many of the ideas I already had about
cost containment in medical care before I signed on, and it has given me
new insights as well.

I know how hard it is for the private practitioner to keep costs
down without strong incentives. Likewise, I know how hard it is to
control hospital costs. So long as third parties pay costs, no one
feels any pressure to watch the dollars - not the physician bent on
satisfying his patient, not the hospital interested in keeping beds full
and building its reputation, and certainly not the patient wanting for
himself all of the miracles dangled in front of an eager public by the
media. It is vital to enlist the cooperation of all three by whatever
incentives can be devised if runaway costs are to be checked.

In an HMO the costs of lab tests, hospital days, and referrals all
come out of the fixed prepaid pot, and if any of these is ordered
unnecessarily, the whole HMO suffers - our employees have less to work
with and each member's coverage is diminished. Gradually all of our
health professionals are responding to this logic, prodded by a tight
review system and by efforts to educate the younger practitioners about
the distinction between what is medically necessary and what merely
treats their own insecurity.

Some of the unenthusiastic staff reaction to cost-control measures
was not unexpected. I also anticipated the resistance of many of our
HMO members. Under the fee-for-service system some patients go from one
physician to another, seeking treatment from prescriptions to surgery
that they are convinced they need.

Naturally it shocked some of them to discover that our HMO
physicians occasionally might decide that a particular service requested
was not essential. Payment might even be denied! Even members
considered visionary HMO advocates were aggrieved when such restraints
were applied to them. One of our HMO board members even cautioned me
not to refer him to a certain physician because this surgeon would
insist on sending him home from the hospital before he wanted to go.

People enrolling in HMOs sometimes have been led to expect miracles
from preventive medicine, when their needs really are not unique at
all. Preventive care involves application of basic medicine:
Identification and treatment of hypertension, elimination of smoking,
reduction of obesity, and immunization. There is no magic formula. HMO
members have the same illnesses, need the same care, and seek the same
reassurances as any other group of patients. I look upon an HMO as a
health cooperative, and physicians are involved (in our size HMO) when

the financial decisions are made. Its buying power can be used to make advantageous financing arrangements, whether in the purchase of drugs, hospital care, or outside specialty care. To make it all work, though, it is absolutely essential that patients themselves be motivated to keep costs down.

It is, however, extremely hard to alter members' habits and expectations. A recent encounter illustrates member reluctance to be guided in the paths of economy. Two years after lung surgery a woman developed another related problem. Her former physician recommended further surgery - at a handsome fee. Our physician staff thought that the fee was too high, so we asked two outstanding thoracic surgeons in town what they would charge for this procedure. Both of these much better qualified surgeons quoted fees of about half. The member, however, still insisted on seeing the more expensive but less qualified physician.

In another instance the member's employer, a person known to be highly critical of the medical profession and always "outraged" at health care costs, called to complain because our HMO refused to pay for a long in-hospital treatment of a chronic alcoholic employe. The HMO staff agreed that only the acute phase justified hospital care. Because we planned to provide outpatient care instead of expensive inpatient hospital care, this "cost-conscious" industrialist threatened to discourage enrollments in our plan.

I have learned that HMO members have certain expectations of the organization when they join, and these are more exacting than they would be for fee-for-service care. They expect to receive appointments much sooner and to spend less time in the waiting room. They also have a preconceived idea that HMO physicians are all general practitioners in the old-fashioned sense, and it has been necessary to emphasize the specialty qualifications of our board certified internists, pediatricians, family practitioners, and obstetrician-gynecologists.

We have found that the best insurance against member dissatisfaction lies in honest marketing. It also helps to have established a reputation for reasonableness. We make every effort to accommodate legitimate requests for care, even if they deviate from the plan, so long as they do not penalize anyone else. Over time, as our staff and patients have become more stable, our problems have decreased. But every new bulge in enrollment brings some new problems and renewed need for education.

An HMO is a microcosm reflecting the medical problems of society at large, including those of cost. People can make or break the medical system, both in the miniature model and on a national scale. The structure of an HMO is designed to provide reasonable discipline, incentive, and reward to both its staff members and its patient members for the exercise of restraint in the utilization of available health care.

Hospitals and physicians are blamed routinely for escalating health care costs, when in fact the pattern of extravagance has evolved in large part in response to patient demand. We can belabor the hospital and the physician as much as we want, but until the people needing the care decide that they genuinely want costs to be contained, costs will continue to soar.

External Readings: Medical Practice

Geyman, JP, "Future Medical Practice in the United States," Journal American Medical Association 245:1140-43 (March 20, 1981).

"Will Private Practice Be Worth the Hassle?" Medical Economics pp. 54-86 (February 1, 1982).

Patient Care 16:142-162 (October 30, 1982).

Gustafson, CG, "How Others See Us - A Peer Review Perspective," Minnesota Medicine 65:595-99 (October 1982).

Weed, LL, "Physicians of the Future," New England Journal Medicine 304:903-07 (April 9, 1981).

Cousins, N, "The Physician as Communicator," Journal American Medical Association 248:587-89 (August 6, 1982).

Avorn, J & Soumerai, SB, "Improving Drug-Therapy Decisions Through Educational Outreach," New England Journal Medicine 308:1457-63 (June 16, 1983).

Ottensmeyer, DJ & Smith, HL, "Rural Health Care," New England Journal Medicine 306:74-78 (January 14, 1982).

Roberts, NK & Cretin, S, "The Numbers Game, or is Small Beautiful?" New England Journal Medicine 304:666-67 (March 12, 1981).

Harris, CJ, "Evaluating an HMO..," Occupational Health & Safety 51:41-45 (February 1982).

"Why Informed Consumers are Choosing HMOs," Patient Care 16:67-80 (October 30, 1982).

"What is Management Medicine?" Patient Care 16:2,225 (May 15, 1982).

"This Practice Makes Management Medicine Work," Patient Care 16:101-24 (May 15, 1982).

External Readings - Medical Practice (continued)

McCue, JD, "The Effects of Stress on Physicians and Their Medical Practice," New England Journal Medicine 306:458-63 (February 25, 1982); 307:563-64 (August 26, 1982).

Peck, RL, "What Would You Face Starting a Practice Today," Physician's Management 22:52-58 (January 1982).

"What Bothers Doctors Most About Doctors," Physician's Management 22:143-48 (June 1982).

Manuel, BM, "Toward Practice Productivity," Bulletin American College Surgeons 67:4-6 (April 1982).

"Hospital Jobs vs Private Practice," Medical Economics pp. 276-86 (May 10, 1982).

"What Doctors Think Makes a 'Good Doctor'," Physician's Management 22:113-23 (February 1982).

Felknor, R, "Keep Your Practice From Becoming Routine," Physician's Management 22:28-38 (May 1982).

"What Makes a Hospital Special," Emergency Medicine 14:179-215 (March 15, 1982).

Preston, T. The Clay Pedestal: A Re-Examination of the Doctor-Patient Relationship. Seattle: Madrone, 1981. 226 pp.

Selzer, R. Letters to a Young Doctor. New York: Simon & Schuster, 1982. 205 pp

LeMaitre, GD. How to Choose a Good Doctor. Andover, MA: Andover Pub. Group, 1979. 169 pp..

Eisenberg, JM, et al. (eds.). The Physician's Practice. New York: John Wiley & Sons, 1980. 274 pp.

Cooper, IS. The Vital Probe. New York: WW Norton, 1981.

McCue, JD. Private Practice: Surviving the First Year. Lexington, MA: The Collamore Press, 1982. 285 pp.

American Medical Association. Alternative Health Care Delivery Systems: The Individual Practice Association. Chicago: AMA, 1980. 40 pp.

American Medical Association. Health Maintenance Organizations. Chicago: AMA, 1980. 192 pp.

Chapter VI

CAREER PLANNING: CONFRONTING THE JOB MARKET

Decisions concerning a career as a clinician involve careful consideration of two factors: The particular specialty which seems likely to command your interest for a lifetime as well as national requirements for doctors with such training. Most students apparently give far more weight to the former than the latter. Since the actual demand for specialized professional services may constitute a fundamental constraint in achieving your career goals, some understanding of the general manpower question seems essential.

When imbalances occur in the supply/demand for physician services, market solutions are difficult to attain because of the long period between acceptance into medical school and entrance into the job market. Adjustment is exacerbated by a host of variables such as technology, which influences physician productivity, changes in the delivery and financing of health care services, and the difficulty of discerning the net result of these forces. Students contemplating or actually pursuing a medical career, of course, may ignore external pressures when the demand exceeds the supply; but personal and social risks rise when an opposite condition obtains.

The Problem

During the late 1960s and early 1970s, national health manpower policy emphasized the need to increase aggregate physician supply. "Federal support of medical education provided incentives for dramatic increases in the number of physicians, with the result that medical school enrollments nearly doubled during that period. In addition, the number of foreign medical school graduates (currently 22 percent of physicians in the United States) doubled during the same period."[1]

Today, medical schools are graduating about two new physicians for every one who retires or dies. Moreover, the supply of doctors has been projected to jump by over 40 percent between 1978-1990 while the population growth is expected to be much less. Although an "appropriate supply" of physicians is subject to varying interpretation,[2] an excess provokes concern that increased competition among clinicians will fail

---

[1] Fruen, MA & Cantwell, JR, "Geographic Distribution of Physicians: Past Trends and Future Influences," Inquiry 19:44 (Spring 1982).

[2] Iglehart, JK, "How Many Doctors Do We Need?" Journal American Medical Association 254:1785-1788 (October 4, 1985).

to produce significant decreases in medical charges and even result in an overuse of health services.

Interpretation

A comprehensive critique of the supply/demand enigma is beyond the purposes of this book. Nevertheless, there are several factors whose combined impact suggests that the physician surplus often predicted for 1990s may be more manageable than disastrous.

(1) The magnitude of the surplus varies according to the source. One projection by the research arm of the U.S. Congress placed the excess of physicians at 150,000 by 1990. The most comprehensive study, conducted by the Graduate Medical Education National Advisory Committee (GMENAC) produced an estimate which is less than one-half of that amount. However, a revised figure issued by the Bureau of Health Professions projects a surplus of only about 30,000.

Regardless of the expected level, some of the potential imbalance may be offset by slight reductions in recent medical school admissions, decreases in the number of doctors admitted to certain residency programs, and regulations restricting the employment of foreign medical graduates. The impact of these forces is demonstrated by 1985 data which show that while more than 92 percent of U.S. senior medical students have secured residency appointments over the last few years, the percent of unmatched graduates of foreign medical schools reached 60 percent among of U.S. foreign medical graduates and 78 percent among alien foreign medical graduates.[1]

(2) The need for physicians in the future ultimately bears some relationship to the growth of the population in general. However, when the composition is changing (such as when the proportion of individuals employed, retired or aged is rising), the effective demand for physician services may be understated in official projections.

(3) The number of female physicians is expected to rise from 50,000 in 1980 to 100,000 by 1990.[2] Yet, "women physicians tend to work fewer hours per week and per year and also tend to see fewer patients per hour than do their male counterparts."[3] Indeed, the hourly patient load of female physicians, in a study of practice covering five specialty areas, averaged only 62 percent when compared to male

[1] American Medical News 28:37 (November 15, 1985)

[2] American Medical News 24:4 (December 11, 1981).

[3] Reinhardt, UE, "The GMENAC Forecast: An Alternative View," American Journal Public Health 71:1151 (October 1981).

physicians.[1] Consequently, when the projected GMENAC surplus of 15 percent is adjusted for this factor, the true excess might be much closer to seven percent.

(4) Because some ncn-clinicians fail to maintain their license while others do but forsake employment in practice settings, the true supply of clinicians tends to be inflated.

(5) Physician investment in IRA/Keogh plans makes it economically feasible for some proportion of doctors to take early retirement. To the extent that this phenonmenon occurs, any excess supply will be ameliorated. Indeed, the National Industrial Conference Board reports that around 30 percent of all workers age 55 to 64 have already left the labor force.

(6) Even though the nation may be confronted with a general surplus of physicians, the mal distribution of doctors, although reduced in recent years, may still yield some employment opportunities.

Public health experts contend that an adequate level of medical service requires one primary care physician for every 2000 persons. Yet in 1984, 33 of 77 communities in Chicago had only one such physician per 3500 population. Ratios of this type, though, can be influenced by a host of factors such as the nature of transportation facilities and the extent to which specialists actually provide primary care. However, physicians seeking practice opportunities should investigate pockets of shortages that persist within certain areas. While the average household income in these communities seldom approaches that of the more affluent suburbs, insurance coverage may mitigate part of the difference.

The diffusion problem is also illustrated by the concentration of psychiatrists where 50 percent of the clinicians are located in five states and the District of Columbia, areas that account for only 33 percent of the population. Consequently, if your area of interest seems over supplied, consider how a possible mal distribution can be turned to your advantage. Further, some specialties will probably continue to manifest a shortage regardless of the national supply of physicians.

(7) Additional elements render interpretation of the supply-demand equation difficult. A number of physicians with board certification in one field practice in another (see Table I-1). Further, some specialists provide a significant amount of primary care and vice versa. Further, most of the services rendered by a physician are subject to his/her discretion and hence include a degree of elasticity which tends to confound research studies endeavoring to predict manpower needs and supply. Finally, the growing importance of technology associated with the performance of certain procedures may lead to higher requirements for specialists and sub-specialists than indicated by

---

[1] Ibid., p. 1152.

traditional measures of supply or need, i.e., physician-to-population ratios.

To summarize the labor market prospects for medical school graduates, the likelihood of a physician surplus before 1990 seems to be widely accepted. The magnitude of the excess, however, may be much closer to 30,000 or even lower. Moreover, the consequences of a surplus may be mitigated to the extent that doctors pursue specialties with a possible shortage (see below) and positions as non-clinicians.

Career Planning in the Face of Uncertainty

How can a medical student plan his/her career when the job market for certain specialties may be overcrowded by the time employment is sought? While job guarantees for future graduates are beyond the power of books on career planning, at least four strategies can be recommended to help confront a surplus.

Apply Probability. The GMENAC projections of physician supply relative to national requirements for 1990 have been classified and ranked in Table VI-1. Although the precision of these figures has been criticized by Reinhardt (op. cit., pp. 1149-1157) and others, the dispersion among specialties provides an important reference for guiding career selection. Readers will note that of the 37 fields examined, a shortage was projected for 12. Consequently, the probability of entering an area with an excess supply should fall sharply if specialties on the left side of the Table receive priority consideration.

Even if there are cogent reasons for completing a residency in cardiology, the area with the greatest projected relative surplus, some physicians may improve their employment chances simply by qualifing for pediatric cardiology, a field with a potential shortage. While reliance on relative specialty rank may not overcome constraints in the form of personal preference, paucity of residency positions, or an overwhelming physician surplus, careful study of these rankings could minimize selection of a specialty that lacks economic viability.

Aggressive Follow-Up. Optimal career selection often necessitates adoption of validating techniques such as talking with faculty and clinicians in private practice as well as monitoring appropriate newsletters and journals. The latter often contain the presidential address where the incumbent assesses the status of the specialty including the manpower outlook for the field. Further, has the relevant specialty association or board, or the American Medical Association,[1] issued an updated critique of the GMENAC projections or conducted an independent study?

---

[1] Journal American Medical Association 253:2878-2880 (May 17, 1985).

Table VI-1

GMENAC Projections of Physician Shortage and Surplus for Selected Medical Specialties,
Ranked According to Percent of Deviation from Estimated Requirements for 1990, USA

Shortage Based Upon Estimates	Projected Amount	Surplus Based Upon Estimates	Projected Amount
50% or more		**10-24%**	
Pediatric Endocrinology	575	Urology	1,600
Pediatric Hematology-Oncology	1,150		
Child Psychiatry	5,100	ALL PHYSICIANS	67,750
25-49%		**25-49%**	
Neonatology	600	General Pediatrics	7,500
Pediatric Nephrology	150	Pathology	3,350
Emergency Medicine	4,250	Orthopaedic surgery	5,000
Physical Medicine/Rehab	800	Ophthalmology	4,700
		Allergy & Immunology	900
10-24%		OB/GYN	10,450
Psychiatry - General	9,500	Infectious Disease	1,000
Preventive Medicine	1,460	Plastic Surgery	1,200
Pediatric Cardiology	150	Thoracic Surgery	900
1-9%			
Hematology-Oncology	800	**50-74%**	
Anesthesiology	1,550	General Surgery	11,800
		Radiology	9,800
Approximate Balance		Neurology	3,150
Pediatric Allergy	----		
Surplus Based Upon Estimates		**75-99%**	
		Nephrology	2,100
1-9%		Rheumatology	1,300
Gastroenterology	100	Neurosurgery	2,450
Dermatology	350	Pulmonary Medicine	3,350
General Internal Medicine	3,550		
DO/MD General/Family Practice	4,250		
Otolaryngology	500	**100% or more**	
Endocrinology	1,800	Cardiology	8,950

Note: Tabulation excludes nuclear medicine. Moreover, figures for anesthesiology, neurology, pathology, physical medicine/rehabilitation, preventive medicine and radiology, as well as non-enumerated fields with a projected supply of about 9,700 physicians, may be subject to a greater error than other specialities that were modeled.

Adapted from: McNutt, DR, "GMENAC: Its Manpower Forecasting Framework," American Journal Public Health 71:1118 (October 1981).

Does the office of student affairs in your nearest medical school compile data on this problem?

Pursue Frontiers. While information on opportunities among emerging sub-specialties is often sparse, those who find it difficult to foresee employment in the traditional and perhaps over crowded fields may refer to the final section of Chapter III, "Additional Professional Areas," investigate frontiers that may be identified through professional associations listed in the Appendix, or ask faculty members to recommend unique opportunities with which they are familiar.

Consider Non-Clinical Roles. While most students enter medicine because of the challenges associated with patient care, 10 to 12 percent, either initially or subsequently, elect to serve in a non-clinical capacity. If your reading of Chapter IV or experience confirms a possible interest in such a position, then specific techniques designed to locate a non-clinical post should be followed.

Medicine: Professional & Public Perceptions

The type of professional services provided by a particular specialty will probably represent the primary basis for the selection of a medical career. However, the decision making process would be incomplete if it neglected the experience of doctors already in practice and the opinions of the patients whom they serve.

A Louis Harris poll reported that "half of all American physicians have sufficient doubts about the future of medical practice that they would not recommend it as highly today as they would have in the past."[1] This disenchantment factor, though, was not due to a deep-seated personal dissatisfaction about the nature of their work, but to two characteristics emanating from external forces - concern about a predicted surplus of physicians, plus government and third-party regulation of their practices and fees. For example, nine out of ten physicians interviewed believe that external controls on fee reimbursement "are either likely to happen or are already in effect."[2] In addition, similar surveys have documented problems associated with the rising expense of professional liability insurance and malpractice actions, and the paper work required for processing third-party claim forms.

While all career options, including medicine, can be expected to manifest certain negative components, some perspective may be gained by recalling John W. Gardner's admonition: "We are all faced with a series

---

[1] American Medical News 25:3 (June 4, 1982).

[2] Ibid.

of great opportunities brilliantly disguised as insoluable problems." With respect to medicine, this field offers not only the chance to treat the health problems of individual patients, but the possibility of devising more beneficial and cost-effective ways of providing and paying for medical care as well.

Fortunately, the public's view of medicine implies a strong basis for being optimistic about this area. Ninety-four percent of 1,504 individuals interviewed reported they were satisfied with every aspect of their most recent visit to a physician. In addition, 80 percent felt that doctors are genuinely dedicated to helping people.[1] Moreover, no other profession ranks higher in terms of prestige or status, especially taking into account the perceived stress associated with medical practice.[2] Finally, in a Gallup Poll covering the public's perception of honesty and ethical standards among 25 professions and occupations, physicians ranked third.[3]

The Economic Setting

As noted earlier, earnings from professional practice, especially in certain specialties and/or selected communities, may be affected whenever the supply exceeds the demand for clinical services. For purposes of career planning, though, a brief review of the sources of professional income and the level of earnings seems appropriate.

Source of Income. We reported previously that 63 percent of the income received by office-based physicians in private practice was derived from reimbursement supplied by third-party programs. The balance, 37 percent, came directly from the personal resources of their patients.

The source of income can also be examined in terms of compensation formulae associated with different types of delivery units. Approximately three-fourths of all non-federal, office-based physicians receive the majority of their income from some means of payment other than salary.[4] Although the survey results displayed in Table VI-2 identify five methods of physician compensation, fee-for-service represents the predominant means governing clinician earnings.

---

[1] These attitudes may be subject to erosion since the same survey reported that 62 percent of the sample were "beginning to lose faith in physicians" while 60 percent said that physicians were "too interested in making money." American Medical News 26:3 (January 7, 1983).

[2] American Medical News 24:11 (December 4, 1981).

[3] apharmacy weekly 22:131 (August 19, 1983).

[4] Kahn, HS & Orris, P., "The Emerging Role of Salaried Physicians: An Organizational Proposal," Journal Public Health Policy 3(3):285 (1982).

Table VI-2

Distribution of 4,588 Office-Based Physicians by Type
of Practice and Method of Income Distribution, USA, 1980

Type of Practice	Income Distribution Basis	Percent of Survey
Solo	Fee-for-Service	54.0%
Partnership or Group	Fee-for-Service	7.4
Partnership or Group	Salary and Profit-Sharing	15.7
Partnership or Group	Equal Distribution	11.3
Partnership or Group	Straight Salary	7.4
Partnership or Group	Other	3.7
Partnership or Group	Unstated	0.5

Source: AMA Periodic Survey of Physicians. Quoted in Kahn, HS & Orris, P. "The Emerging Role of Salaried Physicians: An Organizational Proposal," Journal Public Health Policy 3(3):286 (1982).

If our point of reference is changed to jobs held by all medical school graduates, however, we find that physicians on some form of salary now "constitute approximately one half of all active physicians in the United States."[1] This pattern occurs because more than 210,000 physicians (including residents) work either for a government agency or their salaried income is received from (1) clinics, health maintenance organizations,[2] or university/college student health centers, (2)

---

[1] Ibid., p. 284

[2] One doctor reported on his reason for joining an HMO: "I was uneasy accepting reimbursement for treating illness. I was uncomfortable trying to decide whether the expense of an x-ray or other ancillary investigation is beyond the financial capability of some patients." In summarizing the motives of physicians generally, he noted (1) the desire to lead a well-rounded life, with time for family, recreation and vacation; (2) since many physicians are married and have families by the time they are ready to begin practice, they cannot afford the expense of furnishing an office and can not wait for income while trying to build up a practice from scratch; (3) some physicians may not feel adventurous enough to go from the shelter of training in a hospital to the unsheltered private practice office; (4) some physicians join prepaid plans in order to get a stake to set up their own offices. Orris, P. (ed.). The Salaried Physician. New York: Academy Professional Information Services, 1982. p. 19.

hospitals,[1] (3) teaching, (4) research or (5), administration. Moreover, if the corporatization of American medicine continues as predicted,[2] the percentage of physicians deriving a majority of their income from a salary arrangement may approach 60 percent before the end of this century.

When the remumeration package is determined externally by an employer, the nature of fringe benefits could become an important factor that influences not only your total income but comparative assessment of alternative career options. Thus doctors who take salaried positions will need to consider the scope and value of such fringes as vacation/holiday allowances, sick leave, life and health insurance protection, reimbursement for attendance at professional meetings and continuing education seminars, etc.

Level of Earnings. Average physician income derived from private practice is noted below in Table VI-3. While these figures imply that

Table VI-3

Average Net Annual Income from Medical Practice, 1984

Type of Physician	Average Net Income Before Taxes
All Physicians	$108,400
Surgery	151,800
Anesthesiology	145,400
Radiology	139,800
Pathology	118,000
Obstetrics/Gynecology	116,200
Internal Medicine	103,200
Psychiatry	85,500
Pediatrics	74,500
GP/Family Practice	71,100

Source: American Medical Association. Socioeconomic Characteristics of Medical Practice. Chicago; AMA, 1985.

---

[1] "Approximately 60 percent of the physicians with a hospital contract have a salary arrangement." American Medical News 25:9 (April 9, 1982).

[2] Starr, P. The Social Transformation of American Medicine. New York: Basic Books, Inc., 1982. pp. 420-49.

physicians enjoy a comfortable living, some interpretation seems appropriate. (1) Because the duration of medical training (12 years on the average) is longer than that required of any other occupation, the number of years over which full income can be received is reduced accordingly. (2) Three-fourths of the medical school graduates leave school with a substantial debt, often more than $21,000.

(3) During the years of residency (usually four) annual income seldom exceeds $25,000. (4) Further, the typical clinician spends an average of nearly 52 hours in patient-care activities each week,[1] almost one and one-half days more per week than the typical full-time employee in manufacturing.[2] Should increased competition occur, though, physician income may decline as the number of hours per week falls.

(5) Average real income (nominal income adjusted for inflation) for physicians fell between 1970-81 by nearly six percent.[3] Thus current earnings levels may be overstated when relative criteria are invoked.

(6) Since the average cost of running a doctor's office exceeds $85,000 per year, gross earnings must be sufficient to cover this outlay. In terms of relative cost, personnel expenses rank highest, and are usually followed in order by office expenses (rent, utilities, insurance), medical supplies, and medical liability premiums. Moreover, for high-risk specialties in some states such as surgery and OB/GYN, these premiums may exceed $25,000 per year. In short, the typical clinician must possess sufficient management skills to operate a business that generates nearly $185,000 in revenue each year.

(7) If your attraction for medicine is based on economic reasons, you are probably missing your calling - chief executive officers of large industrial and commercial firms command a mean annual income (salary plus bonus)[4] of $488,790 a figure nearly five times the net compensation derived from medical practice. In addition, their unique fringe benefits, generally unavailable to physicians, such as stock options, may raise the true income for business executives by another 10-20 percent.

---

[1] When account is taken of professional activity away from the office, such as reading journals and attending medical society meetings, the true figure may exceed 55 hours per week.

[2] Clinicians in private practice, however, are likely to take five weeks vacation whereas the average industrial worker may have less than three.

[3] American Medical News 25:9 (October 1, 1982).

[4] Forbes (June 6, 1983).

A critique of the economic dimensions associated with medical practice should also include such factors as the number of months required before the revenue of a new solo practitioner even meets office expenses, the continuing decline in the importance of solo practice,[1] income instability of certain specialists whose earnings depend heavily on referrals received from other clinicians, the low incomes of physicians located in rural and ghetto areas, and the impact of Medicare/Medicaid regulations on charges levied by hospital-based physicians, etc.

In summary, while economic criteria represent a valid element in your career planning equation, questions introduced by the inexorable march of technological developments, the increased emphasis on group practice and corporate structure, the cost-containment posture of health insurance programs, to say nothing about the supply/demand relationships that characterize many specialties, combine to make predictions about earnings difficult. Perhaps the safest conclusion is that the dynamics of medical practice imply that few prospective clinicians can neglect, with impunity, the economic aspects of professional service.

Initiating Your Job Search

If medicine is typical of the job market generally, 60-80 percent of the vacancies will not be filled by traditional search techniques - i.e., responding to public notices about open positions, placing your name on a register, or sending unsolicited curriculum vitae en mass to various employers. On the contrary, a majority of positions are likely to be secured, either by promotion from within an organization, or through more informal but carefully directed methods such as personal visits to a short list of potential employers and networking - i.e., using job leads generated by personal contact with friends, colleagues and through active participation in the affairs of a professional association;[2] and, referral by faculty and peers who have been impressed with your credentials.

It is difficult to predict what strategy will yield the greater number of employment interviews or the best job for a particular candidate. Since at least 8,000 physicians obtain employment annually via

---

[1] Solo practitioners accounted for only 55 percent of all patient visits made to doctors engaged in the office practice of medicine. advancedata, 88:2 National Center for Health Statistics (March 16, 1983).

[2] The training obligations of a medical resident, to say nothing of the financial hurdle, may preclude heavy involvement in the activities of professional societies, especially attendance at annual meetings. However, these functions often provide a major means by which you can formulate career objectives and pursue employment opportunities. In short, procrastination may be the vehicle for courting disaster.

the formal route, both approaches should be explored until you can determine which job-finding model may work best for you. If the anticipated physician surplus materializes, some graduates will discover that multiple strategies are needed to find a satisfactory position. While it is still possible for a doctor to hang out his shingle and thus by-pass the employer market altogether, the number of physicians entering solo practice has been falling steadily for decades.

Search activities, of course, are simplified by confining your efforts to either the clinician or non-clinician model. While the techniques utilized for probing both are often similar, the pathways pursued can be quite different. If you are still having difficulty resolving this dichotomy, re-examine Chapters III, IV and V. Further, reference to a basic text that treats the administrative function[1] may also be helpful in determining the extent to which you may prefer increased managerial responsibilities.

Orientation. A brief simulation exercise is recommended to help sharpen your perception of the specifications - professional, economic and personal - that you will be seeking in a new position. By following these steps, you will learn certain aspects of the labor market such as the frequency with which jobs in particular specialties are being advertised. If this figure is low, you will need to move rather quickly into the networking model noted above.

(1) For four-six months prior to the date when you expect to initiate your actual job search, set aside several afternoons or evenings each month. Use these periods to monitor 10 to 15 references that seem likely to contain vacancy notices in your field. Those involving clinical posts appear regularly in more than 100 professional journals. Your speciality focus should reduce the useful sources to less than a half dozen. Regardless of your preference, include as basic references the Journal of the American Medical Association and the New England Journal of Medicine. If your interests lie in a non-clinical post, examine the monthly newsletter and journal published by the American Public Health Association, the classified section of the Wall Street Journal, and ads in two sections of the Sunday New York Times, "The Week in Review," and "Business."

When an interesting opportunity is advertised, copy and store in a file or workbook. If you are searching for a clinical position, Figure VI-1 illustrates notices likely to be encountered. If you are searching for a non-clinical post, Figure VI-2 furnishes appropriate examples, some of which suggest practice opportunities as well. Because of specialty training, your actual file will probably exhibit a much narrower focus than indicated by these samples.

---

[1] Drucker, PF. Management Tasks, Responsibilities, Practices. New York: Harper & Row, 1973.

- 325 -

Figure VI -1

Selected Announcements Seeking Physicians for Clinical Positions

UNIVERSITY HEALTH SERVICE twelve month position in primary care to young adults with major responsibility for sports medicine program. Completion of residency and board eligibility preferred. Significant sports medicine/trauma experience required. Student population of 26,000; accredited health service. Semi-rural community of 30,000 with many cultural advantages.

CARDIOLOGIST. Experienced. BC with expertise in invasive procedures, and a special interest in cardiac rehab and preventive medicine. 180 physician multispecialty group with adjacent 447-bed hospital. Clinic is located in a progressive community with expanding university and private college. Cultural and recreational facilities, beautiful setting, good schools, excellent pension program, no investment required. Service organization.

ORTHOPAEDIC SURGEON for 336-bed GM&S Medical School affiliated VA Hospital Residency program in Medicine, Neurology, Surgery, Orthopedics, Otolaryngology, Ophthalmology, Urology and Dentistry. Board certification and interest in teaching preferable. Licensure in any state sufficient.

FAMILY PRACTICE PHYSICIAN. General Hospital seeking a physician with obstetrics, general acute care and basic surgical qualifications. Salary guarantee is negotiable. Housing and office space is available.

INTERNIST: BC/BE to join a 6-physician department in a 23 physician multispecialty group. The clinic offers an excellent practice opportunity, an incentive pay system with a guaranteed minimum income the first year, liberal fringe benefits and time off. No buy-in requirement.

ALLERGIST NEEDED in 155 Doctor multispecialty clinic; clinic and adjacent 288-bed hospital are located in Big 10 University community of 100,000; teaching positions are available in medical school for those with academic inclination; liberal fringe benefits and salary lead to equal ownership.

PULMONARY PHYSICIAN to head 18 bed respiratory care unit. Also to answer consultations, perform bronchoscopies and interpret pulmonary function test. 441 bed hospital with eight-bed ICU is associated with major medical school. Non-discrimination in employment.

ENDOCRINOLOGIST: Full-time position at University affiliated community teaching

hospital with large housestaff program. Exciting well-rounded clinical practice and ample teaching activities. Some clinical investigation is expected and encouraged.

STAFF PSYCHIATRIST WANTED for modern comprehensive community mental health center containing inpatient day treatment and outpatient services within one building immediately adjacent to a modern 330-bed general hospital. Duties would entail primarily adult inpatient and outpatient services with some case supervision of multidiscipline staff. Duties also include some child and adolescent services, primarily outpatient. Competitive and negotiable salary with excellent fringe package which includes annual sick, personal, bereavement and education leave, disability, health and malpractice insurance.

DERMATOLOGIST: Needed For 21 physician multispecialty clinic. Drawing area pop. 170,000; city pop. 20,000. Excellent school system. Scenic mountains and lakes. Regional med. ctr. Excellent benefit package and CME.

PEDIATRICIAN; BC/BE. ALLERGY-NEONATOLOGY interest desired. Beautiful upstate New York Finger Lakes region. BC pediatrician well established practice. Guaranteed salary. Partnership opportunity.

GENERAL SURGEON: BC/BE to replace retiring surgeon in a 16 physician multispecialty group practice (2 surgeons, 2 OB/GYN, 6 internists and 6 pediatricians). Two year salary guarantee with full partnership available at beginning of third year.

NEONATOLOGIST(S): SUBURBAN PHILADELPHIA Area, Community Hospital, 1800 deliveries per year. Expanding Neonatal and Perinatal Program. Start immediately, excellent salary and benefits. Fine schools and gracious suburban living area, proximity to six medical schools.

VASCULAR SURGEON with recent training for association with Board certified general and vascular surgeon in dynamic growing practice. Fellowship and Board eligibility a must. Excellent pay and benefits.

OB/GYN NEEDED for a very scenic town of 8,000 in middle Tennessee, 95-bed, modern hospital with excellent facilities offers an excellent working environment. Doctors in town will provide coverage, also 24-hour ER and anesthesia coverage. Excellent financial package includes net guarantee, and office space adjacent to the hospital.

Figure VI-2

Selected Announcements Seeking Physicians for Non-Clinical Positions

CHAIRMAN, DIVISION OF RESEARCH: The Clinic Foundation, a world-renowned center for medical excellence, has an exceptional opportunity for a resourceful professional capable of directing our acclaimed Division of Research. In this challenging role, you will be charged with providing the leadership necessary to plan and direct a dynamically innovative Program of Research. You will apply your expertise through diverse channels which include providing direction and counsel to distinguished staff of 44 PhD and/or MD level senior scientists; chairing various Research Committees; representing the Division both internally and externally; and conducting your own research projects. The background of the successful candidate will include a distinguished record of achievement in clinical and basic scientific research which has led to recognition of individual expertise in more than one specialized field. In addition, the candidate will possess at least 10 years' experience in an administrative/management post which successfully demonstrates sound leadership abilities. An MD or PhD or MD/PhD degree is required.

ASSOCIATE DIRECTOR: The National Institutes of Health invites applications for the position, Associate Director for Medical Applications of Research. This is a Civil Service position in the Senior Executive Service with a salary range from $52,247 to $57,673 per annum. Candidates may be eligible for Physicians Comparability pay up to $10,000 per year. Alternately, may be eligible for appointment in the Commissioned Corps of the US Public Health Service. The individual selected, if not presently in the SES, must serve a one-year probationary period. The Associate Director is responsible for assisting major units of NIH in the use of appropriate methods for identification and evaluation of clinically relevant new knowledge emerging from NIH and other programs and for effective transfer of this information to the health-care community.

ASSOCIATE DIRECTOR: Medical Communications: Continued expansion of our operations has created an excellent opportunity on our corporate staff for a physician with experience in internal medicine, pediatrics of family practice to assist the Director in internal and external medical communications such as: respond to mail and telephone inquiries; provide medical approval for advertising and promotional material; maintain liaison with professional and governmental agencies; provide instruction and guidance to Field Sales Force. Excellent verbal and written skills are required.

DIRECTOR MEDICAL TERMINOLOGY: The Association is conducting a research for a new director of its Department of Medical Terminology and Nomenclature. Major responsibilities will involve the ongoing preparation of two medical information and terminology publications; the adoption of nonproprietary names for new drugs; and the continual updating of drug nomenclature. The individual appointed to this position must be knowledgeable in chemistry and drugs and have strong administrative capabilities. MD/PhD required.

CHIEF, BUREAU OF DISEASE CONTROL: Manage and coordinate staff of 58 and budget of $1,150,000 in a large county health department serving a population of 1.5 million. Oversee TB control, VD control (busy clinic with over 36,000 visits per year) immunization and epidemic control and public health laboratory. Also coordinate activities with 13 primary care facilities and large teaching hospital. Requirements: Physician with eligibility for Arizona license, at least three years of disease control program administration experience, board eligibility or certification in preventive medicine and/or master's degree or equivalent in public health.

ACADEMIC GERONTOLOGIST: Faculty member in Gerontology. Department of Medicine in the University's College of Human Medicine is seeking a qualified full time Faculty Member in Gerontology for appointment at the Assistant or Associate Professor level. MD degree required. Applicant must be Board Certified/Eligible in Internal Medicine. Must have commitment to teaching & strong interest in research.

MEDICAL DIRECTOR: The Connecticut Hospice Inc., Co., the pioneer organization of terminal care in the US is seeking an individual to provide overall medical direction. Medical Director serves as Chairperson of active medical board. The Connecticut Hospice, Inc. is licensed as a short-term hospital, special hospice and certified by Medicare as a general hospital with a hospital based home care program. Qualifications: Board Certification in a related specialty preferably family practice or internal medicine. Familiarity with community based and institutional health care delivery; demonstrated interpersonal interdisciplinary skills. Experience in hospice care preferred. Salary negotiable. Current medical director seeking a two year leave of absence to obtain board certification. Medical school appointment possible.

Figure VI-2

Selected Announcements Seeking Physicians for Non-Clinical Positions (continued)

DIRECTOR OF CNS CLINICAL RESEARCH: The qualified candidate will be responsible for planning and coordinating clinical research programs, phases 2-4 with innovative CNS active compounds. This includes the design and implementation of clinical trials and the reporting of results, as well a directing staff in the security of clinical data to be used in the preparation of submission of new drug applications. To be considered for this position candidate must possess an MD degree and at least four years of post graduate training in the neurosciences. The ideal candiate will be research oriented, well versed in neuropharmacology and familiar with clinical trial methodology.

VICE PRESIDENT MEDICAL AFFAIRS: Our major midwestern health care institution associated with a medical school is seeking a corporate officer to head up the Medical Affairs Division. The Vice-President, Medical Affairs will be responsible for the medical education and residency programs, medical staff office coordination, general hospital administration, assurance of high quality medical care and liaison between medical staff and administration.

HMO MEDICAL DIRECTOR: Blue Cross and Blue Shield offers a career opportunity for a physician who has interest and experience in working with alternative delivery health care programs. The individual will have primary responsibility for the medical management of a federally qualified Health Maintenance Organization including development of medical policy and responsibility for physician recruitment. The incumbent should be licensed to practice medicine in the state or have taken the FLEX exam within the last ten years. The individual should possess strong administrative and communication skills. Clinical experience in group practice is necessary and HMO experience is preferred. We are providing an excellent salary.

COMMISSIONER OF HEALTH: As chief executive officer, the Commissioner directs policy and operations of the Department, including responsibility for the preservation and control of communicable diseases, environmental health services, laboratory services and health research. The current operating budget is $106 million and there are 3,700 full time employees. The successful candidate must possess a NY State license to practice medicine, a Master's degree in Public Health, or in Business Administration, or Public Administration with a major in a recognized health field, and a minimum of eight years of experience in public health administration or teaching.

MEDICAL CONSULTANT: Firm is rapidly expanding its health promotion and medical cost containment services. MHRM is one of the nation's premier compensation, employee benefits and employee communications consulting firm with offices in 23 cities and international affiliation. MHRM is dedicated to helping its clients reduce medical costs and improve employee well-being. The ideal candidate will be a confident, agressive MD with a Masters in Public Health and/or experience with utilization review systems and/or medical cost containment. Excellent salary and benefits as well as growth potential to the right candidate. If you are interested in joining a professional organization in the delivery of leading edge concepts in health promotion and medical cost containment, we invite you to investigate this opportunity.

MEDICAL SERVICES DIRECTOR: Assistant health commissioner position for a $12 million health department. We are seeking an individual to plan and supervise sexually transmitted disease, alcoholism, pediatric dentistry, and laboratory programs. This person will function as the medical spokesperson for the department and serve as medical consultant to all other programs, including a comprehensive ambulatory care system, community home health services, immunization clinics, and WIC program. This position will also provide an opportunity for clinical and/or faculty affiliation. Applicants must be licensed or eligible to be licensed to practice medicine in Ohio and must have one year's experience in a public health agency or possess a Master's degree in Public Health or health-related field. Salary established by Board of Health.

ASSOCIATE DIRECTOR CLINICAL AFFAIRS (Diagnostic Division): Leading health care company; position offers the successful candidate a unique chance to demonstrate general management skills and high visibility within the company. You will be responsible for developing and monitoring research protocols and selecting clinical investigators as well as providing technical design support to R & D relating to radiopharmaceuticals and contrast media. You will also review marketing material, provide support to our sales force and coordinate clinical data for presentation to Federal Regulatory Agencies. Credentials should include an MD Degree preferably with a specialty in Radiology or Nuclear Medicine and at least two years experience in a similar position or three years related experience in a clinical setting. Familiarity with imaging products essential.

When jobs of interest are posted for which your current qualifications are inadequate, such as the requirement of five plus years of experience, do not discard but file in an appendix for further examination. These notices can help determine the background you need to qualify for similar positions that may appear in the future. Alternatively, such as a post seeking a vice president for research and development in the pharmaceutical industry, write later to the successful candidate to see if an assistant with your qualifications may be needed.

(2) After 30 to 50 job announcements have been accumulated, classify according to variables that you deem important such as the type of patients who may constitute the bulk of your practice, the possibility of university affiliation, geographic location, etc. Now analyze the contents of your survey. Among other factors, determine the extent to which the desired professional attributes seem more brief than extensive. This may signify that the organization is taking a flexible approach to the task of filling a given job. Further, what unique duties and/or benefits have been observed? Perhaps you will be seeking special situations which offer a limited work week, the chance to participate in a multi-specialty group, or possibly a combination of clinical and administrative duties. Regardless of your employment goals, this informal screening process should help establish the relative frequency with which particular types of positions may exist in the market place, and serve to fill out your profile for an ideal position.

In developing your strategy for confronting the job market, recall that the formal job search model (primarily public notices of vacancies and registeries) requires relatively little lead time. Moreover, your approach can be more passive than active - just read the advertisements and apply. On the other hand, if you rely on more informal techniques, considerable lead time may be needed to build your network of personal contacts. In addition, active cultivation of individuals who may be interested in your employment status can be very time consuming.

Job hunting is a fine art often encumbered by great inefficiency. Moreover, the vast majority of readers probably have little experience or an extensive information network to rely upon in pursuing full-time professional employment. Students perceiving the need for further assistance may wish to interrupt consideration of this volume temporarily and consult several of the references cited in Figure VI-3.

The Real Job Search. If you elect to follow the traditional search model, start by using sources which generated the largest number of opportunities during the simulation exercise. Then augment this base by subscribing to one or both of two comprehensive registers which are published six time a year by the American Medical Association. The first contains announcements pertaining to job openings and is entitled, "The Opportunity Placement Register." The second, "The Physical Availability Register," represents an efficient vehicle for declaring

Figure VI-3

General References for Finding a Job

Allen, J. How To Turn An Interview Into A Job New York: Simon & Schuster, 1983. 100 pp.

Bolles, RN. What Color is Your Parachute? Berkely, CA: Ten Speed Press, 1985. This non-conventional approach to the job search process is widely-regarded as the bible in the field. It is revised annually and has been a perennial best-seller.

Figler, H. The Complete Job Search Handbook. New York: Holt, Rinehardt & Winston, 1979. This volume outlines twenty skills that should facilitate your search for a new position.

Dolan, RC. Fresh Starts: Charting A New Career. Chicago: Pluribus Press, 1984. 225 pages.

---

your entrance into the labor market. Subscribers do not need to be a member of the AMA in order to utilize either service. Further details can be obtained by telephoning (312) 645-4704 or by writing to the AMA at 535 North Dearborn, Chicago, IL 60610.

While your specialty background will tend to delimit the type of positions that can be sought at this juncture, the following check-list may be helpful:

* consider a primary care shortage area. The U.S. Bureau of Health Professions periodically publishes an updated list in the Federal Register.

* contact the Medical Program Officer at the
  - U.S. Air Force
  - U.S. Army
  - U.S. Navy

* contact the U.S. Veterans Administration

* contemplate a non-clinician position.

* explore opportunities in another country where English is the native language or your foreign language proficiency could enhance your candidacy.

> examine the Appendix for non-traditional approaches to locating your best career in medicine.

In conclusion, this overview of career options has attempted to lay the foundation for determining whether medicine warrants a lifetime commitment. As your exploration continues, the road map developed above should serve as a valuable guide to this important process.

APPENDIX

Planning a career in medicine may be approached via an alternative model. This Appendix, therefore, enumerates organizations established to facilitate the contributions of physicians as clinicians and, in some instances, as investigators.

Appendix A utilizes the structure for Chapter III to list specialized groups that support medical practice in their respective fields. Appendix B recognizes 38 additional associations whose functions usually extend beyond the classification scheme adopted above. Some appeal to more than one medical discipline while others (e.g., Orthopsychiatric) include professionals from allied health areas. Many of these societies sponsor newsletters or journals, offer student memberships, hold meetings at least once a year, compile information on career and fellowship possibilities, and/or publish research studies relevant to their interests. Thus they may represent a rich resource for learning more about career opportunities and perhaps unique roles within the vast field of medicine as well.

Appendix C lists the medical specialty boards currently established in the United States. Because of the key function performed by these groups in raising the standards of medical practice, you may wish to contact the appropriate organization to gain additional perspective about your preferred option(s) and certification requirements.

Since our basic objective is to help readers identify differentiated professional activities and related job options, important general purpose societies, such as the American Medical Association with a membership of some 200,000 physicians, have been excluded. However, both the AMA and its student affiliate, AMSA,[1] represent a primary resource for career information that should not be overlooked.

Although more than 190 organizations are enumerated below, the data exclude most with less than 400 members or an unspecified enrollment. However, at least 50 sub-speciality groups exist in a number of areas such as asthma, chemosurgery, clinical and climatological, lung, maxillofacial surgery, pediatric urology, prolotherapy, thermology and transplant surgery. Details about these societies, as well the scheduled meetings of all groups, is published in the final July issue of Journal American Medical Association under the category "Organizations of Medical Interest." This source also supplies information about associations based upon national origin, gender, race, region, and place of treatment (such as the university).

---

[1] American Medical Student Association, 1910 Association Drive, Reston, VA, 22091.

Appendix A

PROFESSIONAL SPECIALTY ASSOCIATIONS

(1) Allergy and Immunology

+American Academy of Allergy & Immunology
611 E. Wells Street
Milwaukee, WI 53202
414/272-6071

American Association of Certified Allergists
P.O. Box 520
Mount Prospect, IL 60056
312/255-1024

American Association of Clinical Immunology &
    Allergy
P.O. Box 912, DTS
Omaha, NE 68101
402/551-0801

American Association of Immunologists
9650 Rockville Pike
Bethesda, MD 20814
301/530-7178

American College of Allergists
800 E. Northwest Highway, Suite 101
Mount Prospect IL 60056
312/255-0380

(2) Dermatology

+American Academy of Dermatology
1567 Maple Avenue
Evanston, IL 60201
312/869-3954

American Society for Dermatologic Surgery
1567 Maple Avenue
Evanston, Il 60201
312/869-3959

International Society of Tropical Dermatology
200 First Street, S.W.
Rochester, MN 55905
507/284-3736

(3) Endocrinology

Endocrine Society
9650 Rockville Pike
Bethesda, MD 20814
301/530-9660

(4) Family Practice

+American Academy of Family Physicians
1740 W. 92nd Street
Kansas City, MO 64114
816/333-9700

North American Primary Care Research Group
Medical College of Virginia, Box 251
Richmond, VA 23298
804/786-9625

Uniformed Services Academy Family Physicians
2315 Westwood Avenue, P.O. Box 11083
Richmond, VA 23230
804/358-3950

(5.0) Internal Medicine - General

+American College of Physicians
4200 Pine Street
Philadelphia, PA 19104
1-800/523-1546

+American Society of Internal Medicine
1101 Vermont Avenue, NW Suite 500
Washington, DC 20005
202/289-1700

Society for Research & Education in Primary
    Care Internal Medicine
4200 Pine Street
Philadelphia, PA 19104
1-800/523-1546

(5.1) Cardiology

American College of Angiology
1044 Northern Blvd., Suite 103
Roslyn, NY 11576
516/484-6680

American College of Cardiology
9111 Old Georgetown Road
Bethesda, MD 20814
301/897-5400

+American Heart Association
7320 Greenville Avenue
Dallas, TX 75231
214/750-5300

(5.2) Gastroenterology

American College of Gastroenterology
13 Elm Street, P.O. Box 1565
Manchester, MA 01944
617/927-8330

+American Gastroenterological
    Association
c/o C.B. Slack
6900 Grove Road
Thorofare, NJ 08086
609/848-1000

American Society for Gastroentero-
    logical Endoscopy
13 Elm Street, P.O. Box 1565
Manchester, MA 01944
617/927-8330

(5.3) Geriatrics

+American Geriatrics Society
Ten Columbus Circle, Suite 1470
New York, NY 10019
212/582-1333

Gerontological Society of America
1411 K Street, NW, Suite 300
Washington, DC 20005
202/393-1411

(5.4) Hematology

American Society of Hematology
6900 Grove Road
Thorofare, NJ 08086
609/848-1000

(5.5) Infectious Disease

Infectious Diseases Society of America
6431 Fannin, Suite 1728
Houston, TX 77030
713/792-4929

(5.6) Medical Oncology

American Society of Clinical Oncology
435 N. Michigan Avenue, Suite 1717
Chicago, IL 60611
312/644-0828

(5.7) Nephrology

American Association for the Study of
    Liver Diseases
K. Kaiser; Slack Inc.
6900 Grove Road
Thorofare, NJ 08086
609/848-1000

(5.8) Pulmonary Medicine

American College of Chest Physicians
911 Busse Highway
Park Ridge, IL 60068
312/698-2200

(5.9) Rheumatology

American Rheumatism Association
1314 Spring Street, NW
Atlanta, GA 30331
404/872-7100

(6) Neurology

+American Academy of Neurology
2221 University Avenue, SE, Suite 335
Minneapolis, MN 55414
612/623-8115

American Association for the Study of
    Headache
5252 N. Western Avenue
Chicago, IL 60625
312/878-8977

American Neurological Association
P.O. Box 14730
Minneapolis, MN 55414
612/378-3290

Federation of Western Societies of
    Neurological Science
c/o Dr. G.E. Gauger
1411 East 31st Street
Oakland, CA 94602

(7) Pediatrics

Ambulatory Pediatric Association
1311-A Dolly Madison Blvd., Suite 3A
McLean, VA 22101
703/556-9222

+American Academy of Pediatrics
141 Northwest Point Road
Elk Grove Village, IL 60007
312/228-5005

American Pediatric Society
450 Clarkson Avenue, P.O. Box 49
Brooklyn, NY 11030
212/270-1692

National Perinatal Association
1311-A Dolly Madison Blvd., Suite 3A
McLean, VA 22101
703/556-9222

Society for Pediatric Research
c/o Dept. of Pediatrics
School of Medicine, UNM
Albuquerque, NM 98131
505/277-6628

(8) Psychiatry

Academy of Psychosomatic Medicine
70 W. Hubbard Street, Suite 203
Chicago, IL 60610
312/644-2623

American Academy of Child Psychiatry
3615 Wisconsin Avenue, NW
Washington, DC 20016
202/966-7300

American Academy of Psychiatry & the Law
1211 Cathedral Street
Baltimore, MD 21201
301/539-0379

American Academy of Psychoanalysis
30 E. 40th Street, Room 608
New York, NY 10016
212/679-4105

American Association of Suicidology
2459 S. Ash
Denver, CO 80222
303/692-0985

American Association on Mental
    Deficiency
1719 Kalorama Road, NW
Washington, DC 20009
1-800/424-3688

American College of Psychiatrists
P.O. Box 365
Greenbelt, MD 20770
301/345-3534

+American Psychiatric Association
1400 K Street, NW
Washington, DC 20005
202/682-6000

American Psychoanalytic Association
309 E. 49th Street
New York, NY 10017
212/752-0450

American Psychosomatic Society
265 Nassau Road
Roosevelt, NY 11575
516/379-0191

American Society for Adolescent
    Psychiatry
24 Green Valley Road
Wallingford, PA 19086
215/566-1054

American Society of Clinical Hypnosis
2250 E. Devon Avenue, Suite 336
Des Plaines, IL 60018
312/297-3317

Association for the Advancement of
    Psychotherapy
114 E. 78th Street
New York, NY 10021
212/288-4466

Association for Child Psychoanalysis
c/o Dr. N. Gray
P.O. Box 27
Guilford, NY 13708

Society of Biological Psychiatry
Box 3870, Duke Medical Center
Durham, NC 27710
919/684-5225

  (9) Surgery - General & Special Focus

American Association for Hand Surgery
110 Lockwood, St., Suite 438
Providence, RI 02903
608/273-8940

+American College of Surgeons
55 E. Erie Street
Chicago, IL 60611
312/664-4050

American Society of Abdominal Surgeons
675 Main Street
Melrose, MA 02176
617/665-6102

American Society of Contemporary
    Medicine, Surgery & Ophthalmology
211 E. Chicago Avenue, Suite 1044
Chicago, IL 60611
312/787-3335

American Society for Surgery of the Hand
3025 S. Parker Road, Suite 65
Aurora, CO 80014
303/755-4588

Association of Military Surgeons of
    the U.S.
10605 Concord Street, Suite 306
Kensington, MD 20895
301/933-2801
    (Note: Surgeons probably represent a
    minority of the membership.)

International College of Surgeons
    (U.S. Section)
1516 N. Lake Shore Drive
Chicago, IL 60610
312/642-3555

Society for Surgery of the Alimentary Tract
c/o Dept. of Surgery
University of California
Los Angeles, CA 90024
213/825-9425

Society for Surgical Oncology
13 Elm Street, P.O. Box 1565
Manchester, MA 01944
617/927-8330

Society for Vascular Surgery
13 Elm Street, P.O. Box 1565
Manchester, MA 01944
617/927-8330

  (10) Cardiothoracic Surgery

American Association for Thoracic
    Surgery
13 Elm Street, P.O. Box 1565
Manchester, MA 01944
617/927-8330

(10) Cardiothoracic Surgery (continued)

+American Thoracic Society
1740 Broadway
New York, NY 10019
212/315-8700

Society of Thoracic Surgeons
111 E. Wacker Drive, Suite 600
Chicago, IL 60601
312/644-6610

(11) Colon and Rectal Surgery

American Society of Colon & Rectal Surgeons
615 Griswold, Suite 1717
Detroit, MI 48226
313/961-7880

+International Academy of Proctology
North Shore Towers 271-17V
Grand Central Parkway
Floral Park, NY 11005
212/631-5291

(12) Neurological Surgery

American Academy of Neurological &
   Orthopaedic Surgeons
2320 Rancho Drive, Suite 108
Las Vegas, NV 89102
702/385-6887

+American Assoc. of Neurological Surgeons
22 S. Washington Street, Suite 100
Park Ridge, IL 60068
312/692-9500

Congress of Neurological Surgeons
c/o University of Maryland Hospital
22 S. Greene Street
Baltimore, MD 21201
301/528-2905

(13) Obstetrics and Gynecology

+American College of Obstetricians
   & Gynecology
600 Maryland Avenue, SW, Suite 300
Washington, DC 20024
202/638-5577

American Fertility Society
2131 Magnolia Avenue, Suite 201
Birmingham, AL 35256
205/933-7222

(14) Ophthalmology

+American Academy of Ophthalmology
1833 Fillmore Street, P.O. Box 7424
San Francisco, CA 94120
415/921-4700

Association for Research in Vision
   & Ophthalmology
Wykagyl Station, Box C-1002
New Rochelle, NY 10804
914/636-2154

+American Society of Contemporary
   Ophthalmology
211 E. Chicago Avenue, Suite 1044
Chicago, IL 60611
312/787-3335

(15) Orthopaedic Surgery

+American Academy of Orthopaedic
   Surgeons
222 South Prospect Avenue
Park Ridge, IL 60068
312/822-0970

American Fracture Association
P.O. Box 668
Bloomington, IL 61701
309/662-4491

American Orthopedic Society for
   Sports Medicine
70 W. Hubbard Stret, Suite 202
Chicago, IL 60610
312/644-2623

Scoliosis Research Society
222 South Prospect Avenue
Park Ridge, IL 60068
312/822-0970

(16) Otolaryngology

American Academy of Otolaryngic Allergy
1101 Vermont Avenue, NW, Suite 302
Washington, DC 20005
202/682-0456

+American Academy of Otolaryngology -
  Head & Neck Surgery
1101 Vermont Avenue, NW, Suite 302
Washington, DC 20005
202/289-4607

American Laryngological, Rhinolog-
  cal & Otological Society
5305 E. Huron Drive, Suite 3-B15
Ypsilanti, MI 48197
313/434-3341

American Otological Society
200 First Street, SW
Rochester, MN 55905
507/284-2369

American Rhinologic Society
2929 Baltimore, Suite 105
Kansas City, MO 64108
816/561-4423

(17) Pediatric Surgery

American Pediatric Surgical Association
1500 East Duarte Road
Duarte, CA 91010

(18) Plastic Surgery

American Academy of Cosmetic Surgeons
15415 Sunset Blvd.
Pacific Palisades, CA 90272
213/459-5832

American Academy of Facial Plastic &
  Reconstructive Surgery
1101 Vermont Avenue, NW, Suite 304
Washington, DC 20005
202/842-4500

+American Society of Plastic &
  Reconstructive Surgeons
233 N. Michigan Avenue, Suite 1900
Chicago, IL 60601
312/856-1818

(19) Urology

American Association of Clinical Urologists
21510 S. Main Street
Carson, CA 90745
213/549-3470

+American Urological Association
1120 N. Charles Street
Baltimore, MD 21201
301/727-1100

(20) Anesthesiology

American Society of Regional Anesthesia
P.O. Box 11083
Richmond, VA 23230
804/359-3557

+American Society of Anesthesiologists
515 Busse Highway
Park Ridge, IL 60068
312/825-5586

Society of Cardiovascular
  Anesthesiologists
P.O. Box 11083
Richmond, VA 23230
804/257-7154

(21) Emergency Medicine

American Association for the Surgery
  of Trauma
c/o Dept. of Surgery
Rhode Island Hospital
Providence, RI 02902
401/277-5005

+American College of Emergency Physicians
P.O. Box 619911
Dallas, TX 75261
214/659-0911

(22) Nuclear Medicine

American College of Nuclear Medicine
145 W. 58th Street
New York, NY 10019
212/582-3919

American College of Nuclear Physicians
1101 Connecticut Avenue, NW, Suite 700
Washington, DC 20036
202/857-1135

+Society of Nuclear Medicine
475 Park Avenue South
New York, NY 10016
212/889-0717

(23) Pathology

American Association of Neuropathologists
c/o J.M. Powers, MD
171 Ashley Avenue
Charleston, SC 29425
319/353-3429

+American Association of Pathologists
9650 Rockville Pike
Bethesda, MD 20814
301/530-7130

+American Society of Clinical Pathologists
2100 W. Harrison Street
Chicago, IL 60612
312/738-1336

+College of American Pathologists
5202 Old Orchard Road
Skokie, IL 60077-1034
312/966-5700

Int. Academy (US/Canada) of Pathology
1003 Chafee Avenue
Augusta, GA 30904
404/724-2973

International Academy of Pathology
c/o Leslie H. Sobin, MD
Armed Forces Institute of Pathology
Washington, DC 20306
202/576-2871

(24) Physical Medicine & Rehabilitation

American Academy of Physical Medicine
& Rehabilitation
30 N. Michigan Avenue, Suite 922
Chicago, IL 60602
312/236-9512

American Association of Electromyography &
Electrodiagnosis
732 Marquette Bank Bldg.
Rochester, MN 55904
507/288-0100

+American College of Rehabilitation
Medicine
30 N. Michigan Avenue, Suite 922
Chicago, IL 60602
312/236-9512

Association of Academic Psychiatrists
8000 Five Mile Road, Suite 340
Cincinnati, OH 45230
513/232-8833

National Spinal Cord Injury Association
149 California Street
Newton, MA 02158
617/964-0521

(25.0) Preventive Medicine - General

American College of Preventive Medicine
1015 15th Street, NW
Washington, DC 20005
202/789-0003

(25.1) Aerospace

Aerospace Medical Association
Washington National Airport
Washington, DC 20001
703/892-2240

(25.2) Occupational Health

American Academy of Occupational Medicine
2340 S. Arlington Heights Road
Arlington Heights, IL 60005
312/228-6850

+American Occupational Medical
    Association
2340 Arlington Heights Road
Arlington Heights, IL 60005
312/228-6850

(25.3) Public Health

American Association of Public
    Health Physicians
c/o Nassau Co. Dept. of Health
240 Old Country Road
Mineola, NY 11501
516/535-2260

+American Public Health Association
1015 15th Street, NW
Washington, DC 20005
202/789-5600

(Note: Physicians are active in the following sections: Community Health Planning; Environment; Epidemiology; Food & Nutrition; Gerontological Health; Health Administration; Injury Control & Emergency Health Services; International Health; Laboratory; Maternal & Child Health; Medical Care; Mental Health; Occupational Health & Safety; Population & Family Planning; Public Health Education; Radiological Health; School Health Education & Services; and Statistics.)

(26) Radiology

American College of Medical Imaging
P.O. Box 27188
Los Angeles, CA 90027
213/275-1393

+American College of Radiology
20 N. Wacker Drive
Chicago, IL 60606
312/236-4963

American Radium Society
925 Chestnut Street, 7th floor
Philadelphia, PA 19107
215/574-3179

American Roentgen Ray Society
880 Woodward Avenue., Suite 105
Pontiac, MI 48053
313/338-0491

American Society of Neuroradiology
1415 W. 22nd Street, Suite 1150
Oak Brook, IL 60521
312/920-8002

American Society for Therapeutic
    Radiology & Oncology
20 N. Wacker Drive, Room 1660
Chicago, IL 60606
312/236-4963

+Radiological Society of NA
1415 W. 22nd Street
Oak Brook, IL 60521
312/920-2670

Society for Pediatric Radiology
c/o Dept. of Radiology
Duke University Medical Center
Durham, NC 27710
919/681-4678

(27) Clinical Nutrition

American College of Nutrition
P.O. Box 831
White Plains, NY 10602
914/948-4848

+American Society for Clinical Nutrition
9650 Rockville Pike
Bethesda, MD 20814
301/530-7110

(28) Clinical Pharmacology

American College of Clinical Pharmacology
19 S. 22nd Street
Philadelphia, PA 19103
215/563-9560

(28) Clinical Pharmacology (continued)

American Society for Clinical
    Pharmacology & Therapeutics
1718 Gallagher Road
Norristown, PA 19401
215/825-3838

+American Society for Pharmacology
    & Experimental Therapeutics
9650 Rockville Pike
Bethesda, MD 20814
301/530-7060

Society of Toxicology
475 Wolf Ledges Parkway
Akron, OH 44311
216/762-2289

(29) Critical Care

Society for Critical Care Medicine
223 E. Imperial Highway, Suite 110
Fullerton, CA 92635
714/870-5243

(30) Forensic Medicine

American Society of Law & Medicine
765 Commonwealth Avenue, 16th floor
Boston, MA 02215
617/262-4990

National Association of Medical
    Examiners
c/o St. Louis University Hospital
1402 S. Grand Blvd.
St. Louis, MO 63104
314/664-9800

(31) Genetics

American Society for Human Genetics
P.O. Box 6015
Rockville, MD 20850
301/424-4120

(32) Holistic and Wellness Medicine

American Academy of Medical Preventics
6151 W. Century Blvd., Suite 1114
Los Angeles, CA 90045
213/645-5350

American College of Preventive
    Medicine
1015 15th Street, NW
Washington, DC 20005
202/789-0003

American Holistic Medical Association
6932 Little River Turnpike
Annandale, VA 22003
703/642-5880

(33) Human Sexuality

American Association of Sex Educators,
    Counselors, & Therapists
11 Dupont Circle, NW, Suite 220
Washington, DC 20036
202/462-1171

Society for the Scientific Study of Sex
P.O. Box 29795
Philadelphia, PA 19117
215/782-1430

+ Major organization within the indicated category.

Appendix B

SELECTED SPECIAL FOCUS ASSOCIATIONS

Acupuncture Research Institute
313 W. Andrix Street
Monterey Park, CA 91754
213/722-7353

Addictionology, American Academy of
c/o Douglas Talbott, MD
3985 South Cobb, Suite 210
Smyrna, GA 30080
404/435-2570

Alcoholism & Other Drug Dependencies,
   American Medical Society of
12 West 21st Street
New York, NY 10010
212/206-6770

Anatomists, American Association of
Box 101 MCV Station
Richmond, VA 23298
804/786-9477

Artificial Internal Organs, American
   Society for
Box C
Boca Raton, FL 33429
305/391-8589

Automotive Medicine, American
   Association for
40 Second Avenue
Arlington Heights, IL 60005
312/640-8440

Bariatric Physicians, American Society of
7430 East Caley Avenue, Suite 210
Englewood, CO 80111
303/779-4833

Blood Banks, American Association of
1117 N. 19th Street, Suite 600
Arlington, VA 22209
703/528-8200

Burn Association, American
c/o Good Samaritan Medical Center
1130 E. McDowell Road, Suite B-2
Phoenix, AZ 85006
602/239-2391

Cancer Education, American
   Association for
c/o Radiation Oncology, U.M.D/NJ
100 Bergen Street
CRTC Bldg., Room A-1020
Newark, NJ 07103
201/456-5365

Cerebral Palsy & Developmental Medicine,
   American Academy of
P.O. Box 11083
Richmond, VA 23230
804/355-0147

Cleft Palate Association, American
331 Salk Hall
University of Pittsburgh
Pittsburgh, PA 15261
412/681-9620

Clinical Investigation, American
   Society for
Zeigler Bldg., Room 531, Univ. Stn.
Birmingham, AL 35294
205/934-2218

Clinical Research, American Federation for
P.O. Box C-5371
Seattle, WA 98105
609/848-1000

Clinical Research, Central Society for
c/o VA Lakeside Medical Center
333 E. Huron Street
Chicago, IL 60611
312/951-5610

Clinical Scientists, Association of
c/o University of CT Medical School
Dept. of Laboratory Medicine
63 Farmington Avenue
Farmington, CT 06032
203/674-2328

Cytology, American Society of
130 S. Ninth Street, Suite 810
Philadelphia, PA 19107
215/922-3880

Electroencephalographic Society,
    American
2579 Melinda Drive, NE
Atlanta, GA 30345
404/320-1746

Electroencephalographic Association,
    American Medical
850 Elm Grove Road
Elm Grove, WI 53122
414/797-7800

Epilepsy Society, American
179 Allyn Street, Suite 304
Hartford, CT 06103
203/246-6566

Experimental Biology & Medicine,
    Society for
630 W. 168th Street
New York, NY 10032
212/795-9223

Group Practice Association, American
1422 Duke Street
Alexandria, VA 22314
703/838-0033

Hospital Medical Education,
    Association for
1101 Connecticut Avenue, NW, Suite 700
Washington, DC 20036
202/857-1196

International Health Society
1001 East Oxford Lane
Englewood, CO 80010
303/789-3003

International Physicians, American
    College of
3030 Lake Avenue, Suite 12
Fort Wayne, IN 46805
219/424-7414

Medical Instrumentation, Association
    for the Advancement of
1901 N. Fort Myer Drive, Suite 602
Arlington, VA 22209-1699
703/525-4890

Medical Systems & Informatics,
    American Association for
1101 Connecticut Avenue, NW, Suite 700
Washington, DC 20036
202/857-1199

Microbiology, American Society for
1913 Eye Street, NW
Washington, DC 20006
202/833-9680

Orthopsychiatric Association, American
19 W. 44th Street
New York, NY 10036
212/354-5770

Pain, International Assoc. for Study of
1309 Summit Avenue, Room 101
Seattle, WA 98101
206/292-7521

Physicians Practicing the Transcendental
    Meditation & TM-Sidhi Programs,
    American Association of
P.O. Box 417
Fairfield, IA 52556
515/472-8195

Planned Parenthood Professionals,
    Association of
810 Seventh Avenue
New York, NY 10019
212/630-4702

School Health Association, American
1521 S. Water Street, Box 708
Kent, OH 44240
216/678-1601

Sports Medicine, American College of
P.O. Box 1440
Indianapolis, IN 46206-1440
317/637-9200

Substance Abuse, Association for
    Medical Education & Research in
c/o David Lewis, MD
Division of Biology & Medicine
Brown University, Box G
Providence, RI 02912
401/863-1109

Ultrasound in Medicine, American Inst. of
4405 East-West Highway, Suite 504
Bethesda, MD 20814
301/656-6117

Utilization Review Physicians,
    American College of
1108 N. Second Street
Harrisburg, PA 17102
717/737-5660

Venereal Disease Association, American
P.O. Box 22349
San Diego, CA 92122
619/453-3238

Appendix C

AMERICAN MEDICAL SPECIALTY BOARDS

American Board of Allergy & Immunology
3624 Science Center
Philadephia, PA 19104   (Founded 1972)
215/349-9466

American Board of Anesthesiology
100 Constitution Plaza
Hartford, CT 06103   Founded 1938)
203/522-9857

American Board of Colon & Rectal Surgery
615 Griswold, Suite 1717
Detroit, MI 48226   (Founded 1934)
313/961-7880

American Board of Dermatology, Inc.
c/o Dr. C.S. Livingood
Henry Ford Hospital
2799 West Grand Blvd.
Detroit, MI 48202   Founded 1932)
313/871-8739

American Board of Emergency Medicine
200 Woodland Pass, Suite D
East Lansing, MI 48823   (Founded 1979)
617/332-4800

American Board of Family Practice, Inc.
2228 Young Drive
Lexington, KY 40505   (Founded 1969)
606/269-5626

American Board of Internal Medicine
3624 Market Street
Philadelphia, PA 19104   (Founded 1935)
215/243-1500

American Board of Neurological Surgery, Inc.
148 Clinical Sciences Building, UNC
Chapel Hill, NC 27514   (Founded 1940)
919/966-3047

AMERICAN MEDICAL SPECIALTY BOARDS (continued)

American Board of Nuclear Medicine
900 Veteran Avenue
Los Angeles, CA 90024   (Founded 1971)
213/825-6787

American Board Obstetrics & Gynecology, Inc.
4507 University Way, Suite 204
Seattle, WA 98105   (Founded 1930)
206/547-4884

American Board of Ophthalmology
111 Presidential Blvd., Suite 241
Bala Cynwyd, PA 19004   (Founded 1915)
215/664-1175

American Board of Orthopaedic Surgery, Inc.
444 North Michigan Avenue, Suite 2970
Chicago, IL 60611   (Founded 1934)
312/822-9572

American Board of Otolaryngology
220 Collingwood, Suite 130
Ann Arbor, MI 48103   (Founded 1924)
313/761-7185

American Board of Pathology
112 Lincoln Center
5401 W. Kennedy Blvd.
Tampa, FL 33622   (Founded 1936)
813/879-4864

American Board of Pediatrics
111 Silver Cedar Court
Chapel Hill, NC 27514   (Founded 1933)
919/929-0461

American Board of Physical Medicine &
    Rehabilitation
Norwest Center
21 First Street, SW
Rochester, MN 55902   (Founded 1949)
507/282-1776

American Board Plastic Surgery, Inc.
1617 John F. Kennedy Blvd.
Philadelphia, PA 19103-1847 (Founded 1939)
215/568-4000

American Board of Preventive Medicine, Inc.
Dept. Community Medicine, School of Medicine
P.O. Box 927
Dayton, OH 45401   (Founded 1948)
513/278-6915

American Board Psychiatry & Neurology
One American Plaza, Suite 808
Evanston, IL 60201   (Founded 1939)
312/864-0830

American Board Radiology, Inc.
300 Park Avenue, Suite 440
Birmingham, MI 48011   (Founded 1934)
313/645-0600

American Board Surgery, Inc.
1617 John F. Kennedy Blvd., Suite 1561
Philadelphia, PA 19103   (Founded 1937)
215/568-4000

American Board Thoracic Surgery
14640 East 7 Mile Road
Detroit, MI 48205   (Founded 1948)
313/372-2632

American Board of Urology
Norwest Center, Suite 520
21 First Street, SW
Rochester, MN 55902   (Founded 1933)
507/282-6500

INDEX

Medical Career Scorecard

for _____

Interesting or very interesting	Moderately interesting	Little or no interest
_____	_____	_____
_____	_____	_____
_____	_____	_____
_____	_____	_____
_____	_____	_____
_____	_____	_____
_____	_____	_____
_____	_____	_____
_____	_____	_____
_____	_____	_____
_____	_____	_____
_____	_____	_____
_____	_____	_____
_____	_____	_____
_____	_____	_____

Instructions: When you complete each numbered section in this volume, as well as the External Readings, record the number of each in the appropriate column above. Seek corroborating information for fields that appear most frequently under "Interesting or very interesting."